LEARNING
E-Commerce
Business Analysis & Design

Nancy Stevenson

Acknowledgements

I'd like to thank Chris Katsaropoulos for trusting me with this project; Jennifer Frew and Elsa Johannesson for their terrific work, which turned my scribblings into a book; and my husband Graham (as always) for his patience and support.

Nancy Stevenson

Managing Editor

Jennifer Frew

Educational Reviewer

Lots Pinnyei

Design and Layout

Elsa Johannesson

Elviro Padro

Acquisitions Manager

Chris Katsaropoulos

Web Album Designer

Elsa Johannesson

Cover Design

Amy Capuano

Published by DDC Publishing

For information, address DDC Publishing, Inc., 275 Madison Avenue, New York, NY 10016
http://www.ddcpub.com

DDC Publishing Inc. Printing

10 9 8 7 6 5 4 3 2 1

Table of Contents

Introduction

Welcome to the world of E-Commerce, a brave new world of exciting technology and global interaction. This book is designed to expose you to the many facets of E-Commerce, from buying and selling to Web-store design; from marketing online to legal issues in E-Commerce. By the time you finish reading this book, you should have a broad understanding of the challenges E-Businesses are facing and meeting today.

The book is organized into Parts, Lessons, and Themes. Each Part addresses a central theme, such as Social, Legal, and Ethical Issues of E-Commerce; the Lessons contained within each Part break these topics up into sections, such as Evaluating Copyright and Trademark Compliance and Ethics and Morality Online. Finally, Themes within each Lesson examine specific issues, such as Fraud or Business Ethics.

Each Theme provides information about technology, business methods, and concepts with five Web site examples to help you understand these learning points. At the end of each Theme you'll find an analysis of three of those sites in more detail, looking at specific features and practices on these Web sites. Each example is followed by questions that encourage you to explore the site online and test your knowledge or apply critical-thinking skills.

At the end of each Part is a Capstone project. This project builds the foundation of an E-Commerce venture throughout the course of this book, using a sample E-Commerce company, All Creatures Publishing, as an example. The projects challenge you to apply the knowledge you've gained in that part to perform some of the tasks involved in running an E-Commerce company, such as designing its Web site or creating a competitive analysis. Each Capstone projects starts with a recap of major concepts covered in that Part, and then provides a description of the project. Ideas for researching the project and information about the technologies involved, with specific Web sites that might be helpful, are also included.

Although every attempt was made to include mainstream Web sites that will be around for some time to come, nothing is forever online. Some of these sites may have disappeared or changed their identity or moved their location by the time you read this book. The descriptions and screenshots in the book, as well as the home page of each site in the Web Album on the accompanying CD, will give you enough to understand the basic elements of the site and the concepts presented. However, nothing replaces actually visiting a live Web site to see how companies are doing business online; if you can no longer find the site itself to explore, search for a similar site with the many search engines available to you on the Web. If a site is included in an E-Business Analysis section but is no longer available, explore the same issues discussed here on a similar site, and answer the questions at the end of the analysis for the currently active site.

Finally, included in the margins for each theme and project section are some special elements to provide additional insight or background information. These include:

Notes, which offer background or additional information about concepts and business issues.

Buzzwords, which highlight definitions of new terms as you come across them in the text.

Technical Notes, which provide some insight into the technology behind E-Commerce, and in some cases give you an idea of how programmers actually build E-Commerce solutions with HTML and other programming languages.

Web Album on CD-ROM

The Web album includes the home pages for all of the Web sites in the book. These home pages can be used as classroom examples. The album can be viewed without an Internet connection.

System Requirements

- Windows 95 or later
- An installed Web browsers (e.g. Microsoft Explorer, Netscape Navigator, etc.)

To Launch the Web Album

1. Open Windows Explorer (right-click on **Start** button and click **Explore**).
2. Be sure that the CD is in your CD-ROM drive. Select the CD-ROM drive letter from the All Folders pane of the Explorer window.
3. Select the file **start.htm**.
4. Double-click the file to open it.
5. Opening this file will launch your Web browser.
6. No software installation should be necessary.
7. Double-click on any site name listed on the left side of the Album window.

If you follow the above procedure and your browser does not launch, Windows will bring up a list of applications to use to launch the file. Select one of the available Web browsers from this list.

NOTICE: The links on these sample Web pages are not active. Only the home pages can be viewed.

Internet Cautions

ACCURACY: Be cautious not to believe everything on the Internet. Almost anyone can publish information on the Internet, and since there is no Internet editor or monitor, some information may be false. All information found on the World Wide Web should be checked for accuracy through additional reputable sources.

SECURITY: When sending information over the Internet, be prepared to let the world have access to it. Computer hackers can find ways to access anything that you send to anyone over the Internet, including e-mail. Be cautious when sending confidential information to anyone.

VIRUSES: These small, usually destructive computer programs hide inside of innocent-looking programs. Once a virus is executed, it attaches itself to other programs. When triggered, often by the occurrence of a date or time on the computer's internal clock/calendar, it executes a nuisance or damaging function, such as displaying a message on your screen, corrupting your files, or reformatting your hard disk.

Part I

Application of Electronic Commerce

The Advantages of E-Commerce
- Explore how the Internet is exposing businesses to a wider audience
- Learn about the speed and convenience of buying and selling online
- View various uses of online content
- Understand the impact of immediacy of information delivery
- See how E-Commerce supports company branding

NOTES

See How Advertising Online Works at E-Commerce Times

- **E-Commerce** is simply the process of buying and selling online. However, many activities surround that buying and selling process, including designing and maintaining an efficient Web store, providing customer service, processing payments, marketing and advertising, and actually fulfilling orders by shipping the product or supplying the service. E-Commerce Times, an online publication, makes money online not from selling its **e-zine** to readers, but by selling advertising space on its site.

Buzzwords

E-Commerce is the process of buying and selling products or service online. E-Commerce is one function of *E-Business*, which encompasses any business activity performed online.

An *e-zine* is an online or digital magazine.

E-Commerce Times Success Stories Page

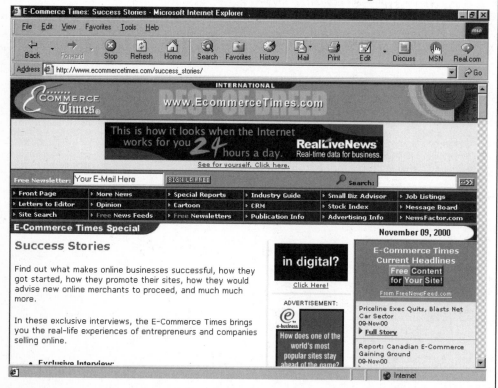

- E-Commerce is changing the way most companies do business. Part of this change is the immediacy of the Web. Customers can access companies 24 hours a day, 7 days a week. Keeping information about a company and products current is easier and less expensive; rather than reprinting an expensive brochure or catalog, a company can simply make a change to the Web site to get up-to-date information to millions of customers in a matter of minutes. An e-zine, such as E-Commerce Times, can deliver up-to-the-minute news in a way no printed publication ever could.

- Note the list of stories in the E-Commerce Times TechNews Headlines; stories are posted there that happened as recently as the last 5-15 minutes. Other E-Commerce uses of this immediacy of information delivery are for online investing with up-to-the-minute stock quotes; online auctions where the most current bid can be tracked minute-to-minute; and banking online where a customer can check account balances and checking account activity at any time of the day.

Find Out How People are Finding Success in E-Commerce at fourthchannel.com

- The selling side of the E-Commerce equation is very important. Many companies, such as fourthchannel, offer advice and services to help companies understand how to sell online. One of the strengths of the Internet is that when you sell, you can reach millions of people at one time. In many cases, you reach customers you never would have found before. fourthchannel suggests that there have traditionally been three sales channels: face-to-face, telephone, and paper-based. The Internet offers a fourth sales channel to businesses.

fourthchannel's Home Page

- Because you can't see a visitor to an online store the way you can see a visitor to a retail store, one very important piece of the E-Commerce sales puzzle is finding ways to get to know your customers. You can do this by having visitors register on your site, storing customer data obtained when a customer places an order, and using a process called **data mining** to track traffic and observe online behavior patterns of visitors and customers.

Technical Note
Data mining is the practice of sifting through data to establish patterns. In E-Commerce, data mining is done with software programs that automatically analyze data, such as buying patterns of customers.

- Traditional selling techniques are still valid in E-Commerce, including identifying your target markets, closing the sale, and retaining customers for repeat business. The difference in E-Commerce is that more of the control of the sale is placed in the customer's hands in a self-service environment. In addition, online technology offers ways to automate selling functions and tie them into retail sales operations.

Omaha Steaks Takes a Bite Out of E-Commerce

- One of the important elements of E-Commerce is Web content. Content is the information that is provided on a company's Web site, whether it's in the form of pictures, video sequences, text, or downloadable files. This content isn't always purely product-related. To attract customers to a site, content is often an added-value element. For example, at Omahasteaks.com, customers can look up recipes for the food that they can buy on the site. Although customers don't need recipes to buy and cook an OmahaSteaks steak, the company provides this content to bring customers back to their site as a repeat customer.

- Content management is the practice of keeping content on a Web site current and interesting. This responsibility sometimes falls to a **Web Master**, the marketing department, or a special Web group dedicated to site design and content management. In some cases companies provide **white papers** or regular newsletters that are of interest to their customers. Although the major goals of creating good content are to make a sale and to bring repeat traffic to a site, many companies feel that a beneficial side-effect is the creation of a more-educated customer.

OmahaSteaks.com Home Page

Buzzwords

A *Web Master* is the person responsible for maintaining a Web site. The Web Master updates the content and handles any technical concerns.

A *white paper* is a technical or informational background document. For example, you'll find white papers on Microsoft's site about products.

Note

Offering value in Web site content is very important in getting customers to return to your site. Make sure you update content frequently and offer interesting information, valuable contests or discounts, and useful tools or downloads to your customers.

■ Because OmahaSteaks is selling food, visual images of the food help to encourage the customer to buy. Typically when designing a Web page all images the site will use are stored in a central file, and a command to retrieve the image file and use it on the Web page is included in HTML code. By using a Web management tool such as Web Express, you can view the properties of any image on a Web page, including the name of the source file for the image.

Viewing Image Properties of OmahaSteaks.com

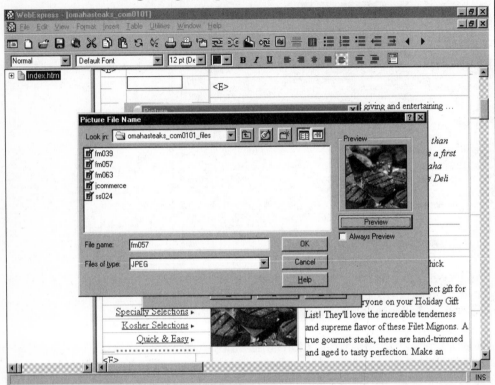

Personalizing Your Online Travel Experience at Atevo Travel

■ Many consider the Internet impersonal and argue that customers want face-to-face contact in a buying and selling transaction—or at least voice-to-voice contact. For that reason many companies have put an emphasis on creating a personal experience online. Atevo Travel, for example, offers a personal travel page where you can share your travel experiences with others. Other sites greet you by name when you arrive, present you with recommended buying lists based on your buying history, or provide personal shopping representatives to assist you.

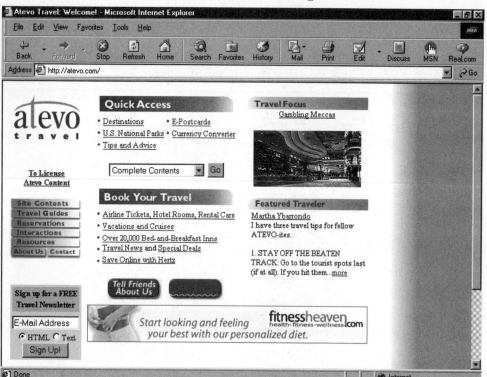

- Service companies, such as travel agencies or car rental companies, use personalization as a way of identifying how each customer prefers to use their service to make the buying experience easier. For example, if a travel company "knows" that you always prefer to fly in business class and you always want a low-fat meal on planes, it can store that data, and save you the trouble of entering it each time you order plane tickets. By simply storing this personal record, an E-Commerce business gives the customer the impression that there's somebody at the business who knows and understands his or her buying preferences. This often results in customer loyalty to that business.

What Happens When the Post Office Becomes an E-Business?

- The US government is made up of many businesses, including the United States Postal Service. You might think the Post Office has no competition to beat, but think again. With various overnight carriers competing for delivery business, and e-mail replacing **snail mail**, the Post Office has to attract customers just like any other business. In fact, USPS.com is an excellent example of how E-Commerce gives a traditional **bricks and mortar business** the ability to reach a large customer base and reposition itself in the marketplace.

- E-Commerce is forcing businesses to reinvent themselves. Once the place you went for stamps, the Post Office now offers customers the ability to pay bills online, buy postage online, and send documents securely over the Internet. Another government agency, the Internal Revenue Service, has made similar strides, allowing taxpayers to file tax returns electronically.

Buzzwords

Snail mail refers to any type of mail that is not sent electronically.

Bricks and mortar is a term for a physical business presence, typically a retail store. *Clicks and mortar* is a term used for a business that maintains an online store.

USPS.com Home Page

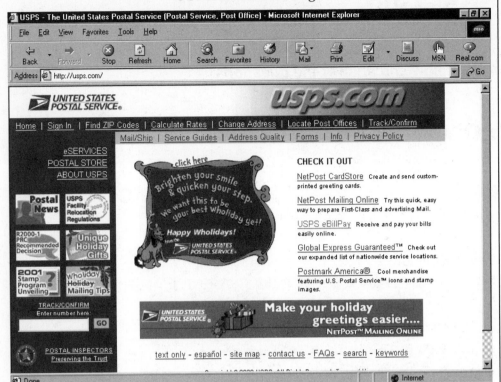

- According to their Web site, USPS eBillPay uses SSL (secure sockets layer); this ensures that your connection and information are secure. USPS eBillPay also uses 40-bit or 128-bit **encryption** (depending on what your browser supports) to make your information unreadable as it passes over the Internet.

Buzzword

Encryption refers to the use of cryptography to convert data into a code so that it can be transmitted over the Internet, yet remain unreadable until it is unencrypted at its destination.

E-BUSINESS ANALYSIS

Take a look at each of these sites (full URLs are located at the end of the exercise), then read the site analysis below and answer the questions.

CASE STUDY: OMAHASTEAKS.COM

- Omaha Steaks has created a site that is rich in content. They include an entire recipe book online, accessed through various categories such as Poultry and Desserts. They also offer a Butcher's Corner with advice about choosing the right cut of meat, as well as information about safe handling of food.

Omaha Steaks Home Page

- One of the reasons that content on OmahaSteaks.com is so successful, is that there are several logical ways for consumers to get to it. For example, you can find products by meat type, such as Seafood or Lamb. But you can also look under Quick & Easy to find products that can be prepared quickly. You can look up products through the Specialty Selections menu, which includes foods like side dishes, appetizers, and desserts. However, some of those same products might be found under the Kosher Food menu or gourmet gift plans. Giving customers several places to find what they want is a convenience bricks and mortar stores can't offer.

Overstock Specials Page

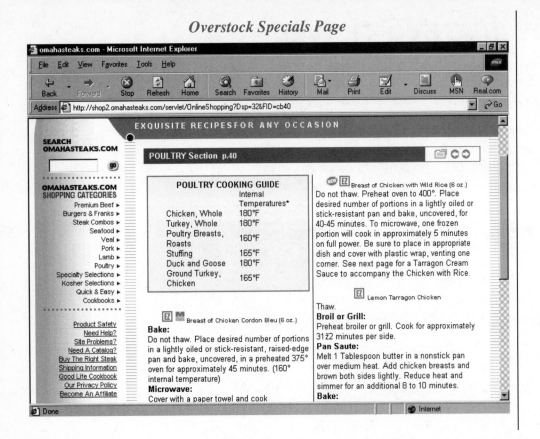

1. How does providing recipes help to sell food at OmahaSteaks.com?

   _____

2. In what ways does OmahaSteaks promote buying food for a gift on its site?

   _____

3. Describe the interests of OmahaSteaks typical customer; how does the site content support that community?

   _____

CASE STUDY 2: ATEVO TRAVEL

■ Travel sites, such as Atevo Travel, face the challenge of time. They must provide immediate and up-to-date information to customers, because travel fares change frequently and specials come and go quickly. They must also provide virtually immediate booking of reservations, because travel carriers and hotels can fill up if there's any delay between the placing of a reservation and its confirmation. For that reason they have to maintain contact with hundreds of travel partners including airlines and hotels.

Atevo Travel Home Page

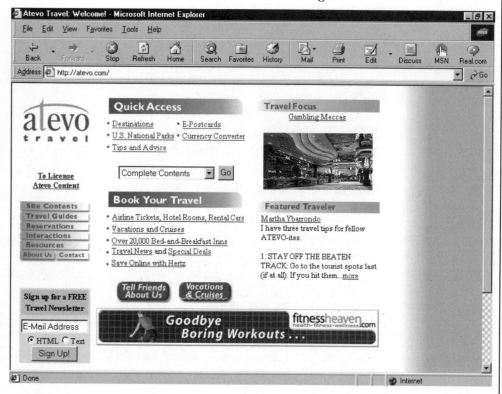

■ One of the ways that travel Web sites generate profit is by selling travel specials that visitors might not otherwise be aware of. Special travel deals often involve a limited time for booking and travel, as well as limited availability. Atevo promotes special deals both on its home page and with detailed descriptions of specials. Note that on their Special Deals page they offer a link to quickly e-mail the deal information to someone else, thereby taking advantage of immediate online word-of-mouth to increase business.

Special Deals Page

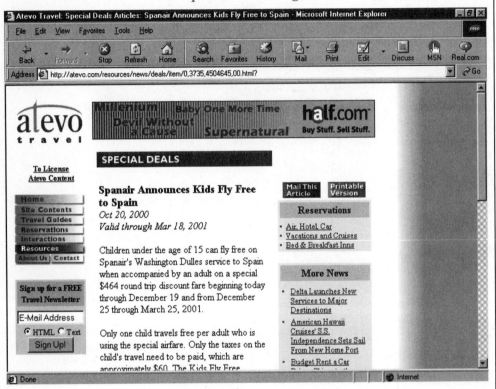

1. Atevo has a feature that allows visitors to tell friends about their site; how does this serve Atevo's business goals?

   _____

2. In what way does the Atevo Web site try to inspire impulse purchases?

   _____

3. At what point is a fare guaranteed to a customer at Atevo.com?

   _____

CASE STUDY 3: USPS.COM

- The United States Postal Service focuses on customer convenience on its site, with features such as the NetPost Mailing Online, which helps businesses prepare advertising mailings; and eBillPay, which allows customers to make immediate payment of bills online. Notice that the only advertising on this page is for USPS and its services; as a government agency, it cannot take outside advertising.

USPS Home Page

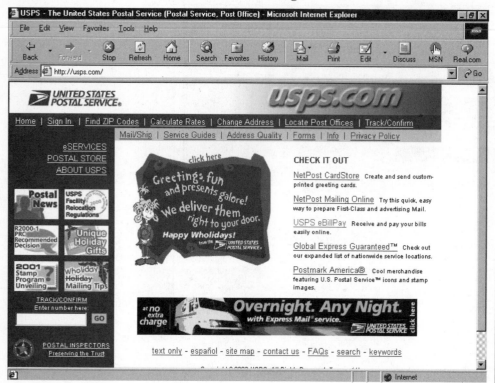

- EBillPay offers several features to attract customers, including security, viewing bills online, making automatic payments, and access 24 hours a day, 7 days a week. This ability to make use of an online site at any time is one of the most attractive aspects of buying online for many customers. USPS takes good advantage of technology to automate its offline services for the Internet age.

eBillPay Page

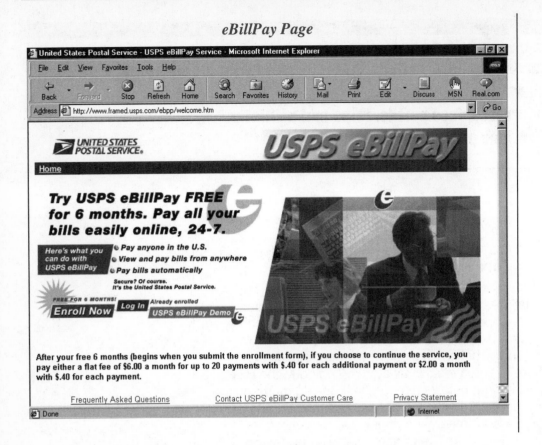

1. What security measures does eBillPay use to protect your privacy?

   _____

2. Using the Calculate Rates feature of USPS.com, figure out what the cost of sending a 10-pound package via 2-day priority mail is.

   _____

3. What services does USPS.com offer that save customers time?

   _____

http://www.ecommercetimes.com
ecommercetimes.com

http://www.fourthchannel.com/
fourthchannel.com

http://omahasteaks.com/
Omaha Steaks

http://www.atevo.com/
Atevo Travel

http://newusps.com/
United States Postal Service

E-Commerce Beyond Your Web Site
- **Examine the integration of a retail store with E-Commerce**
- **Understand how businesses relicense Web content**
- **Explore business partnerships and affiliates**
- **Learn how portals combine content**

NOTES

Study the Relationship Between Bricks and Clicks at Barnes & Noble

- One of the legendary failures of early E-Commerce happened when Barnes & Noble, the retail book chain, set up its online store. Because the .com store was a separate business unit, there was no connection between retail stores and the online version. Customers couldn't get information about where to find a local B&N store by going to the B&N Web site, and they couldn't get help with a purchase they'd made online in a B&N store. When Barnes & Noble figured out that they should convenience the customers by integrating their bricks and mortar business with their online business, their entire operation benefited.

Barnes&noble.com Home Page

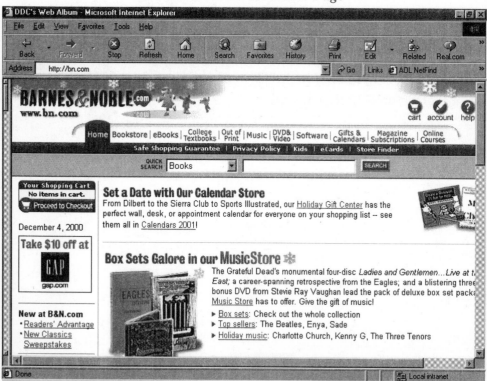

- In the early days of E-Commerce many businesses thought doing business online would be a small adjunct to their real business, and they put minimal effort into integrating the two. In fact, many businesses felt they'd undermine their existing businesses, which had an expensive physical infrastructure to maintain, by selling online. Today, most businesses understand that E-Commerce is inevitable and that it is likely that people will still want to drive to the shopping mall now and then, even though they sometimes buy online. To succeed in business in the future, a business must find a model that integrates the two types of business successfully.

- Booksellers like Barnes & Noble and other businesses are discovering ways to connect their offline and online businesses. Some stores are putting kiosks in their retail locations so shoppers who don't find the book they want can go right to the Web site and order it from the Web store. Most stores provide location directories for their retail stores on their Web site. Innovative ways to handle returns of merchandise bought online in retail stores are being set up. Perhaps the most interesting benefit of this partnership is that booksellers and many other businesses who didn't have much concrete information about their customers and their buying habits, can now get such information from Web sales data.

Groceries Bring Together Online and Offline Operations at Safeway.com

- In a business involving fresh food, ordering online and arranging timely delivery is often a matter of combining the local retail store with the technology of the Internet. If you place an order with Safeway.com, for example, you will most likely still get your groceries from your local grocery store, although this system is sometimes backed up by a centralized grocery warehousing operation. In this model, the Internet provides a sophisticated ordering method and the store offers a new service, home delivery, to complement it.

Safeway.com Home Page

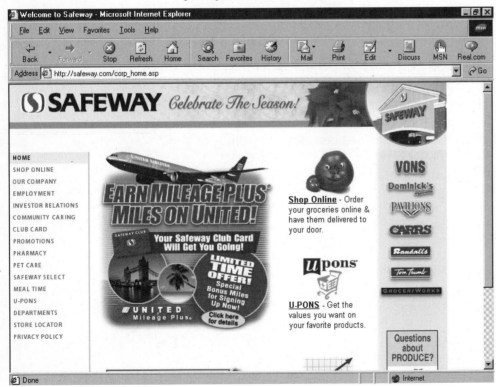

Note

The Store Finder feature on bn.com is a simple search engine you can use to find the address of a store in a database. This feature allows you to narrow your search by checking a series of boxes, such as "Only find stores with a café." Because a database is set up as a series of fields, search engines can return records with no entry in a certain field, any entry in a certain field, or a specific type of entry in that field (such as Yes or No). Database programs use Boolean expressions to search for a condition that is either true or false, using terms such as AND, OR, and NOT.

- The Safeway site offers a discount coupon program that helps to get people into their local grocery stores. You can order these so-called "u-pons" online, and they arrive in the mail. You can then go to your local store and use the coupons. By encouraging use of an offline shopping method from an online site, Safeway is trying to increase sales, control customer buying habits, and keep both business units healthy.

- Safeway.com includes a store locator function that provides graphical maps to pinpoint store locations for customers. Many E-Commerce sites offer brick and mortar store locators to encourage business both online and off. When there is no store in an area, an E-Commerce site should offer a convenient online ordering process so the customer doesn't go looking for a competitor's local retail store.

Learn About a Master of Online Partnerships, AOL.com

- AOL.com has been around for many years as a provider of access to the Internet that also brings together a community of products and services to support their membership. In recent years they've also surfaced with a Web site available to non-AOL members. AOL doesn't provide all of the products and services on its site; instead, they partner with companies such as TD Waterhouse for stock information and Intuit (makers of Quicken software) for financial tools. AOL gets a small profit each time one of their members uses a partner's service, and the partner gets exposure to new customers.

- One aspect of E-Commerce partnering is content relicensing. One company, perhaps a magazine or stock quote business, generates information, and that information is licensed to appear on a partner's site. Because having current, interesting content is a constant challenge for any business with a Web site, there is a real payoff to the cost of a relicensing fees. However, it's essential to monitor these relationships carefully to see if the information the business is providing is really being used and appreciated by the relicensor's customers.

- Online partnerships can get complex. AOL partners with companies to offer special membership deals. For example, if you get an AOL Visa card you get a free month of membership on AOL. The credit card doesn't come from AOL, it comes from First USA. This is a multi-level partnership that is likely to include a payment to AOL for each card obtained through them and increased membership on AOL each time someone applies for a credit card. There is also a promotion involving discounts on rental cars when you use the credit card at Budget Rental Cars. All the partners benefit from increased business, and the customer gets discounts and services they need.

Note

Licensing content to another company's Web site can have several advantages. It can gain exposure for your company's brand, lead customers back to your own Web site, and establish your company as the expert in a particular area.

AOL.com Home Page

- One of the services AOL offers is AOL TV. This is a way to connect to AOL on the Internet through a television over a regular phone line. Many companies are using advances in technology to provide access to their Web sites from televisions, cell phones, Internet appliances, and personal digital assistants. Some of these devices use a standard phone connection, while others take advantage of wireless technology to access a wireless network within certain service areas.

iOwn.com Offers a One-Stop Shopping Experience

- Around 1997 **portals** came to the Internet when major search engines such as Yahoo! began to expand beyond searching to include e-mail, stock quotes, and news headlines. These became sites where someone using the Web could jump off in various directions, making them doorways (or portals) to different areas of interest.

- More recent years have seen the rise of vortals; that is, a portal focused on a **vertical market**. Vortals can focus on an industry, such as the healthcare industry; an interest, such as jogging; an activity such as homebuying; or even a demographic such as senior citizens. iOwn.com is a vortal dedicated to the homeowner; it offers access to real estate services, mortgage companies, contractors for home improvements, and more.

Buzzwords

A *portal* is an entry to the Internet. It is intended to be the first place people see when using the Web. A portal site includes a search engine and may offer e-mail or other services to encourage people to use the site.

A *vertical market* is a specific industry or area of focus. Healthcare is a vertical market, as is the travel industry, and those interested in gourmet food or pets. Businesses target vertical markets through specialized products, promotions, or advertising, and sometimes even specialized businesses.

iOwn.com Home Page

- Portals are typically based on an advertising revenue model. They gather so much information in one place that they keep a visitor on the site longer, opening up additional Web pages and generating more advertising revenue. Advertisers on a vortal offer products or services that are of interest to that one vertical market; this offers a great way for them to target customers that are very likely to be interested in what they have to offer.

- The mortgage rate quote tool on iOwn.com searches a database of currently published interest rates from a variety of companies and generates a table listing those rates. You can use checkboxes on this form to ask to see loans listed starting with the lowest interest rates or with the lowest closing costs. This is essentially a sort feature, similar to the sort feature in a word processor that organizes a list alphabetically or numerically from highest to lowest or vice versa. In a database, however, the sorting feature may actually resequence the records in the database by one or more fields.

Learn About Affiliate Programs at Webmaster-Programs.com

- Another form of online business relationship is called an affiliate program. Affiliate programs are a way for one company to generate sales for another company. The affiliate company places a recommendation or advertisement for their sponsor on their site. The company that actually makes the product handles all the ordering and collecting of payments. Each order that is placed with the sponsor via the affiliate site results in a payment to the affiliate. This is called a commission strategy.

- Transaction tracking software is used to keep tabs on how customers get to a site. This tracking mechanism is the way that a company can tell which site generated a sale for them and so credit the commission

Note

One concern an E-Commerce company should have in getting involved in affiliate programs is maintaining its credibility. If they place a recommendation on their site for a product or service and they haven't fully researched the quality of either the product or company, their own customers may come to distrust them. A few dollars of commission is seldom worth a lost customer.

accurately. Tracking software utilizes robots. A robot is a program that runs automatically without human involvement. Often, a robot utilizes artificial intelligence so that it can respond to different situations it may run into.

Webmaster-Programs.com home page

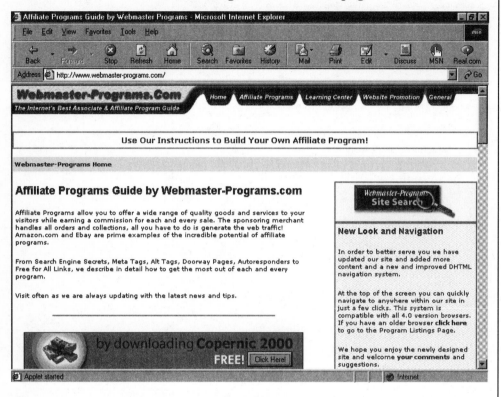

E-BUSINESS ANALYSIS

> *Take a look at each of these sites (full URLs are located at the end of the exercise), then read the site analysis below and answer the questions.*

CASE STUDY 1: BARNES & NOBLE

- Barnes & Noble, a national chain of booksellers, has designed its E-Commerce business to offer an online counterpart to the traditional book buying experience customers can get in retail stores. Barnes & Noble has also made strides in connecting visitors to their site to their stores through features such as the Stores & Events lookup. By using this feature, visitors can see what book signings, readings, or discussions are scheduled at their local Barnes & Noble bookstore. There is also a store locator on the bn.com site.

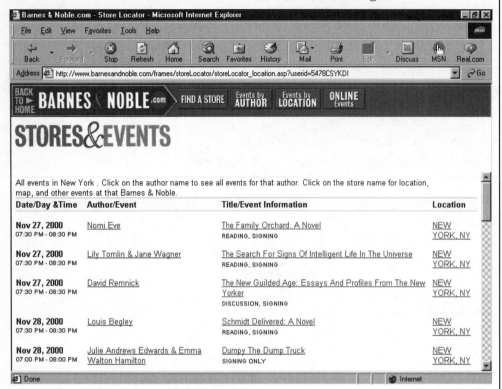

- Barnes & Noble offers services on its Web site that aren't available in their retail stores. Customers have the ability to perform a search for out of print or rare books, to subscribe to magazines, and to buy textbooks. One procedure that Barnes & Noble has instituted at the request of customers is the ability to return online purchases in retail stores. This offers convenience for customers, but it is also a good tactic to drive traffic into Barnes & Noble's retail locations. Note that although customers can get a full refund for an online purchase in a store, B&N suggests a store credit as the first option. A store credit is a way to ensure that the purchase dollars stay with Barnes & Noble.

Barnes&Noble.com Returns Policy Page

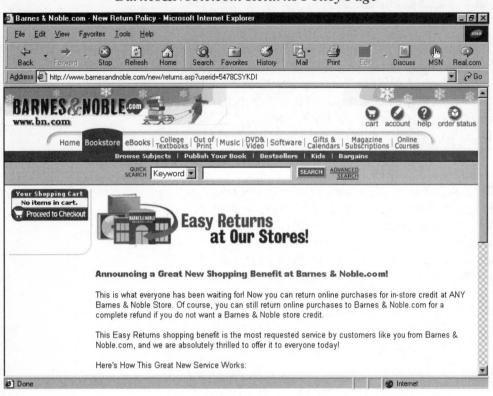

1. What features does the Barnes & Noble Web site offer if you're interested in an out of print book?

   _____

2. Where on a book is an ISBN located?

   _____

3. What are e-books?

   _____

CASE STUDY 2: AOL.COM

- AOL.com's Web site is a fascinating study in how business partnerships can drive content. As you move around the site notice how many features contain a logo or name for a business other than AOL's. For example, go to the Sports Web Channel and you'll see the Total Sports Network's logo in the upper-right hand corner. AOL provides much of its content through these partners, giving exposure to the partner for their name and branding and value to AOL.com's visitors to keep them coming back to the site.

- AOL offers visitors the ability to personalize their content through a feature called My AOL. This model is used by many Internet service providers and search engines, such as Earthlink and Yahoo!. In AOL's case, a My AOL page might contain weather, a stock portfolio, and current news, although a user can customize what content he or she wants to include. Each of these pieces of content is actually provided by an organization with whom AOL has partnered. Visitors can also make their My AOL page their home page (the page that appears every time they log onto the Internet). This ensures that they will visit AOL.com at least once every time they go online.

My AOL Page

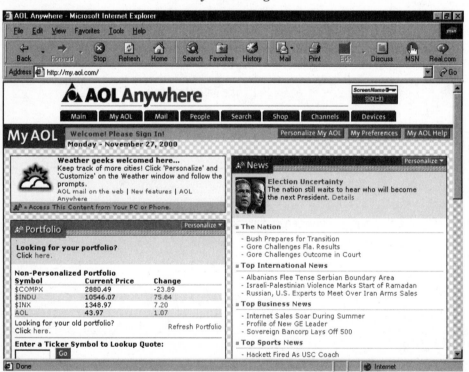

1. Name four partners you can spot by reviewing the AOL.com site.

   _____

2. What company provides TV listings on AOL.com?

   _____

3. In what ways can a visitor customize the My AOL page?

   _____

22

CASE STUDY 3: IOWN.COM

- iOwn.com is a portal for homebuyers. This site is typical of a portal, in that it has a core interest, home owning, and brings together many businesses related to that interest. In this case, visitors can search for a home and realtor, but they can also look for a contractor for home improvements, find mortgage financing, and buy home insurance. Some of those related items bring additional selling opportunities. For example, the insurance page offers not only home owner's insurance, but also life and auto insurance. In this way portals can offer an opportunity for a company to products or services that aren't directly related to their vertical market.

iOwn.com Insurance Page

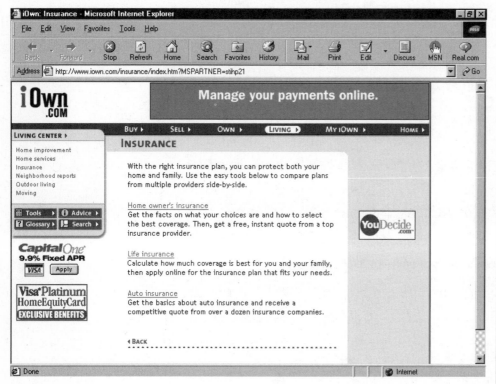

- iOwn.com's home improvement page is run by ImproveNet. On this page visitors can search ImproveNet's database of contractors. Notice that this page asks visitors to register. By registering, a visitor's contact information becomes available to both iOwn.com and ImproveNet. This enables both of them to send notices and special offers to registered users and potentially to sell that contact information to other businesses. Selling lists of potential customers is a very lucrative practice; however because of customer complaints and privacy legislation, most Web sites now offer the option when someone registers of choosing not to receive offers or have information sold to others.

iOwn.com's Find A Contractor Feature through ImproveNet

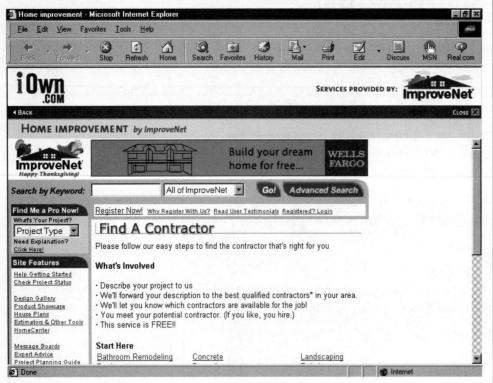

1. How many categories of business can you see represented on iOwn.com (construction, insurance, etc.)?

   _____

2. What benefits does registering visitors have for a Web business?

   _____

3. What is a portal?

   _____

http://bn.com
Barnes&Noble.com

http://Safeway.com/
Safeway

http://aol.com/
AOL

http://iown.com/
iOwn.com

http://www.webmaster-programs.com
Webmaster-Programs

Theme 3

Buying and Selling Activities
- Learn how electronic procurement can save money
- Explore the dynamics of E-Marketplaces
- Discover how businesses are integrating online stores with back end processes, such as invoicing and distribution
- Examine the structure of an online shopping cart

NOTES

Get the Best Price at LendingTree.com

- The central activity of E-Commerce is buying and selling online. This can be in the form of a transaction where a consumer buys from an online store, one business buys from another, or a collective of businesses procures products or services. Around the actual placing of an order are other activities: **transaction processing** (where an order placed with a credit card is processed so the online merchant receives payment); fulfillment (actually pulling the products out of inventory to complete the order); and distribution (shipping of products to customers).

- When businesses buy from businesses, there is often a negotiation or bidding process. This is referred as the purchasing cycle, or on the Internet, as **E-Procurement**. Technology has automated the E-Procurement process; robot software can to go out onto the Internet, search various vendors, and return with a list of prices or even specific bids. Some Web sites, such as Priceline.com or LendingTree.com, even allow consumers to bid out products or services, in effect having businesses compete for our dollars by offering prices they think will undercut their competition.

- At LendingTree.com, customers can enter information about their mortgage requirements, and the service sends out those requirements to dozens of potential lenders, returning the four best bids in a matter of hours. This ability to use technology to shop for the best price is placing more control in the consumer's hands.

Buzzwords

Transaction processing refers to the processing of any online payment by a merchant.

E-Procurement is the process of obtaining bids, negotiating, and purchasing from a company online.

LendingTree.com Home Page

- When you find the right deal and are ready to buy, chances are a transaction system that uses Electronic Data Exchange, or EDI, will be involved. EDI is a system that includes customer input, vendor authentication of that input, and an electronic payments program. All EDI systems utilize established security protocols to protect data being transmitted during the transaction.

Learn about E-Marketplaces from Sterling Communications

- E-Marketplaces, also called **B2B** exchanges, are a form of online community. These communities are formed to create a collective of buyers and provide them with access to information, vendors, and services geared toward their industry. For example, several large car manufacturers created one of the first E-Marketplaces, where suppliers of metal, plastics, tires, and other parts and materials used in making cars can bid for their business.

- E-Marketplaces are shifting the buying/selling dynamic. Because those running the E-Marketplace collectively represent huge buying power, those selling within an E-Marketplace are incented to bid aggressively for business. In addition, smaller vendors who might never have gotten their foot in the door of a giant such as Ford or General Motors, now can gain access to the bidding process.

- Many consulting and technology companies, such as Sterling Communications, are springing up to assist businesses in creating and running E-Marketplaces. Several companies have created E-Marketplace software, such as Exchange from Oracle or Commerce One. This software assists in the creation and running of E-Marketplaces and is often customized for a specific marketplace's needs.

Buzzword

B2B stands for business-to-business and relates to any E-Commerce activity between two businesses, as opposed to between a business and customer (B2C) like you or me.

Technical Note

Many E-Marketplaces are designed and hosted by application service providers, or ASPs. This saves any individual business in the collective from having to host the marketplace on their own server.

Sterling Communications Home Page

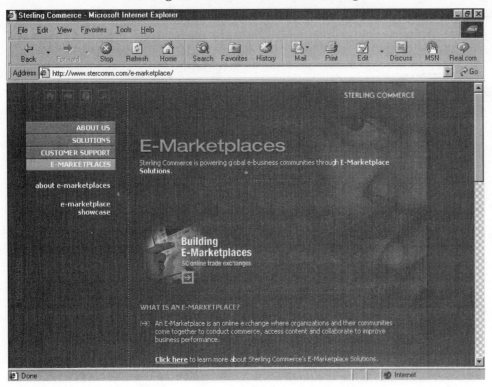

Learn How the Movies Do Business at Filmtrust.com

- One of the important aspects of B2B purchasing online is the ability to automate several aspects of the purchasing process. E-Marketplaces such as Filmtrust.com not only provide access to suppliers, they also provide a system to create and track purchase orders and do online invoicing. In many cases, these systems are designed to integrate with a company's own business systems such as enterprise resource planning, or ERP, software. This type of software links various functions, such as purchasing, inventory, manufacturing, and distribution, so that an activity in one business unit is automatically reflected in updated data in all areas of the business.

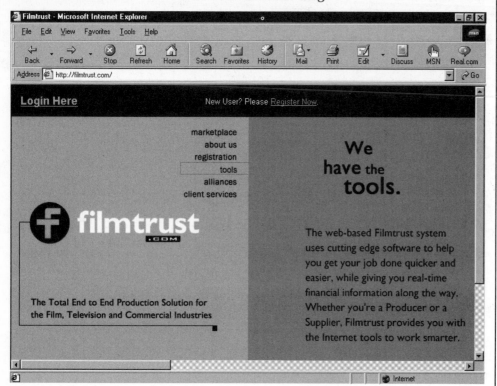

- Some E-Marketplaces are open only to a membership; others, such as Filmtrust, are open to anybody. Most E-Marketplaces establish a set of community rules, which are essentially business practices that anyone who participates must agree to follow. Rules are either created by the entity that runs the E-Marketplace, or by its founding members. One key to the success of any E-Marketplace is building the marketplace membership on both the buying and selling sides. The more members a site gets, the more credibility it gets in its industry and among reputable vendors.

- When you go to the marketplace section of Filmtrust, there are two ways to locate a vendor; one is to select a category of vendor, the other is to look through an alphabetical listing by clicking on a letter from A to Z. Each letter contains a hyperlink to a page that contains all entries for that letter.

Experience How Shopping Carts Work at OpenaStore.com

- A shopping cart is a software application that fulfills the function of an electronic product catalog with an order-processing feature. Customers use shopping cart functionality to select merchandise, compile an order, review or change their selections, and place the order. A shopping cart application on a Web site usually interacts with a company's business software to process payments, track inventory, and fill the order. You can buy shopping cart software, or get it as a customized solution from a vendor who also hosts your E-Commerce store.

- OpenaStore.com is an example of a hosted solution that includes a catalog/shopping cart function, Web site design, and credit card processing. As you'll see in the demo of their shopping cart on their Web site, it's important that a shopping cart provide the opportunity for

Note
Most E-Marketplaces are not currently making a profit for the owners of the sites. As they get more active, however, profit models that include a transaction fee or a membership fee will support the sponsoring entity's involvement.

customers to get help, make changes to their orders at various points in the shopping process, and get information on topics such as shipping and returns policies at any time. A serious issue for E-Commerce businesses is shopping cart abandonment. This simply means that a customer begins placing items in a shopping cart, only to cancel the process or simply leave the Web site before placing the order. One of the major reasons for shopping cart abandonment is when customers become confused with the process, so making your ordering process simple to understand and control is of great importance.

OpenaStore.com Home Page

- Online stores institute security at the point in the buying process when a customer is ready to check out of the store, because this is the point where he or she will transmit personal and credit card information. Online security involves a secure protocol called secure sockets layer, or SSL. SSL was created by Netscape to send private data over the Internet.

Learn How Car Parts Get Where They're Going at iAutoparts.com

- When an online business sells products that it doesn't manufacture itself, it faces a distribution challenge. Take iAutoparts.com as an example. You can use this site to look for a specific auto part from a variety of manufacturers and order the part. Fulfilling each order requires that iAutopart.com obtain the part from a car manufacturer and ship it to the customer.

- iAutopart.com maintains 45 distribution warehouses around the country where they stock many parts. This addresses their distribution challenge to some degree, but they must be prepared to quickly locate and ship parts that they don't have in stock. In their model, they have created alliances with the car manufacturers so that they can obtain both new parts and parts for older models quickly and easily.

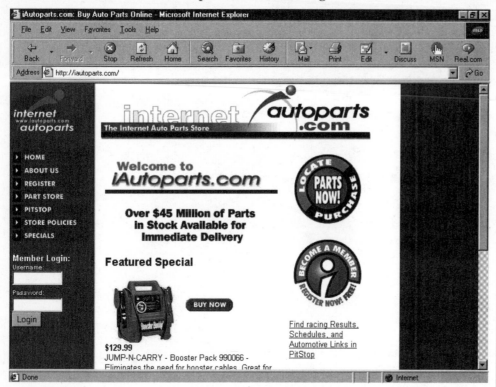

- Warehousing large quantities of materials or products on hand is a huge cost to businesses. Advances in technology have allowed many businesses to implement **just-in-time inventory** practices. Some businesses have integrated their inventory systems with their vendors. A vendor therefore knows when a particular item is running low and they can contact their customer to initiate a replenishment order. Other companies simply use tracking software to alert their purchasing department to inventory status in plenty of time to order more. Because many larger companies maintain several distribution centers in different geographic areas, the time to get new products to a customer is usually minimal. Also, many vendors work with their customers to ship merchandise directly from their distribution centers to customers. This is often referred to as drop-shipping.

Buzzword

Just-in-time inventory involves purchasing practices that allow a business to monitor inventory and replenish it as needed, rather than keeping large quantities on hand.

E-BUSINESS ANALYSIS

> *Take a look at each of these sites (full URLs are located at the end of the exercise), then read the site analysis below and answer the questions.*

CASE STUDY 1: LENDINGTREE.COM

- Financial institutions are moving online in a big way. People are banking online, investing online, and checking credit card balances online. Lending institutions have not been left behind. Companies that offer loans of all kinds are trying to attract customers through their own Web sites. Other sites have been created to offer potential customers access to a wide variety of lending institutions so they can choose the loan product and institution they prefer.

- LendingTree.com is one such site. Here a consumer can request bids on several kinds of loans, ranging from mortgages, home equity loans, auto loans, and even small business loans.

LendingTree.com Home Page

- The customer begins LendingTree.com's bid process by filling out a form with information about the type of loan he or she wants, and information about his or her financial situation, such as income and current debt.

31

LendingTree.com Application Form

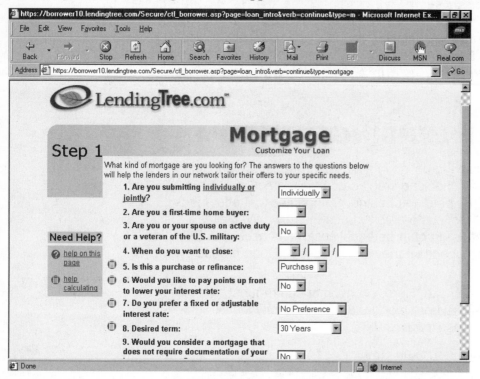

■ The information the customer submits is shared with dozens of lending institutions through an automated system. Within a few hours, those institutions process the application, and place a bid in a private area of LendingTree.com, accessible to the borrower with a password assigned by LendingTree, for review. Each lender also sends an e-mail directly to the customer with the same offer.

Lending Institution Bids for a Customer's Business

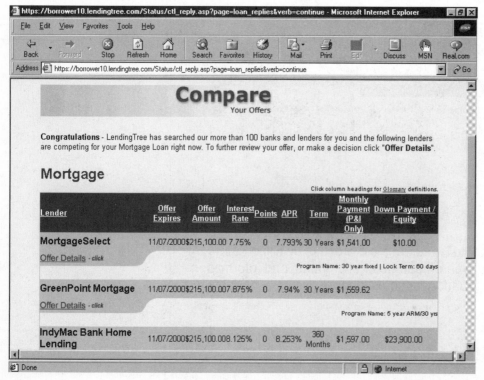

- This approach of aggregating, or bringing together in one place, several businesses is convenient for customers. It also provides another avenue of access to the customers for the lending businesses. However, because these companies will have their products presented to the customer side-by-side with competitors, each business participating in such a site must be very careful to be familiar with their competition's offerings in order to make competitive bids.

- Note that this practice of bringing together several vendors to bid for business is also done on a business-to-business level through E-Marketplaces.

1. What is firewall protection and why does LendingTree.com provide it to consumers?

   _____

2. What security measures might protect a customer providing financial information to dozens of lenders at LendingTree.com?

   _____

3. What help features does LendingTree.com offer in filling out a mortgage application?

   _____

CASE STUDY 2: OPENASTORE.COM

- Openastore.com is a company that provides not only software solutions for E-Commerce, but hosted services. Hosting refers to a business that places another business's online store on its server. Openastore is then responsible for maintaining the server and network functions of that store for its customer. A business that provides software applications, often customized to a client's needs, along with a hosting service, is referred to as an ASP, or application service provider.

Openastore.com Home Page

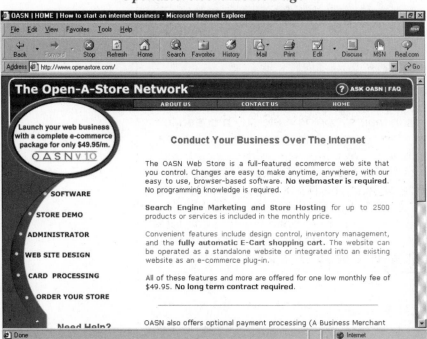

- Openastore.com provides several features to the businesses that are its customers, including Web site design, credit card processing, inventory management, a catalog/shopping cart function, and hosting. The catalog/shopping cart demo on the Openastore.com site shows how their store model provides several functions. Customers can:

  - view a catalog page with product pictures; they can click on a product to see more details

  - get information on ordering options, as shown in the following figure

  - get more information about the company behind the store

  - ask questions of the customer service department

  - review their shopping carts

  - checkout, ordering all the items in their shopping carts by providing shipping and payment information

Openastore.com Demo, Order Options Page

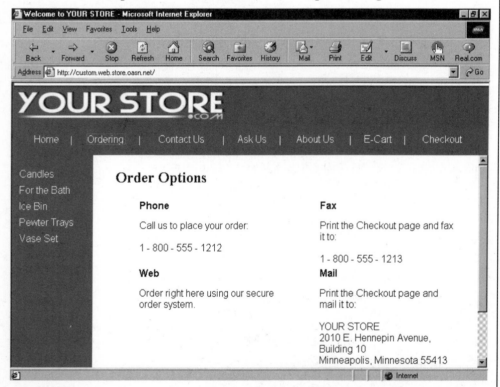

- When customers place products in their shopping carts and proceed to checkout, there are still several steps to complete their orders. First, the customer is given the opportunity to review what's in his or her cart, with information such as Price, Options, Quantity, and Subtotal. The customer is, at this point, offered the option of changing the quantity of items in the cart, or deleting specific items. After filling in shipping and payment information, the customer will be given one more option to confirm that the order is correct. It's important that customers be offered this chance to review an order before placing it, so they don't make a mistake, which can be frustrating for the customer and costly for the business that must manually correct an order.

Openastore.com E-Cart Page

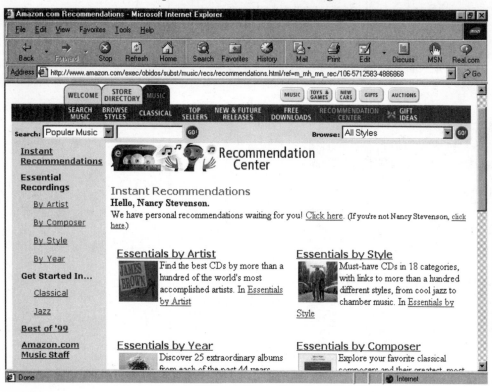

1. What two options for Web site design does Openastore.com offer?

   _____

2. What features does the Administrator element of the openastore.com service offer?

   _____

3. How many products can an OASN store host?

   _____

CASE STUDY 3: IAUTOPARTS.COM

- iAutoparts.com is an Internet auto parts store. The company stocks $45 million car parts and has established alliances with car manufacturers that allow them to purchase new and even older car parts and fill customer orders quickly. Because ordering car parts directly rather than having a mechanic do it suggests that customers will do the work on their cars themselves, iAutoparts.com assumes these are car enthusiasts. Therefore, they include added-value content on their site for this audience, including car racing results and schedules and links to sites related to automobiles.

iAutoparts.com Build Your Own Page

- iAutoparts.com features a page titled Specials. This is the online equivalent of a display on a rack at the front of a retail store. Retail businesses often highlight discounted items, typically because they are overstocked on those items and want to get rid of inventory. Sometimes, these specials are seasonal; for example, an autoparts store might put antifreeze on special when cold weather hits. Selling online offers the convenience of being able to change the display of specials every day by simply placing information about a new item on a Web page. Because this is much easier than building and tearing down physical displays in a store, online stores often rotate promotions on a regular basis.

iAutoparts.com Specials Page

1. Of the three sites analyzed above, which are examples of B2B sites? Why?

   _____

2. Why does iAutoparts.com ask customers to register?

   _____

3. Look at iAutoparts.com's returns policy; what is a core part and how is it treated differently when a customer wants to return it?

   _____

http://lendingtree.com
LendingTree.com
http://www.stercomm.com/
Sterling Communications
http://filmtrust.com/
FilmTrust.com
http://www.openastore.com/
Openastore.com
http://iautoparts.com/
iAutoparts.com

Customer Support Activities
- Learn about customer relationship management online
- Explore customer service policies and procedures
- See how E-Commerce companies provide information to customers
- Understand how outsourcing works

NOTES

Learn About Customer Resource Management at SearchCRM.com

- **Customer resource management (CRM)** is a new term for customer service, and it goes beyond helping customers with problems or questions. CRM puts the focus on building long-term relationships with customers, not just on their satisfaction with any single transaction. searchcrm.com is a portal where you can access customer relationship management news, look up CRM vendors, and research CRM-related Web sites.

searchcrm.com Home Page

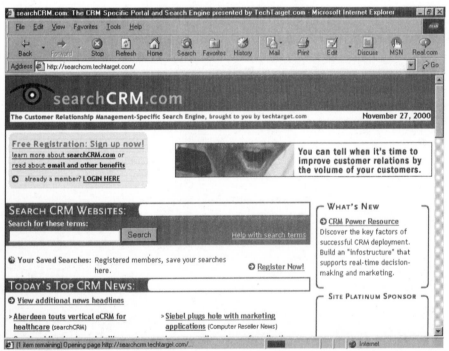

Buzzword
CRM stands for customer resource management. This includes not only traditional customer service, but also initiatives to personalize service and offer benefits that build long-term customer relationships.

- Today there are many companies that provide customer service products or services. For example, you can hire a company whose employees will answer phones as if they were your employees and deal with customer complaints or requests for you. This saves you the cost of staff, extra office space, and phone lines. You can also purchase customer service software that helps you build and maintain a database of customer information so that you can easily pull up records of customer preferences and buying history. searchCRM.com offers Vendor Central, which makes searching for CRM consultants, hardware and software, and various services easy.

- Editor's Picks at searchCRM.com is a good place to learn about the basics of customer service online; it provides a glossary of CRM terms, reviews of books about CRM, links to CRM associations, and case studies to show you how CRM works in action.

- searchCRM.com requires that visitors register to use certain features. This allows the company that runs searchCRM.com to assemble a database of information on its customers, the people who visit and access information on its site.

Learn About Sales Techniques and Legal Issues at CRMXchange

- Online commerce is relatively new; therefore all those participating in it are, to some extent, learning as they go. There is a lot you can learn from the experience of your E-Commerce peers. This site is focused around forums and exchanges for information, advice, and software and hardware for the CRM professional. You can chat about issues, and even sell used customer service phone equipment here.

CRMXchange

- Servicing customers over the Internet brings up a host of legal issues, including customer privacy, intellectual property rights, and adherence to interstate shipping and tax regulations. Go to the Legal Column at CRMXchange.com to get advice about customer-related legal issues such as shipping regulations and privacy initiatives. These columns are written by lawyers who specialize in Internet commerce issues.

- A weekly sales tip for customer service professionals is provided by the President of a New York-based consulting firm that assists people in setting up call center training programs. A call center is the facility at the other end of the 800 number you use to call a company for customer

Technical Note

Customer service makes use of several technologies, including interactive voice response systems, artificial intelligence-driven systems for routing online inquiries to the appropriate resource, and speech recognition software.

service; for E-Commerce, this "call center" may be the place that e-mail from customers is read and replied to. Depending on the nature of the product or service the company sells, the call center may provide technical support, deal with customer complaints, or provide information to help customers get the most out of their purchases.

Federal Express Helps Customers with Customer Service Tools and Services

- One great way to see what's being done in the area of customer service online is to visit sites of companies who are doing it right. Federal Express, which provides shipping services to individuals and companies worldwide, offers customers many self-service tools to make their shipping experience successful. Giving your customer the ability to get information online at any time, without having to speak to a company representative, is one of the advantages of E-Commerce customer support. It benefits the user who often gets more immediate help, and it saves the company money over an in-person interaction.

- Various account management tools at FedEx.com allow a customer to open an account, order shipping supplies, and track shipments online. They can also get information on their privacy rights and what to do if they have to file a claim for a shipping loss.

- Providing information and advice to customers helps them have a more successful buying experience. That helps to generate loyalty to your company and product or service, which typically results in repeat business. For example, if a customer is using FedEx to ship to another country, he or she should be aware of days when shipping services are not available in that country. FedEx provides a lookup tool on its site to research local shipping holidays. Customers can also go to the E-Commerce Builder section for help in running their own online businesses. There is information and free software here to help with order management, business analysis, marketing, and customer management.

Federal Express Customer Service Page

Note

Note the many ways customers can contact Federal Express, including a TDD service for the hearing impaired. It helps your customers if you can provide several ways to reach you, including phone, fax, and e-mail.

- The FedEx privacy policy specifies that cookies may be used in certain areas of the site. **Cookies** are files that are created when a user accesses a site; they are stored on a user's hard drive, and offer a way for the company running a site to track visitor activities and preferences.

Learn How Amazon.com Handles Customer Returns

- Amazon.com was one of the early **E-Commerce business-to-consumer** (B2C) success stories in terms of customer relationship management. Once only a purveyor of books, Amazon has branched out in recent years to offer an auction site, music, software, electronics, and more.

- Go to the Amazon.com Web site and click on Help to reach their customer service area. Customers can obtain information on ordering and redeeming gift certificates here. They can also sign up for a gift registry service, indicating the types of products they'd like to receive and letting Amazon notify potential gift givers of their choices.

Amazon.com Customer Service Page

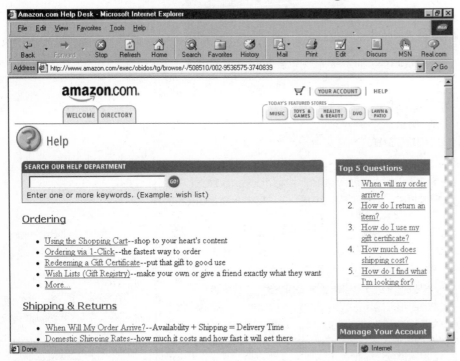

Buzzwords

Cookies are files that are created when a user access a site; they are stored on a user's hard drive and can be used to track online activities.

E-commerce deals with buying and selling activity over the Internet.

Business-to-consumer, also called B2C, refers to business activities directed to a consumer, rather than from one business to another. Activity between two businesses is referred to as *Business-to-Business*, or B2B.

- One detail that keeps some people from buying things online is shipping, especially if the customer is concerned about the possibility of returning a product. A helpful and efficient returns system is very important to convincing customers to buy from you. Amazon.com has a generous returns policy, allowing up to 30 days to return items and even paying for shipping if a product is damaged or there was an error in the order. Amazon does not allow for exchanges, however. Note that the Help page offers a link for self-repair advice to help customers solve their own product problems to avoid the returns process entirely.

- There is a table on the Amazon.com Help page that lists the Top 5 Questions that customers ask with links to the answers. By using a Web page editor, such as FrontPage or WebExpress, you can view the formatting of cells in a table not in code, but as familiar formatting settings, as shown below.

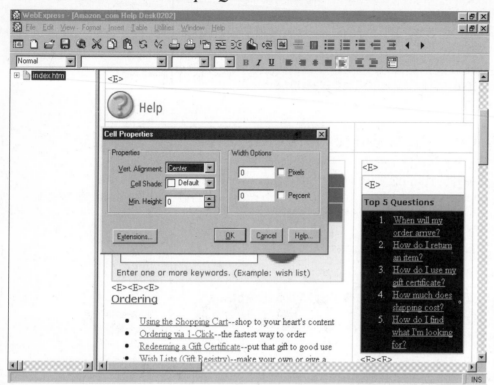

Customize Products at Chrysler.com

- Many car companies, such as Chrysler, have made the leap to the Internet in recent years, offering product information and tools to help customers design and price the cars of their dreams. Customers can click on the Trade-in Value link on Chrysler.com's home page to learn how much their current car is worth before they visit their dealer. The Finance Options service gives information about various possibilities for car loans and leasing; customers can also check out Available Incentives to see if the model they want offers a special rebate or other discount program.

- One of the strengths of the Internet is that it can provide customers with personalized buying experiences, and tools for customizing their purchase to their specific needs. When a customer goes into a bricks and mortar store he or she is usually limited to the items available on the floor; at an E-Commerce store the customer can ask for a product in any available color, size, or style, and even preview how it will look before he buys.

- Visitors can click on a vehicle from the Chrysler.com home page, then use the Build Your Own tool. This feature walks customers through a series of screens to select options such as color, accessory packages, and sound system.

Note
Providing a customer with tools to price and review different product or service options before buying saves your employees time they might spend reviewing this information with customers one-on-one. Be sure, however, to offer a way for customers to get help with these tools if they need it.

Chrysler.com Home Page

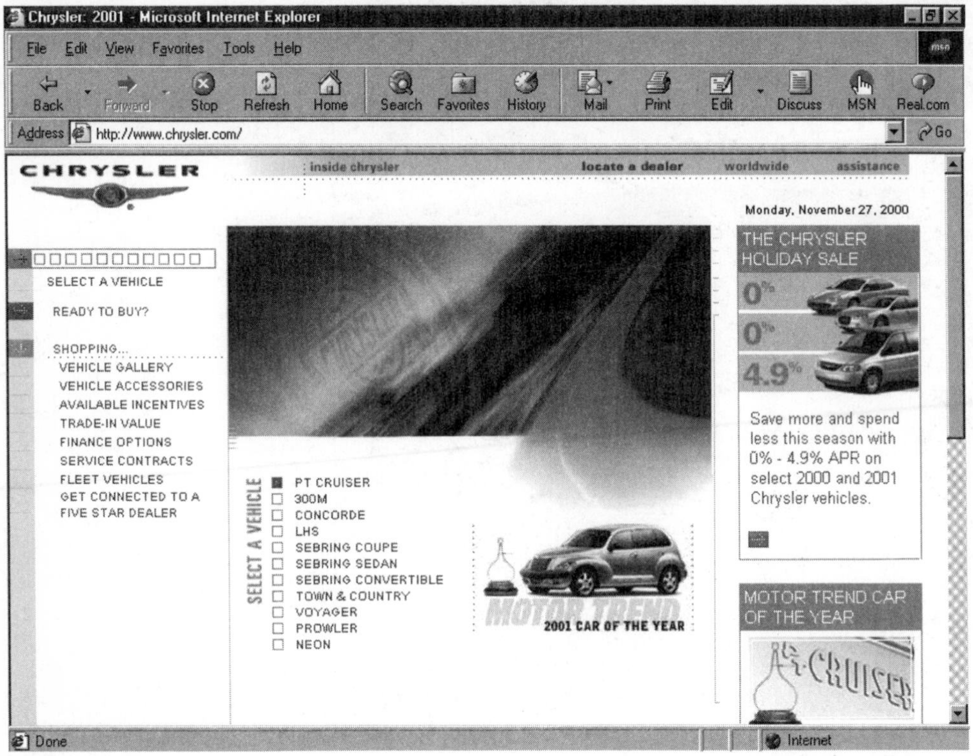

On the Chrysler home page customers are offered a table with all the available models. When a visitor clicks in a box next to a model name, or even passes the mouse over a model name, an image of that model appears to the right of the table.

E-BUSINESS ANALYSIS

Take a look at each of these sites (full URLs are located at the end of the exercise), then read the site analysis below and answer the questions.

CASE STUDY 1: FEDERAL EXPRESS.COM

- Many companies are discovering that providing tools to help customers with their buying experience saves the company money. For example, on the Federal Express site, there are many tools, ranging from package tracking to dealing with international shipping forms.

Federal Express Home Page

■ Providing tools that help customers is a nice thing for a company to do and may help build customer loyalty. But the real benefit to business is the money it saves by not having employees interact with customers. Allowing customers to track their own packages really puts the work on the customers' shoulders, rather than an employee's. What may seem like a convenience may actually be a way for customers to help themselves.

FedEx eBusiness Tools Page

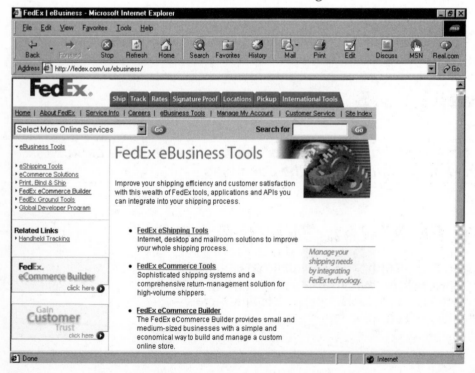

■ The eBusiness Tools listed in the figure on the previous page go beyond shipping help and offer support for customers' eBusinesses. Why does FedEx provide such tools? Consider that if Federal Express helps a company succeed in its online business, Federal Express is likely to get some of that company's shipping business. Other tools such as the eShipping tools shown in the figure below are provided to make the customer's shipping experience go smoothly with the intent that the customer is more likely to ship again with FedEx if all goes well.

FedEx eShipping Tools Page

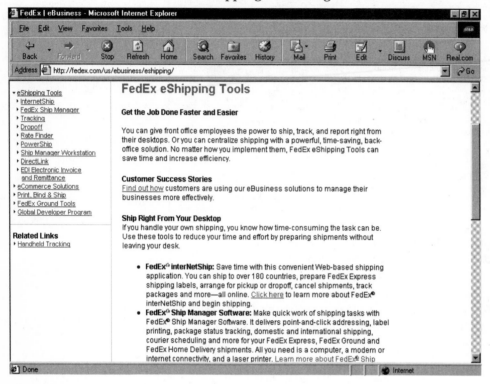

1. What is FedEx InterNetShip and how does it help customers?

   _____

2. How many Express and Ground packages can you track on the Fed Ex site?

   _____

3. What is EDI Electronic Invoice and Remittance?

   _____

CASE STUDY 2: AMAZON.COM

■ Amazon.com puts strong emphasis on personalization on its site. You can see this on its home page, which includes a personalized greeting (Hello, Nancy Stevenson), as well as personal recommendations for products based on the customer's past buying patterns. This tracking of customer preferences by purchase is done automatically, using technology such as cookies and keywords associated with products.

Amazon.com Home Page

- Amazon includes a Recommendation Center feature that allows you to search by categories, such as artist, year, or style. By offering recommendations to visitors, Amazon encourages impulse purchases; that is, purchases of products other than the products the customer came online to buy. Amazon also offers features to help customers discover new categories of products they've never purchased through its Get Started In… feature.

Amazon.com Recommendation Center Page

1. How does Amazon use links in its home page recommendations to cross-sell additional products?

   _____

2. How does the Amazon Wish List feature in the Gifts area of the Web site work?

   _____

3. What does Amazon.com sell in addition to books?

   _____

CASE STUDY 3: CHRYLSER.COM

■ Sometimes a Web site can provide more than facts and figures to customers. For example, the Chrysler.com Web site provides a tool that lets customers build their own model of a car, making choices among colors, features, models, and so on. Once they've made their choices, a suggested retail price is displayed.

Chrysler.com Build Your Own Page

■ The Chrysler Web site also allows customers to look up local dealers through the Locate a Dealer tool, search for current incentives, such as rebates on selected models, and find information on service contracts. Although customers still have to work with a dealer when they're ready to buy a car, this site allows them to do their homework and pin down exactly what they want to purchase. With a product like a car where a price is often negotiated, an educated consumer can help make the purchasing process more comfortable for all concerned.

Chrysler.com Dealer Locator Page

1. What is a suggested retail price?

   _____

2. What criteria can you use to search for a…etc.

   _____

3. What is trade-in value?

   _____

http:searchCRM.com
searchCRM.com
http://CRMXchange.com/
CRMXchange.com
http://fedex.com/
Federal Express
http://www.amazon.com/
Amazon.com
http://www.Chrysler
Chrysler

Learning E-Commerce
Part I, Applications of E-Commerce
Capstone Project

Summary of Concepts

- E-Commerce refers to buying and selling activities over the Internet. E-Commerce includes direct sales to customers, business-to-business purchasing, and customer service and support online. When selling online, businesses must find ways to automate fulfillment (filling orders) and distribution (shipping) of products to make shopping online convenient and affordable for customers.

- E-Commerce provides a way for businesses large and small to reach a wider audience and to get their names in front of millions of people with sophisticated marketing techniques.

- One challenge facing companies is how to integrate an existing bricks and mortar store with an E-Commerce initiative, resulting in clicks and mortar success. Learning how to build and leverage strategic business partnerships is also a key part of doing business online.

- E-Commerce customers are concerned with ease of use through simple ordering and returns processes, a personalized shopping experience, and security for their credit card payments.

Case Study

The Business:

- All Creatures is a small publishing company located in Western Massachusetts. It publishes books on pets and exotic animals, which it sells through retail bookstores. The company currently has 105 employees and a single warehouse located behind their office. The company publishes approximately 80 titles a year. Customers buy their books at local bookstores, or through online bookstores such as Amazon.com. All Creatures, therefore, usually doesn't have direct contact with its end users, the readers of its books.

- The CEO of All Creatures has decided it's time to create an online bookstore to sell their books directly to customers. Although this is not intended to be the major **sales channel** for the company, it will allow them to accomplish three key goals:

  1. They can gather some demographic information about their customers, such as age, income and so on, by taking surveys and collecting personal information during the ordering process. This will help them target their products more accurately to market needs and interests.

Buzzword
A *sales channel* is one outlet for sales of a product or service. For example, a company that sells toys might sell them over the Internet, through toy superstores, such as Toys R Us®, in discount stores, such as K-Mart, or in children's clothing stores in malls.

2. They can establish themselves as a company that offers support to the pet-owning community by providing added value on their Web site. They will offer a regular column about pet-health issues written by a veterinarian, tips from a professional pet groomer, links to pet-related Web sites, and a calendar of pet-related events around the country. This valuable content will help to build loyalty to the publisher among their customers.

3. Through their online store, All Creatures will create stronger brand recognition. When pet lovers search for pet-related information, search engine results will lead them to AllCreatures.com. In addition, the company will establish links from other sites to their own site. In this way the All Creatures name and logo will be placed in front of potential customers on a regular basis. This improved branding is expected to payoff in both online sales and sales through retail stores, as browsing customers spot the name and logo on retail shelves.

Note

A company's brand consists of the recognition among the buying public of its name, logo, and image. Disney, for example, uses Mickey Mouse as one of its symbols and has an image of wholesome family fun. Building up brand recognition attracts customers to buy from a company and creates ongoing customer loyalty.

The Project:

- Make a list of competitive challenges this business would face doing business online, including specific examples of competitors who are already online. Select a couple of competitors' Web sites and see what image they are projecting. What services do they provide customers online? How do they provide information on their products to customers on their Web sites? What are those competitors' strengths and weaknesses, and how could All Creatures learn from them? Work alone or in teams to complete this competitive review.

The Business Model:

- To complete this project, you must begin to understand how a company such as All Creatures would build an E-Business model. Here are three important things to consider:

  1. ***Analyze the target market of the business***: age, gender, interests, and income. Will this customer own a computer and go online to shop? Can this customer afford to pay shipping costs above and beyond the product price? Will most customers be repeat customers, buying more than one pet book in a year? Do customers also buy books as gifts?

  2. ***Identify E-Commerce activities the company must establish***: There are business activities, such as online order processing and shipping, that All Creatures must set up. They will have to obtain a **domain name** and submit their site to search engines. Consider how this business will respond to individual customer questions and complaints: they can design their site so that customers can e-mail them with questions, look up information in a frequently asked questions section of the Web site, or call a number for support of Web site issues, for example. Outsourcing some of these activities might be a good way to handle some of these diverse activities initially.

  3. ***Explore how this business could build its customer base and branding through an E-Commerce presence:*** The Internet can be used to extend a company's image with a Web presence. This company should look for market segments it could reach online that it isn't reaching through existing channels. Think of other types of businesses that cater to the same target market, such as pet stores and pet magazines; All Creatures could create partnerships with these organizations to help sell their books. It might be beneficial for All Creatures to place a store finder feature on its Web site so those who don't want to buy online can find a store nearby that stocks their books. Consider the pros and cons of that approach.

- How have competing publishers addressed these issues on their Web sites?

Buzzword

A *domain name* is the alphanumerical, friendly name for a Web site or other Internet site. For example, www.ddcpub.com, www.microsoft.com, and www.whitehouse.gov are all domain names for Web sites.

Technology

- There are technical issues related to various E-Commerce activities, such as payment transaction processing, transaction security, and software that helps a company integrate its bricks and mortar business with online data.

- Use Web sites and books to learn more about the technology underlying E-Commerce activities, such as:

  - 32-bit encryption and how it can make transactions secure

  - database software used to build a useful customer service database

  - security and privacy tools that are available in Web design software

Books to help:

Learning Microsoft FrontPage 2000 (catalog number Z49)

Learning to Create a Web Page with Microsoft Office 2000 (catalog number Z43)

Learning Databases (catalog number Z60)

Web sites to explore:

http://businessintelligence.ittoolbox.com

Learn about various technologies that help a business gather and analyze data about online customers, manage databases of customer data, and more.

http://www.networkcomputing.com

Find out about how encryption and electronic certificates can help to protect both your and your customers' privacy.

http://www.Microsoft.com/support/kb/articles/Q205/6/98.ASP

Learn about adding secure socket layers to Web pages built with FrontPage Web design software.

Part II

The Impact of the Internet on Business

Theme 5

Changing How People Communicate
- **Learn how people are sharing ideas and work online**
- **Understand technologies that drive online communities**
- **See how project teams form workgroups on the Internet**
- **Take a look at the future of virtual conferencing**
- **Discover how businesses interact with customers in real time**

NOTES

YourBestOffice.com Offers a Virtual Office Accessible From Anywhere

- In today's business world the way people are working and communicating is changing in large part because of the Internet. People can share documents, hold discussions in real time, send e-mail, and share their project schedules online. They can form workgroups that collaborate in writing and via voice and video conference. And they can do all this from their own conference room, or on the road anywhere in the world.

- YourBestOffice.com is an interesting example of a virtual office that makes this kind of interaction possible. This site offers file sharing, file storage, discussion groups, e-mail, and bulletin boards that anybody can use to interact with customers or others in their own company. Because these services are hosted on the Internet, they can be accessed from anywhere in the world, from places where an office network or workstation hard drive might be unavailable.

Note

It is possible for a company to set up its network so that employees who are on the road can access files and programs stored on the network through the Internet. Although hosted office sites include security measures, some companies don't like to put their files on a public site. However for those without such a sophisticated IT (Information Technology) structure, hosted office solutions can be very useful and secure.

YourBestOffice.com Home Page

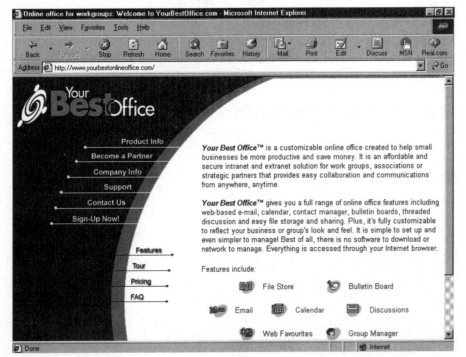

■ One of the benefits of using a hosted office solution such as YourBestOffice.com is that a company doesn't have to maintain a large staff dedicated to supporting a network. Some hosted solutions even provide access to software products, such as Microsoft Office on a licensee basis, so a company could conceivably run all of its daily computing operations outside of its own walls. These online services also provide maintenance and support: YourBestOffice maintains its own servers and provides support for users consisting of a FAQ (frequently asked questions) area, searchable support database, and personal tech support assistance.

O'Reilly WebBoard Supports Online Communities

■ One of the features that makes online communication for business possible is live chat. Live chat is an online discussion that takes place in real time, as opposed to a bulletin board-type of discussion where one person might post a message on Sunday night, which isn't read by someone else until Monday afternoon. In a live chat, those participating type or speak their input, and other participants respond to it immediately. This is called **synchronous** communication, because it is a synchronized conversation, as opposed to a bulletin board-type of discussion, which is referred to as **asynchronous**.

Buzzwords
An online discussion is referred to as *synchronous* when it occurs in real time. An online discussion where there is some delay between participant input is called *asynchronous*.

WebBoard Home Page

■ O'Reilly's WebBoard is a software tool used to build forums and chat rooms for Web sites. A forum is an asynchronous communication area where visitors post comments about a topic that can be read by anyone visiting the forum at any time. A chat room is a synchronous communication area for live discussions. E-Commerce businesses use such forums and chat rooms for customer support, to build communities of customers that make a Web site an attractive destination, or for employees and customers to interact with each other. Some companies, such as book publishers or software companies, sometimes use chats to hold live discussions with authors or other experts. These online events are similar to a call-in radio talk show, where visitors can ask the featured guest questions about a particular topic.

■ Online forums are organized in a structure called *threaded* discussion. One person posts a message, and responses to that message are listed underneath it, with the most recent message at the top. A visitor can follow the thread of this discussion by starting with the oldest message, and reading each one in sequence. Forums typically contain several of these written conversation threads, with the original message marking the start of each discussion.

Project Teams Work Together Online with Microsoft Project Central

■ Project management software, such as Microsoft Project, has been around for many years. This software provides scheduling and resource management tools used by work teams. The most recent version of Microsoft Project includes a feature called Project Central, which supports online collaboration on projects. Members of the team can view tasks to be performed, interact with each other, comment on draft schedules, and update the actual time they've put in on the project on their company intranet or Web site. Most project management software today offers similar features.

Microsoft Project Central White Paper Page

■ Collaborating online is replacing in-person meetings, as well as the distribution of paper documents by hand or mail. Users can be set up to receive updates by e-mail, to get notification of meetings, and to set up meetings with a number of individuals whose schedules must be coordinated. In addition, the ability to copy everybody involved in an effort on key information without having to pick up the phone or print out several copies of a document means that people who need to know are never left out.

- Online collaboration isn't limited to company employees. Increasingly companies are working with vendors, freelance contractors, and even customers, sharing information and getting work done. One technology that helps with this process is viewers. Viewers enable people to view documents created in a software product without actually having the product installed on their computer. Microsoft makes an Office File Viewer available so that anybody can read Office product documents, for example.

Online Conferencing Gets Going with Sites Such as MeetingByWire.com

- Meeting online is not just limited to typing messages into forums or chats. Sophisticated technologies are making videoconferencing a real alternative to in-person meetings. Sound comes through clearly and with no delay, and video images, although still somewhat less than perfect, help participants see each other's expressions and reactions, adding a personal touch to remote conferencing. MeetingbyWire.com is one site dedicated to providing information about conferencing products, especially Microsoft's NetMeeting.

MeetingbyWire.com Home Page

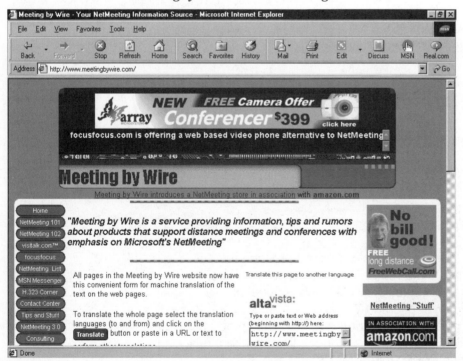

- For businesses today, the ability to have people meet at any time and from any location means huge savings of time and money traditionally spent in traveling to a remote location. The savings in employee productivity are also enormous. In addition, this ease of communication means that it's more realistic than ever for companies to work with vendors anywhere in the world and open remote offices with little concern about employee or information accessibility. Another result of this kind of conferencing is that more and more companies are allowing employees to **telecommute** (work from home).

- Products such as NetMeeting work over IP-enabled networks. IP stands for Internet Protocol, which is part of TCP/IP (Transmission Control Protocol/Internet Protocol). Protocols are essentially the rules that control the transmission of data, and allow dissimilar systems to communicate.

LandsEnd.com Tries Creative Ways to Interact with Customers Online

- E-Businesses are using new technologies to interact with customers as well. LandsEnd.com allows customers to connect with a live shopping assistant through text chat. A customer browsing the site can get advice and information about products, how to order online, or how to determine the right clothing size before making a purchase.

LandsEnd.com Lands' End Live Page

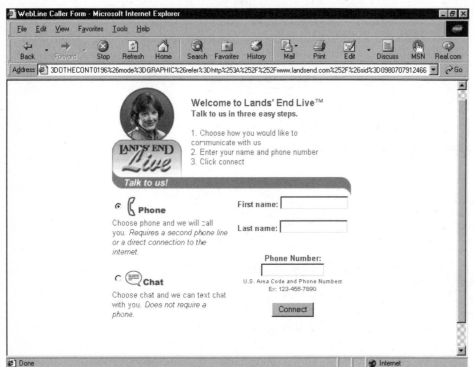

- LandsEnd.com also allows customers to enter their name and phone number while shopping online, and a representative will call and speak with them as they're browsing the Web site. Of course, this requires that a customer have two phone lines, one for the Web connection and one to speak with Land's End. Alternately, if a customer uses a cable modem, he or she is able to both be online and speak on a phone line simultaneously, because a cable modem works over cable TV lines, not phone lines.

- Live interaction with online customers has its pros and cons for a business. Placing employees in direct contact with customers carries with it a higher cost than having customers help themselves. However, the opportunity to ensure that customers have a satisfactory shopping experience, coupled with the opportunity to sell additional products to customers while they're online, might offset those personnel costs in the end.

Buzzword

Telecommuting is the practice of allowing employees to work from home, in essence commuting by telephone, rather than by car.

E-BUSINESS ANALYSIS

> *Take a look at each of these sites (full URLs are located at the end of the exercise), then read the site analysis below and answer the questions.*

CASE STUDY 1: YOURBESTOFFICE.COM

- YourBestOffice.com allows users, for a small fee each month, to take advantage of a variety of network-hosted features. Essentially, this service can set up a personalized environment for a company, with the company name and logo, and provide user support. Companies can set up access for users, allowing employees, vendors, and even customers to access files or discussions. Companies can also post and update a calendar of important company dates. They can restrict access to confidential information. A company could even maintain copies of important files on this site, to protect themselves in case of damage to or downtime on their own company network.

Introducing Your Best Office Page

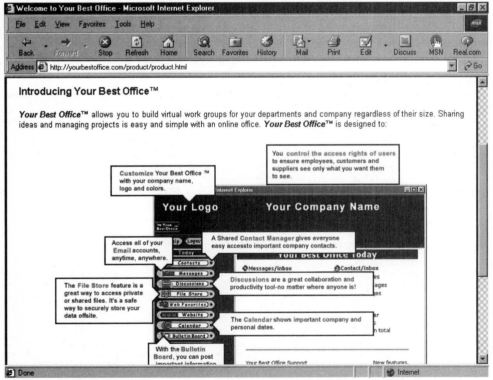

- The YourBestOffice.com site includes a tour of a sample company named Max-T Shirts. This sample shows how all the features of the site are accessed from a central location, personalized with the company name and logo. A handy summary shows the number of items in each area, and even indicates when items on the calendar are overdue. One nice feature here is the Community section; this allows a company to enter information about customers, employees, and suppliers, with e-mail addresses and any other information they wish to include to help build a sense of an online community. The tour of the product offered on the YourBestOffice.com site is very realistic: it allows visitors to actually read messages, reply to them, and read and add comments to discussions, so it gives an excellent idea of how the service works.

YourBestOnlineOffice Sample Company Tour Page

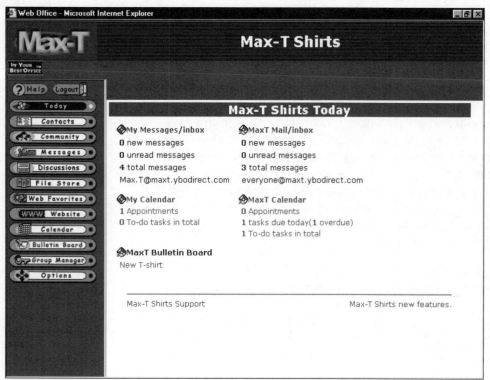

1. What is a shared file?

_____

2. Is a discussion on YourBestOffice.com synchronous or asynchronous?

_____

3. What feature allows users to keep track of to-do tasks?

_____

CASE STUDY 2: MEETINGBYWIRE.COM

■ MeetingbyWire.com focuses mainly on NetMeeting from Microsoft, however it does provide information about some other conference products. The site is run by a Microsoft certified consultant and has areas that provide tips on topics such as audio problems, as well as a NetMeeting Store that is run in conjunction with Amazon.com. The profit model for this site is to get a commission from products bought from Amazon through the site and from fees paid by consulting service customers. The site has more of the appearance of an informational portal than an E-Commerce site, one way for a business to draw customers who then end up making a purchase of some sort.

MeetingbyWire.com Audio Tips Page

- This site also provides some training material on how to use the products it sells. This training takes the form of tutorials using text and screenshots of the software. Providing training on a product can be a good way to ensure that customers are successful with it, and continue to purchase upgrades to their software—hopefully from the site where they got free training.

MeetingbyWire.com NetMeeting 101 Page

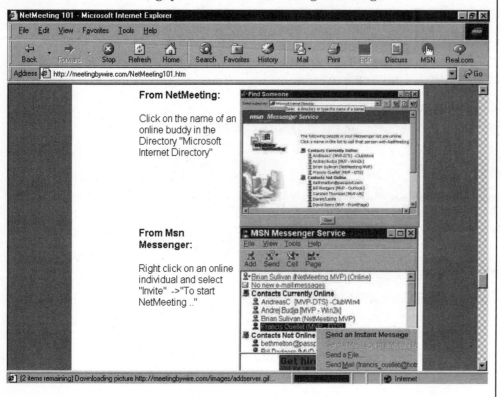

1. What is the possible outcome of providing training to customers on a product?

   _____

2. What does clicking on "Invite" in MSN Messenger do?

   _____

3. Who is MeetingbyWire.com's partner for selling NetMeeting products?

   _____

CASE STUDY 3: LANDSEND.COM

- Lands' End, traditionally a catalog sales company, has moved online in a big way. As a company with a reputation for customer service, they looked for ways to provide a personal shopping experience for their customers. One way that Landsend.com provides help is with their customer support structure, which includes phone, e-mail, fax, and live interaction. Lands' End Live allows a customer to interact with a customer service representative via text chat, or by phone while exploring the online site. This live interaction is supported by Cisco Systems Customer Contact applications.

Landsend.com Contact Us Page

- Lands' End's Personal Shopper is a wizard-like application that lets a customer enter information about his or her clothing preferences and size and select preferences from various styles of clothing. Based on this input, the Personal Shopper recommends products Lands' End believes would appeal to that person. There is even a Today's Task feature that lets a customer enter a specific piece of clothing and the type of event it is to be worn to (business, business casual, leisure) and the application recommends products to the customer. This is a clever way to simulate a sales assistant presence, while actually letting the customer serve himself or herself.

Lands' End Personal Shopper Recommendations Page

1. What is a TTY line?

   _____

2. How can a Lands' End customer track the status of his or her order?

   _____

3. Once Personal Shopper makes a recommendation, how does a customer buy one of the recommended items?

   _____

http://www.yourbestonlineoffice.com
YourBestOffice.com

http://webboard.oreilly.com/
WebBoard

http://www.Microsoft.com/office/project/ProCenWP.htm
Microsoft Project Central

http://www.meetingbywire.com/
MeetingbyWire.com

http://www.landsend.com/
LandsEnd.com

Theme 6

Surveying the Competitive Environment Online
- See whether your product stacks up against the competition
- Explore how decision makers learn about E-Commerce trends
- Search for information on competitors
- Learn how selling to a niche can make you competitive
- Analyze pricing and service as competitive tools

NOTES

ConsumerReports.org Tells You How Your Products Score Against Your Competitors'

- Keeping up with the competition has always been an important part of any business's strategy. Keeping up with online competition is just as important and perhaps more challenging because of the speed with which changes can be made to a Web business site and rapid changes in technology and the E-Commerce market. However, knowing what your competitors are offering customers and how they are positioning their products or services is essential. Knowing this can help you to understand how to stand out from the crowd and get customers to click their way to your E-Commerce site.

- Part of keeping your online business competitive is staying aware of how your specific products compare with other brands. Publications such as Consumer Reports Online provide objective evaluations and rankings of various types of products. You can read their reviews and learn what they liked about your competition and what they didn't like about what you have to offer.

Note
The Bank of Boston publishes a document about analyzing your competition. They recommend something called the SWOT model. Essentially this model suggests that every business look at its Strengths, Weaknesses, Opportunities, and Threats as a basis for a competitive strategy. You can read this document at http://204.183.94.19/bank boston/analyze.asp.

ConsumerReports.org Home Page

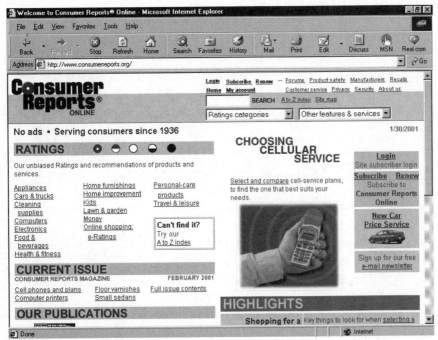

- The information-rich nature of the Internet can make finding your competitors easy in one sense and problematic in another. You can use any of the hundreds of search engines available and search by your industry, your product or service type, or other keywords about your business and come up with a list of your online competitors. However, because there are so many companies online, ranging from one-person operations to huge conglomerates, it's sometimes hard to know if the company names returned by such a search really qualify as competitors. In fact, you may have to visit all the sites to know which ones are even in business any more.

Learn About E-Commerce Trends at CyberAtlas.com

- In order to compete for business online, you have to understand how customers are using the Internet and what kinds of online features and services seem most useful to them. Then, you can make sure you're offering features that help customers to enjoy the online shopping experience. Sites such as CyberAtlas make information about who is shopping online and what appeals to them available to help businesses strategize. The section of this site called The Big Picture contains articles related to the **demographics** of the Internet public.

CyberAtlas.com Home Page

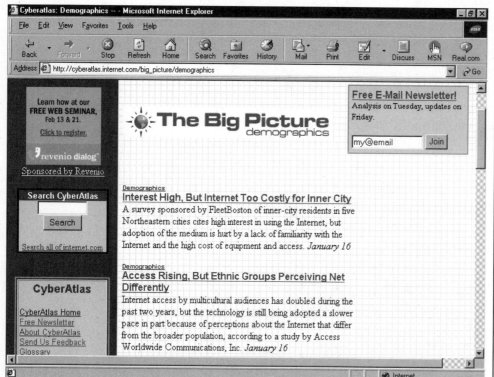

- CyberAtlas also provides information by various markets, such as finance, retailing, and healthcare. Here an online business can see where there are negative trends in their industry and work to lessen the impact on their own business. They can also spot opportunities in these trends and adjust their strategies to take advantage of change in the marketplace before their competitors do.

Buzzword
Demographics are statistical depictions of a population. Demographics can include characteristics such as age range, income, gender, and occupations.

Technical Note
One feature on CyberAtlas.com is a weekly performance tracking of top Web sites, showing which sites are performing well and which have problems. This feature is powered by Watchfire, which is characterized as Web site intelligence software. This type of software can check a Web site for problems such as broken links and forms that don't function properly. Many businesses use this kind of software to ensure that their customers' experience on their site is error-free.

CompaniesOnline.com Offers Information on Companies in Various Industries

- There is a great deal of information on the Internet that a business can take advantage of in analyzing its competition. In addition to simply visiting a competitor's Web site to see how they present themselves online, you can use various sites to get a snapshot of information about them, from the number of employees, to management profiles and new product announcements. For companies that are publicly owned (that is, they issue stock) it is a requirement that they make their financial information available, as well.

- CompaniesOnline.com, a feature of Lycos Small Business, allows you to search for a company by industry, then presents you with a profile of that company, as well as a link to its Web site. Knowing the size and financial backing of a competitor can help you determine where they will be able to meet you head-to-head, for example with price discounts or costly promotions, and where they will be limited either by size of staff or funding.

CompaniesOnline.com Search Page

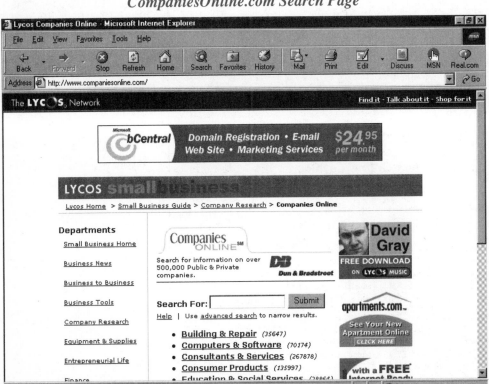

- One way to stay competitive with other businesses in your industry that have an online presence is to be sure that when customers search for businesses they find your Web site. Search engines look for keywords on sites that match the keyword typed into the search engine by a computer user. There's a trick you can use to be sure that your site is listed with every keyword your competitors are using on their site so you're never left out of a search result. Go to a competitor's site and look at the Web page source code. Click View on your Web browser, then select Source (Page Source with Netscape). Look for the words listed in the KEYWORD META TAG area (you can use the Find function of the browser to search for the term 'keyword' in the code) and copy the terms listed there, then add them to your Web page's own source code. Now anyone searching by one of those terms will find not only your competitor's site, but your site, too.

Take a Look at Flowers by the Sea, an Online Business that Sets Itself Apart by Selling to a Niche Market

- Flowers by the Sea is a flower company with a difference. The company specializes in biodynamically grown plants. That means that they use no pesticides or other chemicals in the growing process that might damage the environment. For customers who are environmentally conscious, this might be the flower company of choice. A business can often find success by addressing a **niche**, that is, a small but often passionate segment of their market. In some cases that segment is ignored by their competition. In other instances a competitor's product might satisfy that niche customer, but because they don't position the product so that the niche feature is obvious they are not taking full advantage of the special interest appeal.

Flowers by the Sea Home Page

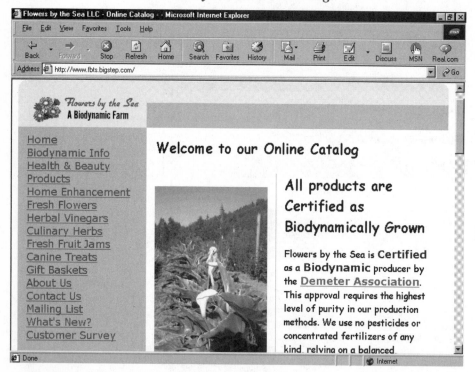

Buzzword
The word *niche* originally referred to a small space where you can display items. In marketing terms, a niche market is a smaller market. For example, toys is a market, but antique porcelain dolls is a niche within that same market.

- There are several good examples of companies that have successfully addressed a niche market need. One is Subaru, which created a niche category of sports utility wagons with its Outback model, a cross between a sports utility vehicle (SUV) and a station wagon. Another example is Wild Birds Unlimited, which sells bird feeders and bird food, along with garden décor. This company examined the pet/animal market and found a niche in bird lovers. One benefit of focusing on a niche market is that you might find you can provide something nobody else is providing. Also, you have a narrow focus for your marketing efforts that can be less time consuming and more productive than a shotgun approach with a broader market.

- If you take a closer look at Flowers by the Sea, you'll notice that they've taken their original niche market and found other ways to serve it. When somebody comes looking for responsibly grown flowers, he or she will also find herbs, health and beauty products, jams, and even organic dog biscuits. All of these are likely to appeal to the same niche market with the concept of healthy and responsibly grown products free of chemicals. Niche markets don't have to be limiting to your company's growth, as long as you stay loyal to the niche concepts and the customer you are targeting as you grow.

USAFlower.com Finds its Customers with Promises of Price and Service

- Take a look for a moment at a competitor of Flowers by the Sea, USAFLower. Where Flowers by the Sea went after the environmentally conscious flower customer, USAFlower targets a broader market. However, USAFlower makes promises of prompt delivery and offers special discounts. If a company's product line has a broad appeal, it should still look to differentiate itself from the competition in some way, for example by the quality of service it provides or by offering better prices.

USAFlower.com Home Page

- A well-known advertising campaign positioned Avis Rental Cars against its competitor, Hertz. Hertz dominated the market, so Avis came up with the slogan "We Try Harder." Essentially they took advantage of the fact that they were in second place in the market to let customers know that fact motivated them to provide better service. The point is that every business has to know its strengths and weaknesses and position itself properly to attract customers. Online, you'll spot companies that stress strengths such as price, service, quality, ease-of-use, breadth of product choice, and speed of delivery. Interestingly, what has caused many online companies to fail is the extreme competition online that has forced them to lower prices or provide free shipping, which in the end, couldn't support a profitable bottom line.

- A company's positioning against its competition can come out in a variety of ways, with a company slogan on a Web site, or even by adjusting the appearance of the Web site to reflect the selling message. Flowers by the Sea, for example, uses a casual font reflecting the natural, back-to-the earth aspect of its products. USAFlower.com places two messages about same day delivery on its site in the first few inches of the home page. A third competitor, 1-800-Flowers, places the slogan "Flowers are just the beginning" at the top of their home page, where pictures of flowers, chocolates, and stuffed toys stress the range of product offerings.

E-BUSINESS ANALYSIS

Take a look at each of these sites (full URLs are located at the end of the exercise), then read the site analysis below and answer the questions.

CASE STUDY 1: CONSUMERREPORTS.COM

- Consumer Reports Online presents unbiased reports and ratings on a wide variety of products. Notice that the site accepts no advertising, and the organization purchases all the products it reviews rather than taking free merchandise from companies, which could cause some favoritism. Consumer Reports Online caters to the general consumer checking on quality of products, but can be used by businesses to check the ratings of their own and competitors' products. The site is organized by types of products, such as electronics and health and fitness. One interesting section of this Web site is Consumer Reports for Kids. This area sports a look that matches the younger market, though the area is probably used as often by parents as by kids.

Consumer Reports for Kids Page

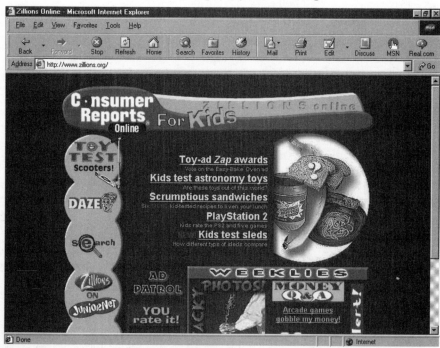

■ Consumer Reports ratings, such as this one on cellular phone plans, give you an at-a-glance way of reviewing competing products from various companies. By clicking on the Details link for any entry you can see information such as roaming charges, cancellation fees, and costs of various options. By checking several items in the Check to Compare column, then clicking on the Compare button at the top of the page, you can view a table listing all the detailed information for the checked items. If you and your competitors' products or services are included in such a report on this site, you've got a great tool for making point-by-point comparisons from your customers' point of view.

Consumer Reports Compare Page

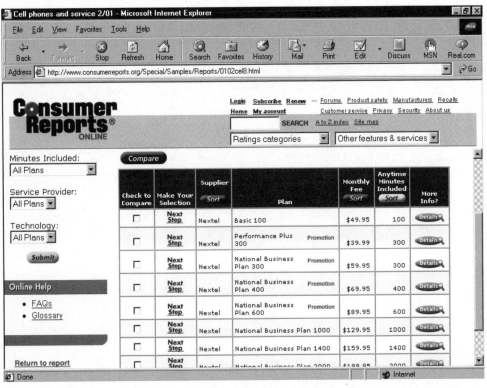

1. What kinds of products are rated on the Consumer Reports for Kids page and how do they match the user demographic?

   _____

2. Which cellular plan offers the most competitive pricing?

   _____

3. Which cellular plans are offering promotions and what are the details of those promotions?

   _____

CASE STUDY 2: FLOWERS BY THE SEA

- Flowers by the Sea is a company that focuses on the niche market of environmentally responsible flowers and plants, foods, and beauty products. This company doesn't push a lot of products with glitzy photos; rather the contents of the site focuses mainly on explaining the company philosophy. The motivation here is to show the consumer how the company is different from the competition so that their choice of where to buy flowers is not based simply on price or fast delivery, but on the type of company they want to do business with.

Flowers by the Sea Page

- Notice that Flowers by the Sea catalog pages don't tout discounts or even mention how quickly your order will be filled. In fact, each item listed on this page notes that availability will vary, meaning they don't even guarantee they can fill your order for that product that day. Certain businesses stress freshness or originality over cookie-cutter products to differentiate themselves. Flowers or fruit, which may or may not be in season, are one example. Another is art; some sites that sell handmade fabrics, pottery, or other artwork may show an example of the product on their site and state that the actual colors or design that you receive may differ from the picture. This kind of sales pitch doesn't work with every customer: the ones who want to know exactly what they're getting, or for whom the hand-picked product has little appeal will go to a competing site.

Flowers by the Sea Catalog Page

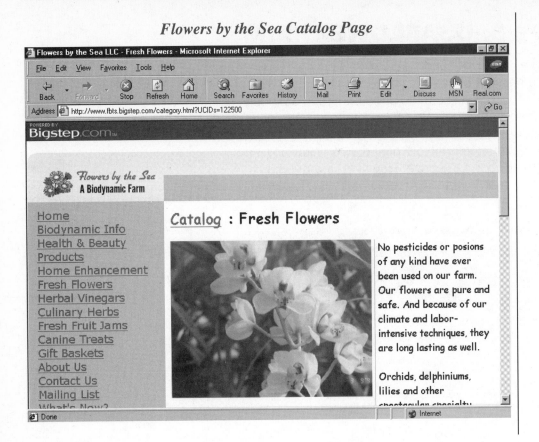

1. Do you think that Flowers by the Sea uses strong branding on its site? Why or why not?

   _____

2. To what kind of customer would the typeface and graphics used on the Flowers by the Sea site appeal?

   _____

3. Does the Flowers by the Sea online catalog show individual product pictures? Why do you think that's so?

   _____

CASE STUDY 3: USAFLOWER.COM

- USAFlower.com makes an interesting study in contrasts to the Flowers by the Sea site. The site has lots of specific product pictures, as well as featured items and specials at discounted prices. Price is definitely a selling point on this site; in fact they provide a comparative pricing chart showing how they stack up to their competition on this point. Interestingly, if you study the chart several competitors cost only a dollar or so more, once delivery fees are added to the price. However, the overall impression for the consumer is that USAFlower is by far the lowest cost site.

USAFlower.com Comparative Pricing Page

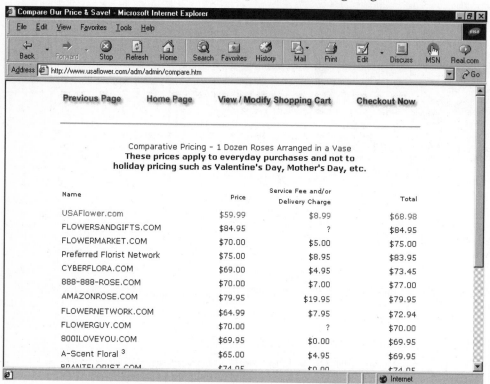

Comparative Pricing – 1 Dozen Roses Arranged in a Vase
These prices apply to everyday purchases and not to holiday pricing such as Valentine's Day, Mother's Day, etc.

Name	Price	Service Fee and/or Delivery Charge	Total
USAFlower.com	$59.99	$8.99	$68.98
FLOWERSANDGIFTS.COM	$84.95	?	$84.95
FLOWERMARKET.COM	$70.00	$5.00	$75.00
Preferred Florist Network	$75.00	$8.95	$83.95
CYBERFLORA.COM	$69.00	$4.95	$73.45
888-888-ROSE.COM	$70.00	$7.00	$77.00
AMAZONROSE.COM	$79.95	$19.95	$79.95
FLOWERNETWORK.COM	$64.99	$7.95	$72.94
FLOWERGUY.COM	$70.00	?	$70.00
800ILOVEYOU.COM	$69.95	$0.00	$69.95
A-Scent Floral [3]	$65.00	$4.95	$69.95
BRANTFLORIST.COM	$74.95	$0.00	$74.95

- In addition to photos of specific products for sale, the site offers several gift-giving guides, such as A Guy's Guide to Giving Flowers. Flowers are mainly purchased as a gift, so by providing advice on giving the right gift the company is helping the customer to have a successful purchasing experience. The site also offers information about State flowers and birth flowers to make a gift more personal. Although this site does have a gourmet gift basket area, the focus is otherwise purely on flowers, unlike several flower sites that have extended their product line to other gift items. For a customer who knows he or she wants to buy flowers, this might be the site of choice over one that clutters his or her experience with other categories of gifts.

USAFlowers.com A Guy's Guide to Giving Flowers Page

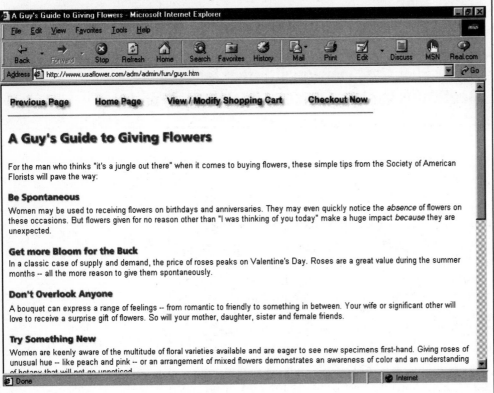

1. Identify two competitor sites to USAFlowers.com.

   _____

2. Do you think USAFlowers.com considers Flowers by the Sea to be a serious competitor for their customer? Why?

   _____

3. How does giving customers advice about giving and taking care of flowers encourage future sales?

   _____

http://www.consumerreports.org
ConsumeReports.org
http://cyberAtlas.com/
CyberAtlas.com
http://www.companiesonline.com
CompaniesOnline.com
http://www.fbts.bigstep.com/
Flowers by the Sea
http://www.usaflower.com/
USAFlower.com

Working Across Borders
- Learn how businesses find international customers
- Explore issues of standardization for the Internet
- Examine how Web sites manage different languages
- Learn about doing business through international partners

NOTES

Take a Look at an International Marketplace at Global Sources

- When a business creates a business Web site, it is potentially making itself available to the entire world. Of course, many Web businesses will only accept orders from customers in their own country, but many others are setting themselves up to handle international E-Commerce. Several challenges exist when doing business globally, including handling different currencies, doing business in multiple languages, **localizing** products, and dealing with shipping and customs costs and restrictions.

- With the challenges of doing business internationally, why do so many companies do it? Businesses buying from other businesses can often buy products and services at significant savings outside of their own country. Sometimes the savings are due to cheaper labor in other nations that makes product prices more attractive, even with the added cost of shipping overseas. In other cases certain natural resources or equipment might exist in another country that make it necessary to buy internationally. Businesses hoping to sell to new customers also see huge potential when they start to look beyond their own country's borders because of sheer numbers of potential consumers.

- Many businesses today are using the Web to find international customers. Some draw business simply by making their Web site available in different languages and handling international transactions. Other businesses actively seek business by bidding for international contracts. Online marketplaces, such as Global Sources, exist to help businesses find customers. At globalsources.com, the focus is on volume orders between one business and another. This site allows visitors to search for international suppliers and post information about their own products for international buyers to review.

Buzzword

Localization is a term used for creating versions of products, such as books or software, that can be used in other countries. Localization typically involves translation and possibly modification of a product for a local market.

Globalsources.com Home Page

- When browser applications view information on the Web, they use certain character sets that recognize various languages. Internet Explorer, for example, uses an autoselect feature that attempts to recognize whether the characters on a page are from a Western European character set, or from languages such as Chinese, Hebrew, Thai, or Japanese. In Internet Explorer, you can select the View menu, choose Encoding, and select a language from the side menu that appears. In Netscape Navigator, you can use the Character Set submenu from the View menu to accomplish the same thing.

Learn About Localization Issues from W3C

- The Internet and World Wide Web were not created by any one company or entity. They evolved through the involvement of many individuals and groups around the world. Some of these individuals and groups created the underlying languages that are used to program Internet sites virtually on the fly, and therefore a variety of standards grew as well.

- The Worldwide Web Consortium, also known as W3C, is one of several organizations that exist to promote standards in Web development. This standardization addresses many issues of internationalization and localization. Basically, they support a uniformity of character sets, languages and writing systems through research, documentation, and conferences. With various programming languages being used to create Web content, this kind of standardization will have a significant impact on the ability of Web businesses to function efficiently for an international audience.

W3C Home Page

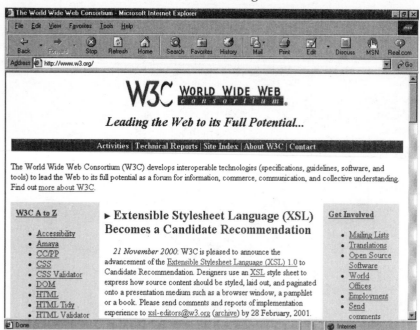

Technical Note

HTML's base character set is Unicode. Where an older character set, ASCII, can deal with 256 character sets, Unicode can handle 65,536 character combinations. That's because Unicode uses two bytes for each character, instead of one. That quantity of characters allows Unicode to incorporate almost all of the languages of the world.

Learn How Babel is Leading the Way Towards Multilingual Web Sites

■ The Babel site is a joint effort of the Internet Society and Alis Technologies, a manufacturer of software solutions for language integration. On this site businesses can get information about creating **multilingual** Web sites. Although use of HTML and its Unicode foundation will work with much of the Web's content, some HTML editors have difficulty handling non-Western languages (that is, languages other than English and other Romance languages that evolved from Latin, such as French, German, and Spanish).

Buzzword

Multilingual simply means using more than one language. A multilingual Web site typically offers a choice to visitors of viewing the site in one of a choice of languages.

Babel Home Page

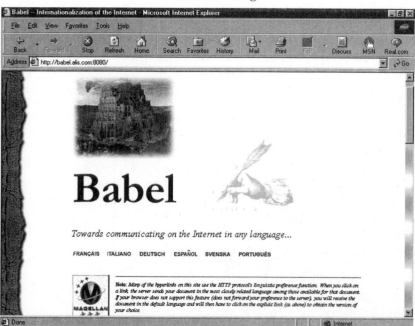

Note

In its early days, the Web made use of the ISO character set. However there was a problem, because ISO only supports Western European languages. It was mostly replaced when HTML came into popular use.

- In addition to providing a Web experience in several languages, any company that truly wants to sell internationally, through the Web or otherwise, has to consider whether they must translate product manuals or safety instructions into other languages. Many global companies produce multi-language documentation for that reason.

Explore the World with Disney

- It's not just language that can separate countries doing business on the Internet. Cultural standards and preferences can also get in the way of smooth business transactions. Disney, the international entertainment giant, does a great job of offering unique Web sites for many countries, designing each to appeal to a particular country's sensibilities. This involves not only use of the country's language, but also graphic images and phrases that appeal to Disney's youthful international audience.

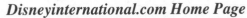

Disneyinternational.com Home Page

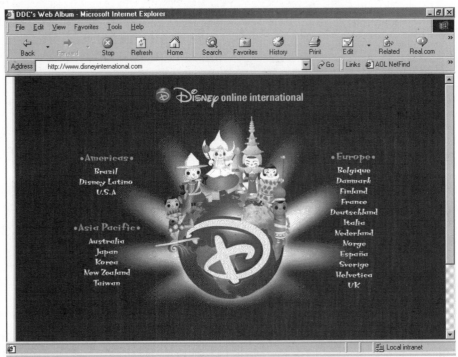

- Setting up such a massive enterprise in so many countries typically involves orchestrating services such as translation, Web design, ticket sales, printing, and so on. Many larger companies set up their own offices overseas staffed by local personnel, but smaller companies may have to rely on international partners to handle all overseas activities. Still others **franchise** or license their products or concepts to international companies, in effect giving them the right to represent the company in their countries.

- When you try to view a site that displays a foreign language such as Korean or Hebrew, you may get a message asking if you'd like to download that character set and install it on your computer. If you choose not to download the set, some text on the site may not be readable. Windows contains various language character sets, although not all of them are loaded on your computer when you install Windows and may have to be installed later from your Windows CD.

Buzzword

A *franchise* is a way for a company to essentially lease its concept and image to someone else. McDonalds and other fast food restaurants use the franchise model, selling the right to operate a McDonald's franchise, and providing advertising, access to McDonald's products, and the use of other McDonald's name to franchisees.

Learn How IBM Worldwide Sells in Other Countries

- Technology companies face unique issues when selling outside of their own country. That's because governments place restrictions on making certain types of technology available to countries who might be adversaries in future conflicts. There are, for example, laws pertaining to software encryption.

- IBM, which sells both software and hardware internationally, must be aware of these restrictions, as well as issues such as electrical current standards for electronic equipment when they sell products into different countries. IBM works with international partners to sell their products, which helps them ensure that they are in compliance with local requirements.

IBM.com Worldwide Page

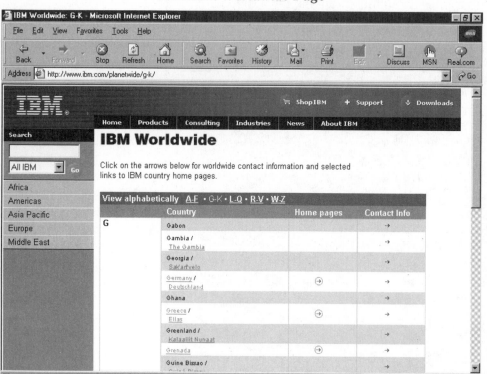

Note
Customs regulations for shipping certain products overseas can be complex. Violating a customs regulation can also carry severe penalties. Many companies rely on professional shipping companies to handle customs paperwork and procedures.

- IBM offers some useful Web pages for those who are interested in developing Web sites in other languages. Visit http://www.ibm.com/developer/ to learn more about Unicode and view their dW machine translation, an automated translation technology.

E-BUSINESS ANALYSIS

> *Take a look at each of these sites (full URLs are located at the end of the exercise), then read the site analysis below and answer the questions.*

CASE STUDY 1: DISNEY INTERNATIONAL

- Visiting Disney Web sites for different countries reveals differences beyond simply translating the text on the page. Take a look at Disney Australia and Disney Taiwan. An obvious difference is their use of images of people native to each country so customers can identify with the company. The sites also sport different graphic images and a different overall look and feel. Note that several of the button links on the Taiwan page use a purely graphic element, with no text label at all. Graphics can provide a universal visual language that helps visitors to easily make choices on a Web page.

Disney Australia Home Page

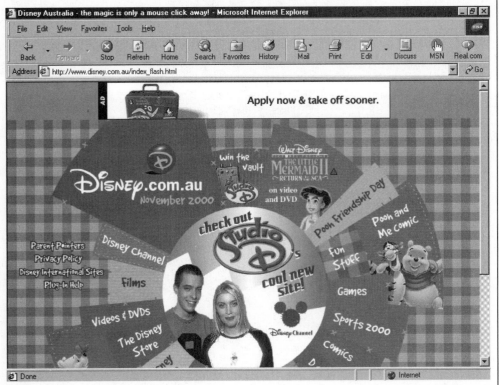

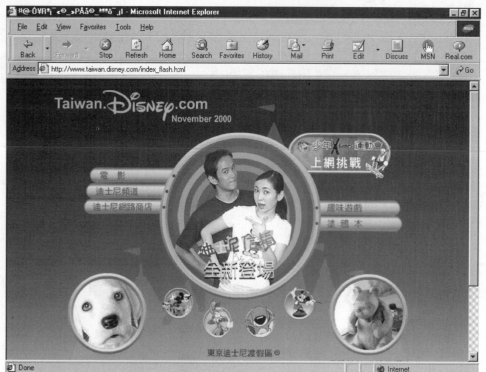

- Disney also operates theme parks around the world. This means that they have to deal with ticket sales in several languages and currencies. The reservation Web page for Disneyland Paris suggests three ways to order tickets for a day at the park: by phone, by using a ticket reservation agent on the Internet to make your purchase, and by submitting an online reservation. Note the universal graphics of a phone, a computer with the word Internet on the monitor, and the @ symbol, which is used represent an e-mail address.

Reservations Page for Disneyland Paris

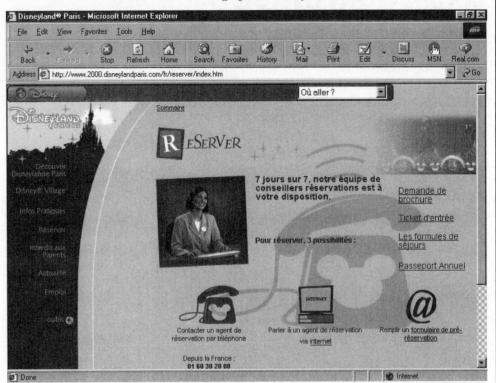

1. How do the poses of the people on the Australia and Taiwan Disney sites differ?

   _____

2. Why do you think Disney doesn't put the name "Disney" in Taiwanese characters on the Taiwan Disney site?

   _____

3. What days of the week can you make online reservations for Disneyland Paris using the Internet?

   _____

CASE STUDY 2: IBM WORLDWIDE

- IBM has been operating as an international company for some time now. They have established a worldwide network of offices and business partnerships. IBM provides Web pages so that customers can research and make purchases from many countries around the world, such as their South Africa site. Note some of the elements on this page that are specific to South Africa: the currency used for the product prices (R2522,00 for an IBM WorkPad), the European style of date (30/01/2001 for January 30, 2001), and the British spelling of the word Center in the link to the IBM Business Centre.

IBM South Africa Home Page

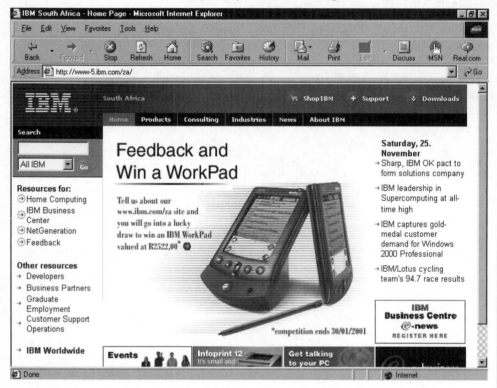

- IBM partners with local companies for many products and services, including training, technical support, and marketing. Their PartnerWorld program helps local retailers to sell IBM products, providing product literature, as well as software technology to help them run their businesses. By using a partner model, IBM ensures that customers in other countries get the support they need.

IBM PartnerWorld Page

1. What is localization?

   _____

2. What types of things would have to be localized for South Africa? How about China?

   _____

3. What forms of support does IBM offer its international partners?

   _____

CASE STUDY 3: GLOBAL SOURCES

- Global Sources, an international business-to-business buying portal, helps connect businesses worldwide by providing both a place to connect and information on international commerce trends. Their Supplier Polls offer statistics on price and supply trends for specific products in certain regions, such as Asia. By reviewing price trends for a product in a particular region, a business can identify markets that offer the best pricing for products.

Global Sources Supplier Poll Page

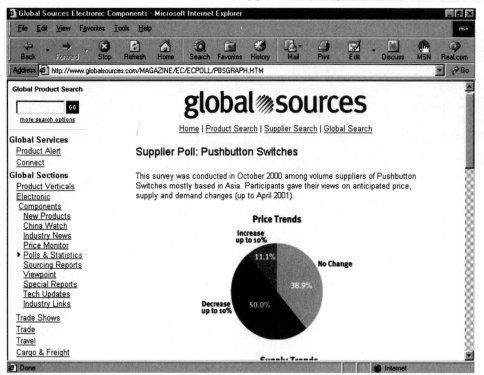

- Global Sources also offers a Supplier Search tool. Buyers can search for suppliers by product or supplier name. They can also use filters to narrow down the geographical area for the search. A filter is a database feature that tells the search tool to exclude certain records, such as those that have the word "Europe" in the Region field. Note that Global Sources keeps information on 94,444 suppliers in 152 countries.

Global Sources Supplier Search Page

1. What might be some benefits of buying supplies and materials from foreign countries? What might be some challenges?

   _____

2. What is a vertical market?

   _____

3. How many suppliers does Global Sources have in their supplier database for Albania?

   _____

http://www.globalsources.com/
GlobalSources.com
http://www.w3.org/
World Wide Web Consortium
http://babel.alis.com/
Babel
http://www.disneyinternational.com/
Disney International
http://ibm.com/planetwide/
IBM Worldwide

Challenges of International Transactions
- Explore currency conversion issues
- See how retail E-Companies are dealing with international sales
- Learn about how money moves from country to country
- Research world trade regulations and issues

NOTES

Explore How Foreign Currencies Compare at Oanda.com

- It's remarkable that in the 21st Century it's still cumbersome to deal with different countries' currencies, but it is. The Euro currency, for example, which was created in an effort to establish a common currency for all members of the European Trade Union, has had a rocky existence. Although the currency is traded on paper, there is no actual money out there to slip into your wallet. All the countries that support the Euro still maintain their own currencies. Reluctance to go to any global or even regional standard for currency is surprisingly stong, and it creates a barrier to easy international E-Commerce.

- One challenge is that currency value fluctuates on a daily basis. If you order a product online from a store in a country other than your own, you are likely to use a credit card for the transaction. Your credit card will be charged in a foreign currency and your credit card company then converts the charge to US dollars when they bill you. That means that the conversion rate may be applied weeks after your purchase. There are several sites on the Internet, such as Oanda.com, that allow consumers to check conversion rates on a daily basis.

Note

Many businesses today either do not get involved in E-Commerce with customers in other countries, or if they do, they set up an office or work with a business partner in other countries and handle those transactions from a separate Web site.

Oanda.com Home Page

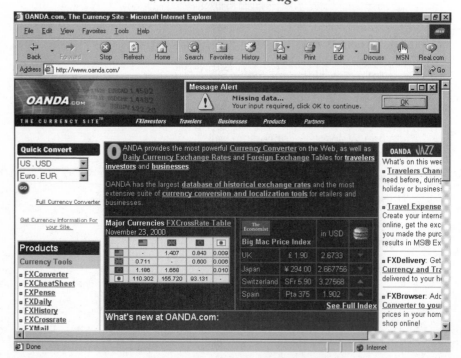

■ Some businesses that routinely make international purchases of supplies or products use purchase orders and are billed for each transaction. On a large order, fluctuations in currency value can make it difficult for a company to anticipate actual billing amounts. To deal with this, US companies often request a fixed price in US dollars from international vendors.

London's Harrods Goes international

■ When a business decides to sell internationally, it typically targets its sales country by country, based on the potential market and issues of doing business with individuals or businesses in that country. Harrods, the specialty department store in London, currently sells within the United Kingdom and in Japan. As of the writing of this book, Harrods had recently re-launched a North American site and were developing a European Web store as well.

Harrods.com Home Page

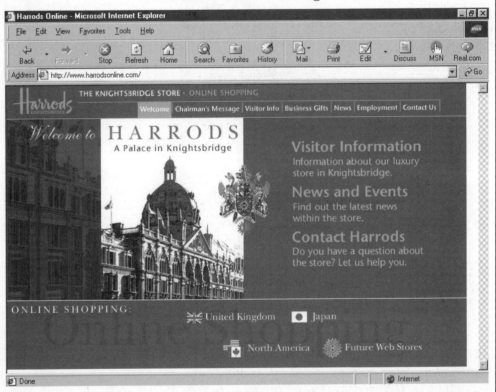

■ In determining which countries to sell to, a business has to consider the market in each country. They must look at information about the number of customers for the type of product being sold and whether potential customers can get the same products more easily or cheaply from local companies. In addition, it's important to understand how many people in that country have access to the Internet and to analyze how comfortable the culture is with buying products online.

■ Another challenge for international business is pricing. A company must take into account any costs of doing business in a country that might cut into their profit margins when setting product prices. If they have to customize a product for a foreign market, for example translating a book into another language, that cost has to be considered. A business must determine what price the local consumer is willing to pay for the product. Typically customers pay for shipping and import duties, so pricing must still be attractive in light of those additional costs.

Explore the World of International Banking at Chase.com

- When companies do business with other companies outside of their own borders, banks with an international presence are sometimes involved with transferring funds or arranging settlement of significant business deals. Banks that deal with international transactions have to deal with a complex system of correspondent and clearing banks to exchange money. One such bank, Chase, maintains offices in 48 countries.

Chase.com Home Page

- The speed with which transactions occur, especially with the instant communication capabilities of the Internet, necessitates virtually instant financial transactions in many cases. With current techology, money can be wired from one bank to another in a single day, even from one country to another.

- Chase maintains links on its Web site to all the Web sites created by its offices in different countries, so that visitors to the Chase site can go to a site for a specific country easily. Of course a company could set up one Web site with Web pages for each country's office, but by establishing links to separate Web sites, there is more flexibility to have each country update its own site and protect it with security on its local server.

Sothebys Offers Rare Merchandise through International Auctions

- Online auctions have been more accepting of international customers, perhaps because the actual transaction happens to a great extent between the buyer and seller. Sites such as eBay allow sellers to post items internationally or locally. The buyer must pay the seller in his or her local currency. Although someone selling an item internationally may pay international shipping, the buyer is expected to pay any customs duties.

- Taxes are another consideration in purchasing internationally. Local sales tax is often applied both in the country where the buyer lives and in the country where the seller lives. In Australia, where sales tax can run to 22% for example, this cost can be significant. Sothebys auction house maintains offices in various countries; these offices can help buyers deal with the ins and outs of customs and taxes when they buy from that country.

Note

An interesting site for information about customs regulations is the World Customs Organization at http://www.wcoomd.org.

Sothebys.com Home Page

- Sothebys includes online catalogs of items for sale on its Web site. Online catalogs are essentially databases of images and text. The items in the catalog can be displayed by category in an online form that may look similar to a printed catalog. Several catalog design software packages are available, including Web Store from iCat and Actinic Catalog from Actinic.

Learn about International Trade Regulations and Trends from the World Trade Organization

- When companies do business in other countries, they are governed by trade policies in each country. The World Trade Organization, based in Geneva, Switzerland, represents the trade interests of its 139 member countries. The WTO sponsors agreements signed by members and other countries that establish how countries will deal with international trade regulations.

World Trade Organization Home Page

Buzzword

WTO's definition of *intellectual property* is "rights given to people over the creations of their minds." Traditionally various forms of art such as music and paintings have been included in this category, but in more recent years other forms have come under scrutiny, such as new product ideas and software interfaces.

- One concern about international commerce is the abuse of **intellectual property** rights, that is, rights that a company has in an idea or content, such as software code or written documents. One example of this is the controversy over written content and music that are distributed over the World Wide Web that has surfaced in recent years. Regulating misuse of this type of material within one's own borders is difficult; regulating it around the world is almost impossible. The ability to distribute such material over the Internet just compounds the problem. This is one reason some companies choose not to sell to certain countries, such as Taiwan, where copyright infringement is rampant.

- Other issues under consideration as E-Commerce continues to grow worldwide are protection of privacy, prevention of fraud, use of public telecommunications lines, and application of customs duties.

Technical Note

The WTO site includes text of speeches made around the world by the Director General. You can download these speeches in PDF format. PDF stands for portable data format and refers to a document exchange software product from Adobe called Acrobat. With Acrobat installed on your computer, you will be able to read documents saved in the PDF format, regardless of what software program they were created in. You can download Acrobat for free from the Adobe site (www.adobe.com).

E-business Analysis

Take a look at each of these sites (full URLs are located at the end of the exercise), then read the site analysis below and answer the questions.

CASE STUDY 1: HARRODS

- If you go to Harrods' Web site, you'll see links for Japan, North America, and Future Web Stores. You'll notice that on the Japanese site both English and Japanese are used. In some cases companies include information such as the company name, product names, or slogans in their native language, because these are known worldwide and carry with them a corporate identity factor. For example, on Harrods' Japan site the site name "Harrods Online Shopping" and the logo for Harrods of Knightsbridge are in English.

Harrods-Japan Online Shopping Page

- Harrods has created a Web page on its main Web site that makes a statement about opening future stores in other countries. They have included an e-mail feature here that allows those interested in having a Harrods' Web store available in their country to contact the store. This is one way for Harrods to begin to gauge potential markets in specific countries. Receiving e-mail from enough potential customers suggests that their country has the technology, and perhaps as importantly, the widespread use of that technology, to make E-Commerce viable.

Harrods Future Webstores Page

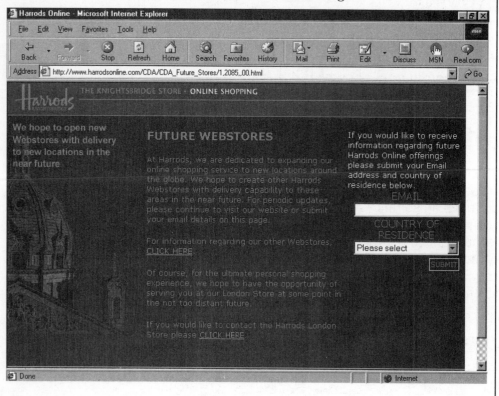

1. What is Harrods' slogan for business gift buyers?

   _____

2. Who is the Chairman of Harrods?

   _____

3. What three ways can you find on Harrods' site to contact them?

   _____

CASE STUDY 2: CHASE.COM

■ Chase is a banking institution with worldwide presence. Businesses can take advantage of Chase's International Equivalent Service to make payments in each of several currencies at the same time. Payment instructions are directed to individual systems in each country for settlement. These payments are accomplished using Standard Settlement Instructions, also known as SSI. Chase also provides global clearing of funds transfers, which simply means that they can make fund transfers from a customer's bank account into other accounts in the local currency.

Chase European Economic and Monetary Union Payments Architecture Page

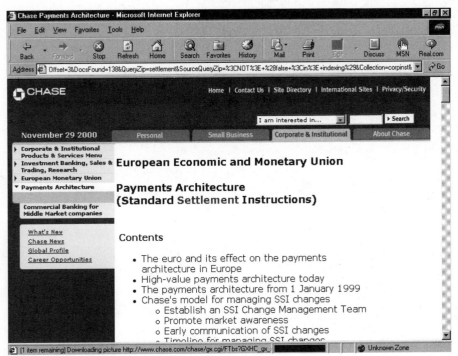

- Chase offers several services specifically targeted to E-Commerce, including an E-Procurement service in conjunction with Intelisys. This process automates purchasing from corporate intranets where purchasing information may be initiated, through the Internet to individual vendors. Chase does this with electronic payments, much as an individual might set up a personal bank account to make an electronic payment of his or her phone bill.

Chase Intelisys Electronic Commerce Page

1. What challenges do regional currencies such as the Euro present to E-Commerce businesses?

   _____

2. What is another term for payments architecture?

   _____

3. What kind of services does Chase provide through its Corporate and Institutional program on its Chase Australia site?

   _____

CASE STUDY 3: SOTHEBYS.COM

- Sothebys is typical of a company that has a global presence because of the uniqueness of what it has to offer (fine art, antiques, etc.) and the strong community of international customers for those products. On Sothebys, as with many Internet auction sites, items are placed online with a starting bid, an estimate of the item's value, and an indication of the time remaining to place bids. Most online auctions stay open for bidding for several days or even weeks. Bidders can return to the Web site and view the current bid at any time during this period and if they choose to, bid again. This allows customers to bid and counter-bid, driving up the final price of the item.

Sothebeys.com Home Page

- Shipping costs for items sold by Sotheby's can vary because of the high value of most items, as well as regulations and tariffs in destination countries. Sothebys charges for insurance coverage for shipping its valuable cargo as an add on to the auction price. Sothebys provides, for the convenience of its customers, information about export regulations and taxes in the US, Europe, and other locales on its customer service page.

- Typical of many businesses today, Sothebys has branched out into service businesses related to its main auction business. For example, you can find information on their Web site about their international real estate group, their appraisal and restoration services, and even financial planning and insurance products. The key to such expansion is to target services or products that would appeal to the existing international customer base.

Sothebys.com Services Page

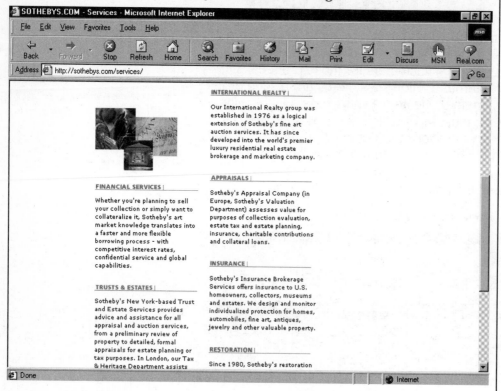

1. Name two other online companies that offer unique products.

   _____

2. How does Sotheby's provide a 'live' bidding experience?

   _____

3. How does eBay's target customer differ from Sotheby's?

   _____

http://www.oanda.com
Oanda.com

http://www.harrodsonline.com/
Harrods Online Shopping

http://chase.com/
Chase

http://www.sothebys.com/
Sothebys.com

http://www.wto.org/
The World Trade Organization

Exploring Profitability Trends of E-Commerce
- ■ **Explore the history of E-Commerce**
- ■ **Learn how E-Commerce influences the larger economy**
- ■ **Study the implications of online usage statistics**
- ■ **Consider what the future holds for E-Commerce**
- ■ **Discover what success online means—and doesn't mean**

NOTES

IDC.com is Part of the Legion of Trendspotting Organizations for E-Commerce

■ Today E-Commerce is a segment of our worldwide economy that analysts and the media pay close attention to, partially because of its enormous potential and partially because sudden and frequent change is part of its nature. E-Commerce wasn't even in existence a decade ago, but today projections from trendspotting companies such as IDC and Forrester place expected E-Commerce spending at one trillion by 2005.

IDC Home Page

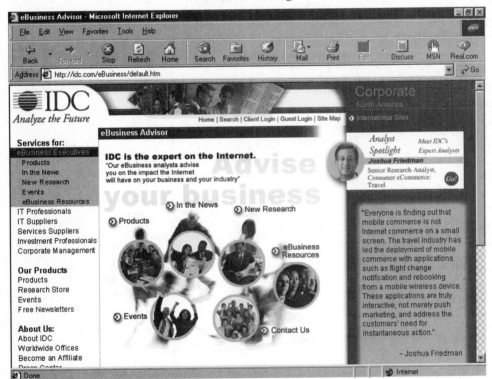

Note

Who were some early players in E-Commerce who have survived? AOL started way back in 1985 as an Internet Service Provider (ISP), but has grown into an online community serving almost 150 million members, counting all of its various businesses such as CompuServe. Amazon.com, one of the first online retailers with staying power, began in 1995 and in that time has served 29 million online customers.

■ From around 1993 to 1996, the Internet was mainly a home for academics and a few technologists who could stand to read through text postings in newsgroups. In fact, when buying and selling began late in 1994, Internet traditionalists fought the trend, wanting to keep the Internet as a pure medium for exchange and sharing of information and technology.

- By 1997 and 1998, people had begun to spend money online, but a Web marketing campaign consisted of e-mails to newsgroups, and most online businesses were still processing credit card payments by hand. 1998 brought a rush of investment in any E-Commerce venture that sounded vaguely interesting, but unfortunately many of these ventures were driven by technologists rather than people with a good grounding in business. The wild speculation in any business that was online led to a crash of inflated stock prices in 2000, with many people predicting doom and gloom for E-Commerce. Analysts took this roller coaster ride along with the rest of us, and in reality few of their projections probably came true, so unexpected has been the rocket-like path of E-Commerce.

CyberAtlas Helps You Follow E-Commerce as Part of the Larger Economy

- So where does that leave E-Commerce as we move through the early years of this new millennium? It's a difficult time to make predictions because a lot is in flux. Internet-related companies are closing and downsizing, even while online spending is reaching unprecedented highs. The reality is probably that the overinflated hopes of the late 1990s are now reaching a more realistic level, and E-Commerce efforts going forward will follow more closely the profitability models of traditional businesses. E-Commerce is here to stay, and it has become an important part of the world's economy.

- Predictions are still rampant, however it is often useful to focus on today's facts rather than tomorrow's guesses. Sites such as CyberAtlas provide information on what is happening with consumer spending online and the Internet economy in general. Many of the statistics and studies discussed on these sites position E-Commerce as a segment of the world's economy by industry, country, or even within a single company.

- Another type of information presented on these sites that is helpful to see how E-Commerce interacts with the general economy consists of updates on activities of so-called Internet companies. These might be software or hardware manufacturers, or technology consulting firms supporting E-Commerce. Watching how the companies who support E-Commerce are doing gives some indication of how E-Commerce itself is doing. As was seen in 2000, when E-Commerce begins to falter, it causes ripples throughout the general economy.

Note

Although E-Commerce is a growing force in the economy, business-to-consumer E-Commerce spending only totals one percent of all US spending.

CyberAtlas.com Home Page

- CyberAtlas doesn't perform research; rather, they gather studies and data from a variety of organizations such as IDC and Gartner Group. In reading statistics about any topic, but it seems especially about the quickly changing Web, you'll find that different studies provide different results. That's because studies are done with a segment of the population, and the conclusions about the responses of that segment are broadened to represent the entire population. For example, a study could include only 200 people, but if 40 percent of those people said they buy online, the reporting organization will conclude that 40 percent of all Internet users buy products online. The accuracy of a study is affected by the size of the segment interviewed, and the quality of the research methods of the organization sponsoring the study.

Estats from Emarketer Provides Market Research for the Online Economy

- Estats is another site that reports various statistics about E-Commerce. Typical reports on such a site might include the size of the Internet population, the activities of that population (for example, of the 242 million people who go online, how many invest online), and the demographics of that population (how many are women, or aged 50-65, for example).

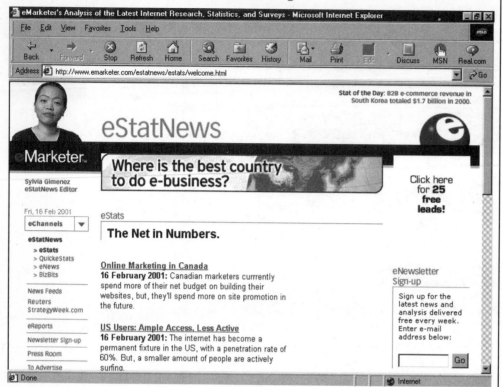

- Statistics on Internet usage are very telling. For example, in 1995 there were 22 million people online (about twice the population of New York City). The year 2000 ended with 242 million people browsing the Web— over ten times as much in five years. It is based on that kind of growth and the study of current trends that organizations have predicted an Internet population reaching 765 million by the end of 2005 (according to CommerceNet Research Center).

- Statistics about actual Internet usage are typically more accurate than some other information, because technology allows sites to record accurately each visit to a site by a unique visitor, and each page that visitors view, as well as actual online transactions performed. Software exists that can compile those statistics from Web sites, providing a pretty accurate picture of activity out there. What's less sure are statistics about who those visitors are: Who can guarantee, for example, that somebody visiting a site from Jane Smith's Internet account is actually Jane Smith and not John Smith? It's not even foolproof to count on data gathered from forms that people fill out online with their personal data, because people may not provide true information, fearing invasion of their privacy. The anonymity of the Web makes some statistics hard to get, even as the technology available for gathering this data improves.

WebTomorrow.com Takes a Look at Where This is all Leading

- So how do you take all these projections and statistics and make sense of where E-Commerce is and where it's heading? The answer may be, you don't. Projecting the future of E-Commerce is just as tricky as predicting the future of the general economy, and nobody's really mastered that skill. If economists could predict exactly what will happen next year, it would be like having a list of winning lottery numbers the day before the drawing. Although economy professionals use a variety of scientific approaches and formulas that have some validity based on historic trends, in the end they are using mathematical calculations to predict human behavior. Perhaps the best you can do as a student of E-Commerce is to visit a variety of sites such as WebTomorrow.com on a regular basis, read a variety of studies and opinions, and then draw your own conclusions.

WebTomorrow.com B2B Trading Hubs Page

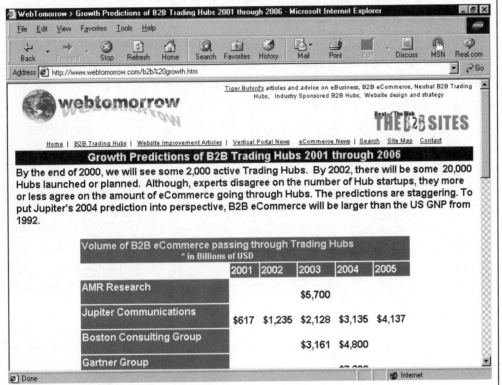

By the end of 2000, we will see some 2,000 active Trading Hubs. By 2002, there will be some 20,000 Hubs launched or planned. Although, experts disagree on the number of Hub startups, they more or less agree on the amount of eCommerce going through Hubs. The predictions are staggering. To put Jupiter's 2004 prediction into perspective, B2B eCommerce will be larger than the US GNP from 1992.

Volume of B2B eCommerce passing through Trading Hubs * in Billions of USD					
	2001	2002	2003	2004	2005
AMR Research			$5,700		
Jupiter Communications	$617	$1,235	$2,128	$3,135	$4,137
Boston Consulting Group			$3,161	$4,800	
Gartner Group					

- It is reasonably safe to assume, barring some global economic or technological disaster, that people will continue to move onto the Internet. Several countries where the fees to access the Internet are currently high, or where the technological infrastructure isn't yet big enough to support large number of users in their populations, are moving slowly towards broader Internet use. As technologies improve to protect online information and purchases, and as the general population begins to feel more comfortable with online privacy and security, it is likely that more people will buy things online. In addition, more widespread use of wireless devices such as Internet-enabled cell phones and personal digital assistants such as Palm will provide easier and more frequent access to the Web.

- The world of business-to-business (B2B) E-Commerce is also likely to continue to save companies money by streamlining business practices and providing cost savings from online purchasing practices. In fact to date, much more money is being spent in the B2B sector than in the business-to-consumer (B2C).

Note

Studies have shown that B2C spending reached $37 billion in the year 2000. B2B spending, on the other hand, totaled a whopping $218 billion in the same year.

eComInfoCenter.com Offers Stories of Success and its Flip Side

- Another way to get an understanding of how E-Commerce has fared is to look at individual companies and see who has succeeded and who has failed. For example, Amazon.com, one of the survivors of several years of E-Commerce chaos and growth, tells an interesting story. Started in 1995, the company grew to serve 29 million customers by the year 2001, selling in over 160 countries. Starting with only one product, books, the company has now added CDs, videos, DVDs, games, toys, and electronics, and even an auction site. Revenues totaled 2.76 billion in the year 2000. How profitable is Amazon? It's not. After five years the company hopes to make its first profits by the end of 2001.

eComInfoCenter.com Success Stories Page

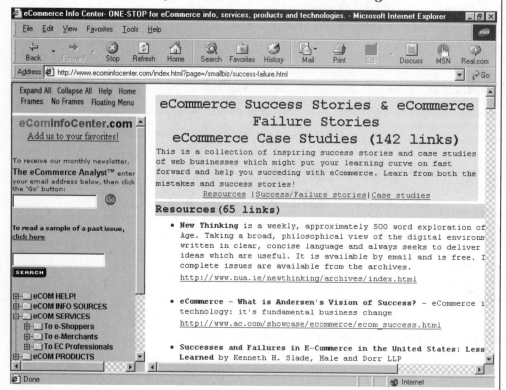

> **Note**
> E-Commerce wisdom says that a company must plan on at least five years of operation before they realize a profit. Since E-Commerce itself is only slightly older than five years, the truth of this estimate is unclear.

- Sometimes it's hard to tell which are success stories and which reflect failure. Internet companies are notorious for needing a long lead-time before they become profitable. One reason for this is the cost of getting a new customer. Depending on the company and product, it can cost from $20 to $40 to get a new customer. If your average product price is $15.99 and a sizeable percentage of your customers only buy once, you are probably losing money.

- Supporting those customers is also costly: where a customer service phone call can cost a company $1, an online customer support exchange can cost $2.35 or more. One reason why online support can be costly is the time it takes to understand a problem. Whereas a phone support encounter typically involves only one contact, with e-mail several exchanges often have to happen before the problem becomes clear to the customer service person. Writing and reading several e-mails takes more time than a few minutes on the phone.

E-BUSINESS ANALYSIS

Take a look at each of these sites (full URLs are located at the end of the exercise), then read the site analysis below and answer the questions.

CASE STUDY 1: IDC.COM

■ IDC is one of a group of trendspotting organizations, which also includes Forrester and Gartner. The business world looks to these companies to predict where E-Commerce is going. IDC compiles vast amounts of data and performs studies, then sells this information in the form of reports. These reports can cost several thousand dollars. On IDC's Web site they provide articles and snippets of information to whet the appetite of would-be buyers. In addition, there is information about various industry events and briefings sponsored by IDC.

IDC.com Events Page

■ IDC places certain pieces of information about their reports online, such as the table of contents and an abstract (a one or two line encapsulation of the focus of the report). Often there is also a featured article by an analyst on the same topic. Businesses whose future can rise or fall based on accurate industry predictions often have a huge budget for this kind of data. When you consider the benefits of having good data in planning a business's future, several thousand dollars spent on that information is a good investment.

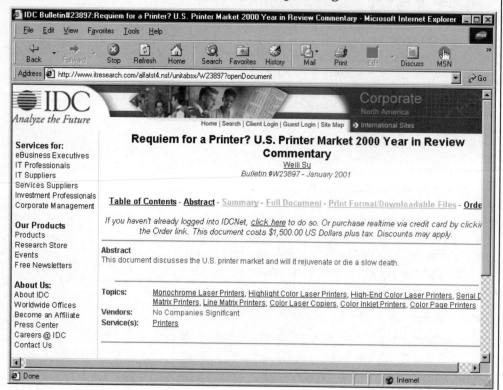

1. Where will the next Asia/Pacific IT Forum take place?

   _____

2. Which individuals at companies might benefit from attending an IDC-sponsored event?

   _____

3. Name three trendspotting organizations involved in E-Commerce.

   _____

CASE STUDY 2: CYBERATLAS.INTERNET.COM

- CyberAtlas provides statistics on a wide variety of Internet-focused topics. One of its regular features is the Top 25 Web Properties by month. The criterion for this data is organizations with the highest traffic to their sites. Not surprisingly this ranking for January 2001 shows that search engines and Internet access communities such as AOL and MSN topped the list. As you move down the list other logical candidates such as weather channels and news organizations appear. Two E-Commerce sites in this listing included the eBay auction site and American Greetings, the latter assumedly for exchange of online greeting cards.

CyberAtlas Big Picture Page

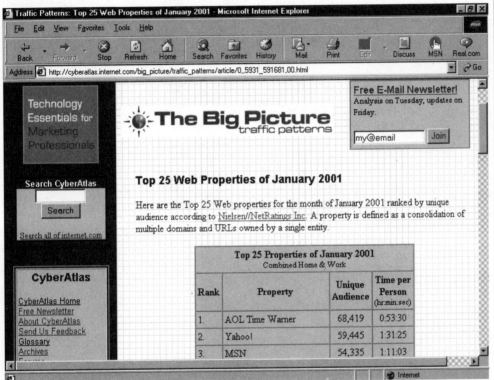

- Other reports on CyberAtlas summarize Internet usage statistics. Most of the information they provide actually comes from other companies, such as the Nielsen NetRatings company. In the week ending December 31, 2000, the average Web user in the US visited five sites and spent a little over half an hour on each site. What was the total estimated Internet usage in the world that week? 158,756,922 hours!

Nielsen NetRatings Page

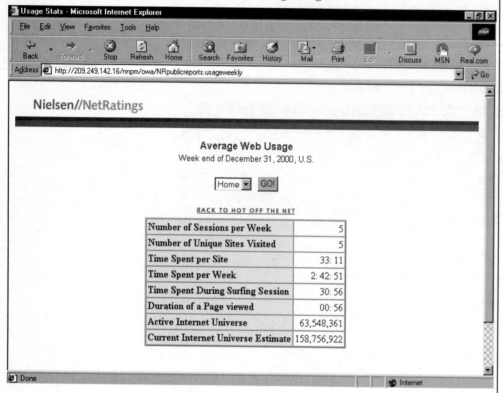

1. What was the top Web property last week?

   _____

2. How many unique visitors did MSN have last week?

   _____

3. How much time did the average Internet user spend online in that same week?

   _____

CASE STUDY 3: ECOMINFOCENTER.COM

- eComInfoCenter.com offers news about E-Commerce that helps you to do your own trendspotting. The site is set up in two frames: the frame on the left allows you to locate articles by topic area such as B2B or eCom Services, and the right hand frame displays articles from various publications. The separate frames allow you to scroll these two areas separately. Currently this site has links with 40,000 information sources.

eComInfoCenter.com Page with Accenture Publication Displayed

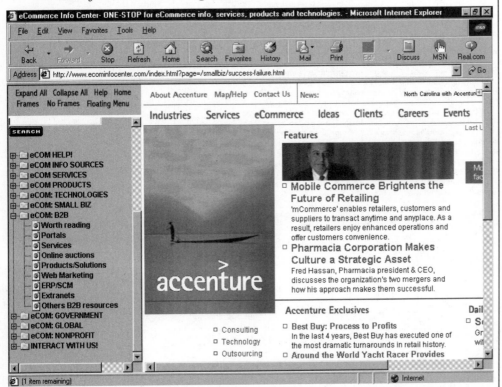

- eComInfoCenter.com not only offers E-Commerce publications and articles all from one central page, it also generates a monthly newsletter, *The eCommerce Analyst*. This kind of summary of media coverage for a topic such as E-Commerce can help busy business people to stay informed. To read this or other publications on screen, a visitor can click and drag the border between the two frames. This can cause the information in a condensed frame to become distorted or unreadable, however.

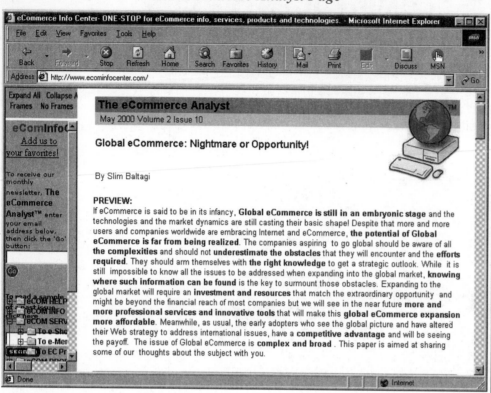

The eCommerce Analyst

May 2000 Volume 2 Issue 10

Global eCommerce: Nightmare or Opportunity!

By Slim Baltagi

PREVIEW:

If eCommerce is said to be in its infancy, **Global eCommerce is still in an embryonic stage** and the technologies and the market dynamics are still casting their basic shape! Despite that more and more users and companies worldwide are embracing Internet and eCommerce, **the potential of Global eCommerce is far from being realized**. The companies aspiring to go global should be aware of all **the complexities** and should not **underestimate the obstacles** that they will encounter and the **efforts required**. They should arm themselves with **the right knowledge** to get a strategic outlook. While it is still impossible to know all the issues to be addressed when expanding into the global market, **knowing where such information can be found** is the key to surmount those obstacles. Expanding to the global market will require an **investment and resources** that match the extraordinary opportunity and might be beyond the financial reach of most companies but we will see in the near future **more and more professional services and innovative tools** that will make this **global eCommerce expansion more affordable**. Meanwhile, as usual, the early adopters who see the global picture and have altered their Web strategy to address international issues, have a **competitive advantage** and will be seeing the payoff. The issue of Global eCommerce is **complex and broad**. This paper is aimed at sharing some of our thoughts about the subject with you.

1. What impact will mobile commerce have on retailing, according to Accenture?

   _____

2. How do you fit more of an article on eComInfoCenter.com's page?

   _____

3. According to The eCommerce Analyst, what should companies aspiring to go global not do?

   _____

http://idc.com
IDC.com

http://cyberatlas.internet.com
CyberAtlas

http://www.emarketer.com/estatnews
EStatNews

http://www.webtomorrow.com
WebTomorrow.com

http://www.ecominfocenter.com
eComInfoCenter.com

How E-Commerce is Saving Companies Money
- Learn about E-Procurement on the Web
- See how smaller businesses can compete
- Explore the supply chain
- Look at E-Marketplaces and B2B purchasing
- Learn how naming your own price can save money

NOTES

PurchasingNet.com Offers Businesses Cost Savings

- One of the best opportunities for enhancing profitability of business today isn't the money that comes from selling online, but the money that is saved from buying online. Termed **E-Procurement**, purchasing online using a variety of approaches and technologies is streamlining the process and offering more competitive pricing for all kinds of industries. E-Procurement is being driven by consultants, trading communities that provide a place for buyers and sellers to interact, and new technology. PurchasingNet.com offers such E-Procurement technology solutions.

PurchasingNet.com Page

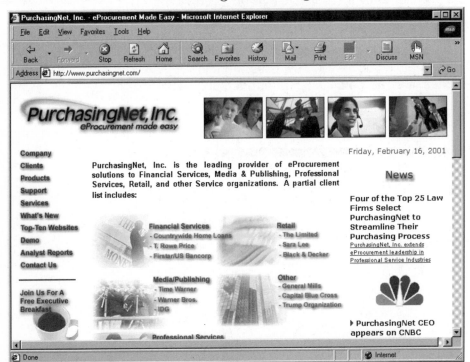

Buzzwords

E-Procurement is the practice of buying products or materials online and the automation of the purchasing process through software and online efficiencies.

A *requisition* is a company-internal form requesting permission to make a purchase.

- Although the function of purchasing has been around for a long time, it has become a technology-dependent discipline in recent years. Purchasing software can automate the buying process by generating **requisitions**, routing them online for approval, coordinating inventory control, and managing the payment of invoices. In addition, technology for gathering pricing or bids from hundreds of sources around the Web in an instant is becoming a common practice.

- The traditional model of making a business purchase is for someone to fill out and submit a requisition to someone else for approval. Once a requisition is approved, a **purchase order** is cut. A purchase order is a company contract to make the purchase, and is typically accepted by other companies as promise of payment against which they invoice the actual cost. In many cases, purchasing professionals in the buying company will find a source for the purchase—a vendor who offers the best price and support for the product—and place the order. E-Procurement software can automate every stage of this process.

Sorcity.com Helps Sellers Find New Customers

- No longer are businesses limited to doing business with vendors in their own town or even country. With E-Procurement technology, businesses are now able to locate new vendors they might not have had access to in the past. The time investment to set up accounts with vendors used to keep companies to working with one or two vendors for a product for years. Today, with automated account set up and access to a wealth of eager vendors online, companies often change vendors from purchase to purchase, based on who is offering the best price. Of course, there is risk in changing vendors so frequently: a new vendor might not be as efficient as a familiar one, and frequent change undermines vender relationships that purchasing agents may need to fall back on for special favors.

- The other side of this expanded universe of purchasing options is the opportunity opened up for sellers. Currently there is a television advertisement where a large Japanese company gives a contract to a tiny Texas vendor because that company provided a competitive bid online. Suddenly small companies can get their foot in the door of previously inaccessible large companies by gaining access to new customers in online trading communities. Sites such as Sorcity.com offer one such community.

Sorcity.com Home Page

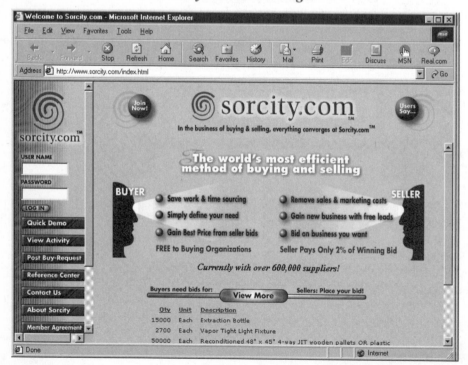

Buzzword

A *purchase order* is accepted by vendors as a document to place an order and a commitment to pay for the purchase.

Note

Some bidding sites offer instant pricing by scanning online catalogs and returning prices listed there. Others such as Sorcity follow the reverse auction model.

- Sorcity.com follows a reverse auction model: a business posts a description of the materials or supplies they want to buy, then sellers make a bid. Their bid is the price they are willing to offer the item for. The winner of the auction is the seller with the lowest price, although a buyer might want to research other criteria, such as company reputation, credit history, or service policies before making a final commitment.

iSourceOnline.com Addresses Needs of Supply Chain Management

- According to Rockford Consulting group, supply chain management is "the process of moving goods from the customer order through the raw materials stage, supply, production, and distribution of products to the customer." E-Procurement is one piece of the supply chain: it is the point at which you might purchase raw materials or manufacturing or distribution services. A typical supply chain example would be the auto industry. A customer places an order for a car with certain accessories in a certain color. The car manufacturer must process the order, if materials aren't already in stock they must order the materials to build the car, manufacture the car, and transport it to the local car showroom to be delivered to the customer.

- Recent technologies and the Internet itself have not only automated the supply chain process, they have also integrated various systems of companies to make the whole process faster and less expensive. A large part of the savings come from the sharing of data: when a customer order is put into the system back at the local car dealer, that information is available to the purchasing manager to buy the raw materials, to the manufacturing supervisor to get the car built, to the transport company that will schedule its delivery, and the accounting department that will bill the dealer for the cost of the car. Managing this whole process efficiently can result in significant cost savings. iSourceOnline.com is one of many sites that provide information on the latest advances in supply chain management.

iSourceOnline.com Page

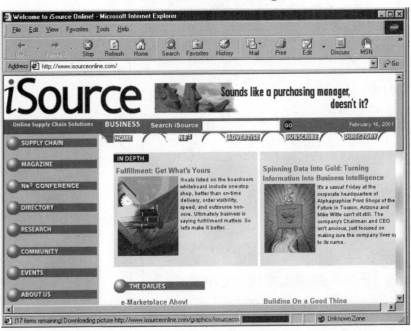

- One of the ways that good supply chain management saves companies money is by reducing the requirement for materials on hand. Companies today can place an order for materials and obtain them in a day or two because they can transmit the order in seconds online. In addition, there is a trend among suppliers to set up localized distribution centers so they don't have to ship materials across country but perhaps only across one state. In addition, companies are sharing their inventory data with vendors so vendors can anticipate shortages and initiate a new order in a timely way. All of this means that a company doesn't have to maintain its own warehouse to store materials prior to use. They can keep a small supply on hand and reduce the high overhead involved in maintaining a large inventory.

Alibaba.com Reveals the Magic of E-Marketplaces

- E-Marketplaces are an outgrowth of E-Procurement practices and technologies. An E-Marketplace is a purchasing community. Many E-Marketplaces are focused around a particular industry. There are E-Marketplaces of auto manufacturers, pharmaceutical companies, aerospace manufacturers, and construction businesses, for example. In these E-Marketplaces an automakers, for example, can find hundreds of suppliers of materials, such as steel, plastic, or molded cup holders; a construction business can find companies who sell nails, lumber, and even the kitchen sink.

- Some E-Marketplaces include suppliers of a wide variety of products and services, not just focused on a single industry. Alibaba.com is an E-Marketplace featuring 27 industries, such as apparel and fashion, chemicals, and industrial supplies. Both suppliers and buyers on Alibaba can post offers of materials for sale or materials needed. Products range from petroleum to dining room furniture.

Alibaba.com Page

- Some E-Marketplaces are member-based, meaning that a company must join the marketplace to be able to make purchases or offer products there. This is more typical of the industry-specific e-marketplaces. One interesting thing to note about the dynamics of e-marketplaces is that they often require the cooperation of competing companies to start up. Even though they share their savings with the competition, companies have worked together to establish industry-focused e-marketplaces and share the management of those marketplaces among them.

Priceline.com Offers Savings to Everybody Through a Name-Your-Own Price Policy

- One online procurement site that is open to individuals and businesses alike is Priceline.com. This site allows visitors to state the price they want to pay for something, then vendors bid for their business. This site started with hotel rooms and airline ticket deals, but has branched out to include rental cars, car purchases, long-distance phone service, and home financing.

Priceline.com Home Page

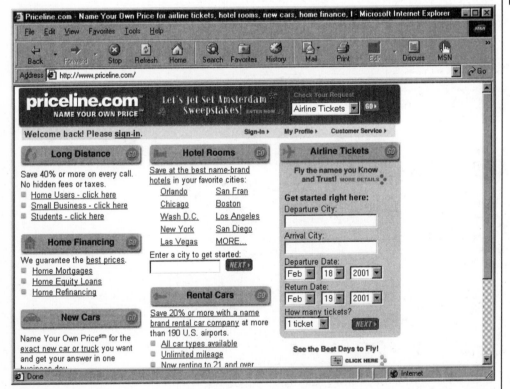

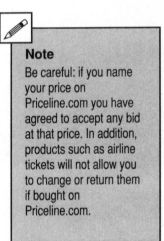

Note

Be careful: if you name your price on Priceline.com you have agreed to accept any bid at that price. In addition, products such as airline tickets will not allow you to change or return them if bought on Priceline.com.

- Priceline.com started with hotel rooms and airline tickets because those are commodities that are time-driven. That means that as a hotel night or airline flight date approaches, those companies run the risk of having an empty room or a vacant airplane seat. Rather than get nothing from these unused items, the companies are willing to offer greater discounts to those who are willing to book them at the last minute. This kind of on-the-fly ability to shift pricing and offer discounts is being tried by many businesses today, largely because of the speed with which deals can be struck online.

E-BUSINESS ANALYSIS

CASE STUDY 1: SORCITY.COM

- Sorcity.com is a reverse auction site, where businesses can post a request for an item they wish to buy and suppliers can 'bid,' stating the price they will offer the item for. To use the site you have to set up your reverse auction by filling out a form. This form asks for a timeframe for the auction, any specific suppliers you'd like to notify of the auction, information about the items you want bids for, and any special terms and conditions. This last might include specifying who pays for shipping and who insures the product while it's in transit.

IDC.com Events Page

- Sorcity.com also places several tools on its site that are useful to purchasing professionals, such as a currency exchange rate listing, time zone conversions so they can contact vendors in other countries, and calculators to convert engineering and metric units into their US counterparts. There's even a link to the Federal Acquisition Regulations for those doing business with the government.

Sorcity.com Resources Page

1. In a reverse auction, who makes a bid, the buyer or seller?

   _____

2. Is Sorcity.com a B2B or B2C site?

   _____

3. What are NAICS codes?

   _____

CASE STUDY 2: ISOURCEONLINE.COM

- iSourceOnline.com focuses on the supply chain, that process that stretches from the time a customer places an order till the moment it is delivered and paid for. One useful item on this site is a Supply Chain Value Activities chart. This chart shows in detail the various activities involved in the supply chain and the various participants in it. You can download and print this chart for reference.

iSourceOnline.com Global Enabled Supply Chain Page

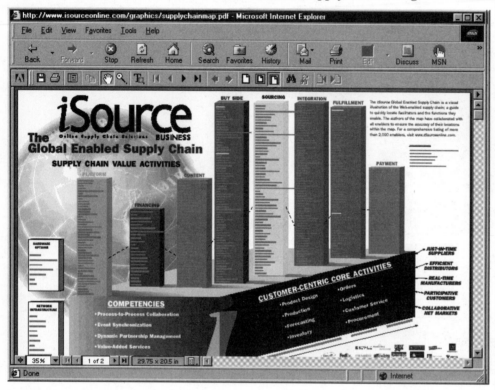

■ iSourceOnline.com includes an online monthly magazine. The articles in this magazine offer some nice functionality to readers, who can click on links to e-mail the articles or get a printer-friendly version. But beyond those features, you can click a link to see any related articles from the magazine archives, or fill out a message form at the end of the article to begin a discussion about it. Discussions are posted to the Community area of the Web site. Finally, near the end of each article is a list of companies mentioned in the article, with a link to each company's home page.

iSourceOnline.com Magazine Article Page

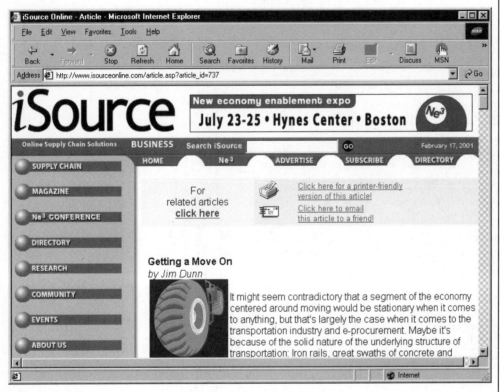

1. What is the supply chain?

   _____

2. Name at least four elements of a typical supply chain.

   _____

3. What conference does iSourceOnline.com sponsor?

   _____

CASE STUDY 3: PRICELINE.COM

- Priceline.com allows its visitors to name the price they want to pay for a product or service and have companies bid for their business. For long distance service, businesses can buy so many minutes of calls to a particular state or country. They must use their business phone line to make the calls. What's nice about this feature is that you don't have to change long distance providers; you just call a number and dial an access code to use your pre-paid minutes. If your company was going to do a project with a company in France that would last three months, you might save money by buying 100 minutes of phone time to France through Priceline, for example.

Priceline.com Long Distance Page

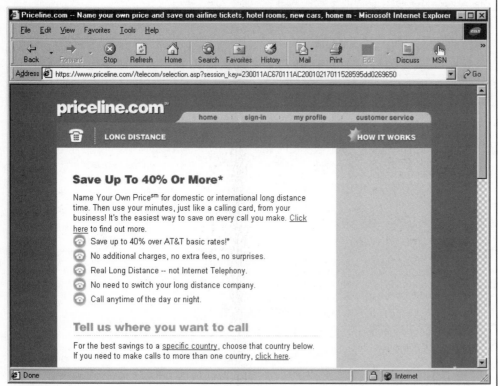

- Companies and individuals can also save on buying a new car or truck on Priceline. With this process there are several pages of details to fill out, essentially specifying the model of car you want with options such as special equipment packages and color. Priceline provides you with a calculator for financing a vehicle, which is helpful. It was interesting to note that in working through this process when I put in a price lower than the dealer's invoice amount, I was advised to change my price, and in fact could not complete the purchase process at lower than dealer invoice.

Priceline.com New Car Page

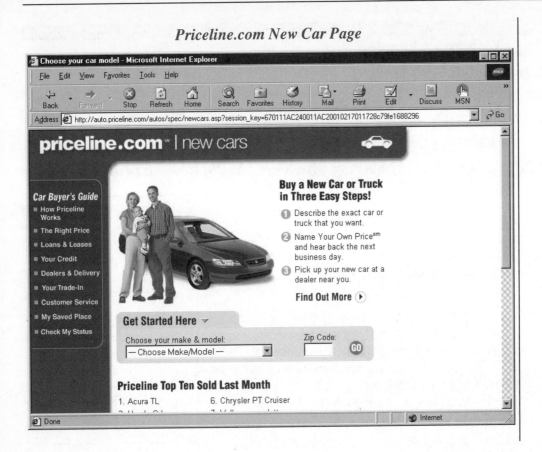

1. How much can you save on long distance calls on Priceline?

    _____

2. Do you have to make long distance calls you purchase at Priceline at a certain time of day?

    _____

3. Why do you think you have to enter your Zip Code to use the new car purchasing feature?

    _____

http://www.purchasingnet.com
PurchasingNet.com

http://www.sorcity.com
Sorcity.com

http://www.isourceonline.com
iSourceOnline.com

http://alibaba.com
Alibaba.com

http://www.priceline.com
Priceline.com

Keeping a Web Store Running
- **Learn all about Web servers**
- **Discover the role of IT in setting up and running a site**
- **Take a look at the option of renting software**
- **See how wireless servers work**
- **Learn what application service providers (ASPs) have to offer**

NOTES

You Can Find a Wealth of Information About Servers at ServerWatch.com

- The term **server** is thrown around a lot these days, sometimes referring to software, sometimes to hardware, and sometimes as the cause of all woes (as in "the server is down"). What is a server? Technically a server is software that can respond to requests. A Web server responds to requests from browsers, delivering Web pages in HTML format. Often, people also refer to the hardware that server software is installed on as a server.

- Server hardware can be a sophisticated mainframe, or a simple desktop computer. However, because of the high volume of traffic on Web servers, high-end hardware is preferable. The Internet is made up of millions of Web servers talking to each other over a series of networks. When a business builds a Web site, it must place it on a server for people to access it with their browsers. A business can either install their own servers, or use one that is hosted by another company. You can learn about various types of servers at ServerWatch.com, part of Internet.com.

Buzzword

A server is a type of computer software that responds to requests. On the Web, a server responds to requests from browsers for Web pages.

ServerWatch.com Home Page

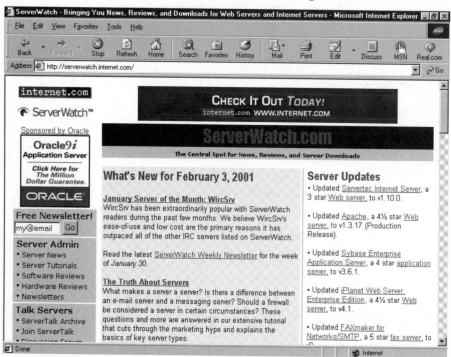

- There are many brands of server software available from companies, such as Microsoft, Oracle, and Sybase. Servers exist for different operating systems, such as UNIX, Macintosh, Windows, and Linux. Servers can also be set up for different functions, such as mail servers to handle e-mail, list servers to handle mailing lists, and audio/video servers to handle multimedia.

ITtoolbox.com Supports Information Technology Professionals

- Today's companies follow different models of getting a site up and running depending on their size and internal technical staff. Employees who manage a company's computers are referred to as either information technology (IT) or information systems (IS) professionals. Sites such as ITtoolbox.com help keep IT workers up to speed with the constant changes in technology. Some businesses keep IT employees on staff full time who can set up and maintain servers and support the technical needs of a Web business. Other companies have employees deal with on-site computer needs, but outsource some or all of their E-Commerce technology needs.

ITtoolbox.com E-Business Page

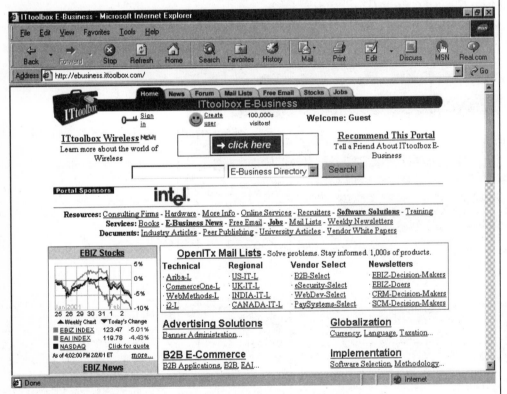

- If a company depends on its Web site for a large portion of its income, it is vital that that site function properly at all times. Because a Web site is open 24 hours a day, 7 days a week, and can get a huge number of visitors, the demand on technology is great. There are much-publicized instances of businesses, such as AOL, whose servers have crashed because they didn't have the technical infrastructure in place to handle this demand. When a Web site crashes, a company can lose millions of dollars in a single day, and perhaps more seriously, customers who experience technical problems with a site may never come back.

Note

Some businesses use off hours to make repairs or perform maintenance tasks on their servers. Diagnostic and back-up software can be set up to run at 3 in the morning on Sunday, for example, when it is hoped few people will be inconvenienced by the offline time.

- In the E-Commerce world it's not just server software that's involved. E-commerce operations rely heavily on databases for features such as catalogs and online help and specialized software for functions such as processing transactions, providing customer service, and tracking site activity for marketing purposes. All of this software must be installed, in some cases customized, and updated when new versions come out; this software maintenance falls on IT workers, or third party vendors.

Learn How Companies are Renting Software from Sites such as Findapps.com to Help Them Succeed

- With so much technology involved in an E-Commerce business, new models of software use are appearing. One approach is for a company to rent software. Although any company that uses a software product on its network is technically licensing it from a software company, new businesses have sprung up to deal with the licensing and upgrading of software products for companies. One such company, Application Rental Guide, offers businesses a variety of software products. In some cases this can be a more cost-effective way to access software, and it takes the burden of installing and updating the software off of an internal IT staff.

Application Rental Guide Home Page

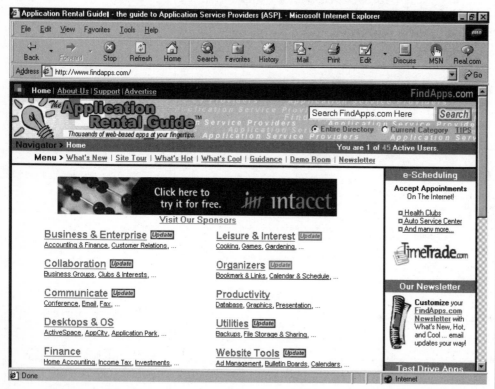

- Companies that host software applications and make them available to companies for a fee are called **application service providers**, or ASPs. ASPs offer a way for smaller and mid-sized companies to place a portion of their IT function with a company that is dedicated to 24-hour a day operability. Because the ASP model is becoming so popular, there are now companies springing up called aggregators. Aggregators manage multiple ASP relationships for companies. In a sense they are like an advertising agency that manages the placement of ads for a company and manages those relationships.

Buzzword

As *application service provider* (ASP) delivers hosted software solutions to a company online. An *aggregator* is a company that manages multiple ASP relationships for clients.

- Some ASPs offer more than simply a word processing program online. Many are taking on entire business functions, such as handling all online transactions or providing customer support. These companies not only host a software application, they provide consulting and administrative services. Companies that outsource any portion of their E-Commerce site operation must also make a commitment to monitoring that service. If an ASP is not delivering good performance, it can have a serious impact on an online business's success. When a company signs on to use an ASP's service, it is typical to sign a service level agreement; under these agreements, the company is charged by the level of service they use.

iPlanet Offers Servers for the Wireless Community

- The world of wireless computing is exploding, and new technologies are developing to support it. Wireless servers such as those offered by iPlanet are essentially like any other server, except that they understand the wireless application protocol that drives delivery of information to wireless devices and can respond to those requests. You can convert a standard server into a wireless server by programming it to recognize a document created with **wireless markup language** (WML) rather than HTML.

Buzzword
Wireless markup language (WML) is the language used to create documents that are delivered to wireless devices.

iPlanet.com Home Page

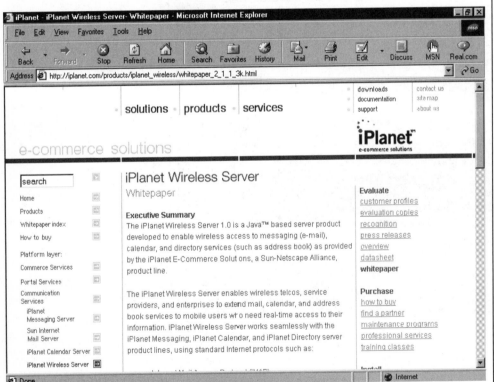

Technical Note
WML is loosely based on XML and HTML, all of which are markup languages. Any markup language is simply a method of telling a receiving system how to read a document. WML tells wireless devices how to read the content being sent to a cell phone, PDA (personal digital assistant), or pager.

- Wireless gateways work a bit differently. A gateway is something like a hi-tech traffic cop: it takes requests from wireless devices and sends them on to standard Web servers. Internet service providers often run wireless gateways and only allow access to certain partner-Web sites through them.

Commerce One.net Offers a Marketplace for E-Commerce Services

- With all the software, hardware, and service options available to E-Commerce businesses today, it's a challenge to determine the best mix of solutions. There are essentially three options available: to build and run applications internally, to buy an off-the-shelf software solution and use it to run your E-Commerce shop, or to outsource software and service functions to an ASP or consultant. Certainly smaller businesses might need to outsource some functions simply because they can't afford to set up the infrastructure to perform those functions. But even larger companies tend to use a mix of internal expertise and outside help.

- E-Businesses can find many of the products and services they need to set up their online business on the Internet. E-Marketplaces such as Commerce One.net provide a good starting point for exploring the huge world of product and service providers for E-Commerce.

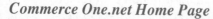

Commerce One.net Home Page

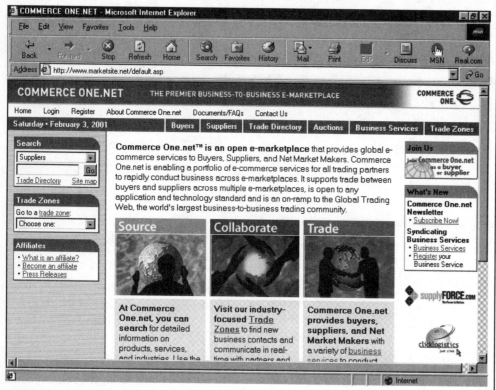

E-Business Analysis

> *Take a look at each of these sites (full URLs are located at the end of the exercise), then read the site analysis below and answer the questions.*

SITE 1: APPLICATIONS RENTAL GUIDE

- Applications Rental Guide is a good site to learn about the world of ASPs because they have a well organized help function, which they call Guidance. Their Guidance page features categories of information, such as Definitions and Projections & Trends; these categories will vary depending on what topic you request guidance on. The site includes articles and definitions from a variety of publications and sites. You can sort these items by name or other criteria, such as date or number of hits. The site also allows visitors to write reviews of the various articles to help guide others as to their usefulness.

Applications Rental Guide Guidance Page

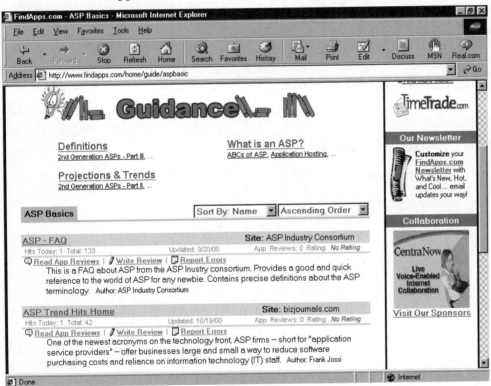

- The Application Rental Guide offers demos of the software it licenses to customers. The demos appear with sample files to give the user an idea of how the application is used in the business world. The technology used to deliver this software actually lets Windows-based applications be used from any computer, regardless of whether it uses a Windows operating system. A user has to have a Java-enabled browser to use the online software, and those with slower computers may experience some delays. Accessing software hosted online is best when done from a computer with a fast processor.

Application Rental Guide Demos Page

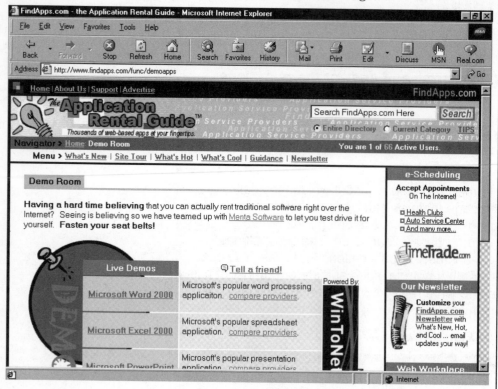

1. What is an ASP?

   _____

2. How does an application hosting site charge for software access?

   _____

3. What is WintoNet?

   _____

SITE 2: COMMERCE ONE.NET

■ Commerce One.net is an E-Marketplace, which means that it is a gathering place for buyers and sellers of services and products. To buy or sell on an E-Marketplace you must register to become a member. Buyers can search for suppliers and read a profile about them. Within the profile is an e-mail link, along with phone and other contact information. On this site you have the ability to sort searches by company, location, or industry. This is useful if you wish, for example, to see all the suppliers in your state in one section of the list.

Commerce One.net Trade Directory Search Results Page

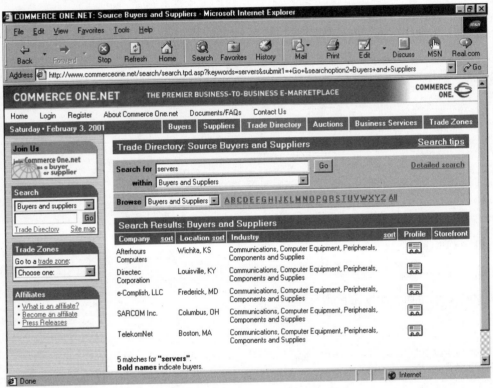

■ One feature on Commerce One.net's Web site is Trade Zones. When you select one of these zones, such as High Technology, you see headlines about that topic. You can move to additional headlines using the Prev, Next, and Front Page navigation links. An interesting feature is the Executive Summary. When you pass your mouse over any of the headlines, an Executive Summary of the article appears in a box to the right outlining the key points in a bullet-list format. There are also graphic links to companies in the category along the right side of the page so you can jump to that supplier's profile.

Commerce One.net High Technology Trade Zone Page

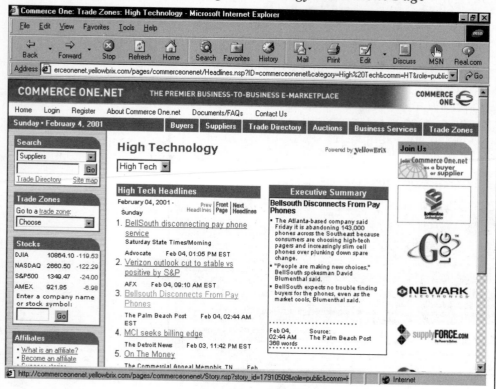

1. Are there any Commerce One.net-listed suppliers of servers in Ohio?

   _____

2. What three items can you sort a trade directory search result by?

   _____

3. Look up today's top headline in the High Technology area of CommerceOne.net; suggest how this headline might relate to or have an impact on E-Commerce.

   _____

SITE 3: SERVERWATCH.COM

■ ServerWatch.com actually has an area where you can download server software. Some of this software consists of demo versions, while others, such as Microsoft Personal Web Server, are actually free. The Top Download area of the Web site lists the servers that had the most downloads from the site that week. When you click on any item in the download list, you go to a detailed description of that product and a download link. Typically the download link actually takes you to the manufacturer's site, with additional data about system requirements you can read before you download.

ServerWatch.com Top Downloads Page

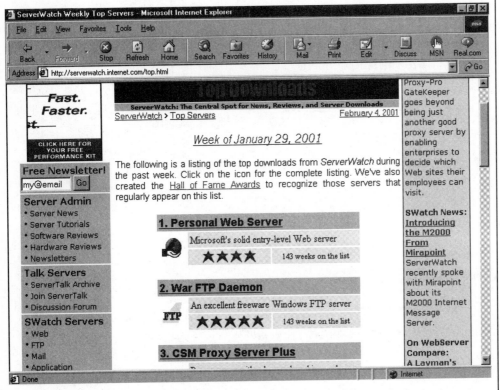

■ ServerWatch.com also includes a WebServer Quick Compare table. Each server name on this list is linked to a very detailed chart providing specifications for operating systems supported, protocols used, and so on. At the bottom of the Quick Compare page is a Power Search link. The Power Search contains a checklist of features, such as Can Require Password or Supports Virtual Servers. You can check the features you want and the site searches only for servers that have those features.

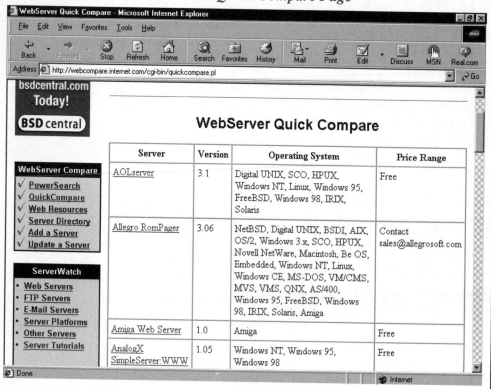

WebServer Quick Compare - Microsoft Internet Explorer

File   Edit   View   Favorites   Tools   Help

Back   Forward   Stop   Refresh   Home   Search   Favorites   History   Mail   Print   Edit   Discuss   MSN   Real.com

Address http://webcompare.internet.com/cgi-bin/quickcompare.pl

bsdcentral.com
Today!
BSD central

WebServer Quick Compare

WebServer Compare
✓ PowerSearch
✓ QuickCompare
✓ Web Resources
✓ Server Directory
✓ Add a Server
✓ Update a Server

ServerWatch
• Web Servers
• FTP Servers
• E-Mail Servers
• Server Platforms
• Other Servers
• Server Tutorials

Server	Version	Operating System	Price Range
AOLserver	3.1	Digital UNIX, SCO, HPUX, Windows NT, Linux, Windows 95, FreeBSD, Windows 98, IRIX, Solaris	Free
Allegro RomPager	3.06	NetBSD, Digital UNIX, BSDI, AIX, OS/2, Windows 3.x, SCO, HPUX, Novell NetWare, Macintosh, Be OS, Embedded, Windows NT, Linux, Windows CE, MS-DOS, VM/CMS, MVS, VMS, QNX, AS/400, Windows 95, FreeBSD, Windows 98, IRIX, Solaris, Amiga	Contact sales@allegrosoft.com
Amiga Web Server	1.0	Amiga	Free
AnalogX SimpleServer:WWW	1.05	Windows NT, Windows 95, Windows 98	Free

Done   Internet

1. What is the Hall of Fame Awards on ServerWatch.com?

   _____

2. What is the cost to buy War FTP Daemon in its full version?

   _____

3. What operating systems does Amiga Web Server support?

   _____

http://serverwatch.com
ServerWatch.com
http:/ittoolbox.com
ITtoolbox.com
http://www.findapps.com/
Application Rental Guide
http://iplanet.com/
iPlanet.com
http://www.commerceone.net
Commerce One.net

Leveraging E-Commerce in Your Business Model
■ **Learn about enterprise resource planning**
■ **See how ERP connects to E-Commerce**
■ **Discover how data mining can benefit an organization**
■ **Explore the tools used in data mining**
■ **Find out what companies can learn from Web site analysis**

NOTES

CIO.com Offers Enterprise Resource Information for Corporate Decision-Makers

■ Enterprise Resource Planning, commonly referred to as **ERP**, is a modular system of software products that integrate the operations of an entire business (the enterprise), ranging from finance to marketing to human resources and product distribution. The essense of ERP is the ability to share information across an enterprise through a centralized database, called a **data warehouse**. Most ERP software comes in modules related to the individual functions of a business. Consultants customize those modules and the way they interact for an individual business and its industry.

■ ERP seeks to speed processes and improve communications in an organization because every department has shared access to data. If a customer places an order, that order is on record for the billing department, shipping department, and customer service department to access as soon as it enters the system. Unlike older systems, where each different department had to enter order information into their own database as the order moved through the company, ERP involves less data entry, less errors introduced, and better customer service.

■ CIO.com is Web site geared towards information executives in companies. Its Enterprise Resource Planning Research Center offers articles and data about ERP that help IT (Information Technology) professionals stay on top of advances and changes in the ERP field. When an organization adopts an ERP system the process is referred to as an ERP implementation. ERP implementations can be very costly, involve dozens of consultants, and take years to complete. However the eventual savings in productivity and money are often well worth the effort involved.

Buzzwords
ERP is a software system designed to integrate the operations of an entire business through a centralized database called a *data warehouse*.

Note
An ERP implementation is usually very costly, ranging anywhere from $400,000 to $3,000,000 plus. Costs involved include the software itself, consultants, employee training, and costs to modify the functioning of the system after it's installed to make adjustments to refine the workings of the system.

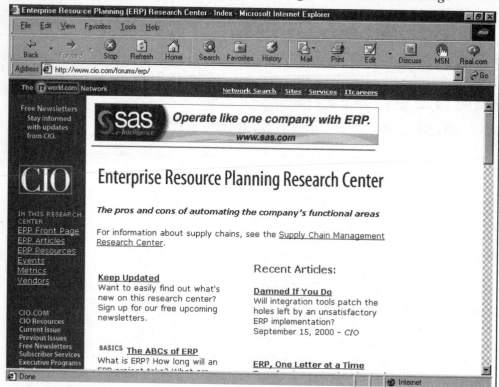

- ERP software is built around data tables; these tables include settings that can be set differently depending on how the business wants its processes handled. One limitation of ERP is that a business must choose one set of settings for each process, so everybody in the company must agree to handle functions in the same way. Because in most companies departments handle things in very different ways, this reeducating of an organization to one centralized process is often difficult.

ERPSupersite.com Offers Information on ERP Vendors, Consultants, and Services

- When a company starts an E-Commerce operation, whether as an extension of its offline business or an entirely new business, everything that happens online is part of the overall business enterprise. If a customer places an order on an E-Commerce site, the order information must be entered into the centralized database, accounting must process the payment, the warehouse must pull the product, and the shipping department must send the order out. If the customer sends an e-mail inquiring about the order, an ERP set up will allow customer service, shipping, and accounting to view the identical data and help the customer, no matter which department such inquiries are routed to.

- In recent years ERP software companies have been paying special attention to E-Commerce to bring online functions—such as customer service and online order processing—into line with offline processes. Special concerns about connecting a traditional business with an Internet business include security of company data and accommodating the 24 hour a day, 7 day a week nature of E-Business.

- As ERP systems grow to encompass online business, more consultants have appeared with expertise in E-Commerce and ERP, and software vendors such as Baan and SAP have created E-Commerce-specific ERP software. The ERP Supersite sponsored by TechRepublic offers a way to find various players in the ERP world, including vendors of ERP software, IT consultants, and business analysts.

Note
Some of the major publishers of ERP software include PeopleSoft, Baan, SAP, and Oracle. Each offers E-Commerce-focused ERP solutions.

ERPsupersite.com Home Page

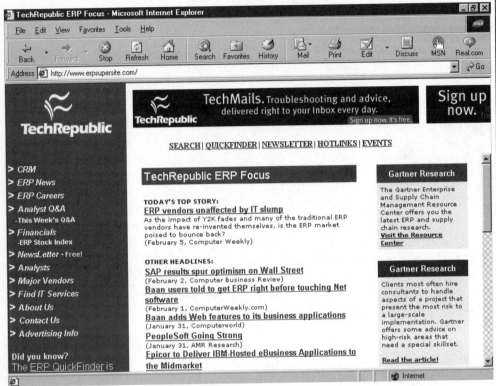

DMReview.com Site Helps You Learn About Current Advances in Data Mining

- One area of business where the Internet has brought great advances is data mining, also referred to as business intelligence, Web mining, or knowledge discovery. Essentially data mining is the practice of looking at information in a database to try to identify patterns of information. Based on those patterns, a business can build models that help them predict what might happen in the future. Data mining is one part of decision support systems; that is, a system of gathering, reporting, and analyzing business data to support management decision-making. Where other methods of data analysis, such as statistics, may simply organize data, data mining software discovers patterns in data that may not be obvious.

- With data mining you might review online sales data to create a model of seasonal buying habits on which you can base future promotions. With the wealth of information made available by ERP's centralized database and the Internet's many data gathering tools, data mining is becoming an important force in E-Commerce. DMReview.com's Web site is one of the many sites that have sprung up in recent years offering support for and information about data mining efforts.

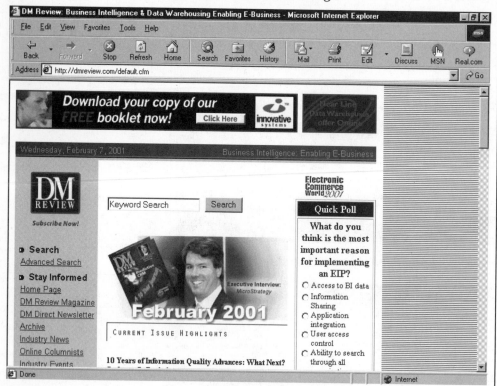

Data mining existed before the Internet, but the wealth of tools available to search the Web and to gather data about online customers makes the data mining even more effective. In addition, the advent of computer systems with enough memory to contain huge databases of information (50 gigabyte and beyond) has allowed businesses to apply data mining to large enough segments of data to provide more robust results.

See How Bots Explore Data Online at BotSpot.com

To assemble the data that decision support systems use, software called **agents**, or **bots**, is often used. Bot is short for robot, and like the robot of science fiction a bot is programmed to carry out a function without human intervention. For example, a bot might perform a search for data on the Web, moving from site to site, and returning data without human involvement. Intelligent bots use artificial intelligence to make some basic decisions or choices based on past experience. Bots are used on E-Commerce sites to inform customers when a product in their category of interest appears, to search for prices on a product from various sources, or to automatically check a Web site for broken links.

BotSpot.com provides information about bots, including listings of existing bots organized by subject, such as Shopping or Data Mining. Many of these bots can be downloaded and used for free. You can explore descriptions of various categories of bots on this site: for example you'll discover that a Chatter Bot can actually talk to you, and Fun Bots play games. In the area of E-Commerce, bots can be used for activities such as searching, E-Procurement, negotiating prices with customers, and even to run interactive banner ads that can 'talk' to customers.

Buzzword

An *agent or bot* is a program that performs a process without human intervention. Intelligent agents can make basic decisions as they search.

BotSpot.com Home Page

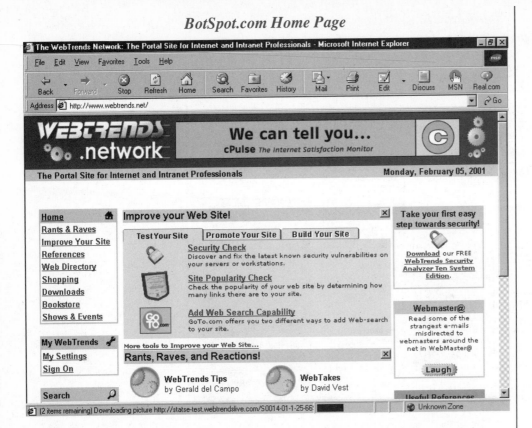

- Bots can cause problems on computer networks, either by discovering data that is confidential or that could be used to damage the network, or by slowing down the network performance. An agent can crawl around a network performing repeated searches and use up computing resources in the process. Some Web masters have developed ways to keep robots out of their networks or Web sites as a result. However, bots are used by search engines to return a site name in search results, so most E-Businesses who want to encourage visitors don't block bots for this reason.

Statracker.com Provides Web Analysis Tools to Business

- In addition to using bots to locate information on the Web, several companies have come out with Web analysis products or services. Statracker.com is one example. Their system generates reports on information such as the number of visitors to a site, referrers (that is, the name of the site the visitor came from when he or she landed on your site), keywords used to search, and what browsers and operating system visitors use. Statracker does not actually provide software to install; rather you paste their code onto your Web page and it enables you to generate various reports.

Statracker Home Page

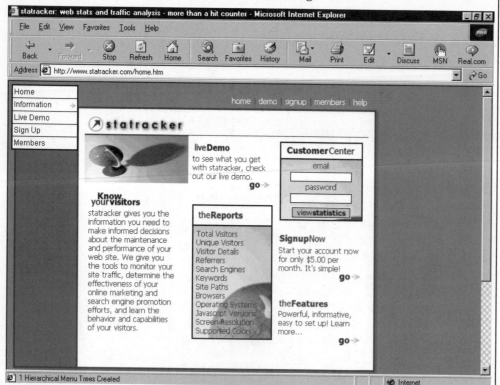

- Management and marketing professionals use Web analysis information in a variety of ways. For example, if you know what referrer sites people came to your site from, you might choose to place a link on those sites to draw similar visitors. Or, if you know which browsers most visitors are using, you might modify your site design to maximize its appearance for the way those browsers view Web pages. A marketing person might use data about what countries visitors live in to develop an international advertising strategy.

- Web site analysis software and services can track traffic to your site, noting total **hits** as well as unique visitors. Each time a person comes to a site, every page that person views is counted as a hit. However, tracking software can narrow that down to show **unique visitors**, that is, the total visitors to your site, not the total pages visited by all visitors.

Buzzwords

A *hit* is recorded whenever somebody displays a Web page; a hit is essentially one visit to any Web page.

A *unique visitor* is a record of the number of people who viewed any part of your site, regardless of the number of Web pages they might have visited.

E-Business Analysis

Take a look at each of these sites (full URLs are located at the end of the exercise), then read the site analysis below and answer the questions.

CASE STUDY 1: ERPSUPERSITE.COM

■ ERPSupersite.com contains various links and search features for finding ERP resources. Their Find IT Services area lets you search by the type of service, such as networking or eBusiness, or use pre-defined searches to search by activity criteria such as firms who can build an online store or install CRM (Customer Relationship Management) software. The search results provide links to more detailed information about each provider. A nice feature of this search tool is that you can check the providers that interest you, then use the Communicate With Providers action to send an e-mail to them all asking for information about their services or asking them to bid on a project.

ERPSupersite.com eMarket for IT Services Page

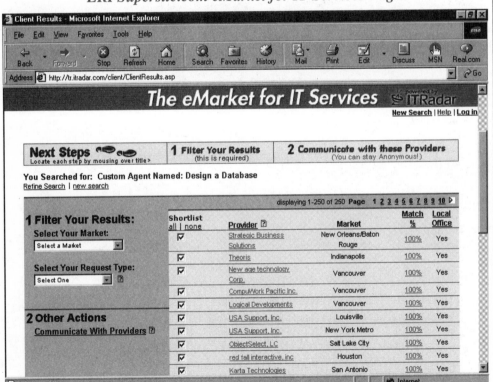

■ If you want to find ERP vendors of software solutions from this site, you can use the ERP QuickFinder feature. This provides an alphabetical list of all ERP vendors, including stock information, product information, and a link to their Web sites. A CRM QuickFinder feature is also available to see just vendors of customer relationship management software, a very hot sector of E-Commerce today. The Press Releases link included in QuickFinder results shows you a list of not only press releases from the company but also current news stories in which the company was mentioned, with links to view the actual releases and stories.

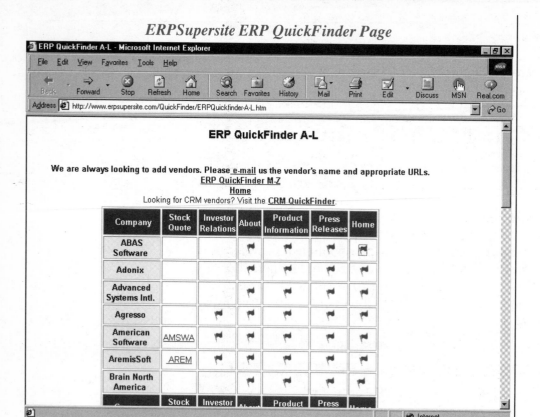

1. What filters can you use to narrow IT Services results?

   _____

2. What is CRM?

   _____

3. What software products does American Software publish?

   _____

CASE STUDY 2: DMREVIEW.COM

- Data mining is in an explosive growth period because it is a recently developed science that has a wealth of new tools at its disposal. DMReview is an online magazine and Web site dedicated to business intelligence. The site includes columns, articles, and news about data mining and decision support systems. The site also runs a weekly poll on a question related to business intelligence or E-Commerce. The polls are always based on a multiple-choice scenario, and the results are summarized in easy-to-read bar charts that show the percentage of people who made each choice.

DMReview.com Poll Results Page

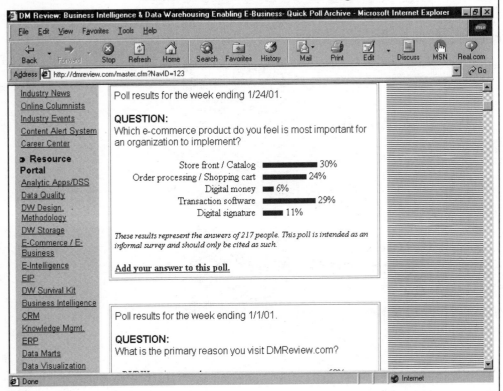

- Another feature of this site is the Content Alert System. You can enroll in this system and choose various topics. Whenever an editorial item such as a product review or column relates to that topic, the site sends you an e-mail alerting you. This kind of alert system appears on many E-Commerce sites, letting customers know when a product of interest to them appears in the company catalog or goes on sale. These systems are often designed around a bot, which sorts through data on the site and matches it to the information provided by visitors.

DMReview Content Alert System Page

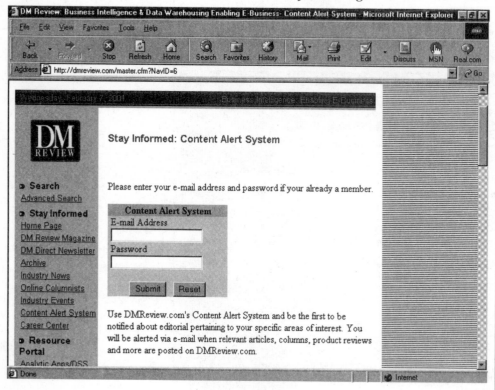

1. What was the result of last week's poll on DM Review?

   _____

2. What is a decision support system?

   _____

3. What kind of software can be used in a customer alert system?

   _____

CASE STUDY 3: STATRACKER.COM

■ Statracker.com offers a system of tracking data about Web sites. The reports that can be generated using this system provide a wealth of information about Web site traffic. Statracker.com includes sample reports you can view online. The Detailed Visitor Report, for example, provides data on each and every visitor to a site, including the time they entered the site, information about their ISP, the referrer site they came from, exactly which Web page they entered the site through, their browser and operating system, and even their computer screen resolution.

Statracker Detailed Visitor Report Page

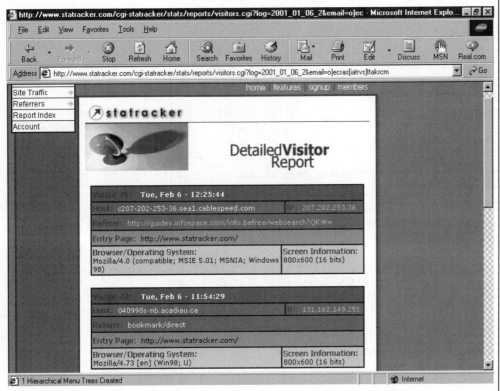

■ Another report, the Country Location Report, summarizes the number of hits on a site by country. They can track this because different countries have different extensions to their domain names. For example, in the United States domains of ISPs and Web sites typically end in .com or .net. However in England they end in .uk, and in Canada, they end in .ca. Knowing the countries of visitors to your site can help you know when you might need to provide content in different languages, or where you might have some international sales potential.

Security Check Sample Report Page

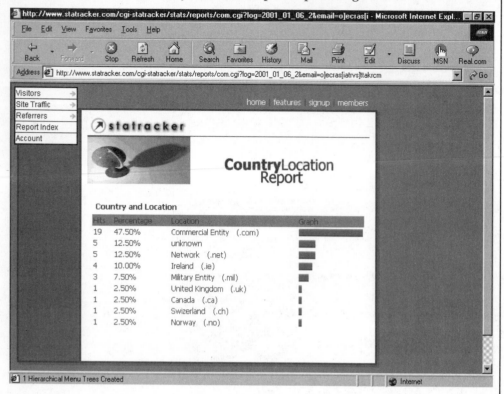

1. What is a referrer site?

   _____

2. What concerns about privacy might tracking of visitors to a site raise?

   _____

3. What extension is used by military entity domains?

   _____

http://www.cio.com/
CIO.com

http://www.erpsupersite.com/
ERPSupersite.com

http://dmreview.com/
DMReview.com

http://www.botspot.com/
BotSpot.com

http://www.statracker.com
Statracker.com

Theme 13	**Technology That Keeps E-Commerce Companies Secure**
	■ **Learn about the role of IT in E-Commerce security**
	■ **Explore the world of corporate intranets**
	■ **Discover what security software has to offer**
	■ **See how to check security and other settings on a Web site**
	■ **Learn about challenges in wireless security**

NOTES

8wire.com Supports IT Professionals with Information on the Latest Technologies

■ The new Internet economy, together with other technology trends, are taking companies out of their isolation and connecting them to customers, vendors, and business partners online. The traditional role of information technology, or IT, professionals is changing as a result of this shift. No longer just the people who install software and back up the network at night, these professionals are now challenged to set up internal Internets, called intranets, and to deal with hackers (theives of corporate data who can sneak in electronically through the back door).

■ IT employees must be able to use security software and design their networks to prohibit outsiders from getting access to sensitive company information. At the same time, they must allow others, such as a supplier checking inventory levels, to retrieve information. One of the fundamental security tools at their disposal is the **firewall**. A firewall is essentially software that stops intranets from being accessed via the Internet. Firewalls are typically set up to block access by search engines or intelligent agents that move around the Internet looking for data, but can still allow outside interaction, such as receipt of e-mail. Sites such as 8wire.com help IT professionals keep on top of the latest security technology, and the latest security threats.

Buzzword

A *firewall* is software that blocks access to a company intranet via the Internet.

Note

Password protection has various loopholes that makes it less than air-tight. Many people save their password so they don't have to type it in each time they log on, making their computer fair game for anyone passing by their workstation. Also, people are notoriously unimaginative in creating passwords; many hackers can easily figure them out.

8wire.com Home Page

- The method of requiring a user name and password to **authenticate** access to a network has only limited value. Besides the concern that people will make their password known either on purpose or inadvertently, passwords are simply strings of characters sent as text. Text sent online can be easily intercepted with network management software tools.

Learn All About Intranets at Innergy.com

- One of the biggest advances in protecting the security of an intranet is a form of encryption that protects communication between a server and browser called Secure Sockets Layer (SSL). SSL finds its best application in E-Commerce settings, ensuring the integrity of information a Web store provides to customers and keeping visitors responses confidential. However, on a company network, SSL doesn't do anything to authenticate a client Web browser, essentially verifying that the person communicating with it has a right to. This makes SSL less useful for protecting an intranet from outside access.

- Innergy.com is a site devoted to the intranet. Innergy.com includes articles on current technology such as digital certificates. Digital certificates are an improvement over simple password protection. Digital certificates are a form of digital identity. A user has to present a digital certificate to gain access to an intranet. Digital certificates can be issued by a network administrator using something called a public key infrastructure (PKI); a public key infrastructure is the framework for issuing and authenticating digital certificates. A key is used to encrypt and decode information.

Buzzword
Authentication is the process of verifying the identity of a computer user.

Note
Although not all secure sites use this designation, if you see a site whose URL begins https://, you can be sure it uses SSL to protect itself and visitors.

Innergy.com Page

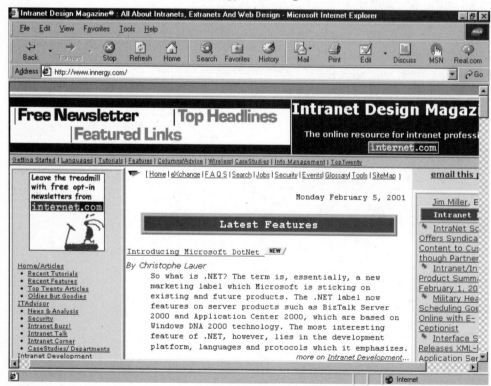

- Companies such as Microsoft have been the victims of hackers in recent years, causing concern about how safe the average company can be against this threat. In reality, encryption solutions, if used properly, can protect sensitive information, even if a hacker does come calling. That's because encrypted information is never stored on a server in its unencrypted form. That means that even if somebody hacks into the intranet, the unencrypted data is not there to be found. That's why information such as credit card numbers collected by online merchants are not at risk, if the company has done it's security homework.

Sun Security Software Helps E-Commerce Businesses Stay Safe

- Sun Microsystems is the company behind the programming language Java and the manufacturer of various software programs, such as Solstice network management software. One of the strengths of Sun is to offer multi-platform products; that is, software that works across operating systems such as Windows, UNIX, Linux, and Macintosh. Sun has a strong product line offering in the area of networking, and their security software is among the best. Their Solaris networking platform offers access control (a way to control who can access a network to protect certain types of data), authentication, and **auditing**. Auditing creates a record of any security-related events; that record can be used to determine the source and severity of a security event.

Buzzword

Auditing is a way of creating a record of security-related events on a network.

Sun Solstice Product Page

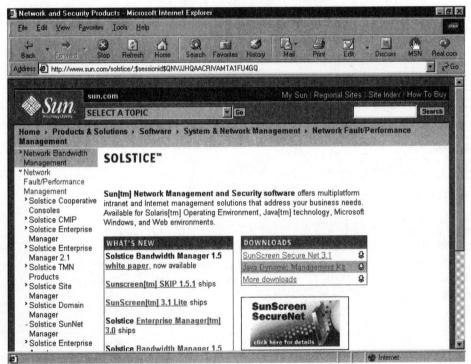

- Some Sun software products can also be used to set up Virtual Private Networks, referred to as VPNs. A VPN uses encryption to protect information between two specific points on the Internet. A VPN would work well in setting up access for a vendor to the area of an intranet where inventory data is stored, for example. However, because VPNs work with two fixed points, they don't provide much flexibility for making changes to access rights or providing access from different locations.

- Routers are the part of a network that, as the name implies, route packets of information to different points on the network. Routers have some role in intranet security because they can be set up with rules that limit how computers outside the network can connect to the network. Routers also can stop certain information from leaving the local network.

WebTrends.net Provides Tools to Diagnose Your Web Site's Security

- In addition to software that can be configured to protect a network, you can use software to monitor and analyze how secure your intranet or Web site are. WebTrends.net offers a security check tool, along with tools for analyzing Web site traffic and even your site's popularity (which it does by checking how many links point to your site).

Webtrends.net Home Page

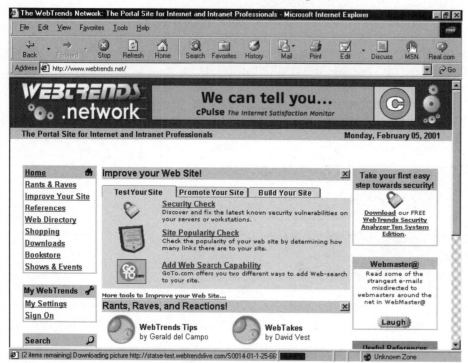

- WebTrends Security Analyzer performs over 1,000 tests on a Web site or network and can fix certain security problems itself. The software uses **intelligent agents**, software programs that can search through a system and detect and analyze what they find there. Both IT staff and company management can use such analyses to make important decisions about a company's security risks.

- Most companies that go into E-Commerce must set up their systems so that the back end of order processing and distribution coordinate with the front end of their Web store. It's this interaction that causes many companies to worry about security, because they have in effect linked their enterprise with the entire Internet, albeit with protections in place. The other aspect of E-Commerce security is that an E-Commerce business is taking confidential information from customers and must protect that information from prying eyes. A combination of a secure intranet and company network and protections on an E-Commerce site itself where customers enter confidential data is essential.

Buzzword

An *intelligent agent* is a program that searches and analyzes a system. Intelligent agents can make basic decisions as they search.

NetworkComputing.com Offers Advice on Security for Wireless Technology

- E-Commerce is going mobile, and whether a company is launching an e-mail marketing campaign or simply having its site accessed by wireless device users, it needs to be aware of security issues related to the wireless world. Sites such as NetworkComputing.com provide articles and information about such up and coming technologies.

NetworkComputing.com Wireless Security Tutorial Page

- Security for wireless devices is essentially the same as for a wired network. However, wireless devices present certain challenges. First, they have much more limited **bandwidth** than a desktop computer connected to the Internet; bandwidth is the capacity of a computer to send data transmissions. With limited bandwidth authentication functions can take a long time. Wireless devices also have limited memory, so certain types of authentication, for example where certificates have to be retained on both ends to decode encrypted data, aren't possible. In addition, the wireless access protocol (WAP) used to connect to wireless devices has some security gaps.

- Wireless Transport Layer Security (WTLS) is the security method used for exchange of information between the Internet and wireless devices. WTLS is the wireless counterpart of SSL (Secure Sockets Layer), but WTLS doesn't offer all the protections of SSL, although WTLS does include encryption capabilities. The area of wireless security is evolving as more and more consumer transactions from wireless devices become available.

Buzzword

Bandwidth is the capacity of a computer to send data transmissions; the bigger the bandwidth, the more data can be sent at one time.

Take a look at each of these sites (full URLs are located at the end of the exercise), then read the site analysis below and answer the questions.

CASE STUDY 1: WWW.8WIRE

- 8wire.com is a Web site dedicated to the IT professional, and it contains some practical and useful features. 8wire provides tools such as tutorials on networking topics and a glossary of technical terms. There's also a feature called The Buck Stops Here where those who have connected with unusually helpful technical support people can sing their praises. One of the site's practical features is Cyber Hotels, which allows users to search for hotels that offer high-speed Internet connections so they can connect with their network while on the road. You can search by city for all hotels or by hotel chain.

8wire.com Cyber Hotels Page

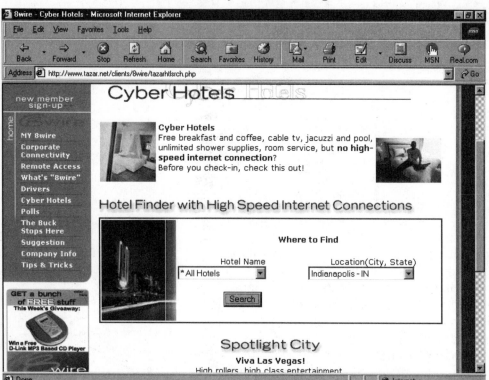

- 8wire tends to offer more practical and useful features than some professional sites, such as the Career Center area. This area has several tools, including an Instant Job Search by keyword, location, and job title. It also has a more detailed search feature called Short Cut Searches. With Short Cut Searches the user can search by company, salary, or industry, or follow links by job type and title, such as Programming/Visual Basic. Finally, users can upload a resume that potential employers can view and request a regular e-mail of job openings through the Tech Agent feature.

8wire.com Career Center Page

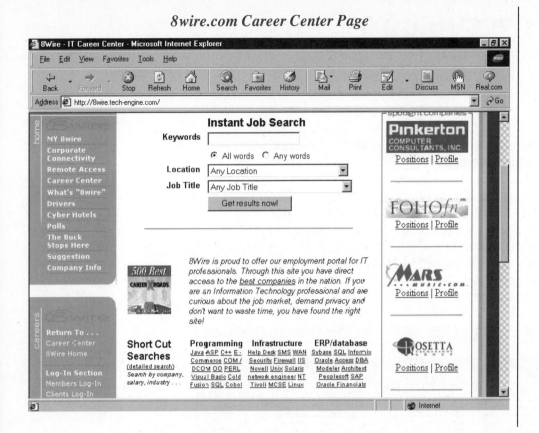

1. How many hotels in Indianapolis have a high-speed Internet connection?

_____

2. How often does Tech Agent send out job updates?

_____

3. What information is contained in a company profile?

_____

CASE STUDY 2: SUN.COM

- Sun Microsystems is one of the giants of programming and networking technology. Its Web site is geared towards users of its products, who are typically technically sophisticated. Although the site contains a wealth of white papers and product information, it also offers some features for the executive visitor. One feature, Persuasion Tools, offers a gallery of presentation templates and graphic art that a visitor can download and use to generate business presentations. This area also offers quotes about technology and statistics about growth in technology sectors. This is a clever way for Sun to help IT managers to convince their management to upgrade their technology infrastructure and hopefully include Sun's products in the mix. Notice that, in the spirit of the cross-platform and anti-Microsoft approach of Sun's Java language, the presentations are offered in PDF format (a document reader that can display documents created in any program) and StafOffice, the suite of applications for Linux, the open source application that is challenging Microsoft's supremacy.

Sun.com How To .Com Page

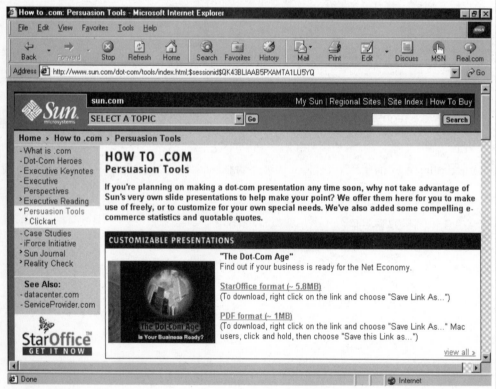

- Open source involves software that makes its source code available to anybody to work with or customize. The Linux operating system and StarOffice suite of applications are examples of open source products. Sun is very dedicated to supporting the open source movement. Its OpenOffice.org group coordinates various projects for developing open source applications. One unusual step they've taken on their Web site is to make a list of these development projects with coordinator contact information available to the general public. By following the links on the Projects and Coordinators chart, you can see software development in progress.

Sun.com OpenOffice.org Page

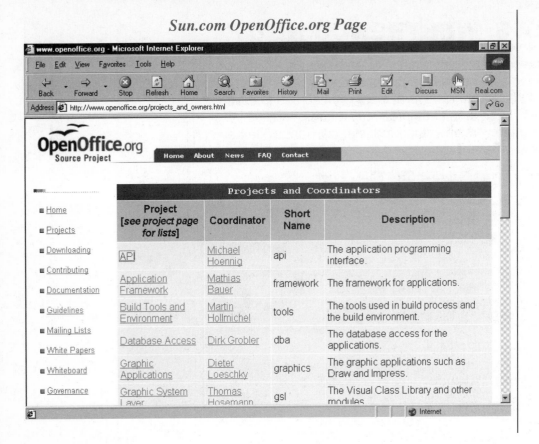

1. What is PDF format?

   _____

2. What is Open Source?

   _____

3. What does API stand for?

   _____

CASE STUDY 3: WEBTRENDS.NET

- WebTrends.com is the corporate home page of WebTrends, while WebTrends.net is touted as a portal for Internet and intranet professionals. Webtrends.net offers several tools you can use to build, promote, or test a site. These aren't free products, but through this site you can download a limited version of the products, view an online demo, or study sample reports.

WebTrends.net Improve Site Tools Page

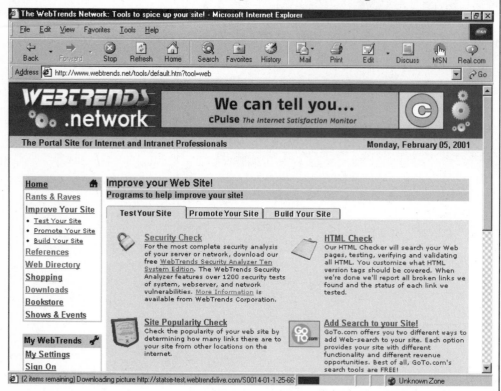

- The sample Security Check report shows the detailed information provided by the software, including tables of risks and vulnerabilities with easy-to-read graphs. Other sample reports for WebTrends products are available on the site. You can search for them by product, or by your job title. With this feature, a marketing professional might see visitor traffic analysis reports, and a finance person could see reports on Internet usage by department. This is a good way to divide up reports, because so many people in an organization can benefit from detailed information about the company Web site's activity and performance.

Security Check Sample Report Page

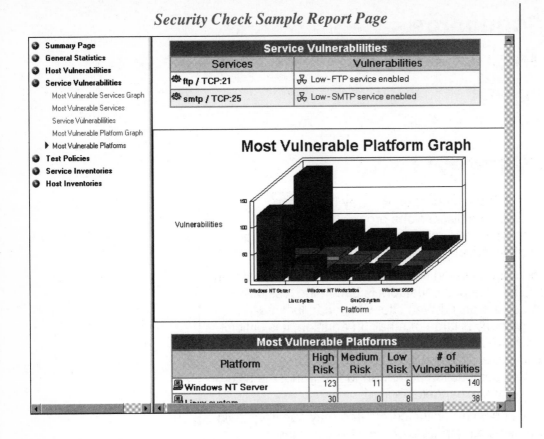

1. What does an HTML Check look for?

   _____

2. What is the name of the free search feature available from WebTrends' site?

   _____

3. In the sample Security Check report, which platform has the most vulnerabilities?

   _____

http://www.8wire.com/
8wire.com
http://www.innergy.com/
Innergy.com
http://sun.com/
Sun.com
http://www.webtrends.net/
WebTrends.net
http://www.networkcomputing.com
NetworkComputing.com

Learning E-Commerce
Part II, The Impact of the Internet on Business
Capstone Project

Summary of Concepts

- The Internet has had a significant impact on the way businesses communicate. E-mail and online discussions provide immediacy of communication, although they have removed the personal interaction many business communications used to involve.

- E-Commerce businesses are learning new ways to identify and deal with competition in cyberspace. Size of competitors is becoming less of a factor because customers see only a Web site, which can look as impressive whether a company is large or small. In addition, it is difficult to claim customer loyalty when it is so easy for a customer to move to a competitor's site with a simple click of a mouse. Also, because businesses are now facing competition from around the world, the size of their competitive universe has expanded.

- E-Commerce is a global endeavor; online commerce may someday help to bridge cultures, currencies, and trade barriers. However, most E-Commerce companies are still constrained from truly operating on a global scale by regulations, language barriers, a limited online customer base in some countries, and currency issues. Companies who operate outside of their own country often do so through partners in other countries, or separate divisions located in another country.

- Current trends in E-Commerce show a definite predominance of business-to-business commerce over business-to-consumer commerce. Businesses buying from other businesses is projected to account for several trillion dollars of activity by 2003. In the business-to-consumer arena, few companies are making significant profit at this time. However, many companies are seeing benefits in their ability to provide improved customer support, as well as savings in their own business operations from using the Internet to perform activities like supply chain management or E-Procurement.

- E-Commerce is driven by technology, including the ability to provide security for online transactions and outsourcing of business activities through Web hosting. Many companies are using technology to streamline the connection of their back-end functions, such as order processing, with their Web site. In addition, data mining technology is providing feedback about customers and their buying habits that will help E-Commerce businesses become more profitable in years to come.

Case Study

The Business:

- All Creatures Publishing would like to take direct sales of its books online in six months. Between now and then, they must do additional work analyzing the practical considerations of starting such a business, including the costs to start-up and the anticipated profit from the business, the impact such a business might have on their current sales partners who sell All Creature books through their own Web sites or bookstores, and the technology the company needs to put in place to deal with the operation of their E-Commerce store, including online **transaction processing**. They must also determine how to set up the store to sell to Canadian, as well as US customers, because they know that their books sell well in Canada.

Buzzword

Transaction processing is the term used for what a business must do to collect a payment from a sale. With a credit card payment, which is typical of online sales, transaction processing involves collecting credit card data, getting authorization for the credit card from the credit card company, and actually getting the money. It also involves keeping records of each transaction for the business.

The Project:

- The CEO of All Creatures Publishing must present a business plan to the board of directors of the company outlining the reasons and methods for launching an online bookstore. In addition to a written business plan, the CEO will give a presentation about E-Commerce, citing trends, benefits, and projected profitability. Assume the role of the CEO and prepare a presentation, alone or working in groups, using presentation software such as PowerPoint. In this presentation you should provide information about trends in E-Commerce, and specifically include information about book sales online. Include statistics about the volume of sales that are being transacted online, projected revenue from E-Commerce in the years to come, and the number of businesses that are moving into E-Commerce. Make the presentation to your class and respond to questions as they play the role of the board of directors.

The Business Model:

- To complete this project, you must research E-Commerce trends on the Internet. Here are three important things to consider:

  1. ***Examine the financial trends***: How much money is being made from E-Commerce today versus two years ago? How much money are analysts projecting will be made two years from now? How much of that money is being made by US companies?

2. ***Look at industry factors:*** Which types of businesses are finding success in E-Commerce? Are other publishers offering books for sale on their own Web sites? How many retail bookstores have also opened online bookstores? Are people buying more or less books than they did five years ago?

3. ***Explore profitability issues:*** How much is the book selling industry making in profits every year from online sales? How long does it take an online business to begin to make money? How much do E-Commerce businesses have to spend on technology to get started?

Technology

- Analysts and companies gather information on their customers and buying trends through software programs that track the volume of traffic on a site and what Web pages are viewed most by visitors. Cookies can also be used to look at online activity of visitors; cookies are files that reflect users patterns of behavior on a Web site; they are created by Web sites and placed on a user's hard disk when he visits a site. Data mining is the area of sifting through data that has been accumulated on Internet user activities and making analyses of that data. Data mining software automates this process.

Books to help:

Learning the Internet: Fundamentals, Projects, & Exercises (catalog number Z57)

Internet Research Projects and Applications: Sales, Marketing, & Management (catalog number RB13)

Learning Microsoft PowerPoint 2000 (catalog number Z40)

Web sites to explore:

http://startupinternetmarketing.com

Learn about market research on this site for new E-Commerce businesses.

http://www.forrester.com

Forrester is one of the leading trend spotters for business. Although they charge for many of their reports, they also provide short articles on E-Business trends.

http://www.publishersweekly.com

Publishers Weekly is one of the major publications for the publishing industry. Look at their Forecasts page to get an idea of where book publishing and sales are headed.

http://www.bookinfor.org/

Run by the Book Industry Study Group, this site tracks book buying trends, including the state of online bookselling.

http://www.business2.com

This is the site of the E-Business-oriented magazine, *Business 2.0*. Read articles about E-Commerce trends and success stories here.

Note

Some companies, such as book publishers or software manufacturers, traditionally sell their products through other companies. For example, books and software might be sold at Walmart or CompUSA or Amazon.com. When such a company decides to open its own store to sell directly to customers on the Internet, it has to consider issues of *channel conflict*. Channel conflict happens when existing sales avenues (or channels) feel that their own sales of a company's products will be undercut by that company selling directly to its customers.

Part III

Social, Legal, and Ethical Issues of E-Commerce

Intellectual Property, Copyrights, and Trademarks
- Learn how companies share content
- Explore possible violations of music copyright
- Discover some new models for intellectual property distribution online
- Learn how free software revolutionized the new economy
- Understand all about trademark violations

NOTES

Meansbusiness.com Shares Others Content, Legally

- The Internet is all about content. Content can mean text, pictures, sound files, video, or animations. Because of all the content floating around out there online, with little to control its distribution and use, legal issues about **copyright** and **trademark** violations come up on a regular basis. A copyright protects written content or artwork, and a trademark protects a company's identifying elements, such as company name, logo, or slogan.

- **Intellectual property** rights are also a concern in the E-Commerce age. Intellectual property is essentially an idea. Examples of intellectual property are the look and feel of a Web site and the idea for a creative work, such as a movie script or song. Intellectual property can also include a business idea or trade secret.

- MeansBusiness.com is an interesting site, because it basically exists to gather content from other sites, condense or otherwise summarize it, and offer it to busy business people. Such a site must establish very clear contracts with the entities from which it is taking content, or it puts itself at risk of being sued.

Buzzwords

A *copyright* protects content. A *trademark* protects a company's identifying elements, such as name or logo.

Intellectual property is the right an individual or group of individuals has in an idea.

MeansBusiness.com Home Page

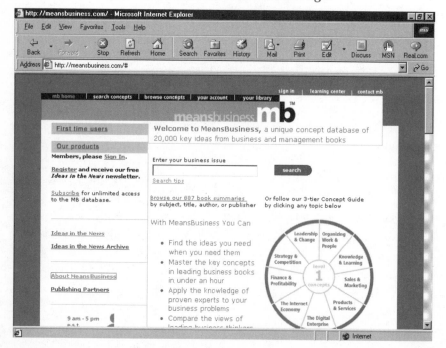

■ Can you be sued for taking a joke or sound file of a song off of the Internet and distributing it on e-mail or a computer disk? Technically, you can, if the originator of that joke or piece of music did not specifically post it on the Internet with a notice that it was free for the taking.

Visit Napster.com, in the Spotlight for Possible Music Copyright Infringement

■ Napster.com began its existence in the midst of controversy. The site touts itself as "the largest file sharing community in the world." The software this site provides allows people to capture media files from others' hard drives over the Internet. Some musicians feel this helps to promote their work; others, and most notably those who manage the music industry, feel this is an illegal infringement (or violation) of copyright.

Napster.com Home Page

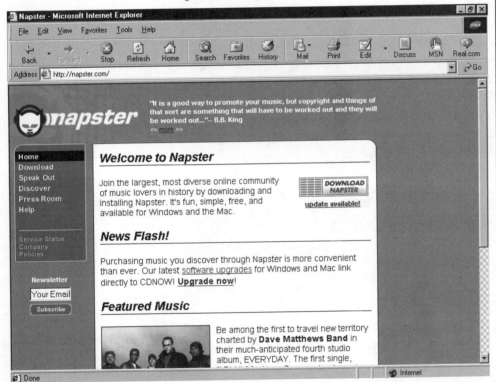

Note

Indicative of the volatility of business models on the Web, Napster itself was on the brink of extinction because of legal battles over copyright issues at the time of this writing. If you can't locate a Napster Web site anymore, search for sites that offer music on a subscription or other non-traditional basis to see how music distribution models have evolved.

■ Music isn't the only item a Web business should be concerned about using without permission. Companies must be careful to get permission when using photographs, quotes of material from other Web sites, and other companies' product logos, for example. Even a quote from a satisfied customer should be verified by obtaining written permission from the customer to use it online.

■ MP3 helped to revolutionize how sound files are shared online. MP3 stands for MPEG, a sound file format, audio layer 3. There are three audio coding schemes in use; layer 3 compresses audio by removing unnecessary information, such as data about sounds the human ear can't even hear. This compression makes sending these large files around the Internet possible.

New Models for Distributing Book Content Online at StephenKing.com

- Master horror writer Stephen King created a stir in the publishing world when he announced that he would bypass his regular publisher and make his latest work directly downloadable from his Web site. King collects a dollar or two for every download, and since he has broken his book up into several installments, he could, theoretically, end up with about 10-13 dollars per book. That's the same as a discounted hardcover book you might buy in a store, of which an author normally receives only a small percentage.

StephenKing.com Page

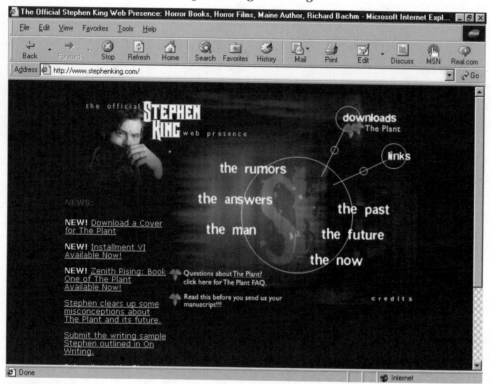

- King isn't the only one distributing books electronically. Book publishers are also selling electronic copies of books, called **e-books**. The ability to distribute intellectual content over the Internet as a new model of doing business is bringing up a great many questions. What does this sort of direct online distribution of intellectual property mean to traditional methods of distribution? How are authors compensated when copies of electronic books get made and sent freely around the world?

- The distribution model being used to sell or even give away materials online isn't the only issue of concern. Once anything has been downloaded from the Web, it can, theoretically, be duplicated and given away or sold to others. Any online business must be concerned if it intends to either sell a media product online, or make information available online.

Buzzword

An *e-book* is an electronic version of a printed book, that is, book contents saved in a computer file format. E-book readers are available that allow you to store and read books from a portable device. E-books can also be read online.

Exploring how Software Distribution Works on the Internet at Redhat.com

- The software industry has experienced some of the same issues as the entertainment industry when it comes to sales of software online. Linux is an open source operating system; that means that the code for the software is freely available to everyone to use or even change. Red Hat is one version of Linux that has enjoyed great popularity. The company makes money selling versions with documentation and support, as well as giving away more limited free versions. This model of making software available to all has threatened software giants like Microsoft. Still, many companies have jumped on the bandwagon and created Linux-based versions of their popular software programs.

Red Hat Linux Home Page

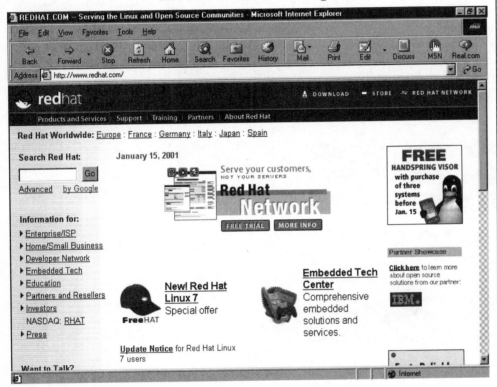

- Concerns about the rights a designer or programmer has in software are important to keep in mind. When E-Commerce companies hire Web designers to design their site, or have company programmers modify the way shopping cart software they have purchased works, they should be careful about legal pitfalls. A Web designer may technically own the design of your site if you don't stipulate in a contract that he or she grants all rights to the design to you; and if you make changes to the way software functions, you may be in violation of the software manufacturer's copyright.

- Source code refers to the underlying code that programmers write to create software. Source code can't do anything by itself; it must be converted into language the computer can understand with a compiler or assembler. Software companies have a great investment in their source code. If somebody manipulates it or duplicates it, he or she can be arrested or fined.

See What the Government is doing about Online Trademark and Copyright Issues at USPTO.gov

- A trademark is a legal protection for a name or phrase that helps to identify a company or product in the public's mind. A trademark has value: it becomes part of a customer's buying decision because he or she associates the trademark with certain characteristics, such as value or quality. A company can register a trademark for their company name, a product name, or even a company slogan.

- The United States Patent and Trademark Office, whose Web site is located at www.uspto.gov, exists to record trademarks and help to monitor any trademark infringements. A trademark infringement occurs when a company or individual uses another company's trademark in a way that suggests some association with that company, or that criticizes the company.

Note
In most cases, companies allow use of their name by other businesses as long as their trademark is properly noted and the use of the name doesn't falsely suggest some relationship or endorsement.

United States Patent and Trademark Office Home Page

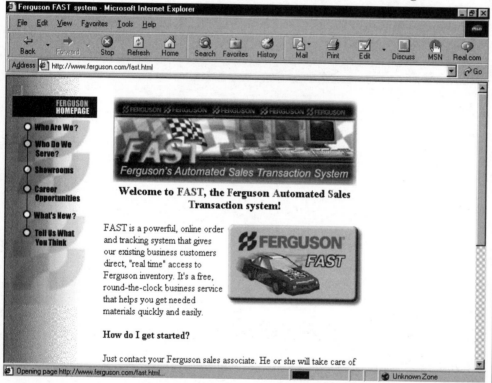

- Many companies periodically scan the Internet to look for any improper use of their trademarks. One trademark violation that is unique to the Internet is the use of a company's name in a Web site address, or URL. For example, Porsche, the sports car manufacturer, had to file a law suit because several Web sites used the Porsche name in their URL address.

E-BUSINESS ANALYSIS

> *Take a look at each of these sites (full URLs are located at the end of the exercise), then read the site analysis below and answer the questions.*

CASE STUDY 1: MEANSBUSINESS.COM

- MeansBusiness.com follows an interesting model of presenting copyrighted material from a variety of sources. The company's editors cull information from publishing sources into three distinct knowledge products: Concept Extracts, Concept Book Summaries, and Concept Suites. Concept Extracts focus on book passages, while Concept Book Summaries provide a collection of extracts from a particular book. Concept Suites are a collection of 8-15 Concept Extracts focused on a central theme or business concept. By consolidating and organizing information in this way, the site provides a valuable service to busy businesspeople.

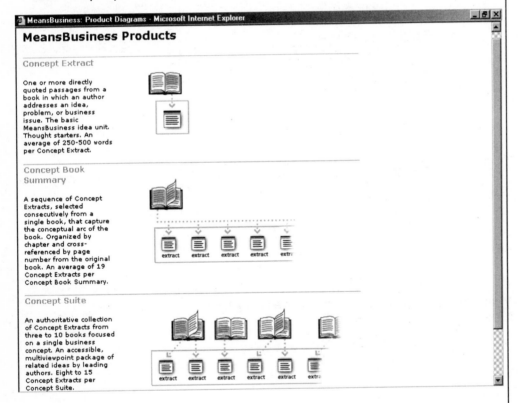

- MeansBusiness.com doesn't just pick information as it pleases; that would put them at risk for copyright infringement. Instead, they partner with publishers to showcase their content. This is a win-win scenario, in that it provides MeansBusiness.com with permission to reproduce and repurpose existing copyrighted material and provides a good way for publishers to excite readers' interest in a book and possibly to purchase it from a bookstore. The Learning Center on MeansBusiness.com presents content from publishers in highlighted sections, such as Ideas in the News and Business Issues in the Spotlight.

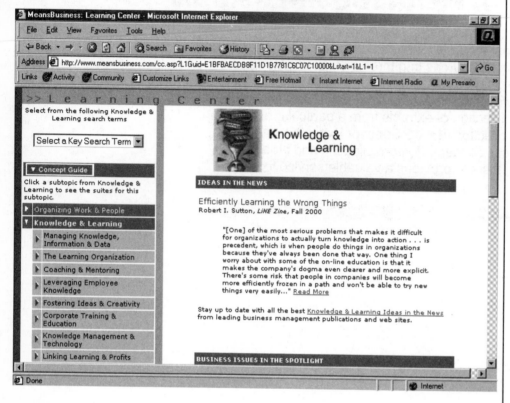

1. What is a concept database on Meansbusiness.com?

   _____

2. What restrictions does Meansbusiness.com place on visitors sharing material from the site with others?

   _____

3. How does the personal Library on Meansbusiness.com help visitors to organize content?

   _____

CASE STUDY 2: STEPHENKING.COM

- Stephen King began his direct distribution sales with a six-installment book titled *The Plant*. His download page is set up so that a customer can download each installment, then come back to pay in a separate step. This honor system form of paying is very unusual in the world of E-Commerce, but it reflects the kind of innovative commerce models being tested online. Customers must have a reader program, such as Adobe Acrobat or Microsoft Reader, to view the downloaded files.

StephenKing.com Download Page

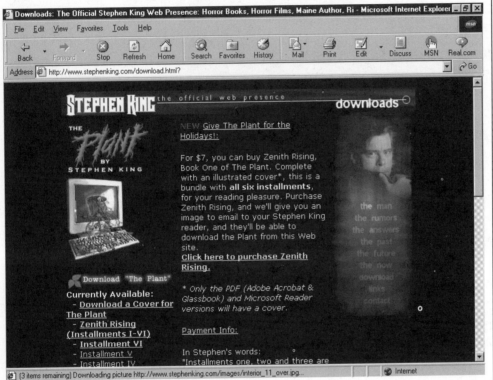

- Stephen King's site is also a good reflection of the kinds of partnerships E-Commerce encourages. Even though he is self-publishing some books, his site also lists books for sale through his publisher, with a link to the publisher's Web site. If you go to his publisher's Web site, there's a link back to Stephen King's site to buy his downloadable books directly from him. Although the publisher may not be making money directly off of King's downloadable titles, this interaction is likely to increase traffic and therefore sales on both sites.

Stephen King's List of Current Titles Page

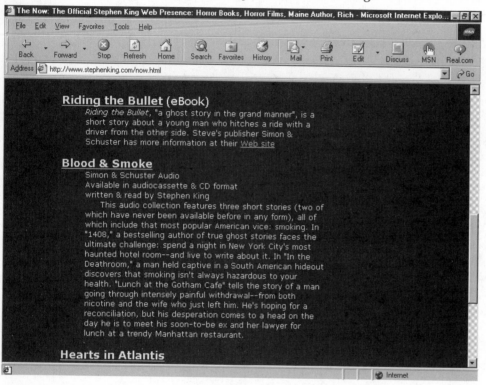

4. What is the name of Book One of The Plant?

   _____

5. How many book formats can you identify from Stephen King's site?

   _____

6. Who is Stephen King's publisher?

   _____

CASE STUDY 3: REDHAT.COM

■ Red Hat is another example of an innovative E-Commerce model. Initially, Red Hat followed the model of the open source community by offering its version of Linux for free. Eventually, it added a packaged version including documentation that it sold in stores; ironically, the company made a great deal of money selling a version of something that was available free online. Some consider that it is because of the included documentation in the retail version; others that people perceive more value in something they have to pay for. Whatever the reason, Red Hat has become a very successful company building on its beginnings of giving away something for nothing as a way to build demand for its product. These days, only a trial version of the network software is available for free download.

Redhat.com Free Trial Download Page

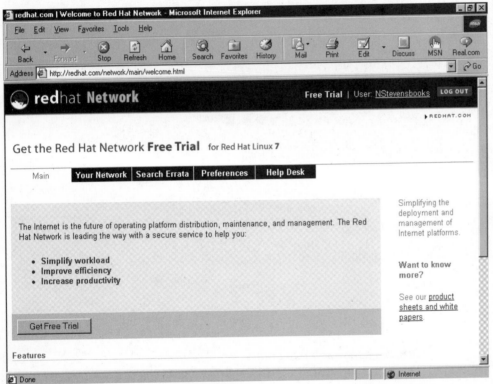

■ Red Hat does offer links to free Linux items, such as documentation and FAQs. The Open Source community in general encourages free sharing of information, but as Linux has become more popular, companies have been forced to charge for Linux-related products and services.

Redhat.com Linux Documentation Page

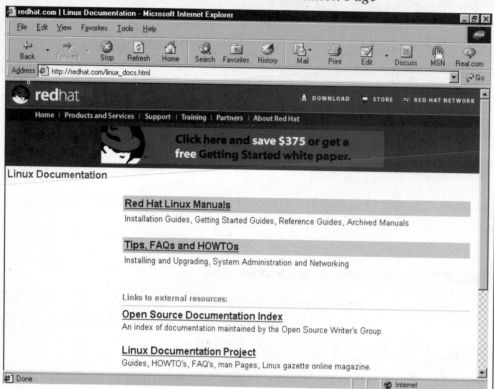

1. What benefits does the Red Hat Network product offer?

   _____

2. What is the name of the site where you can read the Linux Gazette?

   _____

3. What index is maintained by the Open Source Writer's Group?

   _____

http://meansbusiness.com/
Meansbusiness.com
http://napster.com
Napster.com
http://www.stephenking.com
Stephenking.com
http://www.redhat.com/
Redhat.com
http://www.uspto.gov/
USPTO.com

Policing the Internet

■ **Discover who is protecting consumers and businesses online**
■ **Learn about services that search and monitor trademark use**
■ **Explore how domain name disputes are settled**
■ **See how businesses look for copyright violations**
■ **Learn about the future of free expression online**

NOTES

Learn about the Electronic Frontier Foundation's Goal of Online Free Expression and Privacy

■ The Internet is like a Western town without a sheriff. No one entity has control over what people do online, and the potential for business fraud or abuse of personal privacy is great. Several **watchdog groups** have sprung up, such as the Electronic Frontier Foundation, to monitor and advise the public on issues of free expression, morality, fraud, and privacy online.

Buzzword

A *watchdog group* is an organization of people who monitor a situation, such as abuses of privacy or fraud online, and report those abuses to authorities.

Electronic Frontier Foundation Home Page

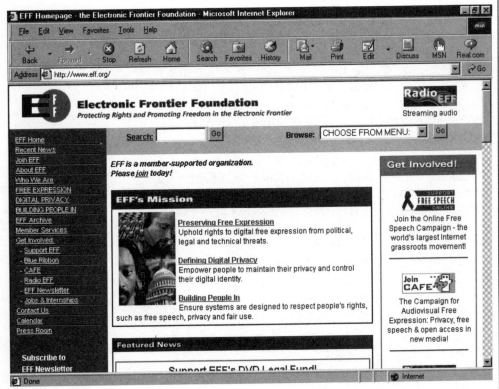

- The dual edged sword of protecting the right of individuals and companies to enjoy free expression online, while also protecting the public from immoral or illegal activity, is a difficult thing to control. The global nature of the Internet, with the opportunity for expression unhampered by any one political or cultural group is something that many people feel should be maintained. However, online fraud and crime is a reality, and to halt these activities some self-governing is required. That's why organizations such as EFF have appeared.

- In addition to non-profit organizations such as EFF, governments are getting involved in patrolling certain activities online. Violations of consumer privacy, deceptive business practices, and morally objectionable material as defined by law are controlled, to some extent, by government. But that control becomes less effective because some laws exist at the state level, and some at the Federal level. Questions of who will enforce a law are difficult to deal with.

- International law further complicates matters. In Europe, personal privacy is defined much more broadly than in the United States to include any personal information, such as marital status or whether an individual wears glasses. Online businesses in Germany are forbidden to offer unconditional guarantees on their products because this is seen as a marketing come-on; US businesses offering such a guarantee and doing business overseas are in violation of German law. Organizations such as EFF help the online community keep abreast of current international legal issues online.

Truste.org Protects Consumer Privacy

- One of the greatest concerns about the use of the Internet and legal protection comes in the area of privacy. In many cases, when a consumer signs up with a Web site or makes a purchase, there is an option included in the process that grants the right for personal information to be sold or solicitations to be sent to the consumer. When a consumer provides information to a Web site, the potential to abuse that individual's privacy by selling or sharing that information is great.

- Truste.org is the site of a non-profit organization that exists to build trust in online activity and its protection of individuals' privacy. The organization issues a seal to sites that meet certain standards in their privacy policies, letting consumers know that the site they are visiting is concerned about their rights. Like several similar groups, one of the goals of Truste.org is to ensure that the Internet community be allowed to self-govern its actions, rather than have government controls applied.

Note

In Europe the European Union has set strict standards for online privacy; U.S. privacy standards are currently voluntary, causing some discrepancies in enforcing E-Commerce law internationally.

Truste Page

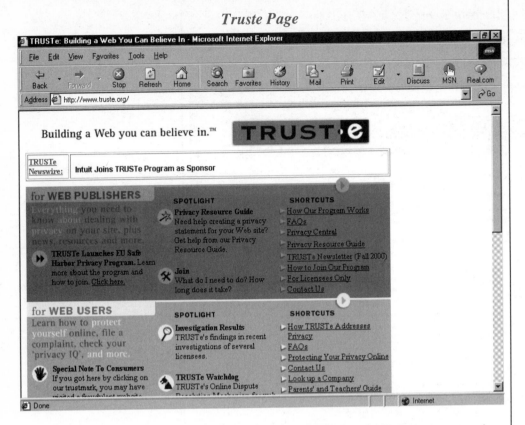

- Truste.org also offers a children's privacy policy seal. Both parents and businesses are concerned about the material that children are exposed to, as well as problems when children make unauthorized purchases online. When a site displays Truste.org's children's policy seal, it has agreed not to allow children under 13 to provide contact information without parental consent, or to entice children with special games or offers. However, with all of these policing sites, the problem of identity is a challenge. Online, you are who you say you are, and children who don't acknowledge their correct age to a site will not have their actions controlled.

NameProtect.com Helps Businesses Protect their Trademarks

- Services and software have appeared to help online businesses protect their trademarks. NameProtect.com offers free trademark searches, name monitoring (to see if other sites are using a name illegally), and a trademark registration service. Protecting a trademark is so important that some larger companies do their own monitoring of how other companies are using their name or trademark using sophisticated search engines.

Note

Did you know that aspirin was once a trademarked name? The product became the general term for a certain type of medication because of common use, and the owner lost the trademark.

- There are a few ways in which a company can protect its trademark. One is to simply use the trademark; if a trademark is not used continuously, it may be lost. Also, a business should take care to use the trademark ™ or registered ® symbol after its name to identify its protected status. Finally, a company should make efforts to stop its name or product name from being used in a generic way. Companies such as Xerox and Kimberly Clark (which manufactures Kleenex) regularly place ads in publications stating that these words are registered trademarks of a particular product, and should not be used to denote a generic copier or tissue.

- Nameprotect.com includes an attorney referral service. Any company setting up business on the Web would be wise to seek out the services of an attorney. Today, many lawyers specialize in Internet law, dealing with the intricacies of online trademark and privacy issues.

Discover Who Regulates Internet Domain Names at ICANN

- According to its Web site, the Internet Corporation for Assigned Names and Numbers (ICANN) is "the non-profit corporation that was formed to assume responsibility for the IP address space allocation, protocol parameter assignment, domain name system management, and root server system management functions previously performed under U.S. Government contract by IANA and other entities." The group sets the standard for resolving disputes concerning .com, .net, and .org site registrations.

ICANN.org Home Page

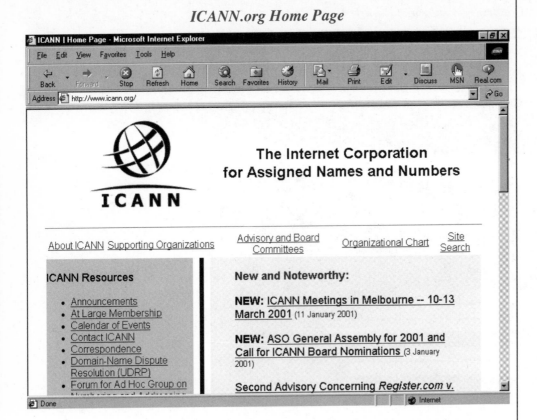

- Browsing the Internet, you'll find many sites that allow you to register a domain name. Those sites all have to apply to ICANN for registrar accreditation. The actual assigning of domain names is controlled through the **Shared Registration System**, or **SRS**. SRS was started in 1999 by the U.S. Department of Commerce to set up a central depository of domain names with .com, .net, and .org extensions. Any ICANN accredited registrar can register domain names through this system.

- Other regions of the world have their own Internet naming organizations such as Reseaux IP Europeens Network Coordination Centre in Europe and the Asia-Pacific Network Information Center. Many countries use country-specific extensions for domain names, such as uk for England and au for Australia.

Buzzword

SRS stands for Shared Registration System, a system of domain name registration set up by the Department of Commerce.

See How Domain Name Registrars Work to Protect Business Rights at Webby.com

- Webby.com is a site that provides Web hosting and domain name registration, as well as Web marketing services. Such services can provide assistance to businesses that want to get a secure certificate for their site. A secure certificate is an icon on a site that lets visitors know that it uses secure socket layer (SSL) protection.

- Companies that host other's Web sites are at risk if their clients' sites violate the law. As part of the terms and conditions of its hosting service, Webby offers a Copyright Violation Report Form. This form can be used by companies who believe their copyright is being violated by a site hosted by Webby.com. Such terms and conditions of service are one way for hosting companies to protect themselves from legal action if a site they host does something illegal.

Webby.com Copyright Violation Report Form Page

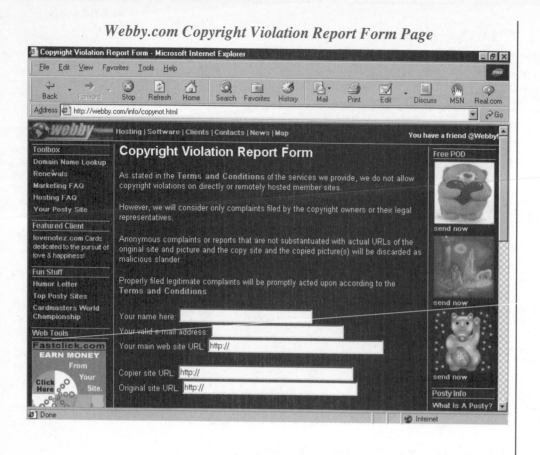

E-BUSINESS ANALYSIS

> Take a look at each of these sites (full URLs are located at the end of the exercise), then read the site analysis below and answer the questions.

CASE STUDY 1: ELECTRONIC FRONTIER FOUNDATION

- The Electronic Frontier Foundation site has a variety of Web pages, including the Blue Ribbon Campaign for Online Freedom of Expression. The page includes links labeled by country flags to access similar campaigns in other regions of the world. By joining the campaign you provide your name and contact information, and the group sends you alerts about political initiatives in your congressional district that they feel threaten online free expression. These alerts are often pre-addressed e-mail forms you can simply send on to politicians to protest an action. This kind of grassroots activity is at the core of many Internet policing efforts.

EFF Campaign for Online Freedom of Expression Page

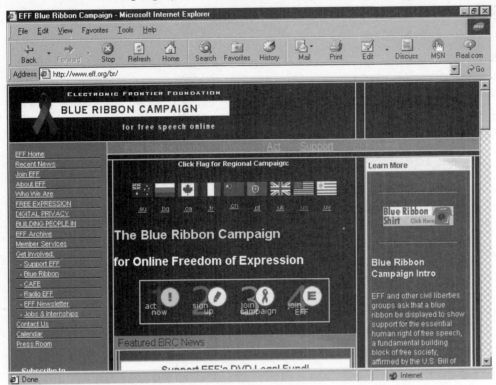

- One way that the EFF.org site seeks to encourage online privacy protection is by educating consumers. The Digital Identity page explains how everything from your grocery store discount card to your online browsing habits are being recorded and quantified to create a digital picture of you and your buying habits. The page also offers links to articles and FAQs to help consumers learn about privacy issues.

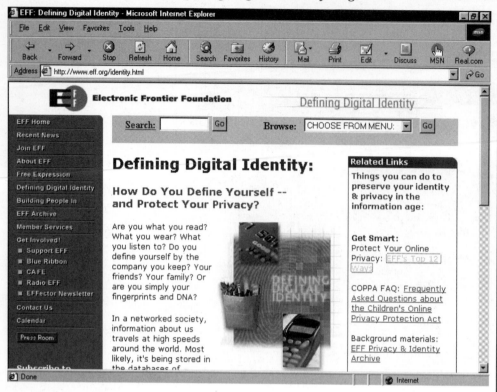

1. What is the meaning of EFF's blue ribbon?

   _____

2. What is the Children's Online Privacy Protection Act?

   _____

3. What is a 'digital identity'?

   _____

CASE STUDY 2: TRUSTE.ORG

■ Truste.org is another non-profit organization focused on privacy issues. Truste approves sites for acceptable privacy procedures. If a visitor spots a privacy violation on an approved site, Truste helps resolve the dispute. Truste also issues a monthly watchdog report summarizing any dispute resolutions that are in progress. Truste provides these reports in both HTML and Microsoft Word format.

Truste.org Watchdog Page

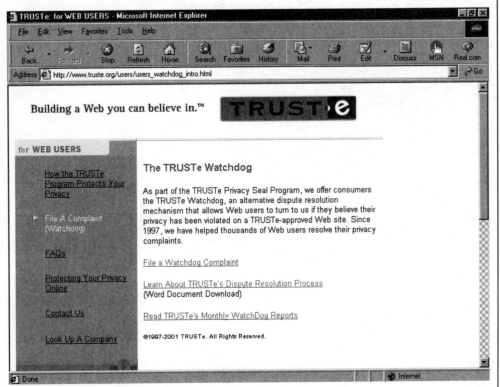

- The Truste program helps users create a privacy statement for their site that works for their business. They offer a model privacy statement on which businesses can base their own statements. Of course, every business has its own privacy requirements based on the type of information they collect from customers, whether they actually perform financial transactions online, and the nature of the product or service they provide. Therefore they must tailor the statement to their site and submit it to Truste.org for approval.

Truste Program Page

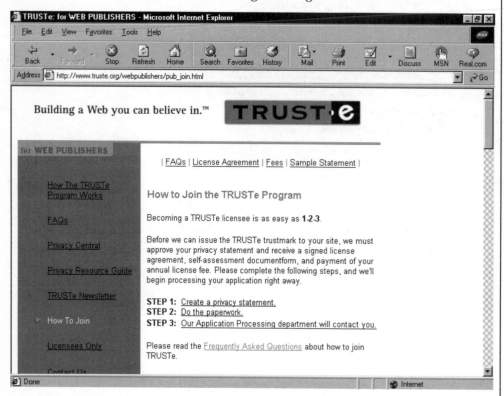

1. Describe Truste's Dispute Resolution Process.

   _____

2. What does a Truste Monthly Watchdog Report contain?

   _____

3. What is the yearly licensing fee to participate in the Truste program?

   _____

CASE STUDY 3: NAMEPROTECT.COM

- Nameprotect.com offers an automated online application for a trademark that saves businesses from having to learn about some of the requirements of the process. Before applying for a trademark, however, a business should perform a trademark search to make sure their choice isn't already protected by another company. Because the fee for simply applying for a trademark is more than $300, this simple step could save a company money.

Nameprotect.com Protect Page

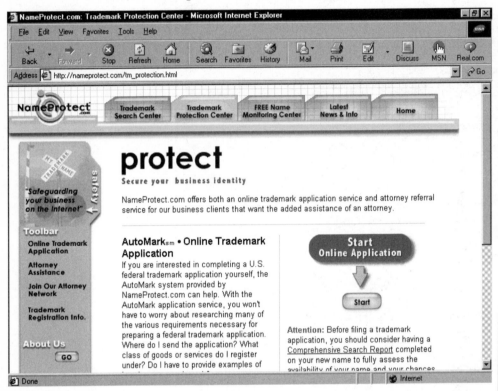

- Nameprotect.com allows you to perform a search of trademarks. You simply enter a term and any matching trademark is listed, along with a description of the business that owns it. However, be warned that these types of free trademark searches are usually not comprehensive; to be sure there is no existing trademark you should perform a comprehensive search, for which companies such as Nameprotect charge a fee.

Nameprotect.com Trademark Search Results Page

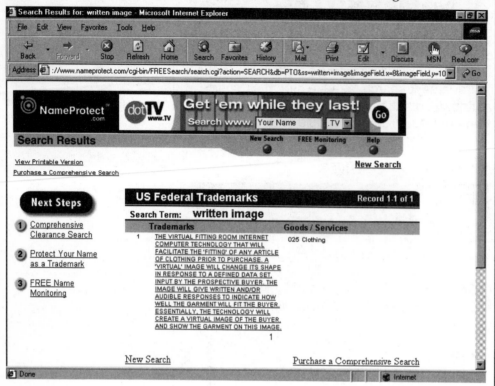

1. How does the AutoMark Online Trademark Application work?

   _____

2. What is the difference between a trademark and a copyright?

   _____

3. How much does a comprehensive trademark search cost?

   _____

http://www.eff.org/
Electronic Frontier Foundation
http://www.truste.org/
Truste.org
http://NameProtect.com/
NameProtect.com
http://www.icann.org/
The Internet Corporation for Assigned Names and Numbers
http://webby.com
Webby.com

How Online Fraud Threatens E-Businesses

- **Learn how anti-fraud software works**
- **See how online auction companies are protecting visitors**
- **Explore the concerns of Internet watchdog groups**
- **Discover what the US government is doing about fraud for online investors**
- **Read an online publication on how to avoid Internet scams**

NOTES

CyberSource Provides a Technology for Preventing Fraud

- Fraud is a legal term for deceitful business practices. E-Commerce fraud is currently estimated to cost online businesses 1.6 billions dollars a year. By 2005, Meridien Research has stated that the number could rise to 15.5 billion. The amount of fraud is likely to increase in direct relation to the number of online transactions in years to come. Still, only about a third of online merchants use anti-fraud technology to protect themselves.

- Companies such as CyberSource and HNC produce anti-fraud software. These software applications work in a variety of ways. Some search for patterns of purchasing activity that seem unusual. Others look for odd buying scenarios, such as a first-time, high-priced purchase that is sent to an address other than the credit card billing address. One problem with these technologies, however, is that they are set to catch only the frauds that are currently in use. As with anti-virus software, any new scheme can slip through the cracks until the technology is updated.

CyberSource.com Home Page

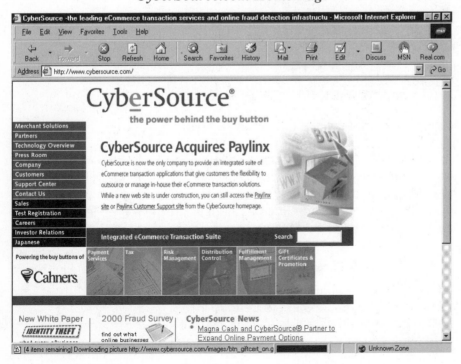

eBay Offers Auction Participants Secure Transactions

- When you purchase something through an online auction, you are buying not from the auction house, but from an individual you never met. Because online auction sites connect individual users to transact business, these sites have been hotbeds of fraud. People have sent money orders to sellers, only to have the product they bid on arrive damaged, not what they thought they were getting, or not arrive at all. To help customers avoid such problems, many auction houses have set up payment systems.

- eBay uses a service called Billpoint to enable customers to enjoy some of the protections of paying by credit card. Users can authorize a payment from their credit card to another's bank account using Billpoint. Because credit cards typically offer some protection against fraud, this makes purchasing in the online auction world somewhat more secure.

eBay Online Payments Page

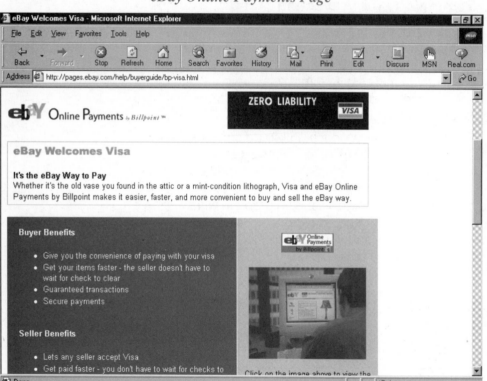

- eBay also offers some protection for cash transactions. If a buyer never receives an item, eBay will reimburse the customer up to $200. In addition, eBay has set up an **escrow** system that buyers and sellers can use. Escrow is a payment system where one person gives money to another person or entity, to be paid to a third person only when certain circumstances have been met. With an online auction, the payment is made only after the merchandise has been inspected by the buyer.

Internet Fraud Watch Keeps an Eye on Online Transactions

- The Internet Fraud Watch is run by the National Fraud Information Center (NFIC), which was established by the National Consumers League in 1992. This non-profit group started dealing with telemarketing fraud, but has found that similar scams are often perpetrated via the Internet. Fraud

Buzzword

Escrow is a method of payment wherein money or an item of value, such as a deed, is given to an individual or entity (such as a bank) to hold until the conditions of the transaction have been met.

can be reported by calling a national hotline or on their Web site. The site also contains fraud alerts reporting recently instituted scams to watch out for.

Internet Fraud Watch Page

Note
Telemarketing fraud has traditionally been aimed at older people. About half of the people who are victims of these schemes are senior citizens. Although the online population tends to be younger, as baby boomers with computer skills retire, fraud against the elderly online will become more of a concern.

- The NFIC reports fraud to the Federal Trade Commission and other agencies so that action can be taken to prosecute online criminals. The organization deals not only with individual victims of fraud, but also with businesses that have encountered fraud either from consumers or vendors.

- With the advent of E-Procurement systems that search large databases of vendors for the best price on products or services, companies are frequently doing business with other companies they've never dealt with before. This is a scenario that lays the groundwork for potential fraud.

See how the Government is Helping to Protect Online Investors at SEC.gov

- The Securities and Exchange Commission (SEC) is a governmental agency that oversees the investment sector of our economy. Online investment has taken off in recent years, with individuals buying and selling stocks and other investments through brokers, or even by setting up their own brokerages and day trading businesses. Because investing can often involve large sums of money, it is an area where online con artists abound.

- Investing fraud is often more complex and harder to spot than typical consumer fraud. For example, one scheme known as pump and dump works this way: A group of investors buys stock in a company at a low price. Then, they go online and begin to plant stories, postings to newsgroups, and even phony press releases characterizing the stock as a hot buy. When enough people buy the stock and the price goes up, the group sells its stock at a huge profit. Those who bought the stock as its price was soaring are left holding the bag when the price levels off again. Because online investors are always looking for the next big tip, they are easy prey for these kinds of scams.

- Some companies who can't meet requirements to be listed on major stock exchanges, such as NASDAQ or the New York Stock Exchange, are traded over the counter. These so-called **OTC** stocks are the most risky for investors because they are not under the backing of an exchange or other entity.

Explore Internet ScamBusters Publication on Internet Fraud

- New Internet scams are being invented every day. That's why services such as the Internet ScamBusters online publication are so useful for tracking the latest trends. Some online scams are simply a waste of time, such as those that circulate damaging computer viruses or chain letters that guarantee you'll get money if you forward an e-mail to 10 friends. Others place charges on your phone bill or credit card for items or services you never ordered, or take your money to get involved in some phony get-rich-quick scheme.

Buzzword
OTC stands for over the counter, a type of stock purchase involving a company that doesn't qualify for membership in a stock exchange.

Note
In another effort to prevent credit card fraud, credit card companies introduced smart cards several years ago. A smart card has a microchip embedded in it. This chip contains personal information about the cardholder that can be used to verify a purchaser's identify.

Internet ScamBusters Home Page

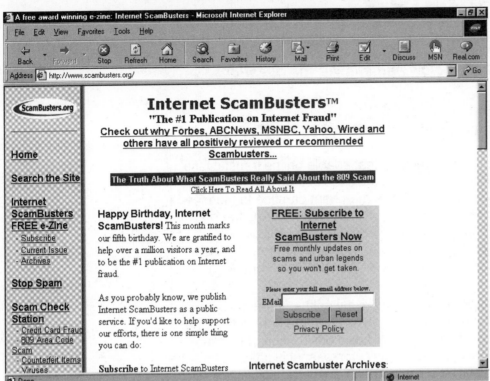

- Another category of scam is the urban legend, where a false story is circulated over the Internet. Recently an e-mail made its way around, for example, saying that the U.S. government was about to institute a 5-cent fee for every e-mail sent. These stories may cause minor panics, or simply make for interesting discussions around the water cooler at work, but if they provide false and damaging information about your online business, they could be much more than an annoyance.

- In order to encourage customers to buy online, most legitimate Internet businesses have policies that cause them to bear the brunt of the cost if someone's credit card is used for an online purchase without his or her knowledge. For that reason, many businesses are actively involved in trying to fight online fraud. A new system of disposable credit card numbers is being tried by some credit companies, such as American Express and Discover, to help combat credit card fraud. Under this system, a credit card number is used only once by a customer, then is no longer valid. This makes stealing such a number from the Web site where it was used meaningless for an online criminal.

E-BUSINESS ANALYSIS

> *Take a look at each of these sites (full URLs are located at the end of the exercise), then read the site analysis below and answer the questions.*

CASE STUDY 1: CYBERSOURCE.COM

- CyberSource produces software products that enable online transactions, including Internet Fraud Screen. This product checks purchaser credit in real time, returning a credit score an online merchant can use to measure the potential risk of accepting an order from that customer. Any fraud screening software brings with it the risk that a merchant will deny a purchase by a qualified customer. This not only loses the merchant a sale, it offends the customer, who may never return to buy from them again.

- Note that the CyberSource Web site provides a wealth of information on Internet Fraud Screen through the related links along the right side of the page. Software companies often back up a basic description of software with information such as how the technology works, specifications for installing the software, and white papers written about the software's functionality. CyberSource even includes details such as a survey on online fraud to help educate potential customers.

CyberSource Fraud Screen Page

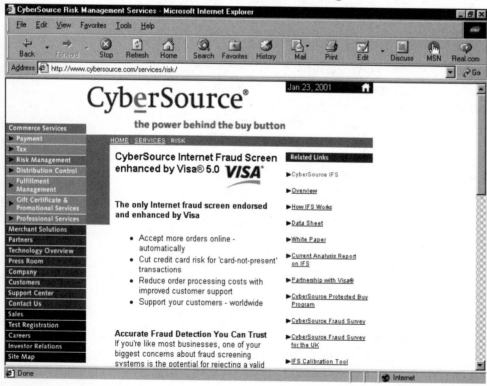

■ The fraud survey on CyberSource.com includes an online slide show, offering bullet points and charts and graphs of data. Visitors can move through the slide show using the navigation arrows. Such a presentation can be set up in HTML, with the navigation buttons actually representing links to another document. Many business presentation software products, such as PowerPoint from Microsoft, allow you to save presentations created in them in HTML and post them to a Web site. Such presentations can also include sound files and animation effects.

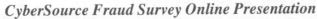

CyberSource Fraud Survey Online Presentation

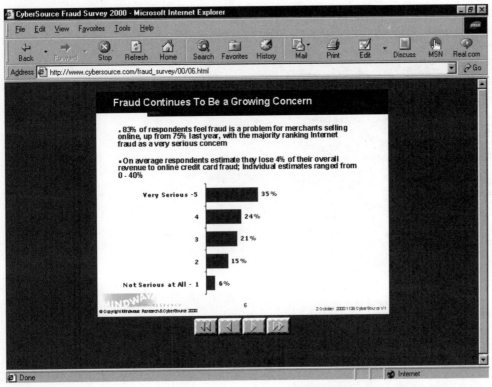

1. What is a 'card -not-present' transaction?

   _____

2. What is an "insult" in a credit card transaction?

   _____

3. What percent of revenue do businesses surveyed by CyberSource estimate they lose to credit card fraud?

   _____

CASE STUDY 2: EBAY.COM

- To protect participants in its online auctions, eBay maintains a feedback forum. This forum is used by those who have purchased or sold items on eBay to report on their experiences with a particular seller or buyer. This information can be used by both buyers and sellers; buyers can see whether a seller has delivered a product as it was described and in good condition; sellers can find out if a particular buyer has paid promptly for past purchases.

eBay Feedback Forum Page

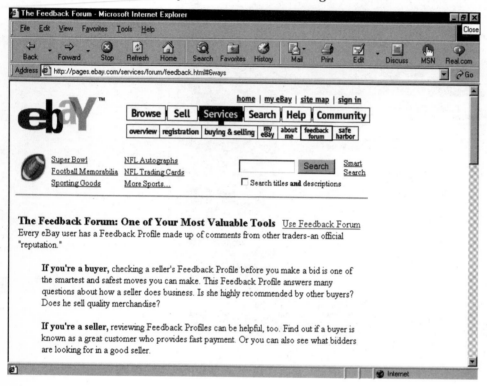

■ Information submitted to the feedback forum is compiled on a member ID card. This card reports positive, neutral, and negative feedback for past transactions. Members can respond to comments on their feedback profile, telling their side of the story. If a member is no longer registered with eBay, his or her feedback submissions are all converted to the neutral category. Since those who quit their membership in eBay are possibly disgruntled, visitors should take that policy into account when viewing total neutral comments reported on any member's feedback profile.

eBay Member ID Card Page

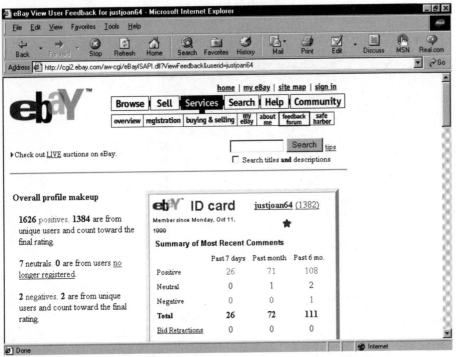

1. How can a seller use the feedback profiles?

   _____

2. What other ways are there for visitors to find out about other members?

   _____

3. What is a 'unique user', as referenced in the feedback profile on eBay?

   _____

CASE STUDY 3: SCAMBUSTERS.ORG

- One area of the ScamBusters site deals with spamming. Spam is essentially junk mail sent to large numbers of people online. Over time as a user's e-mail address is given out to newsgroups, ISPs, and even businesses during online transactions, that address can become available to both reputable and not-so-reputable marketing groups. There are measures a user can take to protect his or her personal e-mail account from unwanted messages and offers. This page on ScamBusters.org provides advice about how to do this, with links to articles and other resources dealing with spam.

Stop Spam Page

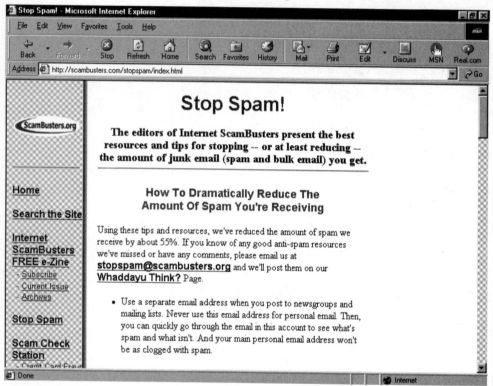

- ScamBusters Web site also contains a Press Area with related links. On one of its press pages they've included a video file of a ZDTV talk show about scams, as well as a file from a radio talk show on the same topic. Visitors to the page can view the video using Real Player, a multimedia plug-in that can be downloaded for free from many Internet sites. Use of actual sound and video files to play back radio and TV programs is a great way for a business to leverage media exposure with visitors.

ScamBusters.org Press Page

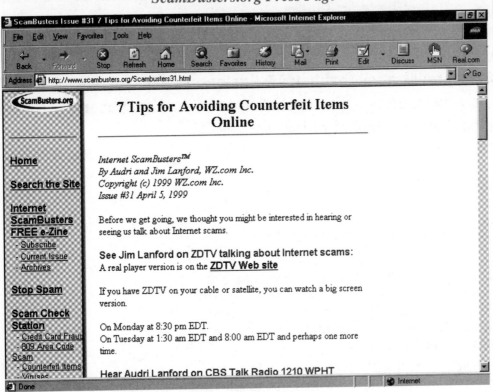

1. What are some measures identified on ScamBusters.com for avoiding spam?

   _____

2. Why is spam a problem for businesses and individuals?

   _____

3. What is a multimedia plug-in and where can you obtain them?

   _____

http://www.cybersource.com/
CyberSource.com

http://www.ebay.com
eBay.com

http://www.fraud.org/
Internet Fraud Watch

http://www.sec.gov/
Securities and Exchange Commission

http://www.scambusters.org/
ScamBusters.org

Theme 17

The Ethics of Doing Business Online

- Consider the responsibility of E-Companies to keep customers informed
- Examine the code of conduct for medical Web sites
- Explore an organization that holds E-Businesses accountable
- Learn how file sharing online is stirring an ethical controversy
- Learn about online content rating systems

NOTES

See How R. J. Reynolds Handles the Public's Right to Information Online

- Many businesses have discovered that the Internet is a good place to provide information for their customers that they'd rather not put into their sales literature or on their product boxes. This information might include less appealing messages, such as disclaimers of company responsibility or information about recalls of defective products.

- Tobacco companies, which sell products acknowledged to be bad for their customers' health, tend to use their Web sites as a way to fulfill an **ethical** and legal obligation to inform customers of dangers or data about health issues related to tobacco, as well as updates on tobacco-related lawsuits. R. J. Reynolds' Web site is a good example of this. They offer information on topics such as the ingredients of their cigarettes, legal settlements, and the dangers of secondhand smoke.

R. J. Reynolds Home Page

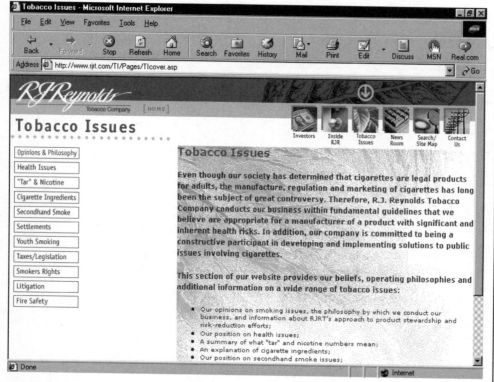

Buzzword

Ethics is a philosophical discipline dealing with good and evil and moral choices. In business, ethics typically concerns adhering to accepted standards of practice.

Technical Note

On R. J. Reynolds Web site they use an arrow above their navigation menu to show the visitors what page they are on. Because older Web browsers that can't read JavaScript might display the code rather than the arrow, the page contains a command to hide the JavaScript from older browsers.

Discover How the Medical Community Polices Itself Online at the Health On the Net Foundation

■ Providing advice or information about health-related issues online involves some special ethical concerns. Because it's difficult to accurately diagnose or prescribe a treatment for people without examining them in person, great care must be taken that visitors to a health-related site take the advice there in the correct spirit. Sites that don't present information correctly, offering warnings and disclaimers, could find themselves legally liable if somebody follows their advice and suffers as a consequence. There must also be careful to provide accurate information.

■ The Health On the Net Foundation is one online group that has devised a code of conduct for medical and health Web sites that it calls HONcode. Sites can become a member of HON, which makes them responsible for adhering to the code. The code stipulates, among other things, that only medically qualified individuals will give advice unless otherwise stated, that sites will make clear that the information they provide does not replace the relationship of a patient and doctor, and that information and identities about visitors to the site will be kept confidential.

Health On the Net Foundation HONcode Page

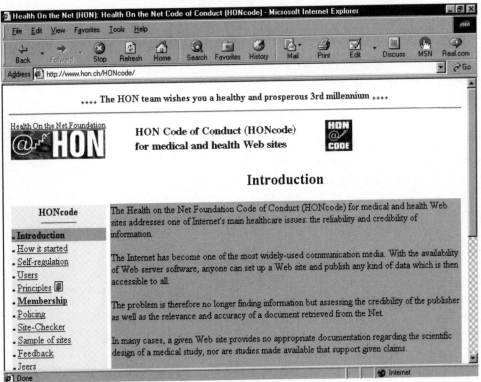

■ As part of its policing effort, if a member site receives a visitor complaint that is also reported to HON, and if the site does not correct the problem, HON may sever the link from its HONcode graphic on the member site. Any visitor clicking on it will no longer be taken to HON Web pages.

See How WebChamber.com Promotes Responsible Internet Businesses

- Many towns in the United States and other countries have established chambers of commerce. These are associations that exist to hold local business members to a certain standard of conduct. In simple terms, these chambers of commerce maintain records of complaints about their members' business activities and make that information available to the public, their potential customers. Online, WebChamber.com is seeking to take on this role to help customers feel comfortable dealing with member businesses.

WebChamber.com Mission Statement Page

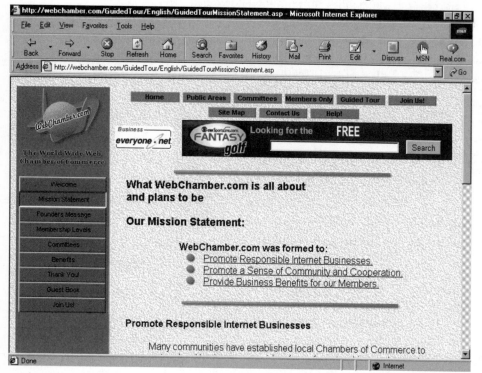

Note
Chambers of commerce for many towns in the United States have established their own Web sites and provide another way to learn about local businesses with an Internet presence. http://www.Chamberof Commerce.com is a site that provides a directory of local chambers.

- In addition to providing a way for the public to monitor online business performance, WebChamber.com provides benefits to business members in the form of discounted business products and an opportunity to network with other members. In the brave new world of online commerce, being able to share experiences with and get advice from other members can be very helpful to an E-Business.

Learn About the Ethical Controversy Surrounding File Sharing at Zeropaid.com

- Part of the culture of the Internet since it first caught on with the public has been freedom of information and a free exchange of ideas. In file sharing, this free exchange has hit an ethical dilemma. File sharing through applications such as Gnutella and Napster is a method of allowing Internet users to share files from one hard drive to another over the Internet. File sharing is often used to exchange MP3 music files; this has caused an uproar in the music industry because it cuts into their market for selling musical recordings. Zeropaid.com is one example of a file sharing portal.

Zeropaid.com Home Page

Technical Note
Applications for file sharing work in one of two ways. Products such as Napster allow two computer hard drives to exchange files through a central server on the Internet. Gnutella and other products allow for **peer-to-peer** access, which simply means that two computers can talk directly to each other on what has been called a "serverless network." Essentially peer-to-peer network setup allows each individual computer to act as its own server.

Buzzword
Peer-to-peer is a network setup where all computers in the network act as servers.

- Although sites that share data or files that are not their own are an annoyance for E-Businesses, most do not profit from this exchange. If a business does try to profit from giving away another company's property, it is a clear target for a law suit. Some music companies have responded to the sharing of music files by coming up with a music subscription model. A user can pay a monthly fee and download any number of music files. This model puts some control—and cash—back in the control of the music industry.

Explore How the Internet Content Rating Association Provides Guidelines for Web Content

- Some products and information that are being sold online can be harmful to children. Online businesses that offer something that is inappropriate to certain segments of society have an obligation to regulate their own activities. However, finding a standard of what's appropriate that everybody can agree on can be tricky. Also, because it's technically impossible to be positive about who is logged onto a site, enforcing such self-regulation can be difficult.

- Web sites that face this conflict have a few choices. They can put a statement on their site saying that it is inappropriate for certain age groups. They can require users to acknowledge a statement that they are over 18 before they are allowed to make purchases on the site. Or, parents can use software that blocks access from their computers to certain types of sites. Some sites offer parental control software for free download on their home page. However, all of these measures still leave loopholes for young users to jump through and view or purchase inappropriate items.

197

- The Internet Content Rating Association is one group that works with Web sites to help the public recognize sites that contain potentially harmful content. This is one attempt to establish a common standard of acceptable content for children online. Businesses can label their site with the correct rating, providing a service to parents and meeting their social obligation to younger Web surfers. ICRA provides a filtering software so visitors to a site can filter out content they prefer not to view.

Internet Content Rating Association Home Page

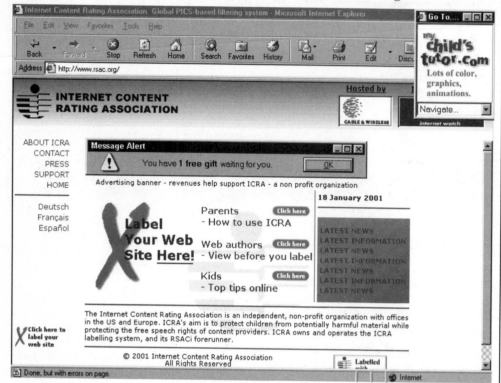

- ICRA offers several categories in its filtering software, including language, nudity and sexual content, violence, gambling, drugs, and alcohol. Web designers rate their own sites as containing or not containing each kind of content. Then users can filter categories of content out and block access. Currently the filtering system can be used by visitors with the Internet Explorer browser, but ICRA is working to make their system compatible with other browsers.

E-Business Analysis

> *Take a look at each of these sites (full URLs are located at the end of the exercise), then read the site analysis below and answer the questions.*

CASE STUDY 1: R. J. REYNOLDS TOBACCO COMPANY

- R. J. Reynolds Web site is informational, rather than a site for selling products. Its audience includes both consumers of their products and stockholders in their business. Assumedly one of their main objectives is to appear as a responsible business that is concerned with public welfare. To that end the site contains no advertising and sports a clean, conservative look. Its Youth Smoking page is typical of its site, with an explanation of the company philosophy towards cigarettes and younger people. With so much information on a site, it's important to be organized. Note the dual methods of navigation this site provides: broader topics are labeled by the graphic icons across the top of the page, and details of those topics are accessible from a text-based menu along the left side of the page.

R. J. Reynolds Youth Smoking Page

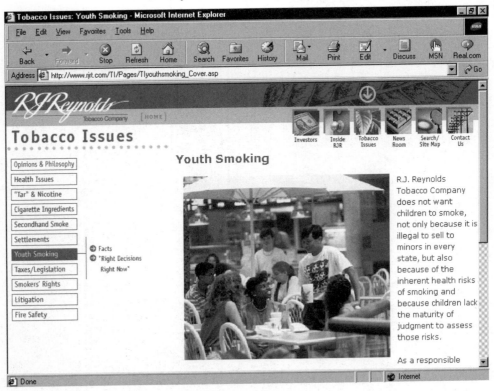

- R. J. Reynolds provides a list of ingredients used in their cigarettes to allay concerns about health risks in addition to the addictive nature of nicotine. The note preceding this list indicates that 'most' of the ingredients have been deemed safe by the U.S. Food and Drug Administration or the Flavor and Extract Manufacturer's Association. Tables are often used on Web sites to set out lengthy lists of information; this table is set up with data on the level of use of each ingredient in cigarettes and uses for the ingredient other than as an additive to cigarettes. To view more details about the function of each ingredient in cigarettes, users can click on each ingredient name to link to more information.

RJRT List of Ingredients Page

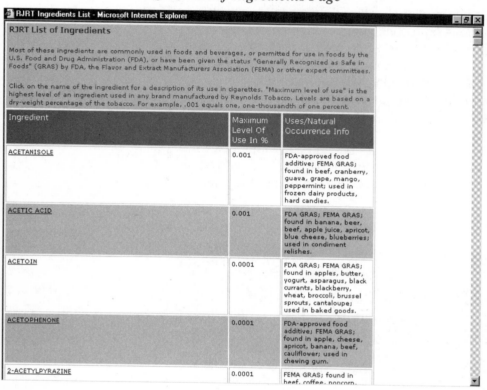

1. What is R. J. Reynolds position on encouraging children to smoke?

   _____

2. What does GRAS stand for?

   _____

3. What is Acetophenone used for in cigarettes?

   _____

CASE STUDY 2: HEALTH ON THE NET FOUNDATION

■ The Health On the Net Foundation site includes a site checker. Internet users can fill out this questionnaire to help them judge if a particular health-related site is adhering to HON's code. Users click on the radio buttons next to an answer under each question, then the results are compiled by the software and a list is generated. The list contains areas where the site differs from the HONcode, with an explanation of the rationale for that requirement. This kind of self-administered test is often found on learning sites, but can also be a useful tool for businesses and associations to get information from their visitors while providing them with a self-driven assessment tool.

Health On the Net Foundation HONcode Site-Checker Page

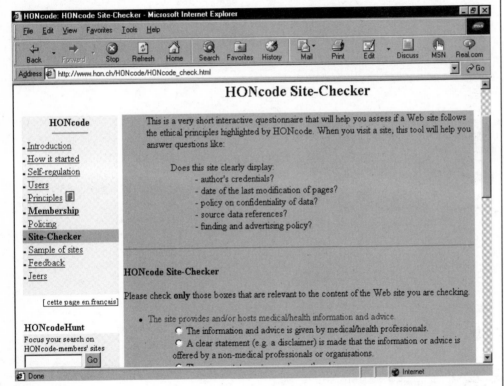

- HON acts as a mirror site for several organizations, such as the World AIDS Conference. A mirror site is a site that contains the same information as another site. Often businesses maintain mirror sites for visitors to obtain downloads of plug-ins or drivers they might need to run a function on their site. Creating a mirror site helps split up the traffic of visitors looking for that information on any one site.

World AIDS Conference Mirror Site

1. What is HONcode?

   _____

2. What elements should a HONcode compliant page display?

   _____

3. What other mirror sites does HON maintain?

   _____

CASE STUDY 3: ZEROPAID.COM

- Although Zeropaid.com stands squarely behind freedom of expression online, even this site sets some limits when it comes to child pornography online. Child pornography is a special concern of Zeropaid.com and other file sharing sites. The site maintains a Wall of Shame as a public service, listing online child pornographers.

Wall of Shame Page

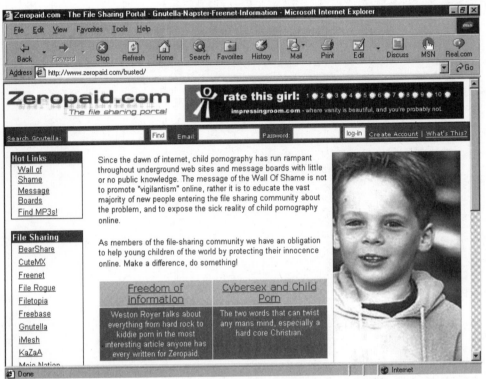

- As part of its commitment to the file sharing community, Zeropaid.com maintains message boards. Message boards allow visitors to share information and make comments on areas of interest. This kind of online communication is called *asynchronous*, because discussions don't take place in real time. Topics on Zeropaid range from feedback on the site and suggestions for the Wall of Shame, to discussions about various file sharing applications and the music industry. Zeropaid has organized these message boards conveniently with a table that lists the boards, the number of topics, posts, and date of the last post. Message boards are one way to get visitors to help each other with a product or technology, sometimes saving businesses customer support time.

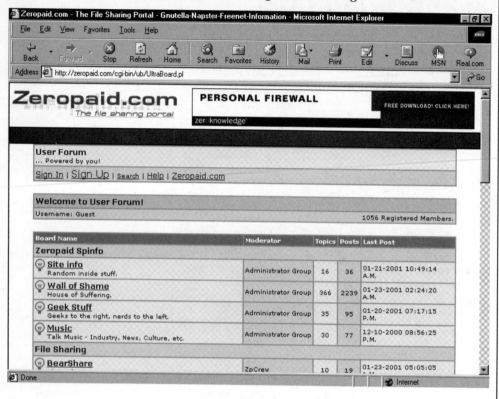

1. What is vigilantism?

   _____

2. What is BearShare?

   _____

3. How many registered members are there on Zeropaid.com message boards?

   _____

http://www.rjrt.com/
R. J. Reynolds Tobacco Company
http://www.hon.ch/
Health On the Net Foundation
http://webchamber.com/
WebChamber.com
http://www.zeropaid.com/
Zeropaid.com
http://www.rsac.org/
Internet Content Rating Association

Learning E-Commerce
Part III, Social, Legal, and Ethical Issues of E-Commerce
Capstone Project

Summary of Concepts

- The Internet provides access to information in unprecedented ways. That access has opened up legal, moral, and ethical challenges for the general public and online business community.

- Legal challenges come in the form of protecting trademark, copyright, and intellectual property rights of individuals and entities. Certain well-publicized violations of these rights, such as the open distribution of musical recordings by Napster, have brought this problem into the spotlight. The rights of a business to make a profit from the value of its brand names and intellectual property are sometimes seen a in direct opposition to the rights of consumers to expression and the unrestricted nature of information online.

- In the area of social responsibility, this same unrestricted environment has brought conflicts of an ethical and moral nature. Proliferation of online fraud, pornography, and poor business practices makes the Internet a challenging place to run a business. Consumers are suspicious and concerned about their personal privacy, as well as about fraud and misinformation. E-Businesses must overcome these perceptions and hold themselves to evolving standards of behavior if online commerce is to succeed in the long term.

- Several groups, both non-profit and governmental, are working to police the Internet for legal and moral violations. The global nature of the Internet makes enforcement difficult, because of differing laws and standards. On the other side of the equation, several groups have been created to work for continued freedom of expression online, arguing that the Internet is the last frontier of unregulated communication and interaction among people.

- E-Commerce is evolving in an environment much like a Wild West town, where freedom and a new frontier offer both opportunity and rewards to responsible people and put a gun into the hand of irresponsible outlaws. Long-term players in E-Commerce will be those who treat customers fairly and act as responsible online citizens.

Case Study

The Business:

- All Creatures Publishing places excerpts of its books on its Web site so that customers can sample their content, much as people browsing in a bookstore can page through a book to decide if they want to buy it. Publishing these excerpts online has proven to be a successful sales tool. At one point All Creatures Publishing partnered with a pet-oriented Web site, Petzforall.com, allowing them to also publish excerpts from books on their Web site in exchange for placing an advertisement for All Creatures Publishing on their home page. Use of these excerpts helped the pet site to provide interesting content to its visitors. Several months ago All Creatures formally ended this relationship because the pet site was accepting some advertisements that the publisher considered in poor taste. Last week the marketing manager of All Creatures was browsing the Web and stopped at Petzforall.com, where she discovered that the company is still including excerpts from All Creatures books on its site in violation of the publisher's **copyright**. The CEO of Petzforall.com feels that because this information is published for all to read on All Creatures Publishing's Web site, it is fair game for use anywhere on the Internet.

Buzzword

Copyright is the right to reproduce, publish, or sell certain materials, such as book content or musical compositions. Copyrighted material should not be used without express permission of the copyright holder. Copyright is granted by the federal government for a specific period of time; many authors or publishers obtain copyrights for their works in several countries to prevent international piracy of their material. Several international laws have been passed to protect these rights across borders.

The Project:

- Have students break into teams of two. Each team should do research online to identify a well-publicized case of copyright, trademark, or intellectual property infringement. (Check to ensure that each team chooses a different case.) Each team should create a presentation to the class outlining the background of the case, describing the two parties in the lawsuit, and the outcome. At the end of the presentation the two people on the team will role play the positions of the two parties in the lawsuit, debating the reasoning for each position. The class should then feel free to ask questions about each party's argument.

The Business Model:

■ To complete this project, you must research legal cases on the Internet. Here are three important things to consider:

1. ***Look for a case that has merit on both sides***: Can you see why each party to the case felt it had cause for its position? Can you identify and understand the motives of each party (profit, freedom of expression, concern about government regulation of the individual, etc.)? Could you broaden the specific case to more global issues of individual versus business or societal rights?

2. ***Identify legal principles involved:*** What basis did the court give for its decision in the case? Did one entity profit unfairly from their actions? Was any contract or promise broken? How does the U.S. Constitution come into play when issues such as freedom of speech are involved in a legal decision?

3. ***Explore various sources of information:*** Read articles from newspapers and magazines about the case, in addition to finding information about the case on legal sites. Look for definitions of legal terms and principles in law dictionaries. See if you can locate an actual court decision on the case to understand why the judge ruled as he or she did.

Note

In book publishing, the copyright for books is often registered in the name of the publisher, although it technically belongs to the author of the work. The author grants the copyright to the publisher for a period of time, allowing the company to reproduce and publish the work. After a book goes out of print, copyright typically reverts to the author.

Technology

■ Certain technologies are being used to help record and monitor trademarks, copyrights, and intellectual property. In the area of sound files, a technology called audio watermarking is used to place an ID on an audio file. This technology allows a music publisher to identify original music files from copies and even to create a fingerprint that points to the original customer for music. If music is pirated, this system helps a company identify who first purchased a recording, so they can pinpoint where the piracy began. Patent, trademark, and intellectual property management software helps lawyers and companies to catalog their various registered marks, while sophisticated databases and search engines assist lawyers in researching whether a particular name or work has already been copyrighted.

Books to help:

Learning the Internet: Fundamentals, Projects, & Exercises (catalog number Z57)

Web sites to explore:

http://megalaw.com

This site is chock full of research tools and information about everything legal. Explore the business topic pages and both Federal and State laws. You can also view video clips of legal discussions from C-Span from this site.

http://findlaw.com

Get information on case law and the Constitution on this site. Also check out the section for students, including law student resources.

http://legalseeker.com

This site offers a section on Internet resources, as well as information on legal procedure. The Intellectual Property and Cyberlaw sections are useful resources for information about online legal issues.

http://freeadvice.com

Hear what people are saying about online legal issues in the legal chat areas of this site and in the Q&A Law Forums. This site also has a section on intellectual property.

Part IV

Exploring the Conduct of an E-Business

Lesson 9: Applying Regulations and Acts to an E-Business
     Theme 18: Protecting Consumer Privacy Online
     Theme 19: Regulating Payment and Taxes for Online Transactions

Capstone Project: Regulations to Control the Conduct of E-Business

Theme 18

Protecting Consumer Privacy Online

- **Read the latest news about electronic privacy**
- **See what the Better Business Bureau is doing to protect consumers**
- **Learn about public policy and self-regulation**
- **See what the Federal Trade Commission is doing to protect children online**
- **Discover how software can protect consumer privacy online**

NOTES

The Electronic Privacy Information Center Provides a One-Stop Information Source on Privacy

- Concern for privacy online has been one of the greatest barriers to consumers embracing E-Commerce. Because E-Commerce transactions typically involve a customer providing personal information, from name and address to credit card account information, many consumers are worried that anyone from a wiley con man to some secret government agency is lurking. But it's not just providing credit card information that worries people. Visitors to online health sites worry that by requesting information about an illness such as AIDS, their insurance company or a potential employer might find out and unfairly cancel their insurance or deny them employment. People who state their yearly income while applying for a mortgage online worry that the IRS will get the information and determine that they didn't declare all their income on their tax return.

- Most online retailers use technological measures such as Secure Socket Layers (SSL) and encryption to protect customer information, and most browsers also offer protection for information you send online. However, all the technology in the world won't protect you if you give your credit card number to a company that consists of a shady character who is planning to skip town with your money next week. Knowing who you're doing business with is important—but difficult online.

- Although there are government agencies such as the Federal Trade Commission that enforce regulations related to Internet fraud or privacy violations, the Internet is a pretty big beat for any agency to police. For that reason, there are many organizations that have appeared to watchdog consumer privacy issues. The Electronic Privacy Information Center is one such site. They provide information on laws and recent scams and offer advice on how consumers can protect themselves when buying online.

Note
In a well-publicized case AOL released information about a member's online activities to the FBI. This raised issues about consumer privacy and the rights of the government to require a Web site to release information. To some degree users should be less concerned with hackers getting at their information and more concerned with a Web site's policy regarding sharing or selling of member information.

The Electronic Privacy Information Center Home Page

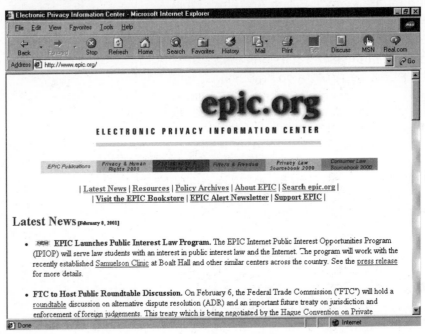

BBBOnline Offers a Privacy Program for E-Commerce Self-Regulation

- BBBOnline, the Web presence of the Better Business Bureau, offers a privacy program as a form of self-regulation for E-Commerce businesses. Those who join this program agree to subject their sites to monitoring and enforcement in the case of a violation of the BBB's policies. The BBB also provides dispute resolution in the case of a consumer dispute. Any business signing up for this program can display a BBBOnline Privacy seal on its site, encouraging customers to feel safe transacting business with them.

BBBOnline.org Privacy Program Page

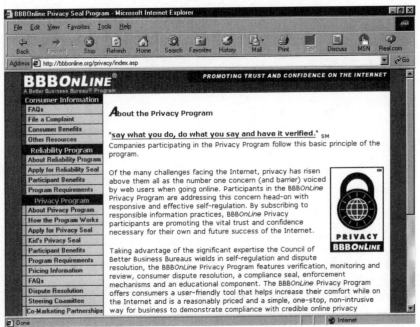

Note

Which is safer, shopping online or in a store? Many point to the situation of providing a credit card to a waiter at a restaurant; there's nothing to stop the waiter from copying down the number and making online or phone charges with it. A Web site using SSL and encryption actually provides more protection than a credit card handed over to a person in a store or café.

- When a customer pays for something online with a credit card, he or she is protected by something called the Fair Credit Billing Act. Under this regulation consumers can dispute unauthorized charges and are only responsible for the first $50 of those charges.

- Another way consumers can protect themselves is to look for a company's privacy policy on their Web site before doing business with them to make sure that they keep personal and payment information confidential. To protect their own privacy, consumers should be careful about authorizing a company to pass on information they provide. Often when customers submit information to become a member of a site, access a service, or make a purchase, there are items to check if they do not want to have their information shared with others. Because customers have no control over where their information might be sent, it's worth the time for them to locate these notices and indicate they do not want information shared with anyone.

The Electronic Retailing Association Offers a Place for Online Retailers to Learn About Public Policy on E-Commerce

- Online retailers have their own interests to protect in the battle for customer privacy. The Electronic Retailing Association is an organization that works with member companies who market through infomercials or online. This association has stated that it is opposed to extensive privacy legislation that ties the hands of online retailers in selling or promoting their businesses to consumers. Instead, the association calls for retailers to place simple statements about their policies on their sites and to follow the model of giving consumers "notice, choice, access, and security."

The Electronic Retailing Association Regulatory &
Consumer Information Page

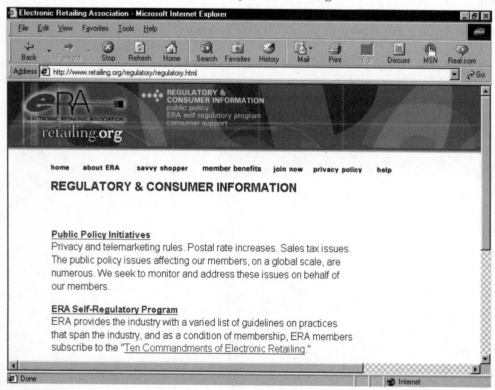

■ The Electronic Retailing Association provides information on typical privacy policies to help its members in drafting their own standards. One company mentioned on their site, AOL, has developed a reputation for protecting the interests of its members. AOL has an eight-part privacy policy, outlined below. It offers a good model for any online business to follow.

1. We do not read your private online communications.

2. We do not use any information about where you personally go on AOL or the Web, and we do not give it out to others.

3. We do not give out your telephone number, credit card information, or screen names, unless you authorize us to do so. And we give you the opportunity to correct your personal contact and billing information at any time.

4. We may use information about the kinds of products you buy from AOL to make other marketing offers to you, unless you tell us not to. We do not give out this purchase data to others.

5. We give you choices about how AOL uses your personal information.

6. We take extra steps to protect the safety and privacy of children.

7. We use secure technology, privacy protection controls, and restrictions on employee access in order to safeguard your personal information.

8. We will keep you informed, clearly and prominently, about what we do with your personal information, and we will advise you if we change our policy.

The Federal Trade Commission Watches Out for Consumers On- and Offline

■ Children's privacy rights online are of great concern to customers and retailers alike. The Children's Online Privacy Protection Act passed in 2000 deals with personal information collected by Web sites from children 13 and younger. This act specifically addresses issues such as when a site must ask for consent from a parent to interact with a child and what information must be included in a Web sites' privacy policy relative to children. The Federal Trade Commission is the enforcement authority for this act.

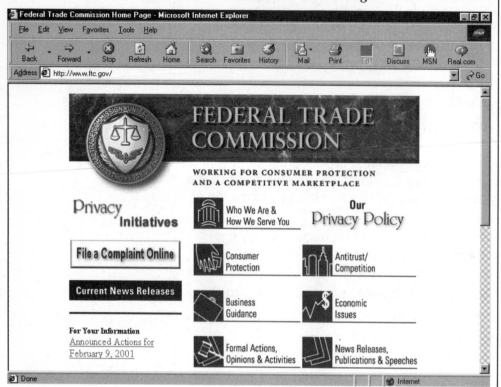

- The Children's Online Privacy Protection Act details what information can and cannot be collected from children online and requires that sites post a notice to parents if it does collect information from children. The act specifies that "individually identifiable" information about a child be protected; this includes name, address, e-mail address, telephone number, hobbies, or anything else that would enable anyone to identify the child or actually contact him or her. In addition, there are limitations on how companies can use tracking software that accesses cookies on a user's hard drive, if that information is tied to a specific individual who is 13 years or younger.

- According to the Child Protection act, a site must provide information at a parent's request about the kind of information that is collected from children and the specific information they might have collected from the parent's child. Of course, the site is required to carefully verify that the person requesting this is indeed the child's parent. Many sites create a form for parents to sign to do this, but some accept an e-mail if it contains a digital signature.

SurfSecret Claims to Protect Online Privacy

- Several software products claim to protect the privacy of people who go online. SurfSecret essentially erases **cookies** stored on a computer hard drive periodically so that the user's history of sites visited and activities performed there is gone. Keep in mind that this will clear out the history record in your browser, a feature many people like to use to quickly return to a recently visited site. The software also automatically empties the Recycle Bin on your Windows desktop after it's erased the cookies, so you can't retrieve any recently deleted documents at all.

Note

You can get more information about The Children's Online Privacy Protection Act at www.ftc.gov/kidzprivacy.gov, or by calling 1-877-FTC-HELP.

Buzzword

Cookies are files that a Web site sends to your system while you're online. The cookie might contain such information as an ID assigned to you by the Web site or preference information you specified while working on the Web site. When you revisit the site, it can read your cookie to recall your preferences or count how often you've visited the site.

SurfSecret.com Home Page

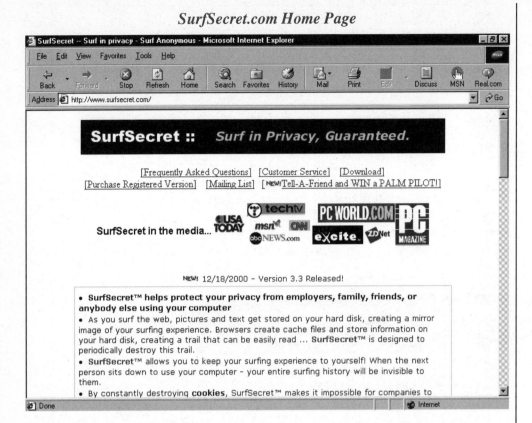

■ Another software product which is free to users is Pretty Good Privacy. This is an encryption software that can be used to send messages and information online securely. Note, however, that this **freeware** is for consumers, not e-commerce businesses, because its terms of use prohibit commercial use. Online consumers should also use antivirus software regularly, because some viruses will actually go to their hard drive and get a copy of information stored there. If you've saved your credit information anywhere online, you could be at risk for such a virus.

■ Other kinds of software to protect people online include programs that shred e-mails, or allow you to anonymously surf the Web with a pseudonym. You can find programs that automatically redirect e-mails so it's not clear where they originated and even to encrypt your entire hard drive. You can even use your computer to make secure phone calls. However, some of this technology poses problems for online businesses who may not always be sure with whom they're doing business. Consumer fraud of businesses is a concern when consumers can assume alternate personalities online.

Buzzword

Freeware are programs other online resources that you can download from the Internet, install, and use for free. *Shareware* software operates on the honor system: if you decide that you like the shareware and want to continue using it, you need to register it and pay a small fee to the shareware author.

215

Take a look at each of these sites (full URLs are located at the end of the exercise), then read the site analysis below and answer the questions.

CASE STUDY 1: EPIC.ORG

■ The Web site of The Electronic Privacy Information Center provides articles, news, a newsletter, and bookstore all related to consumer privacy online. One area of the site even offers up copies of previously confidential documents from various agencies concerning activities such as government electronic surveillance. They include PDF files of these documents, such as the one shown below from the files of the FBI. For security reasons some of these documents have portions deleted.

EPIC Privacy Document Page

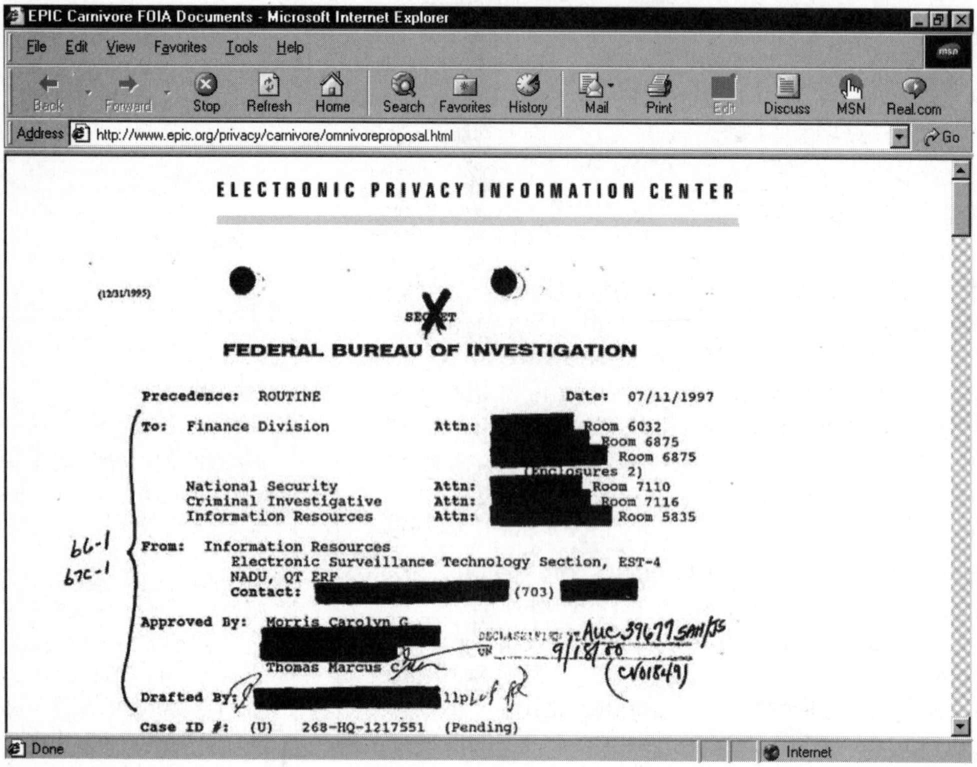

- The site also includes a page called Bill Track that provides summaries of bills currently before Congress that relate to individual privacy. There are also links to go to sites where they can read the actual bills in their entirety. The area is divided up into bills in front of the Senate and those in front of the House of Representatives. Typical topics for these bills are information privacy, financial information privacy, wireless privacy, and regulations regarding how software can be used to track Internet users' activities.

EPIC Bill Track Page

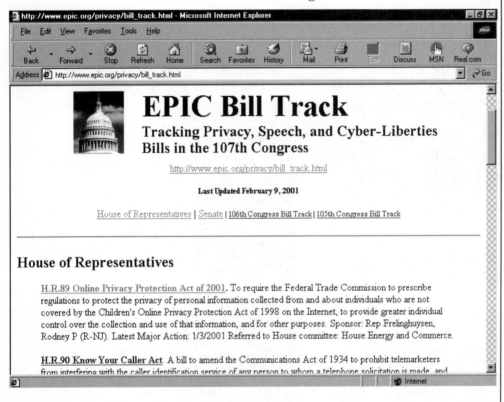

1. What does the Online Privacy Protection Act of 2001 require?

_____

2. What is a PDF file?

_____

3. What are cyber-liberties?

_____

CASE STUDY 2: RETAILING.ORG

■ The Electronic Retailing Association includes a link to an area it maintains called SavvyShopper. This is an interesting site, because it outlines the rights of consumers and regulations protecting those rights broken down by categories such as Name Removal, What If I Change My Mind?, and Unauthorized Charges. Notice that the page is broken into three sections: the major navigation menu for the site is on the left, the specific articles are in the center, and a menu of links for categories of information are on the right. The site includes separate scrollbars for the middle and right sections so users can move around those portions of the page independently. This is done using frames; each frame can hold a separate HTML document.

Savvyshopper.org Page

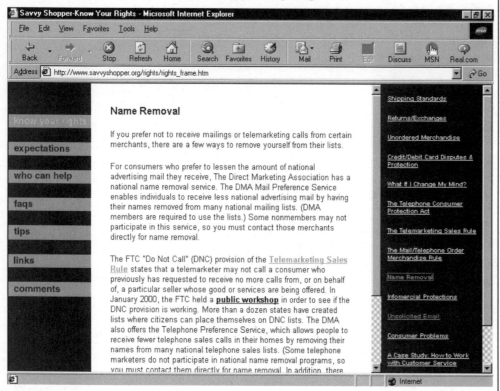

■ Another interesting feature on this site is the search area. They provide several types of information to search by and something called a Word Wheel. Essentially this is a dialog box that you can open, which lists possible topics you can search, with an indication of how many entries there are posted for that topic. You can open this separate window and paste a category into the search text field. You can then use a drop-down list of Boolean operators, such as AND, OR, or NOT, to specify the type of action to take regarding the search term. All of these options provide a pretty sophisticated search feature.

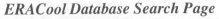

ERACool Database Search Page

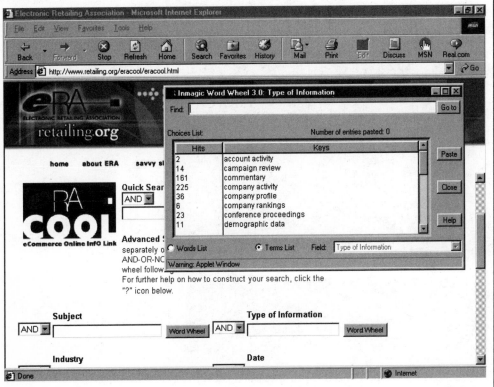

1. What actions can you take to get your name off of mailing lists?

   _____

2. What is the DMA?

   _____

3. Give an example of a search for data that includes a Boolean operator.

   _____

CASE STUDY 3: FTC.GOV

- The FTC Web site contains a link to a mini-Web site called Kidz Privacy. This site addresses the rights of children to privacy. The site has a whimsical interface, using bright colors and graphic images for links that make it fun to explore. The site includes information broken up into areas for parents, kids, and teachers, with links back to FTC Privacy Initiatives.

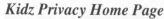

Kidz Privacy Home Page

- The Media area of this site contains links to Web sites that participate in The Kidz Privacy Campaign. These sites post a link to the Kidz Privacy page on their sites and agree to adhere to certain regulations regarding child privacy online. There are also audio public service announcement files on this page that you can playback using an audio plug-in such as RealAudio. You can download the audio files and even the graphics used on the site.

Kidz Privacy Media Page

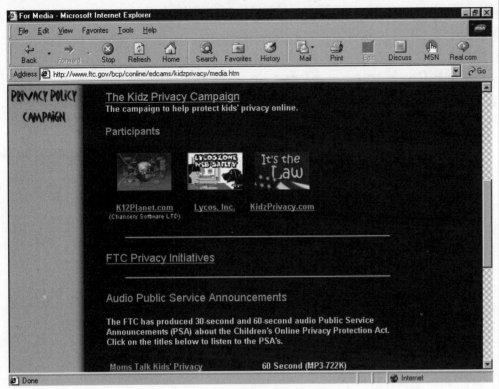

1. What organization runs the Kidz Privacy Web site?

   _____

2. What is the goal of the Kidz Privacy Campaign?

   _____

3. What is a public service announcement?

   _____

LIVE ON
THE
WORLD WIDE WEB!

http://www.epic.org/
Electronic Privacy Information Center
http://bbbonline.org/
BBBOnline.org
http://www.retailing.org/
Electronic Retailing Association
http://www.ftc.gov/
Federal Trade Commission
http://www.surfsecret.com
SurfSecret.com

Regulating Payments and Taxes for Online Transactions
- See how trade policy affects E-Commerce
- Learn about The Internet Tax Freedom Act
- Explore how E-Companies can keep up with tax requirements
- Look at international E-Commerce tax issues
- Learn how the Electronic Signatures Act affects E-Commerce

NOTES

The Center for Trade Policy Studies Offers News and Commentary on Trade Issues

- The Internet started out as a forum for the free exchange of information. In recent years, it has become a forum for commerce, and that changes everything. The exchange of money, entering into contracts, and shipping of products across state and country borders raises issues about taxation, interstate and international commerce, and the format of online payments and contracts. Though some would prefer the Internet stay beyond government regulation and taxation, the reality is that online business is slowly being roped in by the same types of regulations that bricks and mortar businesses are governed by.

- For the most part, E-Businesses are subject to the same laws that other businesses are governed by. State taxes apply to purchases based on the **Nexus**, or physical location, of a business's operations. What's illegal to ship across state lines for a bricks and mortar or catalog business is still illegal to ship for a Web business. Gray areas have centered around issues such as paying taxes on downloaded software or digital content and what state you pay tax to if the Web server that runs your online business is in one state and your business operation is in another. Sites such as freetrade.org, The Center for Trade Policy Studies, provide updates on trade regulations for E-Commerce.

Buzzword
Nexus refers to the physical location of a business entity.

Center for Trade Policy Studies Home Page

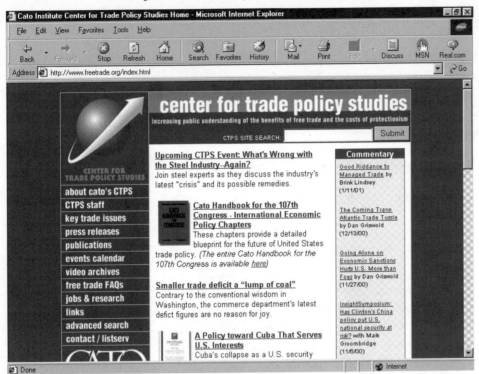

- Free trade regulations generally pertain to the ability of companies to trade across state and national borders and prohibitions against business monopolies. A **monopoly** is a business entity that controls all or most of the market for a particular product, or holds an unfair advantage in selling to a market over competitors. A few well-publicized monopoly cases include the AT&T telephone company monopoly that resulted in a break-up of the business; and Microsoft, which had an unfair advantage because of its ownership of the Windows operating system and questionable business practices. To date, the proliferation of business competition online doesn't seem to provide a climate for growth of monopolies, but as smaller companies are acquired by larger ones, or go out of business, the potential for online monopolies exists.

Commerce.net Offers Reports on E-Commerce Public Policy

- Sites such as Commerce.net provide updates on various taxation and other issues related to E-Commerce. One of the current debates centers around Internet taxation. In 1998 The Internet Tax Freedom Act was passed with certain specific provisions for taxation of online transactions. The Act, which expires in October of 2001, provides a three-year moratorium on any special taxation of Internet service providers and on any multiple taxation schemes (for example where a customer has to pay sales tax to his or her own state of residence and the state the E-Business is located in). The act also established a commission to study the question of whether Internet purchases should be taxed at all. The act further decreed that there would be no federal taxes on Internet access or electronic commerce and that the Internet would be a tariff-free zone; that is, free of any tariffs between countries that would discourage global E-Commerce. It remains to be seen what will happen regarding these issues when the act expires in 2001.

Buzzword

A *monopoly* is a business entity that controls all or most of the market for a particular product.

Note

If you're reading this book after October 2001, you should go to the site that provides information about this act, http://cox.house.gov/ nettax/ for updated information.

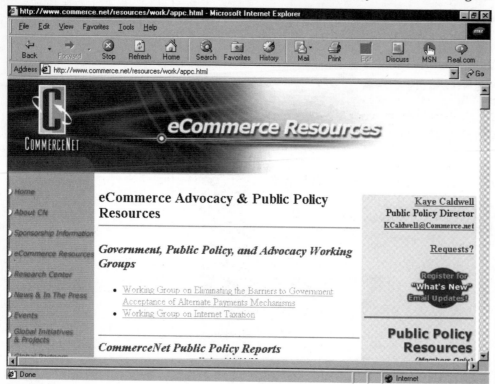

- Another E-Commerce issue being considered for regulation concerns the use of various methods of online payment, for example, digital cash. There are questions about how those payments should be regulated, just as issuance of U.S. currency and credit card use are regulated. In addition, activities such as gambling that are illegal in some states, face scrutiny when offered online. Products that are illegal in one state and not in another are also points of confusion; what obligation does an online store have to understand all the regulations concerning their products in every state and country in the world?

- To consider some of the taxation issues critically, you should consider why companies are taxed by states in the first place. A bricks and mortar store, for example, uses the services of a community, such as roads, police, and water. Traffic to and from the store causes wear and tear on roads and adds to air pollution, which a city or state must spend money to counteract. Sidewalks around the store must be maintained and streets cleaned. Some would argue that an online business doesn't use the same services and so shouldn't be taxed in the same way. However, online businesses maintain offices somewhere and use the highway system to ship their products just as any other business does. The question is probably not whether online businesses should pay taxes, but to whom they should be paid and on what types of products or services.

Note

Certain states have no sales tax: they are New Hampshire, Oregon, Montana, Alaska, and Delaware. If a business is located in these states, they do not have to charge sales tax.

Vertexinc.com Provides Sales Data to Help E-Commerce Companies

- Many laws and regulations affecting E-Commerce are determined and enforced at the state level in the United States. In fact, there are approximately 7,500 sales tax jurisdictions when you take both state and local taxes into account. There are many examples of situations that are treated differently in different states. For example, most states don't impose a tax on services, but a couple, Hawaii and New Mexico, do. If a company arranges for a product to be shipped directly from the manufacturer rather than from their own warehouse, some states require that the tax be paid based on the location of the manufacturer, while others require that the sales tax be based on the location of the company that took the order. Some states treat downloaded software sales as taxable; others do not. These variations can cause a lot of confusion. Vertexinc.com is one site that helps businesses try to make sense of it all.

Vertexinc.com Home Page

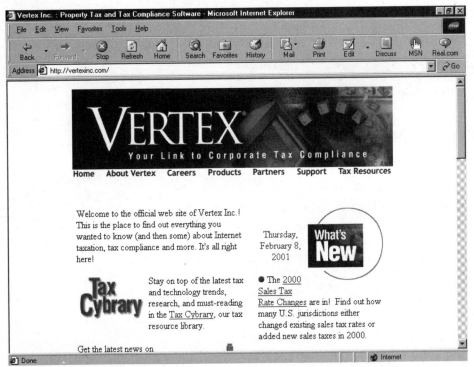

- In fact, sales tax tables like the ones offered on Vertexinc.com can be valuable, especially because sales tax rates can change every year. Also, regulation of Internet businesses is in flux right now, with new situations gaining scrutiny and new legislation being passed. For that reason any online business would be well advised to have both a professional attorney and accountant reviewing its taxation processes on a yearly basis.

- Because keeping track of the large number of tax requirements is complex, several companies produce software to automate sales tax compliance, such as Vertex's Quantum Sales and Use Tax software. Many companies are making reengineering and automating of their tax compliance processes a part of their implementation of an ERP (enterprise resource planning) solution, which centralizes information for an entire organization.

EcommerceTax.com Offers Information on Online Tax Issues Around the World

- Countries around the world are grappling with the challenges of conducting business in a virtual environment. Internationally there are questions not only about who pays taxes and to whom, but also what customs regulations apply and what tariffs will be charged. Underlying all of the discussion is the sincere desire on the part of most countries to have Internet business succeed because it opens up tremendous opportunities for global expansion and profit. Many countries are working together to establish common standards for E-Commerce across borders. EcommerceTax.com provides updates on those efforts.

EcommerceTax.com Home Page

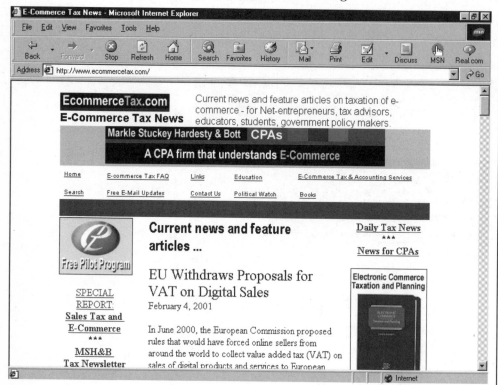

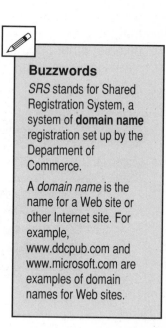
- One area of contention is value added tax, or VAT. Many countries impose such a tax, including Canada and most European Union members. Visitors to those countries pay VAT on purchases, but can have the VAT refunded to them when they leave the country, because it only applies to residents of the country. Recently the European Union tried to impose a VAT on all online sales to people in their countries, regardless of whether the purchase was made from a business in another country or not. This was done so that their own companies could remain competitive with foreign companies. However, this caused such an outcry that the tax on foreign businesses was discontinued. This challenge of taxation and competitiveness with foreign businesses is typical of the intersection of legal, economic, and social concerns brought about by E-Commerce.

- Groups such as the Organization for Economic Cooperation and Development (OECD) are working with various countries to make tax and tariff regulations more unified. One area of concern to these organizations is the so-called "digital divide," which refers to the disparity in the ability to access the Internet among countries. Some countries charge such high rates to access the Internet that their move into E-Commerce has been slower than others. Others lack the technological infrastructure to compete. The next decade should bring some interesting international cooperative efforts to make E-Commerce accessible and profitable for all.

WTOnline.com Offers Insight into the Politics of E-Commerce

- In addition to concerns about free trade and taxation, governments are looking at issues of standardization in online transactions. One such controversy has centered around digital signatures and the standards for business practices regarding E-Contracts. The Electronic Signatures in Global and National Commerce Act of 2000 provides that an electronic signature made online has the same validity as a handwritten signature. Some people are concerned that this exposes consumers to potential fraud, while others say that the act establishes business practices that will bolster consumer confidence in a variety of online transactions.

- WTOnline.com is Washington Technology's Web site and offers information on politics and E-Commerce, with details on federal, state, and local issues. On this site you can also read about international efforts, such as the United Nations' model laws for online commerce. Although these laws don't have any legal standing, they are intended to provide a template for national governments to use in constructing their own E-Commerce laws. It is hoped that this approach will bring some underlying unity to E-Commerce laws around the world.

WTOnline.com E-Sign Bill Article Page

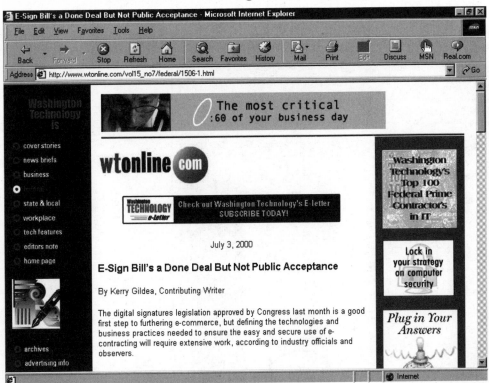

- Digital certification software may have a role in online signatures and contracts because it helps buyers and sellers verify their identities and credit. In addition, standards about how payments are made and accepted are being developed. Much of the standardization and regulation regarding online transactions are tied directly to the state of security technology and enforcement online.

E-Business Analysis

Take a look at each of these sites (full URLs are located at the end of the exercise), then read the site analysis below and answer the questions.

CASE STUDY 1: FREETRADE.ORG

- The Web site of The Center for Trade Policy Studies contains areas that deal with trade issues and offers publications, events, FAQs, and even a video archive of speeches and media appearances related to trade policy. The Publications Library area is nicely designed, with publications broken up into category links indicated by sample publication images. The area contains not only the typical books, papers, and articles, but also transcripts of speeches and Congressional testimony on related topics.

Freetrade.org Publications Library Page

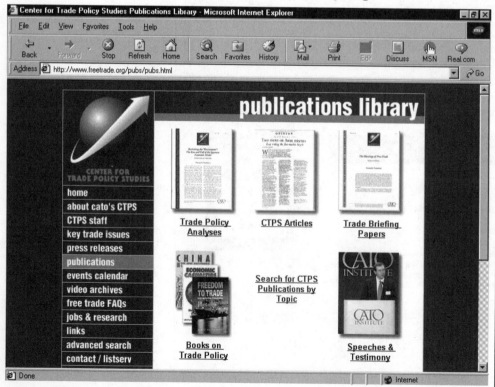

- As you roam around the publications area you'll find a combination of PDF format files, HTML files, video archives, and audio files. One of the publication categories in the Publications area is the Cato Institute Handbook for Congress. When you go to this link, you find that the entire handbook has been placed on the site in electronic form. You can view any section by clicking on that link and reading it online. The online version of the book requires Adobe Acrobat to view it. You can print portions of the book, or purchase a paper edition through an online bookstore.

Cato Handbook for Congress Page

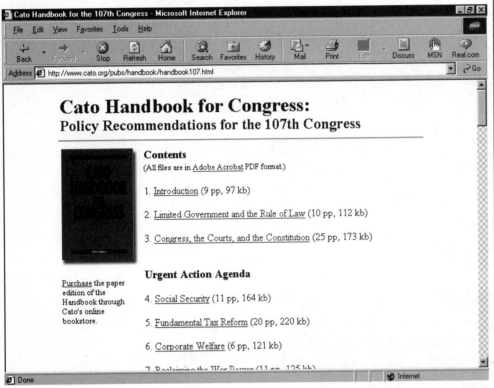

1. What does CATO stand for?

_____

2. What are some sources of Trade Policy Analyses?

_____

3. Is CATO a government agency?

_____

CASE STUDY 2: VERTEXINC.COM

- Vertexinc.com not only sells products for automating tax compliance, its site offers some very helpful information about Internet tax policies and even a glossary of terms related to taxation. They provide information about every state's tax policies, which you can access by clicking on a state from a map. Each summary explains about Internet access taxes (taxes levied on the monthly cost of your ISP), sales tax, any legislation related to downloaded products, such as software or electronic books, and pending legislation.

Vertexinc.com Internet Taxation Page

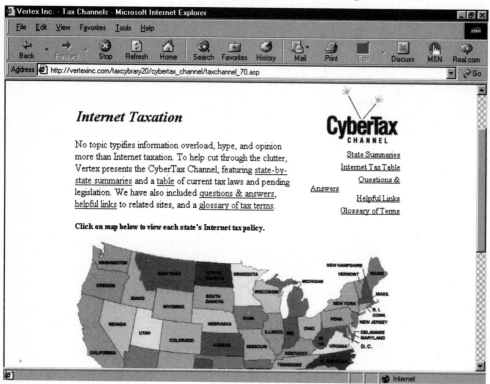

■ Vertexinc.com actually offers a lot of information, which it scatters around its site. For example, its Cybrary page provides links to areas of the site such as the City Business Tax Study, with virtual tours of several major cities to learn about their property tax structures, and WPTX, The Property Tax Station. This is actually neither a radio station nor a location for audio files. It's just a spot where you can find information such as a three-month-tax filing calendar and tax appeals process in every state. Although the graphic symbols that look like small banner ads are a fun way to get to information, there's so much on this site it's not always clear what to click on to get what you need.

Cybrary Page

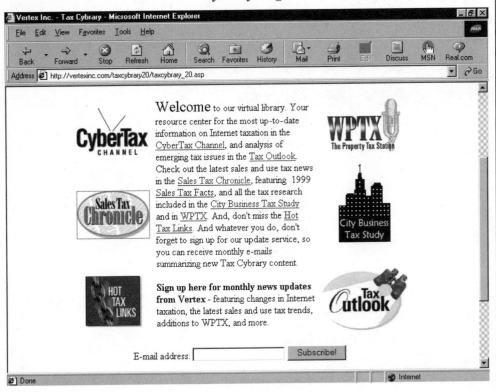

1. What is a virtual tour?

   _____

2. The map with links to individual states on the Internet Taxation page uses image maps to create the links; what is an image map?

   _____

3. What does WPTX stand for?

   _____

CASE STUDY 3: ECOMMERCETAX.COM

- Ecommercetax.com gathers together news and information about taxation and the Internet. A big part of understanding what's happening in that regard is keeping up with what's going on in politics. The Political Watch page of Ecommercetax.com covers activities of Congressional advisory commissions and lobbying (activities by groups trying to influence political decisions) by various industry and special interest groups such as The National Association of Counties. The site also provides links to organizations involved in Internet taxation.

Political Watch Page

- One link on most pages of the Ecommercetax.com site is to the STC Online Sales Tax Calculator. This is a useful tool for online businesspeople, because you can enter your location, the customer's shipping address and the amount of the sale, and get a breakdown of both state and local sales and use taxes. Note that this tool is for "casual use" only; if a company intends to use this calculator regularly in its business, it should subscribe to the service and pay a fee.

The Sales Tax Clearinghouse Online Sales Tax Calculator Page

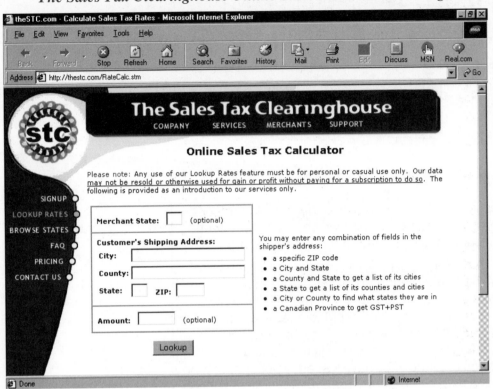

1. What is the Advisory Commission on Electronic Commerce?

   _____

2. What is the definition of lobbying?

   _____

3. In the Online Sales Tax Calculator, where would you enter information about a Canadian Province?

   _____

http://www.freetrade.org/
The Center for Trade Policy Studies
http://www.commerce.net/
Commerce.net
http://vertexinc.com/
Vertexinc.com
http://www.ecommercetax.com
EcommerceTax.com
http://www.wtonline.com
Washington Technology Online

Learning E-Commerce
Part IV, Regulations to Control the Conduct of E-Business
Capstone Project

Summary of Concepts

- Two of the major debates in the area of E-Business are how to protect the privacy of individuals who go online and what involvement government will have in online transactions, especially in the area of taxation.

- To some extent, protection of individual privacy is governed by federal law, but many aspects of the Internet bring up never-before-explored scenarios, and policies of individual businesses with regard to the privacy of their customers is therefore somewhat self-regulated. Most Web businesses agree on the need for protection of children online, and several watchdog organizations are working towards that goal. However, the right of a business to sell or share information about its customers for marketing purposes is still a somewhat cloudy area. In general, security technology such as SSL and encryption have made payment transactions on the Web safe, but customers should still know the business they are buying from and what the privacy and security policies of that site are.

- In the United States, sales tax is applied at the state level, with most E-Businesses applying sales tax at the rate of their state of residence. However, there are still issues of taxation and E-Business that are less clear, including how international customers pay taxes when ordering from another country online. Currently, no federal taxes are applied to online purchases, and many who wish to see the Internet be a home for free commerce would prefer the government to refrain from taxing Web businesses at all.

Case Study

The Business:

- All Creatures Publishing is opening a children's book chat section on their Web site. The area will feature discussions of a series of pet books aimed towards children, as well as areas where children can talk about and post pictures of their pets. The publisher has a privacy statement concerning privacy of customer information when people order books online, but hadn't seen the need before to have a specific children's privacy policy. The new Web page will launch in two months.

Note

The Children's Online Privacy Protection Act regulates what businesses can and can't do regarding visitors to their sites who are under 13 years of age. The act provides that there are certain kinds of information that can be collected from children only with their parents' permission. This includes any information that might help identify a child and make contact, such as name, address, or even hobbies. The act also pertains to how tracking software can and can't be used to track the use of a computer by a child.

The Project:

- Have students break into teams of four. Have each team write a children's privacy policy statement for the All Creatures' Web site. One option is to have two people on the team research and come up with several samples of policy statements, have a third student write the statement, and the fourth one edit it. Then, have all the students on each team research self-regulatory programs, such as BBBOnline's Kids Privacy Seal program, and select one to recommend for use on the publisher's site. Hold a discussion at the completion of the project comparing the privacy statements from the various teams; debate the question of what risks to privacy All Creatures' might create by having children talk about their pets and post pictures of them on their site.

The Business Model:

- To complete this project, you must look for examples of privacy statements online. Here are three important things to consider:

    1. ***Consider sites that cater to children***: Look for toy sites, media sites that target children, such as Disney or HarryPotter.com, or sites that sell music or books to children. What do their privacy policies say and do they place them prominently on their sites? Do any include warnings to children about how to protect themselves online?

    2. ***Look at sites that are aimed at adults:*** Children will go to sites geared towards adults and those sites may not be as attuned to younger visitors' privacy. What obligations do these sites have to protect children, particularly if children aren't even supposed to legally be able to purchase what they sell, such as cigarettes? If a business sells a product that is harmful to children in some way, is it that business's obligation to warn children away from the site? What measures can you find that businesses take to ensure that someone making a purchase from them is over 18?

    3. ***Understand the possible repercussions to an E-Business if it doesn't follow the provisions of the Child Protection Act:*** Read articles from newspapers and magazines about child privacy online, and look at information about legal cases that have addressed this. Check out sites that offer self-regulatory programs for Web sites and see what they tell you about the responsibilities of a Web site towards younger visitors and parents. What responsibilities do parents have for their own children's online activities?

Note

Teaching kids about money and spending habits helps them become better and safer E-Commerce customers. Sites such as Allowancenet (http://www.allowancenet.com) help parents educate kids on money topics. For parents or grandparents who want younger members to experience buying online, they might consider using online currency, such as Flooz. They can send Flooz dollars to kids, then help the children shop online and make a purchase they approve of.

Technology

- There are software programs, such as Net Nanny, that parents can use to restrict their child's access to certain sites. These products are essentially filters that parents use to set parameters for sites that can be visited and sites that can't by using keywords and categories of sites. Parents can also use history features of Web browsers or the cookies on their own computer hard drives to track the sites their children are visiting. As the use of digital signatures becomes more prevalent online, it's possible that the age of a person could be embedded with other information in his or her signature so that a merchant would know if the purchaser is old enough to access a site or make a purchase. Today, however, it is difficult for an E-Commerce site to know the age of every visitor.

Books to help:

Conducting Internet Research (catalog number DC63)

Legal Community Internet Skills (catalog number DC72)

Web sites to explore:

http://parentsoup.com/onlineguide/

This section of Parent Soup provides guidance on keeping kids safe online, as well as information on parental control devices and families online.

http://www.ala.org/parentspage/greatsites

This is a page of the American Library Association that offers links to Web sites that are good for kids to visit. See what some of these kids' sites say about privacy.

http://www.smartparent.com

You can learn about blocking and filtering software on this site aimed towards parents. Look at some of their protection tips and links to agencies and organizations that deal with issues related to the Internet and kids.

http://www.gocrc.com

This is the site of the Children's Rights Council. Here you can get information on legislation related to children's rights, current news about children's rights and privacy, and links to related sites.

Part V

Web Site Considerations: Structure

From Shopping Cart to Checkout
- ■ **Explore the online purchasing process**
- ■ **See how E-Businesses manage customer accounts**
- ■ **Learn about how online orders get processed**
- ■ **Understand payment and returns options for E-Commerce**
- ■ **Learn about outsourcing E-Commerce transaction processing**

NOTES

Take a Look at the Purchasing Process at Bluefly.com

- ■ When a customer buys a product in a retail store, the purchasing process involves possible shopping assistance from a salesperson, the ability to hold and look at products, and personal assistance with completing the purchase itself. With an online transaction, personal assistance occurs only if the customer actively contacts a company by e-mail or phone. Most of the time, the customer is shopping alone, working through a series of screens with written directions and product pictures. That's why structuring your Web site to make the purchasing process intuitive is so important.

- ■ Because buying online is relatively new, and because each E-Company requires its own set of steps to purchase from them, the experience is not as familiar as the one of walking up to a checkout counter in any store in any city. Because customers are not as comfortable, online stores typically build in several safeguards that allow customers to change or cancel an order at various points in the process. They also make it easy for customers to review orders and make changes after the order is placed, but before it ships.

- ■ The tool used for assembling and placing an online order is a **shopping cart**. Bluefly.com calls its shopping cart function a shopping bag. Bluefly follows a typical sales process: the customer uses search tools and an online catalog to locate the product he or she needs. The customer then adds an item to the shopping cart by clicking a button. After adding each item the customer can proceed to checkout, or continue shopping. Most shopping carts place one of each item in the shopping cart by default; the customer is then offered the option of updating quantities before placing the order.

Buzzword
A shopping cart is a program that allows a user to assemble and place an order for products online.

Bluefly.com Shopping Bag Page

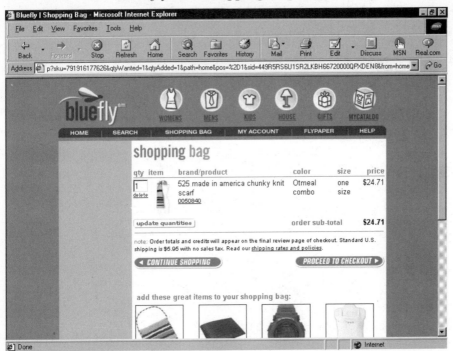

- A shopping cart program typically performs certain mathematical calculations, such as multiplying the quantity of an item times its price; and adding the prices of all the products in a shopping cart together, plus shipping, to reach an order total. To do this, these programs use formulas just as a spreadsheet progam does. A formula identifies actions to be performed on certain information using operators, such as * for multiplication and / for division.

See How Amazon.com Manages its Customers' accounts

- Businesses who are in the business of buying and selling to customers spend a lot of time managing customer accounts. That involves keeping track of customer information including name and address, order history, and payment information, such as credit card number or payment history. E-Commerce businesses also have to track this information. One key difference is that many E-Commerce Web sites are designed to offer customers instant access to their own account information, and in some cases they can even change that information themselves. For example, customers can update their contact information with a new phone number or change the credit card they wish to have purchases charged to. These online data updates must be integrated with the data in the main company records so information is consistent across the business.

- Amazon.com's Web site allows customers to take control of their accounts by tracking orders, canceling orders that haven't shipped, changing shipping or billing addresses for existing orders, and setting up an address book for people they want to ship to frequently. In addition, Amazon.com customers can update their own contact and credit card information. Allowing customers to make these kinds of changes in real time requires a sophisticated data management system on the back-end, one that integrates customer online accounts with order processing, shipping, accounting, and other departments.

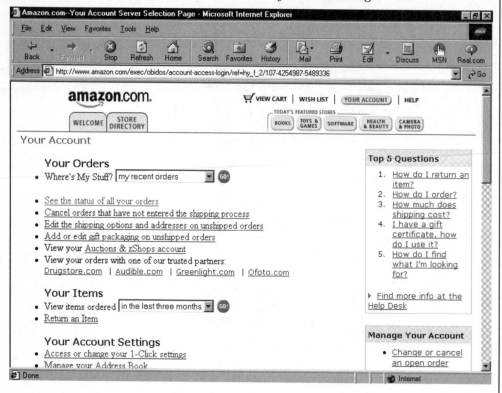

- One category of software that enables this kind of integration of information across an organization is called **enterprise resource planning** software, or **ERP**. ERP is typically a suite of software solutions for various functions in a company, with built-in integration features that allow departments such as manufacturing, shipping, and accounting to update and share information. Some leaders in the ERP software world are SAP, PeopleSoft, and Oracle.

Playing Around with a Shopping Cart at eToys.com

- eToys.com offers repeat customers a feature for one-step purchasing. By using this feature, a customer can skip the tedious task of entering information about their address, credit card, shipping preferences, and so on every time they make a purchase. Instead, they store this information on the site. This makes shopping on such the site much more convenient, so, the business hopes, the customer will purchase from that site again and again.

Buzzword

ERP refers to *enterprise resource planning*, a category of software that integrates various business functions across an organization.

Note

One-step shopping online often involves certain restrictions. For example, eToys.com specifies that no order requiring gift wrap can be made using the one-step feature. Whenever an order has variables, such as multiple shipping addresses, it is often better to use the standard purchasing process.

240

eToys Shopping Cart Page

eToys.com - Shopping Cart - Microsoft Internet Explorer

File   Edit   View   Favorites   Tools   Help

Back   Forward   Stop   Refresh   Home   Search   Favorites   History   Mail   Print   Edit   Discuss   MSN   Real.com

Address   http://www.etoys.com/exec/cart?ACTION=ADD&PRODUCT_ID=50080521&CONTEXT=246541   Go

Your Shopping Cart

Checkout

In Stock

Description	Quantity	Unit Price
Activity Garden	1	$25.00 Sale!
Little Tikes		
This item cannot be gift wrapped.	remove	
Oversize - Extra handling fee may apply.		

Continue Shopping
- Clearance Sale
- Favorites by Age for Boys, Girls
- Toys Under $20

- See all Toys
- Back to Home

✔ Update Quantities

eToys Low Price Guarantee   Subtotal: $25.00

One-Step Checkout

Faster Checkout for return customers:
- No gift wrap
- No gift certificates or coupons
- Ship to one address
- Set your One-Step Checkout settings

Checkout

Regular Checkout for all customers:
- Gift wrap
- Use gift certificates and coupons
- Ship to multiple addresses

Done   Internet

- In many cases companies include information to lure shoppers into additional purchases from the shopping cart page. The Continue Shopping choice itself is one way of doing this, but some sites include suggestions for other purchases that might be of interest to a customer. In some cases these suggestions are simply sale or overstock items, but on more sophisticated sites customers might be offered targeted additional products based on what they have already placed in their shopping carts, or even on their purchasing history. This involves matching past purchases to products from the same category. For example, if you've bought jazz music from a Web site before, suggestions for additional purchases will come from the jazz music category.

- When customers make purchases online **encryption** protects their information. Encryption is a process of changing data into a form that cannot be read by those who are unauthorized. Encryption involves the use of an algorithm, which is essentially a mathematical formula, to scramble data. Only the sender's and recipient's computers have the key to unscramble the data.

Handling Payments Online at Fogdog.com

- When a customer makes a purchase on a site, the processing of that payment isn't so very different from a payment in a retail store or through a phone order, except that electronic encryption technologies are involved to protect data in transit. A business gets credit card information from a customer online, then, using information to authenticate the transaction called a public key, they transmit the information to the bank that issued the credit card. The bank verifies the company's digital signature and the payment, then authorizes the payment (or declines it if the card is invalid or the customer is over his or her spending limit).

Buzzword
Encryption is the process of changing data into a form that cannot be read by those who are unauthorized. An *algorithm* is a mathematical process; it is used to scramble data for encryption.

- Companies setting themselves up for E-Commerce must consider what form of payment they will accept, for example MasterCard, Visa, and American Express. At the moment online purchasing is pretty much limited to credit cards, however other options, such as processing a personal check online or using online gift dollars through sources such as Flooz, are beginning to become available. Companies must also establish returns and exchange policies to deal with refund processing. In addition, taxes may have to be applied depending on the state in which the company and customer are located.

- Shipping charges are an issue with both online and catalog shopping. A customer who buys in a local retail store can walk an exchange into the store, incurring no additional cost. However, if an item is purchased online or over the phone, a customer must be concerned with the cost and effort involved in packaging and shipping the product back. Many online stores such as Fogdog.com will cover return shipping if they made an error in shipping the product, or the product is defective. However, most do not pay for shipping if a customer simply changes his or her mind or doesn't like the product when it arrives. Some companies include a return label with each purchase to make returning it simple; others provide a returns form online that customers can print out quickly and easily.

Fogdog.com Help Page

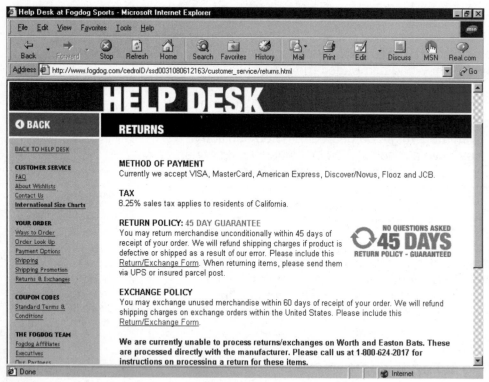

Learn About Expertise E-Businesses Can Draw on to Set up Transaction Processing at Virtualis.com

- Many E-Businesses are turning to other companies to set up and maintain transaction processing for their Web stores. This process is called a hosted service. Companies like Virtualis.com manage the establishment of merchant accounts required to process payments through credit card companies. They also make software available to handle and track online transactions.

Virtualis.com Home Page

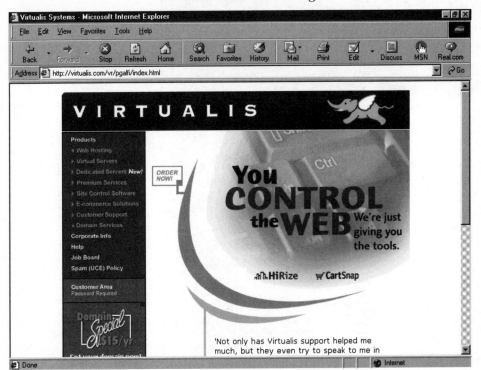

Buzzword

Web hosting is the process of running an application or Web site on a computer server. When a company hires a company to host their Web site, they are hiring them to place and maintain their site on their servers, rather than the company's own servers.

- Many companies who offer E-Commerce services offer a whole range of services, terming them "complete solutions." Virtualis, for example, offers **Web hosting**, software for designing shopping carts and managing a site, customer support functions for E-Businesses, and even a domain name sign-up service.

E-Business Analysis

Take a look at each of these sites (full URLs are located at the end of the exercise), then read the site analysis below and answer the questions.

CASE STUDY 1: BLUEFLY.COM

- The purchasing process at Bluefly.com is set out in a logical way for customers. First, a list of the steps involved in ordering—with an indication of which step a customer is on at any point in time—appears on the left of each order screen. Bluefly requires that you set up an account in order to purchase from them. This makes it quicker for customers to purchase in the future, since basic information, such as address, is stored on Bluefly's server.

Bluefly.com Account Sign-in Page

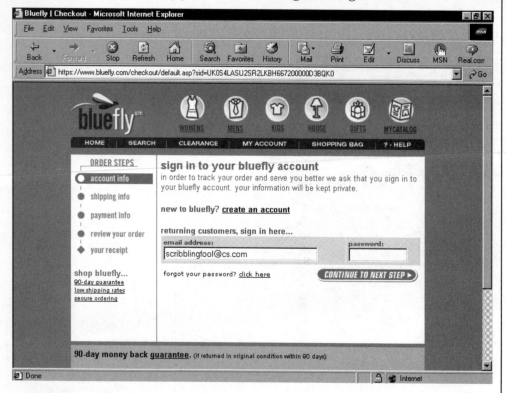

- Bluefly records shipping information as part of creating an account. Note that there is a checkbox a customer can use to easily indicate that the order should be shipped and billed to the same address. Notice that Bluefly will also ship outside the United States, but requires a different form be filled out to do so.

Bluefly Shipping Address Page

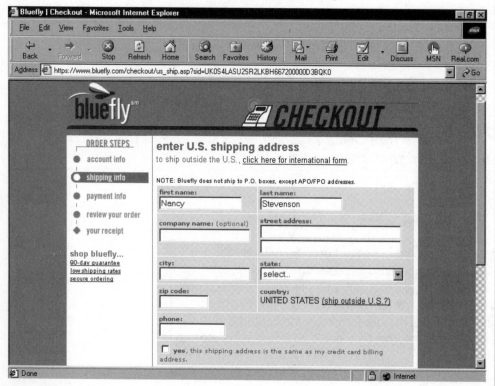

- Most online merchants include some sort of last review step so a customer can be sure that everything he or she has entered is correct before actually placing an order. A good way to design such a page is to provide a link back to each step in the process so a customer can easily make corrections without having to step back through the procedure. Although the policy statement at the top of the page states that changes to an order cannot be made once it is placed, that is usually not the case. An order can typically be changed, but only by contacting the customer service department of the online store before the order ships.

Bluefly Order Review Page

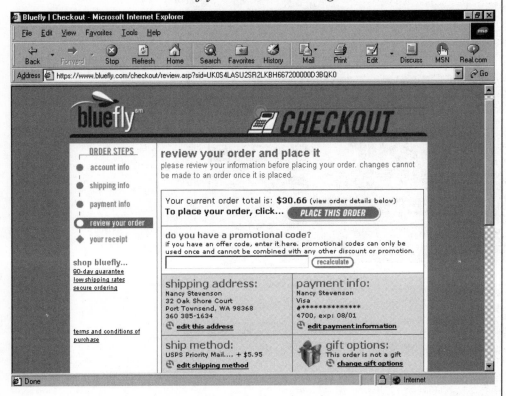

1. Where can you find information about secure ordering during the ordering process at Bluefly.com?

   _____

2. What is Bluefly.com's policy about shipping to post office boxes?

   _____

3. How often can a promotional code be used when purchasing from Bluefly?

   _____

CASE STUDY 2: FOGDOG.COM

■ Fogdog Sports is an online store selling sports equipment and clothing. This site serves both the general consumer and business customers, such as schools, wishing to purchase sports equipment. Their site provides certain features for business purchasers, such as the Institutional Shop and Bulk Sales discounts.

Fogdog.com Group Sales Page

- Business customers often have special needs. They might need help in determining what items or parts they will need, calculating quantities, or figuring discounts for larger orders. At Fogdog, the Institutional feature includes guidance for setting up various sports fields and playing areas, with an indication of what equipment is required for each. When you click on each item on a setup page you are taken to a product page listing models available. From that page you can add products to your shopping cart. The site also provides an alphabetical list of all equipment and related accessories along the left side of each setup page so a customer can access the information in a couple of ways.

Fogdog.com Institutional Field & Court Setup Page

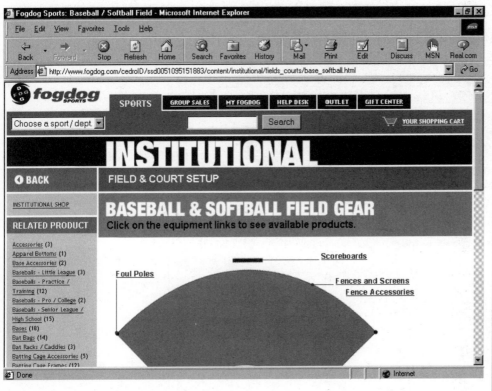

1. What is the difference between Group Sales and Bulk Sales?
   _____

2. How can Fogdog help corporate customers with special promotions?
   _____

3. How many products are available in the category of Bat Bags?
   _____

CASE STUDY 3: VIRTUALIS.COM

- Setting up an E-Commerce site to accept credit card payments involves a few steps. Virtualis explains these steps, which include obtaining a merchant account and choosing a payment gateway. A payment gateway is a software system that you use to automate the processing procedure for online purchases. Virtualis provides not only services to set up the credit card process, it also offers a shopping cart design software that includes credit card forms. However, the forms themselves are useless if a company has not established a relationship with a bank to process payments.

Virtualis.com Merchant Account Page

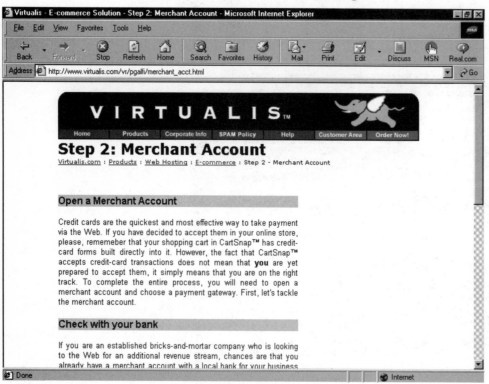

- Virtualis provides a description of setting up to accept credit card payments as a four-step process. Virtualis consults with a company to help them follow these steps, though certain portions involve company participation. For example, obtaining a merchant account requires that a company provide financial and credit history information to a bank. In many cases, a company can use an existing merchant account used for retail orders to process online orders.

Virtualis Payment Gateway Page

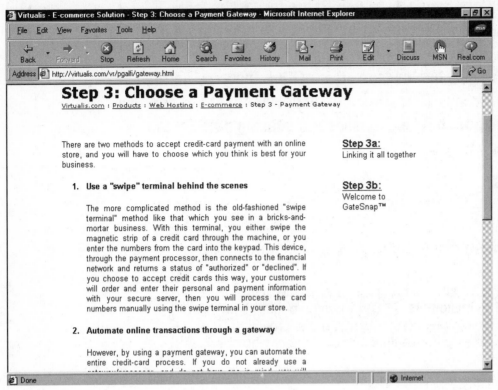

1. What is a merchant account?

   _____

2. What is the name of the payment gateway company that Virtualis recommends?

   _____

3. How can an established retail store use its in-store swipe terminal to process online orders?

   _____

http://www.bluefly.com/
Bluefly.com

http://www.amazon.com
Amazon.com

http://www.etoys.com
eToys.com

http://www.fogdog.com/
Fogdog

http://www.virtualis.com
Virtualis.com

Theme

21

Using a Web Presence to Add Value for Customers
- See how providing information can support selling
- Learn about adding convenience with an online site
- Explore how businesses offer offline features online
- Discover how Web sites can empower buyers of services
- Learn about how businesses are sharing data online

NOTES

See How One Online Pharmacy is Educating Consumers at CVS.com

- When a company determines how to structure its Web site, it has to consider the priorities of its customers. At CVS.com emphasis is given not to selling products such as aspirin and hair spray, but to providing medical information and offering convenience to customers who need prescriptions filled.

CVS.com Home Page

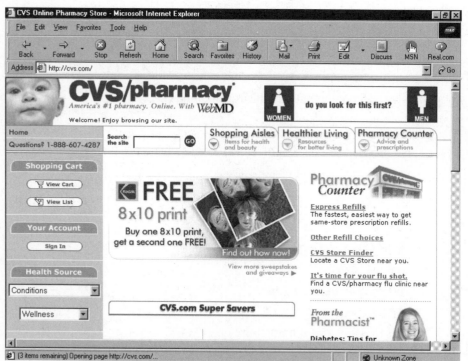

Note
Because specific situations can vary, Web sites giving out any kind of medical or legal information must be very careful to include disclaimers. A disclaimer is a statement that protects a business from being held liable for any harmful outcome a customer may experience by following their advice.

- Although an online business may offer everything a retail counterpart has to offer, an online store may have capabilities that should be brought to the forefront. For example, customers of a drugstore can search a database of medical information online, rather than asking a pharmacist or browsing through books or pamphlets in a store. Customers may lose an in-person presence, but they gain ability to access knowledge in a way that technology makes possible.

■ Online drugstores offer various services for refilling prescriptions, though you typically have to go to the store to pick up the refill. The online business is set up this way to deal with fraud that might occur when selling drugs to the public. When certain businesses set up an online presence they are limited in what they can offer online. This may be because of their own infrastructure (for example not being able to sell internationally because of the inability to deal with foreign currency conversion) or by legal requirements (as with the sales of weapons, drugs, or technology).

Convenience is the Emphasis on Bankone.com

■ Financial institutions have discovered that an online presence allows them to provide convenience to their customers, while saving money themselves. This isn't the first time banks have looked to technology to avoid costly customer one-on-one time with bank employees. Automated teller machines (ATM) have been a major cost-saving venture for banks. Online banking follows the same model of putting the work back in the hands of customers. Banks aren't alone in trying to save money by enabling customers: some businesses, such as airlines, even offer lower prices to customers who purchase online rather than taking the time of a telephone representative to place an order.

■ Certainly being able to check a bank balance at home at 3 a.m. is a convenience for many people. But banks have gone beyond allowing customers to simply check accounts online. BankOne.com, for example, allows you check account activity, order checks, transfer money among accounts, and even invest online. Since people can't actually get cash from their computers, the emphasis is on the convenience of getting information from home on the Web site.

BankOne.com Home Page

Technical Note

Cascading style sheets, called CSS, are used to add control over Web page layout. As with word processor style sheets, CSS define groups of settings for text or an image on a page. CSS layout specifications often relate to the relative position of an element on a Web page.

Technical Note

BankOne.com offers several lengthy pages of information about products and services on its Web site. To make site navigation easy, it uses a Top of Page link at the bottom of most pages. Clicking on this link allows a viewer to move back to the beginning of a page quickly.

Making Play Time Available Online at FAO Schwarz

- In many cases things that customers can do at a retail store can't be replicated in an online store. But some Web designers are getting creative with making virtual counterparts to offline activities. FAO Schwarz, the toy store, provides an intriguing virtual playroom on its site. Using animation software, it allows children to simulate how a toy works.

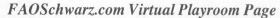

FAOSchwarz.com Virtual Playroom Page

- In any business where the ability to view, touch, or hear a product is important to the buying experience, the online world offers some limitations. However, use of multimedia such as animation, video, and sound files is often a good way to overcome those limitations. And, once a customer has bought a product offline and knows how it sounds, feels, or tastes, repeat purchases online may offer convenience and even savings.

- FAO Schwarz offers an animation **plug-in** to customers that they need in order to view its Playroom animations. If customers haven't downloaded the player already, the site is set up to automatically download it when a customer tries to run an animation. A wide variety of multimedia plug-ins are available on the Internet to provide access to formats that aren't supported by standard browsers.

Making Moving Easy at Alliedvan.com

- There are some businesses that find it impossible to complete a sale online because the variables for each customer are too great and human judgment is required. One such industry is the moving industry. When an individual wants to move his or her home contents from one home to another or one state to another, details about the distance between homes, the number of stories in each home, especially difficult-to-move

Buzzword

A *plug-in* is an application that works with another software program to provide additional functionality, such as the ability to view various multimedia formats.

items such as pianos or appliances, and how their furnishings will be packed all come into play. To make up for their inability to complete transactions online, companies such as Allied Van Lines have tried to provide customer value on their sites by focusing on providing relocation information and advice. Notice that their slogan is Full Service Relocation, putting the emphasis on the general experience rather than on arranging the details of the move.

Allied Van Lines Home Page

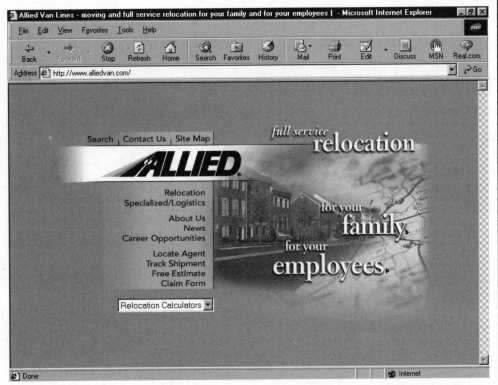

■ To provide relocation information, Allied has made a set of calculators available on its Web site that allow customers to get moving estimates, estimate variables in salary levels in the location they're moving from and the location they're moving to, and view crime information about cities. In addition, they offer the convenience of being able to track a shipment online. Valid moving estimates can only be obtained by e-mailing information about the move to the company and discussing the move with an actual agent.

Learn How Businesses are Servicing Business Customers Online at Ferguson.com

■ When businesses buy from businesses, there is typically more involved than a simple credit card purchase. With large-scale purchases in particular a company must ascertain whether a supply of products is available to meet their needs. The Internet has made it possible for companies to tap into a business's inventory system to check on product availability in real time. This makes the purchasing process faster and more accurate.

Note

The integration of a company with its vendors' product information is an important part of *supply chain management*. Supply chain management is a system of monitoring and controlling the purchase and inventory of materials for manufacturing.

- Ferguson is a supplier of plumbing materials to contractors and industry. They offer an inventory information feature called Ferguson Automated Sales Transaction system, or FAST. To use this system a customer must set up an account with a Ferguson salesperson. With most business-to-business online transactions, a customer account must be set up and credit established before a customer can purchase. In many cases business-to-business payments aren't even done electronically; an invoice for the sale will be sent to the customer to process through standard accounting procedures.

Ferguson.com Automated Sales Page

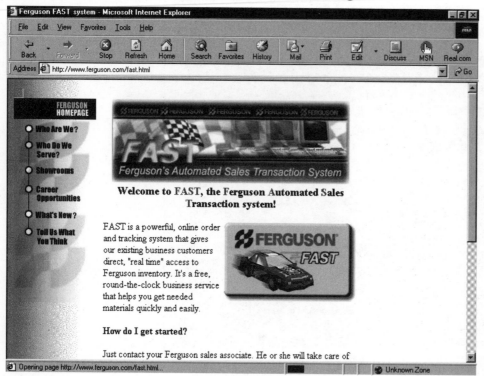

Technical Note

To allow another company to have access to company data, such as inventory, a business must allow authorized entities to go behind a company firewall. A firewall is a system of software controls that limits access to certain types of data on a company intranet. Typically, companies use firewalls in conjunction with other security measures, such as digital signatures, to create a larger security infrastructure.

254

E-Business Analysis

> *Take a look at each of these sites (full URLs are located at the end of the exercise), then read the site analysis below and answer the questions.*

CASE STUDY 1: CVS.COM

- Even though drugstores today sell a wide variety of off-the-shelf products, from candy to housewares, CVS.com makes medical advice and pharmacy services the focus of its Web site. Its home page places the WebMD medical database logo at the top of the page and quick access to its Pharmacy Counter along the right side of the page. Its Pharmacy Counter offers prescription refills and advice. Other features include a drug interaction database, advice column from a pharmacist, and refill reminder service that e-mails you when your prescription might be running out. Because of the regulated nature of buying drugs, visitors must establish an account and fill in certain specific information about a prescription before they can purchase.

CVS Pharmacy Counter Page

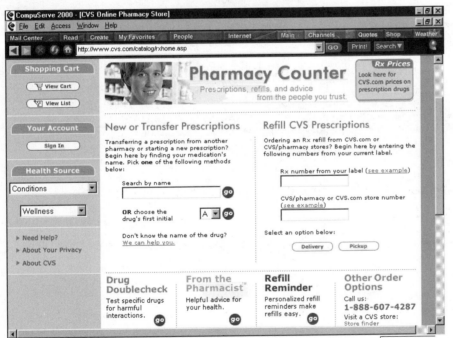

- Although the emphasis on this site is on medical needs, CVS.com does offer a Shopping Aisle section, with products for sale, and even a Photo Center. The Photo Center plays off of the Internet's strengths by allowing customers to send photos taken with a digital camera online for printing, or view photos developed in-store online. The Photo Center also offers film and other photo accessories for sale online, but again, the stress here is on the service they provide for viewing photos, rather than on film product sales. This strategy reinforces the brand trust a drugstore seeks, as the provider for your family's health needs.

CVS Photo Center Page

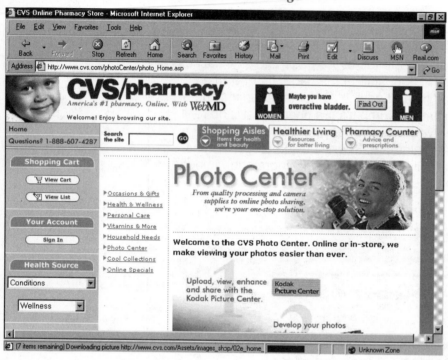

1. How does the CVS Web site encourage use of both local retail stores and the Web site?

   _____

2. How does the CVS Web site attempt to establish the presence of a pharmacist on its site?

   _____

3. What co-branding relationships can you spot on CVS.com?

   _____

CASE STUDY 2: BANKONE.COM

■ Financial institutions have taken to online business in a big way. Sites such as Bankone.com offer a wide variety of services dealing with customer accounts, from viewing account balances and activity to transferring money between accounts. Because banking tends to be a business with a somewhat conservative image, bank Web pages tend to be low-key. Notice that Bank One's Web site doesn't include advertisements or fancy multimedia banners. The pages tend to be information oriented, with little in the way of graphics.

Bankone.com Account Page

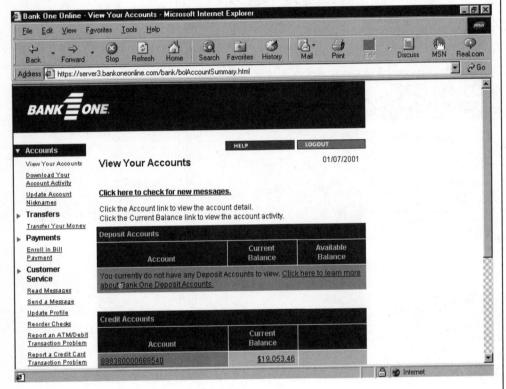

- Because banks earn money off of the money customers keep in their accounts, and not per customer transaction, they are eager to keep employee-customer transactions to a minimum, while still keeping customers happy. Allowing customers to complete procedures such as reordering checks online is a cost savings for Bank One. In fact, ordering checks is something customers cannot do at a physical bank at this point in time without a bank employee's assistance. By thinking of ways to empower customers through technology, businesses can leverage the strength of the Internet, rather than simply trying to reproduce in-person offerings online.

Bankone.com Reorder Checks Page

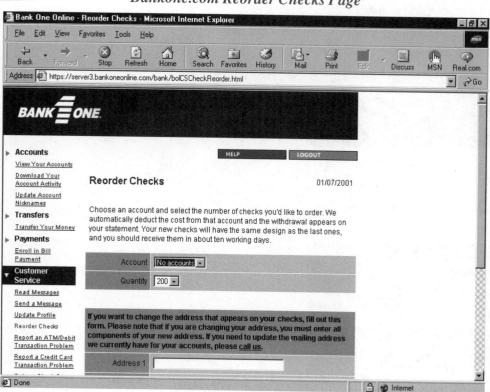

1. How does a customer view account activity from the View Your Accounts page?

   _____

2. What design choices do you have for checks you reorder online?

   _____

3. How would you print out account activity that you access online?

   _____

CASE STUDY 3: FERGUSON.COM

- Business-to-business, or B2B, Web sites often approach their structure in a slightly different way from business-to-consumer. On Ferguson's Web site, for example, the focus isn't as much on how to fill a shopping cart and make a purchase, as how to get advice and information about their products. They include advice for their customers about the whole supply chain process (that is the process of buying supplies, processing them in some form such as manufacturing, and selling and shipping the final product), as well as safety standards (ISO 9000) for their product line.

Ferguson.com Supply Chain Solutions Page

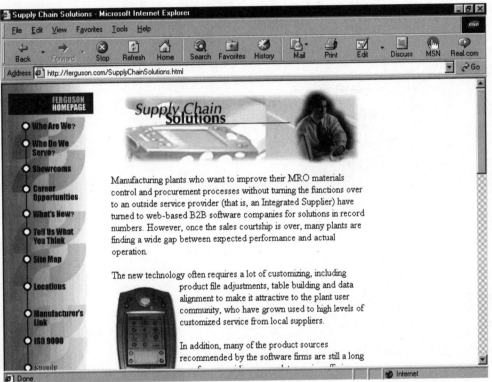

- Ferguson does provide lists of their products online, but because they sell products manufactured by others, they offer a link to manufacturers' sites rather than providing in-depth product information on their site. Customers can then visit those Web sites for more detailed product information. This suggests a close business relationship with manufacturing partners; these kinds of relationships are fundamental to successful B2B interactions.

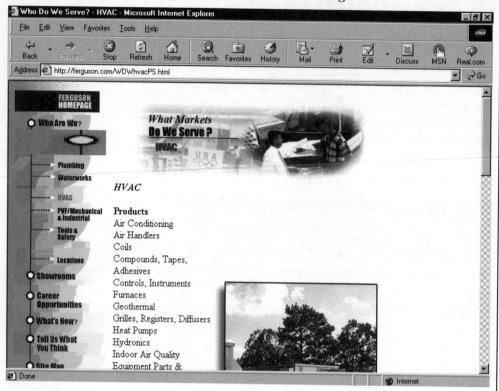

1. What is an Integrated Supplier, according to Ferguson's Supply Chain Solutions?

   _____

2. How does Ferguson use local showrooms to support customers?

   _____

3. What ways does Ferguson provide for customers to communicate with them?

   _____

http://www.cvs.com/
CVS.com

http://www.bankone.com
BankOne.com

http://www.faoschwarz.com
FAOSchwarz.com

http://www.alliedvan.com/
AlliedVan.com

http://www.ferguson.com
Ferguson.com

Marketing Your Online Business
- Learn about how e-mail is being used to market online
- Find demographics and statistics about online users
- Take a look at permission-based marketing
- Discover how newsletters help promote sites
- Explore the world of targeted opt-in address lists

NOTES

How Web Marketing Today and Other Online Publications are Helping to Create the New World of E-Marketing

- When you think about it, online marketing is a very young discipline, having only been around for a decade or so. Of course, some offline marketing techniques can be transferred to the Web. But many companies are also coming up with new ways of reaching people that only the Internet makes possible. The primary tools an online business has at its disposal for communicating a message to online customers are e-mail and the content of its own site.

- Wilson Internet produces a publication at wilsonweb.com called Web Marketing Today. This publication is a good starting point to educate yourself about marketing online, with articles and links to books and other sites. Web Marketing Today is also an interesting study in online marketing for their use of advertising, promotions, and **permission-based** marketing on their own site.

Web Marketing Today Home Page

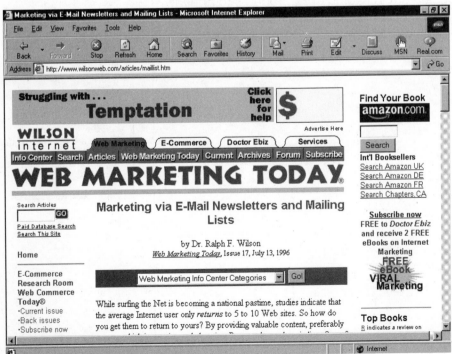

Buzzword

Permission-based marketing, e-mail marketing, and *opt-in marketing* are all terms for the approach of obtaining a visitor's permission to send promotional or informational material to an e-mail address.

- Permission-based marketing, also called **e-mail** or **opt-in** marketing, is based on visitors providing a company with permission to send them marketing or sales messages at their e-mail address. This approach resulted from the generally negative reaction of the online public to unsolicited e-mails and **spam**. Most material sent this way includes an option to have the recipient's name taken off of the list by sending a return e-mail with a message such as "unsubscribe" in the subject line, or by simply clicking on a link and filling out a form.

- An effective marketing device used on the Web Marketing Today site is a pop-up. A pop-up is a window that opens while a visitor is at a site, making some special offer or promoting some product or service. The user must click on a button to close the window. Pop-up windows are often programmed to appear at some point during download or just after a Web page has downloaded to a browser.

eMarketer.com Offers Useful Statistics About the Internet

- Marketing professionals have always valued information about their customers, potential customers, and the competition for their products or services. The Internet offers certain challenges and certain benefits when it comes to this kind of information. Unlike a retail store where you can stand around and observe your customers, notice the predominant age group, gender, and shopping habits, the Internet doesn't provide any in-person contact. However, the Internet is a wonderful information-gathering tool, allowing you to ask customers for information through e-mail and surveys and even observe online shopping habits through several technologies such as cookies (a way to read a record of Web sites a person has visited).

- eMarketer.com is a Web site devoted to compiling statistics on the Internet and how people use it. Knowing the trends of online shopping can help a business target its marketing efforts much more effectively to certain age groups or even types of shoppers. Using this information a company might modify the design or packaging of its products to appeal to its typical buyer, adjust the type of content it places on its site, tailor its marketing messages, and launch e-mail campaigns to targeted mailing lists.

Buzzword

Spam, the electronic equivalent of junk mail, is any unsolicited advertisement sent via e-mail or posted on a newsgroup.

Note

Lists of either street addresses or e-mail addresses can be purchased by companies for mailings. These lists are considered targeted when they contain names of customers with narrowly defined characteristics and have shown a clear interest in a specific area, such as pets or health.

eMarketer.com Home Page

Take a Look at How E-Mail Marketing is Being used by MSN

- So, how does e-mail marketing work? Typically, when you enter a Web site, there are a few ways for the owner of that site to get your permission to e-mail you. One method is to include a checkbox during the sign-up process many sites use to have visitors register. The visitor sees a message that states that unless they check the box (or uncheck it), they will receive promotions and offers via e-mail. Many people don't notice the box or get confused about whether to check it or not. The following figure shows a permission-based e-mail from MSN, with a note before the promotional portion indicating that the recipient opted to receive such offers when visiting 24/7 Media, a partner of MSN.

A Marketing E-mail from MSN

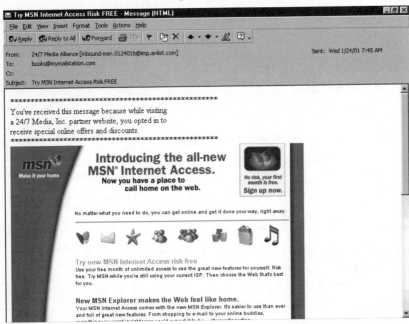

- Marketing e-mails take a variety of forms. The one shown above contains a highly sophisticated HTML document with graphics and a link to a sign-up form. In effect, it is like a magazine advertisement sent online. Other efforts can be as simple as a text-only e-mail introducing some special offer or promotion. A common technique is to include a link within the text to get readers to go to the sender's site, where even more marketing information can be put before them.

IDC.com Uses Newsletters to Reach Online Customers

- IDC is a company that studies trends and sells reports about business and technology. Because they are in the information business, it is only logical that they would use information as a way to drive people to their Web site. IDC sends out several e-mail newsletters on various topics, such as the one about eBusiness trends shown in the figure on the following page. Many online businesses offer some form of free newsletter that visitors can sign up for; when visitors do this, they have given permission to the company to e-mail them, and the user perceives a value to the e-mail.

E-mail Newsletter from IDC.com

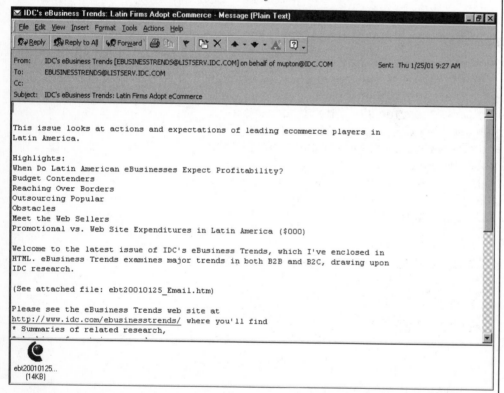

Technical Note
Many online e-mail campaigns including this one from MSN, use LISTSERV, a mailing list management software. LISTSERV handles large mailing lists working on mainframe computers such as UNIX-based servers. Using LISTSERV, a company can scan for subscribe and unsubscribe tagged messages, assembling and modifying lists over time.

- Some e-mail newsletters include the text of the newsletter in the e-mail. Others provide a link to go to a Web site and read the latest newsletter. Still others, such as this one from IDC, attach a newsletter file to the message. Most provide a summary of highlights from the latest newsletter to entice the e-mail recipient to read further.

- One problem with e-mail marketing is that you don't always have control over how polished your e-mail will appear to the reader. That's because different e-mail programs are set up to read certain types of text. An e-mail program such as Outlook from Microsoft, for example, actually accepts messages in three formats: HTML (which can include text formatting, backgrounds, and HTML styles), Rich Text (which does allow text to retain most formatting), and Plain Text. To hit the lowest common denominator of browsers, e-marketers often have to send messages in Plain Text. Plain Text uses a very simple font with no formatting.

Learn About Direct Mail Lists at PostMasterDirect.com

- The mailing list business has been around for many years. Essentially, mailing lists can come from places such as a company database of customers, magazine subscription list, or credit card customer list. Mailing list companies, called brokers, pay for and assemble such lists and sell the use of the lists to companies marketing to potential customers. Mailing list maintenance is very important, because people move, die, or stop certain activities. Therefore list brokers must weed through and update their lists on a regular basis to make them useful and avoid duplicated names coming from several sources.

- Offline mailings carry the cost of purchasing the mailing list, as well as the paper, printing, and postage for each and every item sent. Online, the cost of the list is still there, but the cost of the mailing piece itself may be restricted to paying someone to write the copy or design the HTML layout, as well as the dedicated server time to send thousands of e-mails and deal with bounced-back bad address e-mails. Some companies take all this activity on themselves; PostMasterDirect.com is a typical online list broker business that can handle all aspects of e-mail campaigns for its clients.

PostMasterDirect.com Home Page

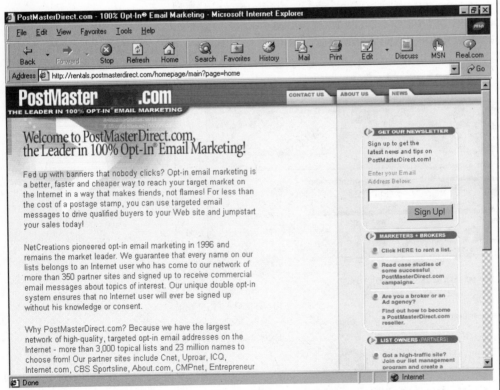

Note
When an e-mail address is no longer valid because a user switched addresses or is simply no longer receiving e-mail, anyone sending a message to that address will have the message bounced back with a note that there is no such address. Companies and brokers involved in online e-mail marketing must constantly update their records to delete such bad addresses.

- When a company sends an offer or promotion using a purchased mailing list, they may or may not have the recipient's permission to send them e-mail. If the list is a well-targeted one, the recipient is likely to have an interest in what the company has to say and may respond to the message. But a company using online direct mail runs the risk of annoying recipients. In fact, the response rate for direct e-mail is about 1.5%, a bit lower than for a printed direct mail piece. That means in a mailing of 100,000 e-mails, only about 1,500 customers will follow-up, and only a percentage of those will actually make a purchase.

E-BUSINESS ANALYSIS

Take a look at each of these sites (full URLs are located at the end of the exercise), then read the site analysis below and answer the questions.

CASE STUDY 1: WILSONWEB.COM

- On this Web site for Web marketers, there are several good examples of Web marketing you can observe. On the home page there is a link for a special offer to receive two free eBooks if you subscribe to one of the site's newsletters. Why should owners of a site give away something just to get people to sign up to receive a free newsletter? Because the value of capturing the name and e-mail address of each visitor is enormous. That information can be exchanged for cash or services from partner sites that use the information to promote their products and services or sold to mailing list brokers. In the case of Doctor Ebiz, which states that it doesn't sell or rents lists of names, the value could come from getting contact names it can promote its other products to.

Web Marketing Today Doctor Ebiz Subscription Page

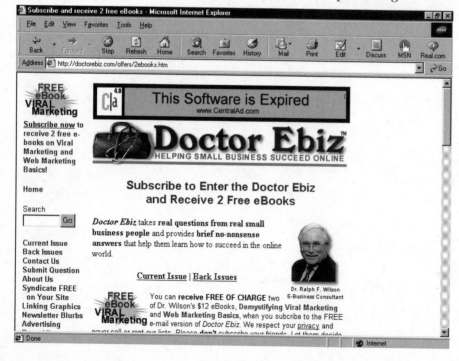

- One important goal of good online marketing is to get a visitor to a site, and keep him or her coming back. You can do that in a variety of ways, including e-mailing people with a link to your site or offering links to your site from another site. Another approach is to try to keep visitors from leaving your site. Wilsonweb.com is set up with several promotional banner ads on the home page. When you click on one of these ads, a window opens taking the visitor to another Web site. By keeping this linked site in a separate window, Wilsonweb.com keeps its own site on the visitor's computer screen. Even if visitors enlarge the partner site window, at some point when they close it, they return to Wilsonweb.com.

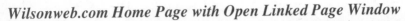

Wilsonweb.com Home Page with Open Linked Page Window

1. What is a mailing list broker?

   _____

2. Does Doctor Ebiz sell or rent lists of subscribers?

   _____

3. What fee-based products or services can you find on Wilsonweb.com?

   _____

CASE STUDY 2: EMARKETER.COM

- eMarketer.com is a Web site that provides statistics on the Internet and its users. The site includes sign-up for free newsletters, as well as features such as eChannels. eChannels are provided for ten different topic areas, including the eMarketing Channel. Note that eMarketer.com offers a combination of free information, such as articles, and information for sale, such as the email Marketing Report at $795. This combination of free content and products or services for sale is a common way to encourage a visitor to explore a site without having to spend money. As he or she spends more time on the site, the hope is that a purchase will eventually be made.

eMarketing Report Page

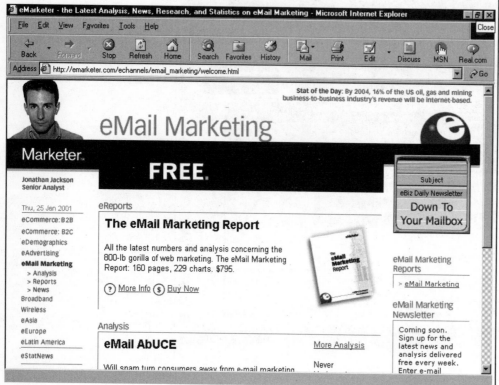

■ eMarketer.com also uses newsletters as a form of permission-based marketing. They have actually targeted several newsletters to those with different interests and let the user know whether the newsletter will arrive in Plain Text or HTML format. The bottom of their subscription form includes a checkbox that is pre-checked. If a subscriber doesn't uncheck this box, they have agreed to get occasional mailings from eMarketer.com. When a visitor provides his or her e-mail address to subscribe, a form asking for optional additional information appears. Although a subscriber doesn't have to provide this information, many will assume they must to complete the subscription process.

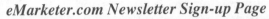

eMarketer.com Newsletter Sign-up Page

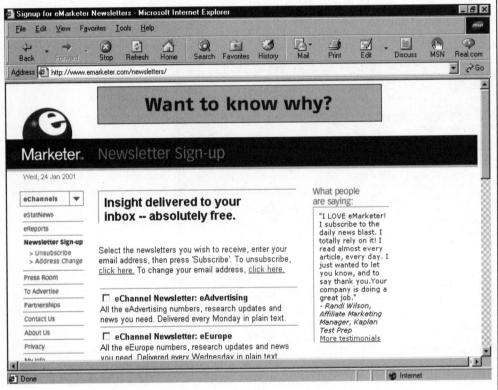

1. What does The email Marketing Report cover?

   _____

2. How can you unsubscribe from a newsletter on the Newsletter Sign-up Page?

   _____

3. Can you change the address to which a newsletter is sent? How?

   _____

CASE STUDY 3: POSTMASTERDIRECT.COM

- PostMasterDirect works with hundreds of online partners to assemble its lists of people who have given permission to get e-mailings; then, it does e-mailings for customers for approximately 30 cents per name. PostMasterDirect.com doesn't give the lists to others; rather it does all the work itself to get customers' mailings out. Notice that PostMasterDirect.com not only manages e-mailings, it also allows individuals to sign up for mailings on specific topics from its site. PostMasterDirect.com maintains a privacy policy for those signing up for mailings; it agrees never to give out their contact information and to send only relevant information to them according to the categories of information they check at sign-up.

PostMasterDirect.com List Member Policy Page

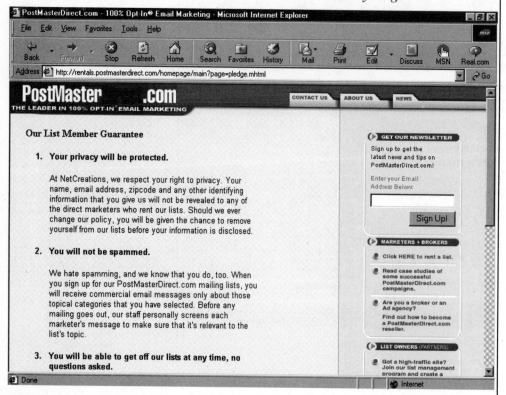

- The sign-up form for receiving mailings from PostMasterDirect.com includes much more than name and address fields. Those signing up provide information about gender, occupation, choice of language, and job function. By providing more information the member can assumedly get much more targeted information from the site. The future of online mailings is probably one where sophisticated programs can take such data and send a female, French-speaking student living in Canada mailings as specific as one from a credit card company written in French offering student credit cards imprinted with designs that might appeal to a woman, rather than a man. The more the online world discovers about us, the more they will know how to offer us exactly the products we will purchase.

PostMasterDirect.com List Member Sign-up Form

Name:	
Email Address:	
URL of your Web Site:	
Work Address:	
City:	
State:	(n/a) ▼
Country:	▼
Zip/Postal Code:	
Language	Of the choices below, which language are you most comfortable with? English ▼
Gender:	Male / Female
Can you receive HTML email?	○ Yes ○ No
Occupation:	WebMaster, Programmer, Technical, Clerical, Administrative, Educator, Business Person, Sales Person, Executive, Investor, Laborer, Student, Unemployed

1. What protects customers against a company changing its privacy policy?

   _____

2. Why is it useful for PostMasterDirect.com to know if a member can receive HTML e-mail?

   _____

3. How can you be removed from their lists once you've signed up?

   _____

http://www.wilsonweb.com/
Web Marketing Today

http://www.emarketer.com
eMarketer.com

http://www.MSN.com
MSN.com

http://www.idc.com/
IDC.com

http://www.postmasterdirect.com
PostMasterDirect.com

Using Links, Portals and Affiliates

- **Learn how portals give one-stop convenience to consumers**
- **Explore how E-Businesses are gaining exposure through affiliate marketing**
- **See how links can provide exposure for your Web business**
- **Discover how vortals bring together enthusiasts**
- **Look at trends in the world of portals**

NOTES

Keyboardmall.com Provides a Portal with a Bit of Everything

- Web portals grew out of what were essentially search engine sites such as Yahoo!. As these sites added links and services that went way beyond their search engine capability, they became the first stop for people accessing the Internet—in effect a door, or **portal**, to all the Internet had to offer. Today traditional search engine sites such as Yahoo and Excite! continue to act as portals, along with Internet service providers such as AOL and MSN, and a wide selection of other sites that offer a broad selection of services.

- Portals such as keyboardmall.com typically include a search engine for locating things online, news services with the latest headlines and links to articles, shopping, and reference materials. In addition, many portals offer free e-mail accounts, a customizable main page, weather reports, and investment portfolio tracking. In short, they have become one-stop access points for Internet users.

Keyboardmall.com Home Page

Buzzword

A *portal* is a Web site that serves as a jumping off point for accessing the Internet. Portals often include a search engine, e-mail accounts, news, weather, and shopping links.

Note

Links, the basis of navigation around the World Wide Web, didn't exist in the beginning of the Internet, but came about with the advent of HTML. The first Web browser, Mosaic, added the navigation control that made popular use of the Internet possible. In the early days of browsers, visitors would be taken to the browser page when they logged on, and browser Web sites continue to be portals of choice for many. Today, however, almost every browser allows users to set any page they wish as their home page (the page that appears by default everytime they log on).

Affiliate Marketing Offers Exposure and Profit at Commission Junction

- Affiliate marketing is a commission-based marketing scheme. In this form of marketing, Web sites form a partnership: Site A accepts an ad or link from Site B, becoming an affiliate. Payment for the ad is based on how many visitors actually come to Site B by following the link on Site A (called a click-through). In some cases payment is tied not only to click-throughs, but to how many purchases are made by people coming to Site B via the link on Site A. Using tracking software, a record is kept of the number of visits and purchases that result from use of the affiliate link. Affiliate marketing is therefore a source of exposure for Site B and a source of income for Site A. Affiliate marketing works best when the links placed on a site appeal to that site's visitors. Therefore a site dedicated to home improvement might be most successful with links to sites that deal with home financing or discount lighting fixtures.

- Some people are more successful with affiliate marketing than others: some smaller Web site owners hope to make big money with the system, only to be disappointed. That's because the key to success with affiliate marketing is to have a site that experiences a great deal of traffic to begin with: if no one visits your site, no one will click through to an affiliated site. As the affiliate marketing industry has grown, services such as Commission Junction have sprung up to manage the process for companies and help them maximize their income from affiliate marketing. These services connect sites with potential affiliates, and deal with the commission accounting and payments.

Note

Lists of either street addresses or e-mail addresses can be purchased by companies for mailings. These lists are considered targeted when they contain names of customers with narrowly defined characteristics and have shown a clear interest in a specific area, such as pets or health.

Commission Junction Home Page

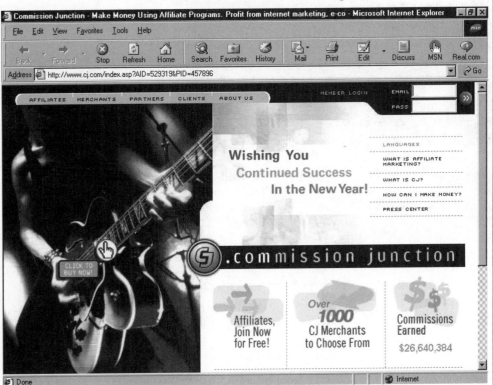

- One key to setting up an effective affiliate marketing program is the software that is used to track and report on activity. Several products have appeared on the market. This type of software can keep track of the number of visitors to a site using a simple counter program, but it can also track what site a visitor has just come from using **cookie** files that record information about Web activity on a user's hard drive. Reports tally the most frequent click-through sites and often interface with accounting programs such as Quicken to manage the affiliate payments.

Automating Links at Links4trade.com

- Many E-Businesses have found that one of the best ways to drive traffic to their sites is by placing links on other sites. When two sites agree to place each other's links on their sites, this is called a reciprocal link. In some cases, companies contact other companies and ask to place a link on their site. On some sites there is a form you can submit to request a link. There are also companies such as Links4trade.com that automate this process for you.

Links4trade.com Home Page

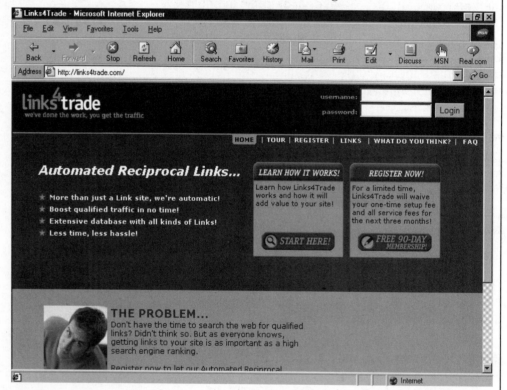

- This exchanging of links has a few benefits for a business. Placing a link to your site on another site gets you more visitors and more visitors can result in sales. In addition, placing an ad or link to a site that complements your visitors' interests can add value to your site as a jumping off point for many areas of interest.

Pet Hobbyist Brings Together Animal Lovers at its Vortal Site

n Where a portal provides a wide array of information and links, a vortal, or vertical portal, provides information and links related to a particular interest. Sites such as PetHobbyist.com offer news, links to businesses,

Buzzword
A *cookie* is a file stored on a user's hard drive that records information about his online activities.

Technical Note
An image link is very similar, except that you need to specify the image file you want the visitor to click on. Links can be created to another page on your own Web site, or to Web pages on another site. It's a good idea to verify links you place on your own site on a regular basis, to ensure that they lead to real addresses and useful information.

forums for discussions, and more, all related to a particular topic. Vortals have also become full-service environments, offering personal finance tools, e-mail accounts, and weather updates alongside their topic-focused content. It's often more effective for a business to target its links in a vortal because the visitor audience is much more narrowly defined than in a general portal.

PetHobbyist.com

- The face of vortals is changing. One current trend is for larger portals to split themselves into vortal segments. For example, About.com highlights 700 vertical areas of interest from within its portal. Some newer vortals are aimed not at interest areas such as pets or gardening, but at communities. For example, iVillage.com is aimed towards women, and zenzibar.com is a portal for alternative cultures (vs. mainstream Western culture).

- Businesses are also coming together in online communities. Enterprise resource and corporate portals are springing up to give company employees a home online where everything about their company can be found in one place. These portals live on company intranets, in-house Web sites for employee use. Typically firewalls are built around an intranet to keep the general public from accessing it.

Traffick.com Touts Itself as "The Portal Portal"

- There are now so many portals, vortals, and corporate portals out there that it's sometimes hard to keep track of them. One site, Traffick.com, is a portal that's all about portals. For E-Businesses that want to develop a logical marketing strategy using links or ads on portals, this site can be a helpful tool.

Note
Traffick.com is also launching a Web site for information about vortals. You'll find this site at verticalmatters.com.

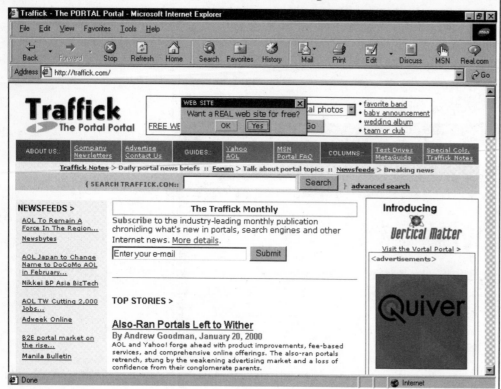

- It's sometimes hard to understand just who is running the content on a portal because Internet partnerships are so complex. Mindspring and Earthlink, ISPs who merged recently, have partnered with Lycos for content. Still, the Lycos search engine maintains its own portal. Some companies are both ISPs and portals, while some browsers such as Netscape also offer a portal to users. Content provider AOL offers Internet access and some member-specific sites, as well as a portal for the general public. In the footsteps of B2B (business-to-business) activity, we are currently seeing P2P (portal-to-portal) activity that has portals striking up relationships with each other that will conceivably make it even more difficult for users to know who they're dealing with.

- One trend in technology that will have an impact on portals in the near future is personalization. Just as many portals allow a visitor to build his or her own customized portal page, placing the news publications and local weather of his choice in one place, the day is coming when Web users will be able to pick and choose content from various portals and Web sites, in essence building their own personal portal. Personalization requires that Web sites become more modular in the way they are structured so that visitors can pick up individual elements of a Web site and move them (or a link to them) to their own page. Some of the largest portals such as Yahoo! have begun to modularize their Web sites in preparation for this change.

E-BUSINESS ANALYSIS

> *Take a look at each of these sites (full URLs are located at the end of the exercise), then read the site analysis below and answer the questions.*

CASE STUDY 1: KEYBOARDMALL.COM

■ Keyboardmall.com is typical of a general interest portal (sometimes called a horizontal portal). On its home page visitors can select a category such as Books & Music, Gifts & Shopping, or Lifestyles. Within each category is a list of more categories; for example, in the Lifestyle category you can choose to look at Home & Garden related items. On the Home & Garden page, items link the visitor to other sites, such as MarthaStewart.com. In addition, advertisements for various products and companies appear on every page of the portal, providing another way for visitors to click through to another location on the Web.

Keyboardmall.com Directory of Lifestyles Links

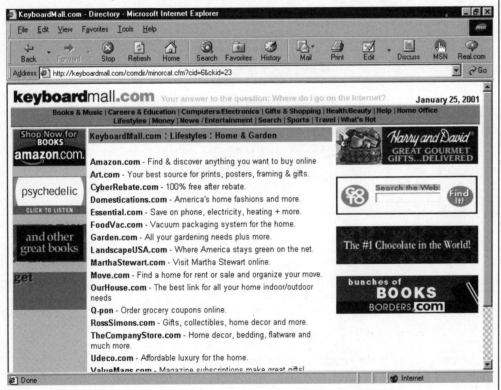

277

- If you use the Search link on the keyboardmall.com site, you are taken to a page that allows you to narrow your search by selecting one of five categories: companies, jobs, people, an Internet Search (that is, a broader search outside of the keyboardmall.com site), and everything else. Portals typically offer a choice of searching methods, including one to search their own site and one to go out on the Internet. Many partner with major search engines to offer search capabilities to their visitors. Keyboardmall.com offers five different search engines: About.com, Ah-ha.com, AtNetWorld.com, FindWhat.com, and TheBestPlacetoSearch.com. Being able to find what you want either on a portal or on the Internet is one of the most important factors for portal loyalty.

Keyboardmall.com Search Page

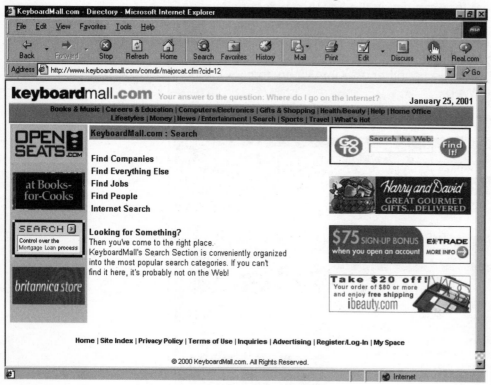

1. What kinds of products does Udeco.com offer?

   _____

2. Identify three links to other companies on the Keyboardmall.com home page.

   _____

3. What search category would you look under to find classified employment ads?

   _____

CASE STUDY 2: PETHOBBYIST.COM

- As a vertical portal, pethobbyist.com caters to pet lovers through its various sections such as DogHobbyist and CatHobbyist. In essence, this vortal starts with a segment, pet lovers, and further narrows it down with these specific species pages that can be accessed with their own domain names or through the PetHobbyist site. Notice that individual interest pages such as DogHobbyist also contain small ads for other PetHobbyist areas to encourage traffic around the site. Also note that, as with many vortals, PetHobbyist.com offers chats and forums to visitors, because visitors share common interests they might want to discuss online. Another interesting feature of the pages on this site is the translation feature: the pages can be viewed in English, Spanish, German, Italian, Portuguese, or French. This is in keeping with the site's claim to be building a global online pet community.

DogHobbyist Page

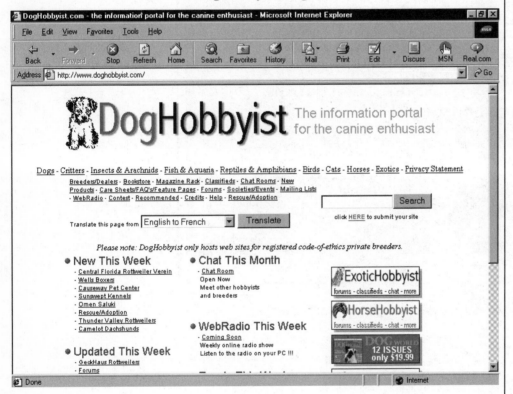

- Pet Hobbyist also includes an Animal Talk Radio area. This page provides a link to the Animal Talk Web site, but it also makes several shows available without leaving PetHobbyist.com. These shows can be run using a Java applet and an audio player plug-in. On the Animal Talk Radio page of Pet Hobbyist there is both a graphic and text link to the Pet Warehouse Network, which sponsors Animal Talk. Perhaps as part of their reciprocal relationship, PetHobbyist.com has an ad under the Cool Links section of Pet Warehouse Network.

Animal Talk Radio Page of PetHobbyist.com

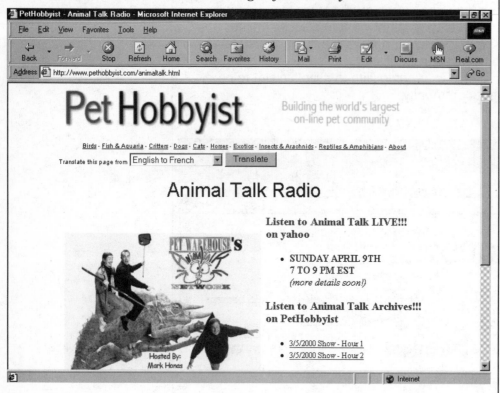

1. What areas of Pet Hobbyist could you visit to get publications on pets?

   _____

2. What is an arachnid?

   _____

3. How is Yahoo! involved in listening to Animal Talk Radio from this site?

   _____

CASE STUDY 3: TRAFFICK.COM

- One of the features Traffick.com offers is TraffickFavorites. This is a set up that lets you access your bookmarked and favorite sites, e-mail address book, files, and documents from any computer. Many portals emphasize the value of using them for e-mail and other functions, because you can access their Web site from anywhere. Some content service providers such as AOL require that you have their software loaded to access their member site, which can cause a problem if you are using someone else's computer. However today those providers also maintain portal sites available to anyone from anywhere.

Traffick.com TraffickFavorites Page

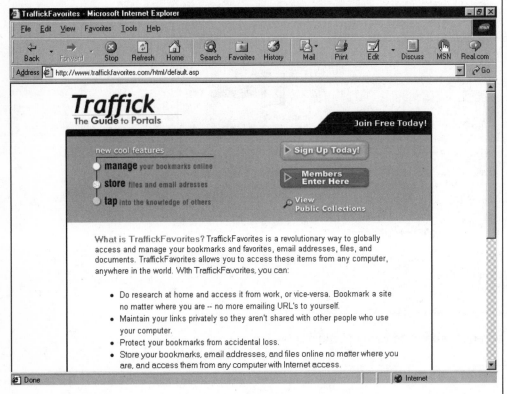

- As a portal about portals, Traffick.com helps you to follow current news on major portals including AOL, MSN, and Yahoo!. Their page about AOL.com is typical. In addition to current AOL news stories, this page gives you access to a forum of comments about AOL, company links, investor information, and a history of AOL. Note that the AOL page includes a link so you can go directly to AOL Anywhere (AOL.com). Information about other, smaller portals can be found in a variety of ways: by reading columns, searching directories of categories such as MegaSearch Sites and Web Browsers, and reviewing articles in the Vertical Portals area of the site.

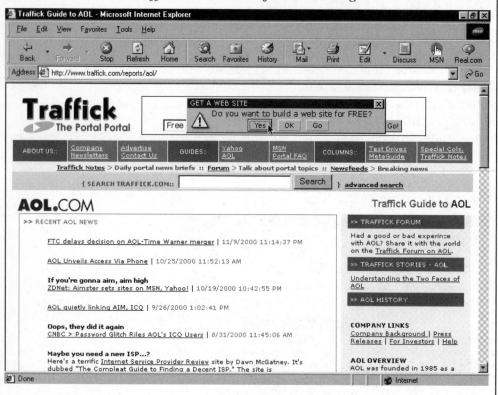

1. What items does TraffickFavorites help you access?

   _____

2. What year was AOL founded?

   _____

3. What features does the advanced search feature of Traffick.com include?

   _____

http://keyboardmall.com/
Keyboardmall.com

http://www.cj.com
Commission Junction

http://links4trade.com
Links4trade.com

http://www.pethobbyist.com/
PetHobbyist.com

http://traffick.com
Traffick.com

<table>
<tr>
<td>

Theme

24

</td>
<td>

Advertising Online
- ■ **See how the online advertising profession is growing**
- ■ **View TV ads online**
- ■ **Learn about M-Commerce and wireless advertising**
- ■ **Discover how E-Business tracks advertising effectiveness**
- ■ **Explore a museum of banner advertising**

</td>
</tr>
</table>

NOTES

Visit the Internet Advertising Bureau to See How the Online Advertising Community is Growing

- ■ Like many areas of E-Commerce, advertising on the Internet is a new and evolving discipline. It is based to a great extent on advertising in a variety of other media, such as print, TV, and radio, because the same tools of text, video, and sound are all available online. But the big difference in advertising in any medium is understanding how people use that medium. How long do people stay on a particular Web page? What kinds of ads running across the top of a Web site (called **banner ads**) catch people's attention as they browse? How frequently should the ad at the top of a page change or run an animated sequence?

- ■ Web advertising professionals who gather on sites such as the Internet Advertising Bureau to learn new tricks are refining online advertising to target people browsing the Web most effectively. The online advertising industry, through organizations such as the IAB, is also working to establish standards in areas such as privacy and spamming. Because no government agency currently controls online content as the FCC does for radio, the industry must monitor its own growth.

Buzzword

A banner ad is an advertisement for another site that runs across the top of a Web page. A *meta ad* is an ad that appears on a search engine, related to a search topic entered by the visitor.

Internet Advertising Bureau Page

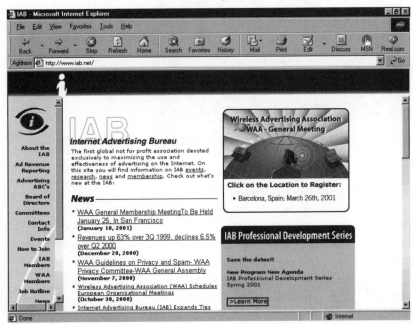

283

- There are different kinds of online ads today. Banner ads, which were simple text and graphic ads originally, now use animated sequences or even video to catch the visitor's eye. Meta ads are ads that appear in search engines related to the keyword of a visitor's search. Because the ad that appears is relevant to the search topic, it is likely to be of interest to the visitor. Not all banner and meta ads appear at the top of a Web page, but because that is the part of a page most people are sure to see if they visit a site, it is the most popular placement.

McDonald's Offers its Own TV Ads to Online Viewers

- Most online advertising is placed on a site other than the advertiser's own, because the goal of most Internet advertising is to draw visitors to the advertiser's site. However, many companies place ads for their own products, or other divisions of their company, on their Web sites as well. McDonald's UK has a very interesting Web site, which includes an area where you can view popular television ads for McDonald's. People can play these ads on their computers using Quicktime software, which can be downloaded from the site. As television and the Internet inch closer to each other through products such as WebTV, we may see more of this crossover of media in advertising.

McDonald's UK TV Ad Page

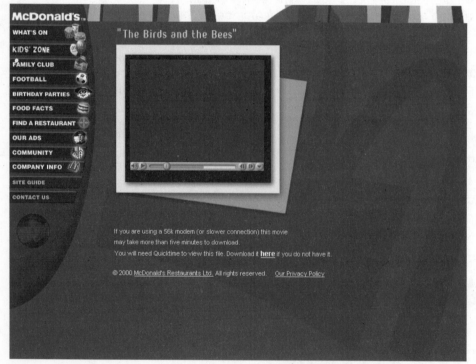

- Other kinds of advertising are evolving online. **Interstitial** ads appear in a separate window while you're waiting for a Web page to appear. These ads often use streaming video to handle larger graphics more efficiently. Although interstitial ads tend to be more successful than banner ads, many people are annoyed by them because they feel they slow down their online experience. **Superstitial** is a recently developed format of interactive ad that can be any size and utilize animation, sound, and graphics. The benefit of superstitial ads is that they don't have as great an impact on a Web site's performance.

M-CommerceWorld.com Opens up the World of Wireless Advertising

- The big news in Internet advertising today is wireless advertising targeted towards the M-Commerce audience. M-Commerce stands for mobile-commerce, which is the universe of wireless devices, such as pagers, cell phones, and portable digital assistants that have become popular in recent years. Because these devices can now access the Internet, they have opened up a whole new way for advertisers to reach consumers.

- At the moment what can be put in front of wireless consumers is somewhat limited. They can read e-mails online and browse certain Web sites. In fact, e-mail advertising campaigns directed towards wireless users have become very hot in the advertising world. It's important to understand that there is a combination of 'pull' and 'push' efforts going on in all Internet and wireless advertising. Push is when an advertiser sends an unrequested ad to a recipient; pull is when someone using a wireless device requests information, say the location of the nearest bookstore.

- m-CommerceWorld.com gives a good overview of what's going on today in mobile/wireless computing. They provide good explanations of dozens of technology buzzwords that are tossed around, including the technology of G3 (a new mobile platform from Motorola) and WAP, the wireless application programming language used to build programs for wireless devices.

m-CommerceWorld.com Home Page

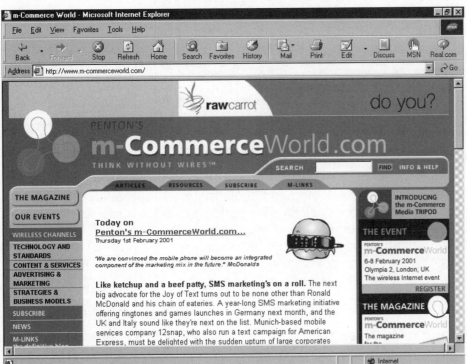

DoubleClick.net Helps Companies Strategize and Track the Effectiveness of Their Online Advertising

- Companies such as DoubleClick are producing software solutions to support the online advertising world. Software exists to help companies organize their ad placement, coordinate online e-mail campaigns, and, perhaps most importantly, to track the effectiveness of their advertising. Companies such as DoubleClick also offer advertising services, consulting on advertising strategies, and media buying. Media buying is a traditional advertising agency function where the agency coordinates the purchase of advertising space for a company for a commission.

DoubleClick.net Home Page

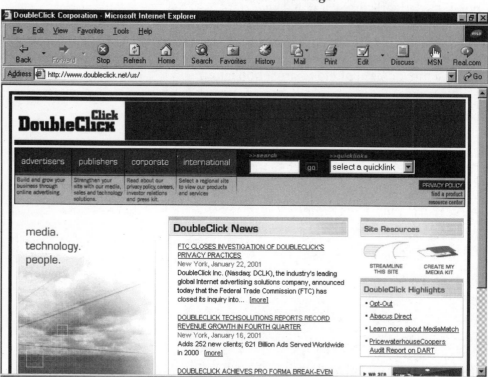

- Using tracking technologies it is possible to track the number of visitors who click on a particular ad, and what post-click activity they perform—for example, whether their click-through to a site from an ad results in a sale. By monitoring the activity from each ad a business places, a company can modify its advertising strategy. It can stop advertising on sites that provide few results, and increase its advertising efforts on the types of sites that seem to provide a better payback.

Visit a Virtual Museum at BannerAdMuseum.com

- Although banner ads are currently lessening in effectiveness and being replaced by new styles of advertising, they still form the backbone of Internet advertising campaigns for many businesses. If you thought banner ads were just annoying distractions from the true Internet experience, you'll have to develop a real appreciation for them. One way to do that is to visit the Banner Ad Museum, where banner ads that have proven most effective in terms of viewer click-through are displayed. The site contains galleries of ads by categories, such as Food/Beverage or

Technical Note

Software that tracks and automatically rotates the banner ads used on various sites is called ad serving software. The technology used can vary depending on the type of ad and others issues, such as browser technology. However most ad serving software deals with regenerating the ad code on a page based on how often the ad is viewed; this is likely to involve both JavaScript and HTML code.

Fashion, as well as galleries by type of media, such as Flash Animation or Java Ads. You can even find banner ads here that involve celebrities.

BannerAdMuseum.com Food/Beverage Ad Page

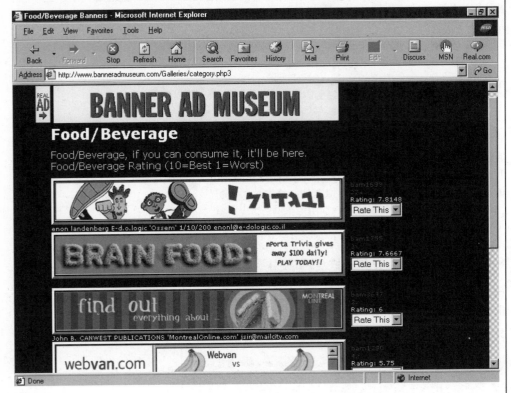

- Banner ads must be well designed to fulfill their key functions. They must promote brand identity of a business or site, deliver some kind of message that either informs or simply intrigues the visitor, and—the most important goal of all—the ad must entice a visitor to click it and go to another site. Accomplishing all this in such a small space is not a simple task. In addition, although banner ads can use animation to display a series of messages, a visitor must stay on a site long enough to view the entire message, which isn't always the case.

Technical Note
A banner ad is essentially a graphic linked to the URL of the advertising company. Banner ads typically employ animated GIF images, although more sophisticated ads use Macromedia Flash or other forms of animation. Many sites limit the file size of a banner ad graphic to 12K to 16K so that its download doesn't greatly impact the performance of the Web page visitors are viewing.

E-Business Analysis

> *Take a look at each of these sites (full URLs are located at the end of the exercise), then read the site analysis below and answer the questions.*

SITE 1: MCDONALDS.CO.UK

■ McDonald's Web site for the United Kingdom is a fun place, full of animations, sound effects, and interesting graphics. The home page is a good example. The page is essentially a virtual McDonald's, which you enter by 'walking through' a set of sliding doors. When you place your mouse over any of the items on the menu on the left side of the page, different areas of the screen are highlighted with explanations of what you'll find in that topic. For example, when you pass your mouse over the Football item, the man standing at the counter holding a soccer ball (British football) is highlighted, and when you move your mouse over birthday parties, the McDonald's employee holding a birthday cake for the two children becomes brightly colored. This is all accompanied by clicking and swooshing sounds that make the site come alive.

McDonalds.co.uk Home Page

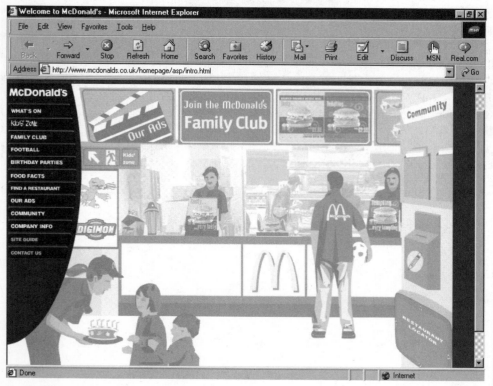

- Subtler forms of advertising on this site include the Kids' Zone. This area offers information on toys offered in the current month as giveaways with Happy Meals, encouraging children to go to McDonald's to eat. The Kids Zone also offers games, a coloring competition, and a feature to send an online card to a friend. The Send a Card feature is another clever advertising gimmick: it lets the kids visiting the site send an e-mail to a friend; that e-mail not only sports part of the McDonald's logo, it has a link at the top to go to the McDonald's restaurant site.

McDonald's Kids' Zone Page

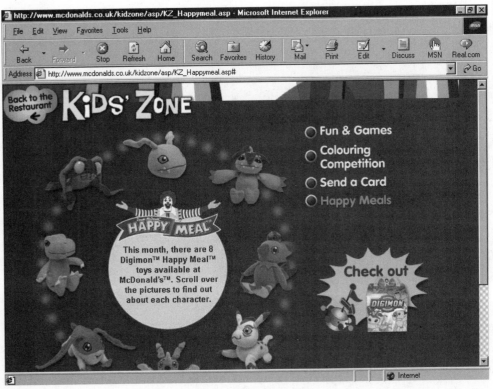

1. What plug-in is needed to play the McDonald's TV ads on their Web site?

   _____

2. What image is highlighted when you place your mouse over the Kids' Zone item on the home page?

   _____

3. What toys are available this month with Happy Meals?

   _____

SITE 2: DOUBLECLICK.COM

■ DoubleClick.com is a company that helps companies coordinate their online advertising efforts. An interesting feature of their site is their personalized media kit, which is essentially a shopping cart that you can place Web page documents in. When you go to any page on this site you can click on the Add to My Media Kit icon, and that page is added to your Media Kit. A Media Kit window appears, showing you the pages you've included. This is a handy way for a visitor to an information-rich site to gather the pages he or she would like to view again or print.

DoubleClick.com Media Kit Page

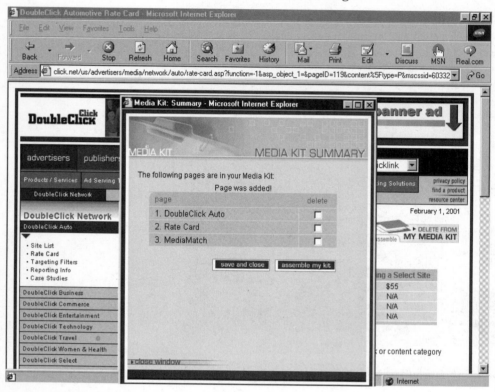

- An interesting feature of the DoubleClick site is called streamlining. By answering some questions about your business interests, you can streamline the site—that is, remove pages that don't pertain to you and move around the site more quickly and easily. DoubleClick.com also features case studies of some of their advertising clients. The case studies are interesting in that they lay out the client's objective and describe what the campaign consisted of in detail. They also show results of the campaign and include comments from the customer. This is a good way to see the various components of a typical media campaign. Some of the case studies also include images of actual ads created for clients.

DoubleClick.com Case Study Page

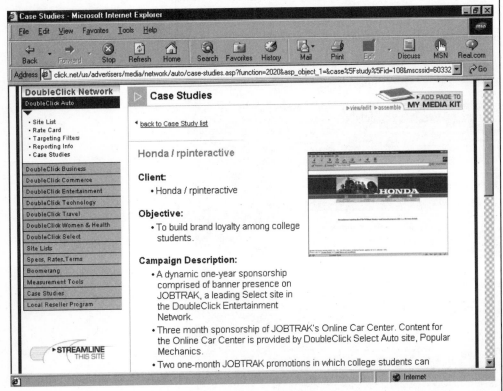

1. How can you delete a page from a Media Kit?

   _____

2. What is the advertiser's objective in the most current featured case study you can find on DoubleClick.com?

   _____

3. How many different types of advertising/promotion can you identify in the Honda campaign?

   _____

SITE 3: BANNERADMUSEUM.COM

- The Banner Ad Museum is devoted to assembling hundreds of banner ads. They include a feature that allows you to view the top ten banners viewed in the previous month. This listing is compiled by Nielsen, the ratings company and includes only U.S. users ratings top banners viewed at home and at work. All the banners displayed both in the Nielsen window and elsewhere in the Banner Ad Museum are fully active, with functional animations. When you view banners in the galleries on this site, you can also provide your own rating on a scale of 1 to 10 from a pop-up list.

BannerAdMuseum.com Top 10 Banners Page

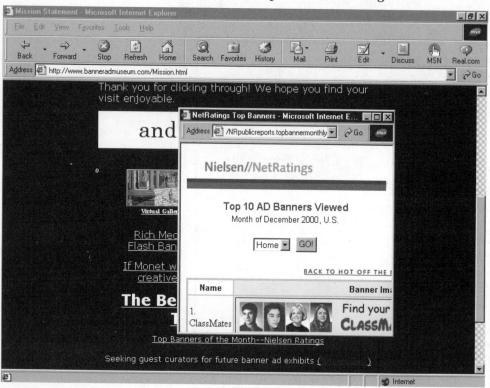

- One more interesting feature on this site shows how various artists' banner ads might look if they were alive today. Click on the "If Monet Were a Creative..." link on the site home page to view these whimsical banner depictions. The Banner Ad Museum also offers a feature that allows you to view your own banner ad as it would appear on various search engines such as Yahoo! or Webcrawler. To use the feature you have to have a graphics file available, which could be any photograph. If you want to test the feature, you can use any image and see it displayed in a typical search engine interface.

BannerAdMuseum.com Your Banner Here! Page

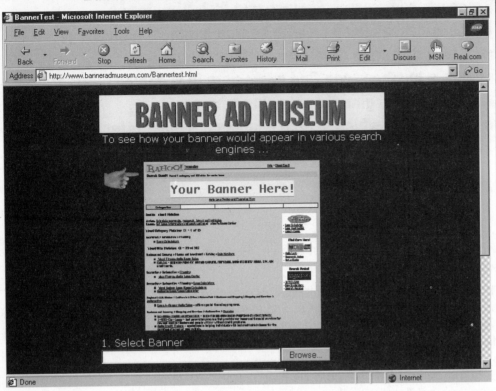

1. Can you identify any common characteristics of the top 10 banner ads in the Nielsen rating feature?

   _____

2. How do work and home categories of top 10 sites differ?

   _____

3. What is the smallest standard size of a banner, according to the banner standards outlined on this site?

   _____

http://www.iab.net
Internet Advertising Bureau
http://www.mcdonalds.co.uk/
McDonald's UK
http://www.m-commerceworld.com/
m-CommerceWorld.com
http://www.doubleclick.net
DoubleClick.net
http://www.banneradmuseum.com/
BannerAdMuseum.com

293

Gaining Exposure from Search Engines and Web Directories

■ Learn how businesses keep up with search engines' technology
■ See how a Web directory organizes listings for visitors
■ Examine how a business can find customers in shopping directories
■ Visit a metasearch engine that is going wireless
■ Get the low-down on which search engines are most effective

NOTES

Search Engine Guide Offers Advice and Information on Search Engine Use for Businesses

■ Search engines provide the avenue by which most Internet visitors find Web sites and information. A search engine is simply an application that uses search tools to locate HTML documents online. Any business can add a search engine to its site, either limited to searching the site itself or capable of searching the entire Web or both. Search sites come in various forms, such as metasearch engines that compile results from several search databases, shopping directories that gather businesses together by their type of product or service, and portals that gather information and links about a particular area of interest.

■ With the profusion of search sites today, it's difficult for both consumers and businesses to know which will provide them with the most value. For a consumer a good search site is one that targets the type of results that prove useful to them; for example some sites weed out non-business-related results which might be helpful for business searchers. For an e-business, it's important to get listed on as many sites as possible, but some sites match a business's customer demographic better than others. Sites such as Search Engine Guide help both consumers and businesses to understand how to find the best search engine solutions and keep current on search engine technology.

Note
In many cases, several search engines are actually based on the same search database. For example, Inktomi, one of the largest search data providers, actually supports six search sites: AOL, Answers, iWon, MSN, HotBot, and Yahoo!. Even so, studies show there is little overlap in search results returned on these sites.

SearchEngineGuide.com Home Page

- Although traditionally search engines search the Web for HTML files by looking for metatag keywords within the documents, new search methods are in development. Google.com has just introduced PDF file searching. PDF files are files saved in the Adobe Acrobat document reader software format. PDF files are more complex to search than HTML files, and they can also be huge documents compared to the typical single-page HTML document. This new capability makes a great deal of material, and especially academic research papers, available to Web visitors. PDF search capability could be used by companies to make white papers accessible to customers without converting them to HTML format.

Web Directories Such as Looksmart.com Offer Information in Categories to Organize the Searching Experience

- Many Web sites have tried to take the basic search engine functionality and add a layer of order to it by placing listings in categories, such as Computing, Shopping, or People. Visitors to sites such as Looksmart.com can drill down through several pages of categories to find information the site has included for that topic, or use the search feature to search the entire Web through one or more Web database. Looksmart editors compile the categories of listings from among those companies in their databases.

295

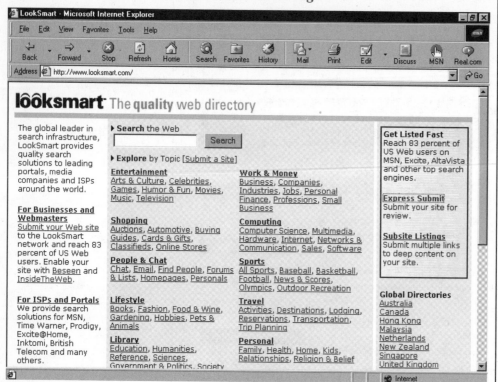

Note
Search engines look for sites by keyword. When a visitor enters a search term, words contained in that term are matched to keywords embedded in the source code on sites.

■ Businesses can submit their names to be included in search databases, usually by simply clicking on a submission link on a Web site and entering information. Most major sites charge a fee for this. In many cases there is overlap among search sites, so a business needs to keep good track of its search engine submissions. For example on Looksmart, if you submit your name you will then be listed in search results on Microsoft's MSN, Excite@Home, Netscape Netcenter, AltaVista, Time Warner, Sony, British Telecom, Road Runner, Prodigy, US West, NetZero, and more than 370 Internet service providers. Centralized search engine listing services such as Searchleap allow you to make multiple submissions at once. These services also help you to understand how sites index their databases and what criteria they use for their searches. Armed with this information you can optimize your keyword strategy, adding keywords to your site that are most likely to be found by major search engines.

■ You can use search engines to help you stay competitive. If you want to see what links your competitors have to their sites, you can do so by going to any search engine and entering link:www.X.com, where X is your competitor's name. You'll get a list of all the sites in that search engine's database that have links to the competition's site.

MySimon.com Organizes Business Listings in an Online Shopping Mall

■ In addition to general search sites, you can benefit from being included in shopping directories, such as MySimon.com. These sites are often used by Web visitors as a centralized location to find a variety of products and services. They can search the site for products or categories of merchandise or they can visit shopping departments. Advertising in specific shopping departments of these malls is a good way to find people who are already looking for your type of product and get them to jump to your site.

MySimon.com Home Page

- Shopping mall sites offer a variety of promotional opportunities. You can get your business included in special shopping guides that advise people about things like buying wedding merchandise and services. Businesses can also offer special promotions or price specials on these sites, or get a product review either from the site editors or visitors to the site. Editorial reviews are basically never negative; customer reviews might contain negative comments, though, so be sure to check in regularly. If you spot a negative customer comment, it's a good business practice to have your customer service department contact that person and solve the problem so the comment might be modified or withdrawn at some point.

- Some search engines use what's referred to as concept searching. Rather than searching strictly by keywords, these engines look for clusters of words in documents. Essentially using various programming techniques, these engines analyze how frequently a word in the search string is used and how often words related to that topic appear near each other. The search engine then concludes that the document is about the requested topic, even if that term isn't specifically used as a keyword. Different engines take different approaches to clustering, but essentially, they attempt to return results based on words in context. A document with the word bridge surrounded by terms such as engineering, structure, and roadway, would be returned in a search for "...suspension bridge." A document with the word bridge surrounded by terms such as dentist, teeth, and mouth, wouldn't.

Metasearch Site Dogpile.com Fetches Wireless Customers

- Dogpile.com is one of the many metasearch engines available, meaning that it returns results from several databases at once for each search. Dogpile offers some refined searching tools. For example, if you want to search for stores in a specific geographical region you can. You can limit searches to business-oriented sites, or search for MP3 or image files. Like several other search engines, Dogpile has also entered the wireless world, connecting its search features to wireless devices such as pagers and cell phones. In addition, it is entering the world of broadband access: this would include cable modems and TV Internet access.

Dogpile.com Home Page

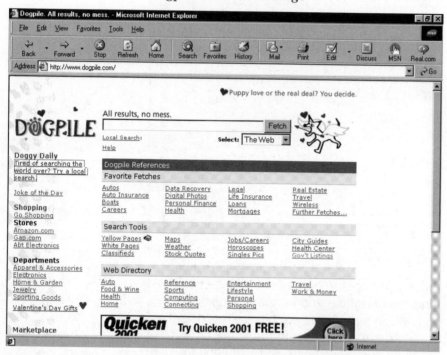

- Search engines are aggressively courting the wireless device market, offering localized content to customers. Localized content offers up information about businesses in the geographical area of the wireless user. So, if you're in Cheyenne, Wyoming with your cell phone you could get a list of local motels, and if you fly over to Miami you can set up your device to get a list of hot Cuban restaurants, Florida style, of course. This offers an essentially an on-the-spot shopping guide that businesses can be part of to influence customer offline buying at the moment of choice. Other devices on the horizon such as a recently introduced refrigerator with Internet access suggest opportunities for gourmet food sites and cookbook publishers.

- Currently, wireless devices are limited by the space they have to display information and the speed of access, which is in some cases as slow as 9.6 or 14.4 kbps. Most still use a monochrome screen, making it difficult to read any kind of detailed information. Most search engines that are available to wireless users offer more limited options than a full search site accessed via a computer. But with increases in speed, the ability to deliver media, such as video, and improvements in screen quality, businesses should look to wireless as an excellent way to reach customers anywhere they go.

SearchEngineShowdown.com Provides In-Depth Analysis of Various Search Engines

- So how does a business know whether one search engine offers advantages over others? Sites such as SearchEngineShowdown.com offer analyses and information about major search engines, with useful comparison charts on their traffic and the accuracy of their search results. In addition, this site offers current news about search engines and changes in their technologies and services.

SearchEngineShowdown.com Home Page

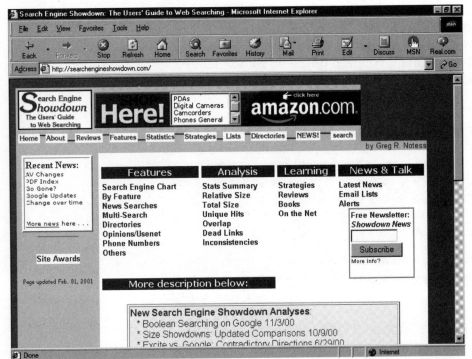

- Search engines aren't all equal. Besides qualifying a search engine by how large its search database is and how many bad links it returns, businesses should be aware of how search engines index their results. For example, Search Engine Showdown provides information on how search engines locate information. Some sites, for example, can return results based on proximity, or how close within a document two terms in a search string are to each other. Others can use truncation or stemming to find portions of or variations on a search term. Although most search engines sort results by their relevance to the search term based on whatever algorithm (mathematical formula) they apply, some will sort results by date, alphabetically, or by the URL of the Web sites.

- The reality for businesses is that getting listed on a search engine is like the old maxim about publicity: even bad listings are good. You should get your business on every search engine you can, because if a visitor turns up your name in a search, he or she might visit your site. But if a business is going to consider advertising or getting some other promotional exposure on a search site, choosing a site that relates to your customer demographic and that offers superior searching with few dead links in the results is a better use of your time and money. Sites such as SearchEngineShowdown.com help businesses understand the real differences underlying search sites.

E-business Analysis

Take a look at each of these sites (full URLs are located at the end of the exercise), then read the site analysis below and answer the questions.

CASE STUDY 1: LOOKSMART.COM

- Looksmart.com is a Web directory with solid search capabilities. The site claims to reach 83% of Internet users in the United States. Looksmart.com currently includes 31 directories covering 13 languages. When you list your site with Looksmart, you also get listed with MSN, excite, AltaVista, iWon, and CNN.com. Getting a site listing with such search engines involves a fee and an approval process. If a business wishes to submit a site to Looksmart, there are a few choices at a few price levels. The site offers an Express Submit feature to submit one URL and have it reviewed for approval within two days. A business can also submit multiple URLs; this is useful for a company that might maintain Web pages for different divisions or a corporate home site and a shopping site, for example. There is also a Basic Submit option; with this option you get a response to your submission in 8 weeks. This submission choice is about $100 less than the cost of Express Submit.

Looksmart Submit a Site Page

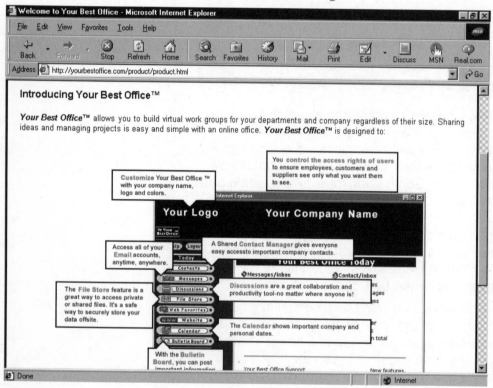

- Looksmart offers a service to Web sites called Beseen.com. This area includes tools to create home pages and a banner ad exchange, as well as a domain name registration feature. In addition, there are applications you can use to include features on your site, such as a chat room, a hit counter, and a search box. If you want Beseen.com to be offered to visitors on your site, you can click on Link to Looksmart's Beseen at the bottom of this page. When you do, you're instructed to copy the HTML code for the button of your choice and place it in your page's source code. This places the button link to Beseen.com on your Web site.

Looksmart's Beseen.com Page

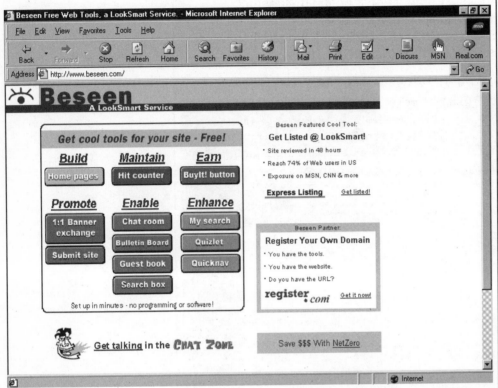

1. What portals will you be listed in the search results of if you list yourself with Looksmart.com?

   _____

2. What is the cost of Express Submit?

   _____

3. What does it cost to use the Beseen.com Hit counter on your site?

   _____

CASE STUDY 2: SEARCHENGINESHOWDOWN.COM

■ Search Engine Showdown has detailed comparisons of search engine features. One category it reports on is the way in which each site deals with Boolean search parameters. Boolean refers to a value that rates some condition of data as true or false. Using that basic premise, you can have qualifiers such as *and*, *not*, and *or*. For example, if the search term New York is entered in a search engine, that engine might look for documents where New *plus* York exist (which is a true value); or, it might also look for documents where New *or* York exist. Users of search engines can use these Boolean parameters to define their search. However, not all search engines allow users to use all of the possible Boolean terms. SearchEngineShowdown.com includes a table showing you which Boolean terms each major search engine allows.

Search Engine Showdown Features Chart Page

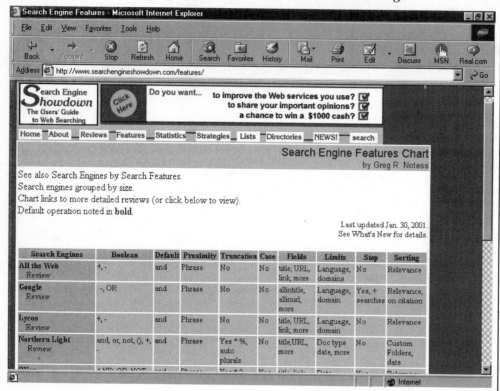

■ SearchEngineShowdown.com also provides in-depth search site reviews outlining the databases the site searches, as well as the strengths and weaknesses of the site (such as how often its data records are updated). These reviews also explain the method of searching used, including what Boolean operators are allowed and whether the site allows for truncation, proximity searching, or case sensitive searches. Reviews also note how many languages a particular site can search by. If you run a business that exports goods to South American countries, you might use these reviews to find a site to advertise on that includes Spanish, German, and Portuguese in its language list.

Searchengineshowdown.com Review Page

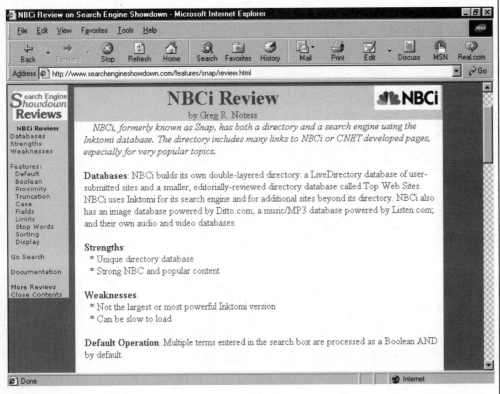

1. What does proximity relate to in a Web search?

   _____

2. What Boolean search terms does Northern Light allow?

   _____

3. What are the weaknesses of NBCi.com, according to SearchEngineShowdown?

   _____

CASE STUDY 3: DOGPILE.COM

- Dogpile.com is a metasearch site that includes Web directories, search tools such as yellow pages and city guides, and a shopping area. Dogpile.com's special search tools include a Local Search feature. With this feature, visitors can look for regional search results, ranging from local weather to local restaurants or maps. The feature is simple to use. When entering a search term the user simply types a comma, then a location name or ZIP Code. Using local search returns results for a certain radius of mileage from the geographic location. For example, if you entered schools,providence,ri, you'd get sites related to education in Providence.

Dogpile.com Local Search Page

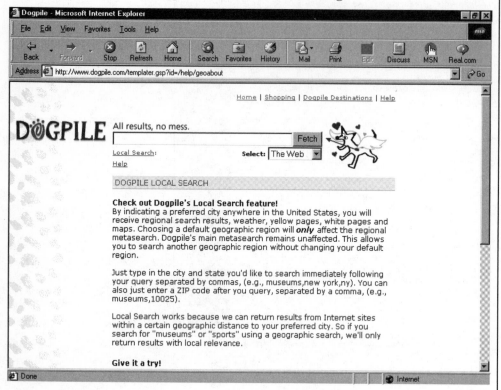

- Dogpile gets its search results from several search engines, so you can't submit a link to Dogpile itself. However, they provide a list of links to those search engines used by their site and a link to a site submission company, GoSubmit.Net. Dogpile does allow you to add a Dogpile search box to your Web site. This is an easy way for you to offer search features to people visiting your site; the benefit to you is that you may keep your visitors on your site a bit longer, and they may return to your site to do searches.

Dogpile.com Submit Site Page

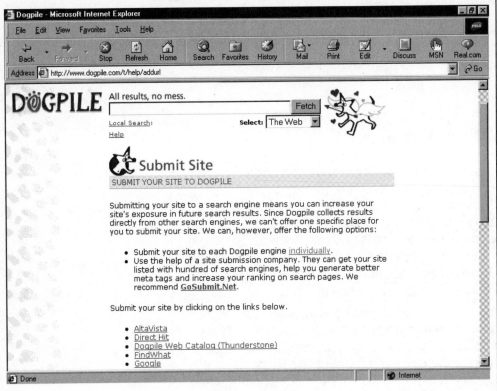

1. What two things do you have a choice of typing after a search term to do a local search?

   _____

2. How do you submit your site for inclusion in Dogpile's search database?

   _____

3. What is the benefit of using a site submission company to list your company on search engines?

   _____

http://searchengineguide.com
SearchEngineGuide.com
http://www.looksmart.com/
Looksmart.com
http://www.mysimon.com/
Mysimon.com
http://www.dogpile.com/
Dogpile.com
http://searchengineshowdown.com/
Searchengineshowdown.com

Learning E-Commerce
Part V, Web Site Considerations: Structure
Capstone Project

Summary of Concepts

- E-Commerce Web sites have a primary mission of buying and selling, so building in the process for making purchases is a primary goal of Web design. The shopping cart is the typical structure for online transactions. Shopping carts allow customers to assemble purchases, make adjustments to quantities, and in some cases choices, such as color and size, and place an order. One-click ordering, pioneered by Amazon.com, has caught on as a way to save return customers from having to enter the same contact and credit card information for each purchase.

- In addition to a purchasing function, most Web sites include added-value content to encourage visitors to return and use the site even when they don't intend to make a purchase. This content might include articles or tables of information related to the company product or service, or tools such as calculators. This content can also serve the important function of helping customers to use a product or service successfully, keeping the need for in-person customer support to a minimum, which results in cost-savings.

- E-Businesses use the Web for various marketing functions, especially to drive traffic to their sites. Often Web sites produce a regular newsletter that they include on their site and also e-mail to visitors on request. Mailing information at a visitor's request is called opt-in or permission-based marketing.

- In addition to articles, newsletters, and a shopping cart, an E-Commerce site typically includes links to other sites and advertising for other businesses. Most Web sites accept advertising both for income and to offer access to related services or products to their customers. Many businesses exchange links; that is, Business A places a link for Business B on their site and in exchange Business B places a link for Business A on its site.

- One final piece of the marketing strategy for E-Businesses is to ensure that search engines return their site address in search results. Companies pay a fee for these listings, and some also place ads or special offers on search sites. Search sites base their searches on databases from various sources, and some sites produce better quality search results than others. Portals are also used by many people to search for information related to a particular topic.

Case Study

The Business:

- When All Creatures Publishing started its Web site, the marketing department had to develop an online marketing strategy. The company designed a Web site that included an easy-to-use shopping cart function, regular articles and features of interest to people who purchase pet books, space for banner advertising, and links to sites with whom they exchanged links. One key part of their strategy was to get their site listed on search sites and to develop an advertising plan centered on topical portals.

Buzzword

Search engines are software programs that provide search functions. Many search sites use one or more search engines to find results in several databases of information. Search engines use *keywords* to perform searches. Keywords are placed on Web sites using HTML meta tags.

The Project:

- Working in teams come up with a list of keywords to include on the All Creatures Publishing site so that search engines will find them in relevant searches. Have each team take an area to brainstorm; for example, one might take the word "pets," one "animals," one "publishing," and another the word "books" and see how many keywords each team can come up with in each category. Then combine the words to form a master list. In addition, have each team come up with a list of the top five search engines they recommend that All Creatures get listed on, based on criteria such as size of the search database, volume of traffic to the search engine, and quality of results (absence of dead links, for example). Finally, each team should recommend three portals that focus on topics relevant to All Creatures' customer demographic where they should place ads. Have each team make a presentation of their search engine and portal recommendations, with explanations for why they chose these over other sites.

The Business Model:

- To complete this project, you must research various marketing and advertising functions on the Web. Here are three important things to consider:

  1. **Think like the customer**: When coming up with keywords for a site, think about terms the customer might use to find a business. Consider verbs, nouns, and adjectives that relate to the same topic. Come up with phrases that are commonly used in conjunction with your industry or product. Which search engines might your customers use and why? Would pet lovers use Dogpile over HotBot? Why?

  2. **Create a customer profile:** In addition to your customers' interest in your product, consider your customer demographic. What age group or gender most uses your products? What kind of income do these people have? Do you sell more to families, singles, or older people? You can use this information to identify portals that these people might go to. For example, if your customer base is made up to a great extent of families with younger children, should you consider a parenting or first time home buyer site as a possible match for your marketing needs?

  3. **Study your competition:** Where is your competition advertising? What keywords are they using on their sites? Try a few sample searches and see what other companies show up in the results. Review their sites to see what kind of content they provide their visitors and what kinds of sites they provide links to. What sites contain links to your competition's site; should you submit links to those same sites so potential customers never see your competitor's name without seeing yours as well?

Note

Companies that publish products such as books or music often include excerpts from their products on their site so that customers can browse and sample before buying. Text-based information can easily be converted into either an HTML or PDF format (Adobe Acrobat format).

Technology

■ Tracking software helps tabulate the activity on a Web site. In Web advertising and marketing, online activity of customers is tracked by such software to provide statistics such as the number of hits on a site, the number of click-throughs from a link on one site to another site, and even customer buying habits. Search sites also use tracking software, as well as software to check their performance. A search site might track the number of dead links reported in a search result or the overlap in searches performed drawing on two search databases. Search sites often use this information to improve the quality of their searches over competing sites.

Books to help:

Learning the Internet for Business (catalog number Z87)

Advanced Internet Research (catalog number DC64)

Internet Research Projects and Applications: Sales, Marketing, & Management (catalog number RB13)

Web sites to explore:

http://clickz.com

This site focuses on marketing, with information on online advertising, media, link management, and Web site content development.

http://www.123link.com

The emphasis here is on link and banner ad exchanges, as well as listings of Web directories.

http://www.pegasoWeb.com

This is touted as the Web Promotion Portal. Here you'll get advice about Web site management and design, as well as information about making the best use of search engines.

http://www.moreover.com/

Web content not only gives your visitors something to look at, it can drive purchases and return traffic. This site offers free content links and information about content management.

http://www.sitepoint.com

This site provides tools and information to build and promote a Web site. There are links to various services, including search engine listing agencies.

Part VI

Web Site Considerations:
Web Design

Successful Navigation Techniques
- Learn how browser controls aide navigation
- Use hyperlinks to move around a Web site
- Explore how navigation bars make browsing easy
- Follow the logic of Web site tables of contents
- Provide ease of use with viewing and printing options

NOTES

Product Searches at Levenger.com.

- The ease with which a visitor can maneuver around a Web site can mean the difference between a sale and no sale, a repeat customer and a customer who never visits your site again. **Navigation**, which simply means how someone moves from one place to another on your site, is the foundation of good structure for any Web site. In E-Commerce, visitors must not only be able to get from place to place and find information; they must also be able to walk through the product purchase process without getting confused or frustrated.

- Navigation is accomplished using a combination of tools. First, the browsers people use to view a Web site offer several navigation tools:

  - there are arrows to move back to a previously visited page or forward to a more recently visited page

  - you can stop a Web page from loading and refresh a currently loaded page if it hasn't loaded correctly

  - there is typically a history function, which allows the user to display a list of all the sites visited during this Internet session and to quickly return to any page on that list.

  - browsers allow users to place bookmarks on pages they will visit frequently.

- Levenger.com, the Web site for a retail business selling products for 'serious readers', shows some examples of other navigation tools. First, hyperlinks under the title Quick Picks take visitors to certain product pages with a single click. Visitors can also move to categories of products, then within each category use other links to find specific products. Many retail sites also highlight selected products on their home page, as with the Eiffel Tower Dip Pen illustrated on the following page. Clicking on that product picture or name takes the visitor immediately to that product page.

Buzzword
Navigation relates to how a visitor moves from one place to another on your site, or on the Internet.

Levenger.com Home Page

Using Navigation Bars at Godiva.com

- In addition to hyperlinks, Web site visitors can move around a site using a navigation bar. A navigation bar appears on every page of a site, providing one-click access to the main areas of the site. On Godiva's gourmet chocolate Web site, there is a navigation across the top of every Web page, offering access to all the areas of the online store, including advice on business gift giving, product information, and recipes using chocolate. In the following figure you can see how this navigation bar includes drop-down menus for accessing specific areas within each topic. This is one way to a lot of topic information on a single screen.

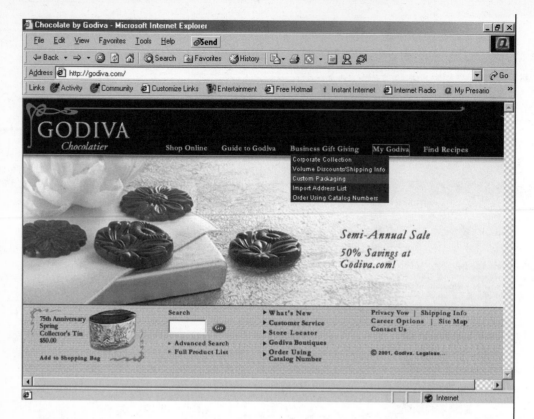

- There is a second navigation device being used on the Godiva site. Along the bottom of this screen there are several links to information about the company business, such as Customer Service, Store Locator, and Career Options. These links are not organized on a navigation bar and so are less obvious to the site user. However, assuming that the main goal of most customers is to find and buy chocolate, placing these in a less obvious design device may be appropriate for most users.

Using a Table of Contents Approach at Fencecenter.com

- Some Web sites provide a method of finding information that essentially requires that visitors drill down through several levels of links to find exactly what they want. This is akin to providing a table of contents for your site in an outline-like form. First the visitor finds a main heading, then a sub-heading, and then perhaps an even more detailed heading that leads the customer to what they're looking for.

- Fencecenter.com uses this drill-down approach. First they offer a list of categories on the left side of the home page. If you click on the Product Tour item, a list of product categories appears. When you click on one of those categories, a list of products is revealed. It is only then that you can click on a product and get the information you're searching for.

Note

If your site will be used by an international audience, consider using pictures or images for hyperlinks rather than text. This helps people who may not be as comfortable reading text in your language to get around.

Fencecenter.com Home Page

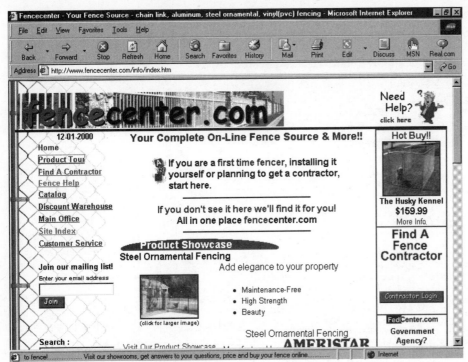

- Although a table of contents approach is logical and meets many visitors' needs, it often requires that you move through three or four pages or levels before you find what you need. If you do use a table of contents approach, you should also provide a search feature so that a visitor who knows exactly what he or she is looking for can go to a specific page more quickly.

Web Developer's Virtual Library Offers Information About Site Navigation

- There are several sites on the Internet that provide help and advice for Web designers. The Web Developer's Virtual Library is one such site. If you go to the area of this site that discusses navigation (click on the Navigation link on the home page) you get links to several pages that describe navigation elements in detail.

- Interestingly enough, the actual Web Developer's Virtual Library site provides limited navigation tools. There are no navigation bars or drop-down menus. There are lists of links and a search feature only. A visitor can return to the home page at any time by clicking on the site logo; this feature is typical of most Web pages, although it's not necessarily obvious to those newer to the Web. This site also places a Home text link on each page.

Technical Note

As the WDVL site points out, designing Web site navigation requires a combination of technical skills, logical organization, and understanding how people think and comprehend spatial relations among things. Never forget your visitor's point of view when designing a Web site.

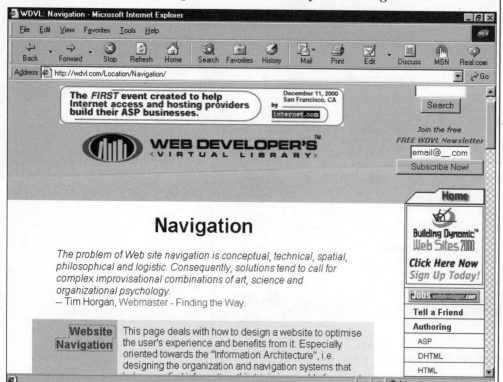

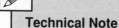

Technical Note

Every time a browser sends a request for a Web page to a server it provides information about itself. This information can be used to send different information to different browsers using scripts, because each browser may read a page slightly differently. This is called content negotiation, because the server negotiates which content it will provide with each browser interaction.

Selling Food the Easy Way at Sizzler.com

- In addition to providing tools to move around a site, a well-designed site offers features that make using the information on the site easier. Those tools include the ability to e-mail a page to a friend with the click of a mouse, to view a page in another format, or to have access to a print-friendly version of the document.

- The Australian site for Sizzler restaurants offers visual menus to customers. They also offer visitors the ability to view the menu in Word format, to view the menu offline, or to print the menu. If you want to provide content you think visitors will want to use once they log off your site, it's a good idea to design these kinds of features into your site.

Sizzler.com Home Page

- A printable version of a page is created by simply providing a link to a version of the page in a different format. The printable format might simply be a Word for Windows document, or it could be an HTML file with a typeface and page layout that gets rid of extra elements on the page, such as advertisements or dark page backgrounds, that make the page more cumbersome to print or read on the printed page.

E-BUSINESS ANALYSIS

> *Take a look at each of these sites (full URLs are located at the end of the exercise), then read the site analysis below and answer the questions.*

CASE STUDY 1: LEVENGER.COM

- Levenger is an E-Commerce site where people who love to read can buy a variety of products, such as papers, pens, and office furniture. This site uses a combination of navigation bars and links to help visitors find their way and is generally well organized. However, finding the information you're looking for is only one part of navigation. When a visitor gets to a product page on Levenger.com, it is not clear what he or she needs to do to make a purchase.

Levenger.com Product Page

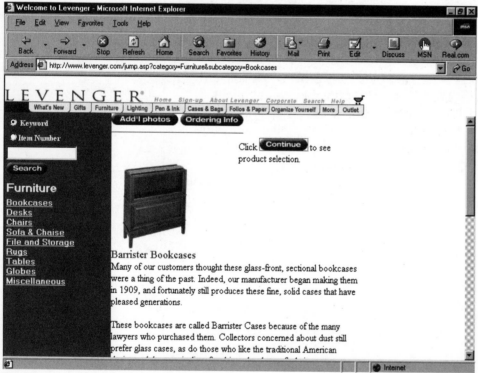

■ If visitors click on the shopping cart icon from this product page to buy the product, the message in the following figure appears telling them that they can't use the shopping cart at this point. To compound a user's frustration, they aren't provided with a link to go to the next logical step to buy the product; they're asked to go back to where they came from and click on another link, labeled Continue. It would be more helpful to indicate on the product page that, to buy this product, the visitor must first view a list of different models and select the one they want. This simple message would save visitors confusion. Because the site designers have provided a page telling visitors they're in the wrong place, they are obviously aware of the potential confusion, but have not fixed the problem at its source.

Levenger.com Empty Shopping Cart Page

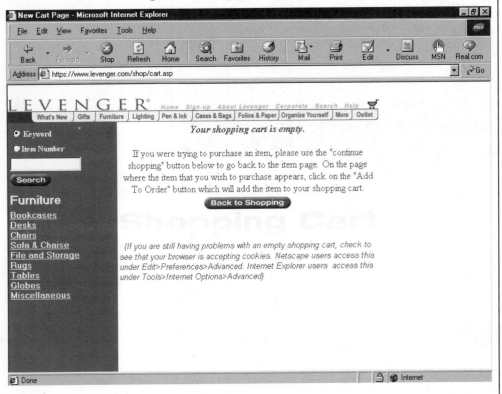

1. How can you get to Levenger's home page from the product page?

_____

2. How could cookies affect how a shopping cart functions works?

_____

3. What will you find if you click on the More item in the navigation bar? Is that content clear from the name "More"?

_____

CASE STUDY 2: GODIVA.COM

- Godiva.com is the online presence of the internationally known fine chocolate maker. The site sports an elegant and appealing design, with deep golds and, of course, chocolate colors. Although the site's shopping navigation bar—including areas such as Shop online, Guide to Godiva, Business Gift Giving, and so on—is always at the top of every page, other navigation elements can vary by page. For example, the Godiva Ice Cream page shown here includes links to Locate Stores and Email Godiva right with the product information. These same links are available on other pages (and even on this one) from the list of links along the bottom (Store Locator and Contact Us, respectively). Including certain links in more than one place on a page can be a way to provide navigation help specific to a page topic.

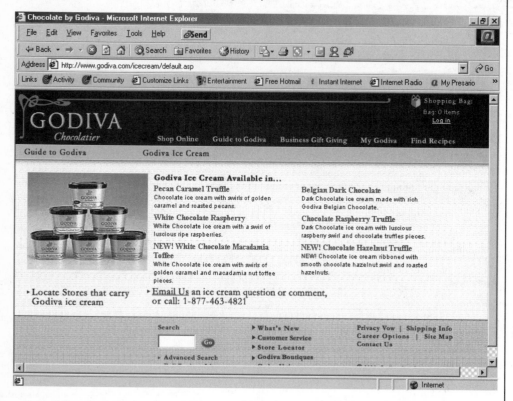

- Notice that on some pages of the Godiva Web site, such as the one shown on the following page, the links that appeared at the bottom of the page have now shifted to the left side of the page. The main navigation bar across the top, however, remains in the same place throughout the site. The move of these links is probably due to design requirements, but it can confuse customers a bit. One thing the designer has done to help is to ensure that wherever the links are, they are always visible on a single page layout—that is, the viewer doesn't have to scroll around the page to find the links. Whether on the left or bottom, they are always visible on the initial portion of any Web page that appears.

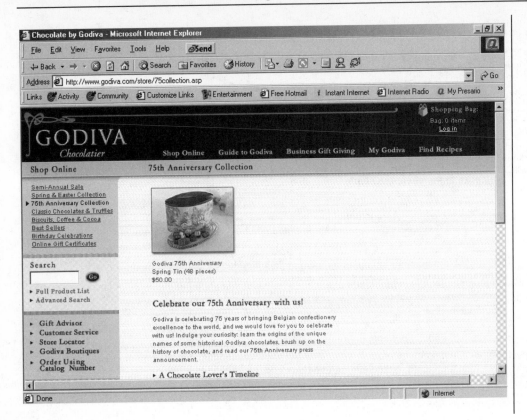

1. How does the Godiva site map categorize the site content?

   _____

2. What area of the site will you find In-Store Promotions in?

   _____

3. Name three places on this site where information on sale products is included.

   _____

CASE STUDY 3: FENCECENTER.COM

■ Fencecenter.com is the Web site of a wholesale fencing supply company. The users of this site consist in great part of construction and fencing professionals. Though not fancy, the site offers some great features, including fencing materials calculators and tools to help you pick the right kind of fence for your needs. The site uses a table of contents form of navigation. When you click on the Product Tour item from the home page, for example, a page appears with a list of product categories and brief descriptions of each category.

Fencecenter.com Product Tour Page

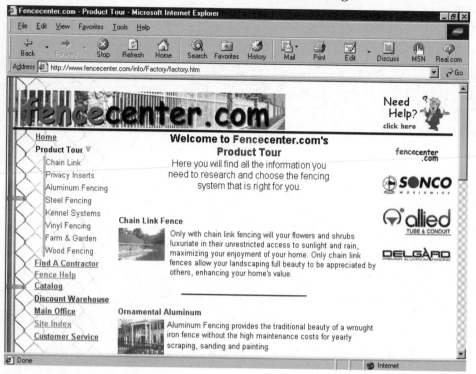

- When you click on any category in the Product list, another page appears, offering a deeper level of detail listing specific products. If you need help at any point in this process, you can click on the Need Help link at the top right corner of the page. This opens a separate window with phone information and an e-mail form link.

Fencecenter.com's Product Level Page, with Help Displayed

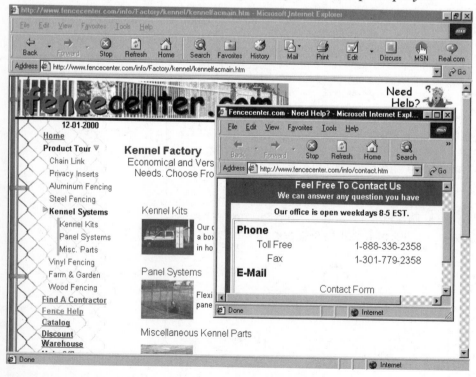

■ The biggest problem with Fencecenter.com involves confusion about how to make purchases. In fact, the site stops short of allowing customers to make purchases. It does allow the visitor to print a purchase list based on specifications they enter, which they can fax to the company to place an order. However, this is not made clear on the Web site until after the customer has gone through several Web pages of information. Customers looking for a shopping cart or purchase feature will be frustrated. A simple message on the home page stating that, at this time, customers are not able to place an order online would make for a much more user-friendly site.

1. What forms of help does Fencecenter.com provide on its site?

   _____

2. How many screens must you view to see pricing of a specific kind of chain link fence?

   _____

3. How does the Site Index help a visitor to find information?

   _____

http://www.levenger.com
Levenger.com
http://www.balduccis.com/
Balduccis.com
http://www.fencecenter.com/
FenceCenter.com
http://wdvl.com/
Web Developer's Virtual Library
http://www.sizzler.com.au/
Sizzler.com

Making Your Site Sell

- See how E-Commerce sites use promotions to sell
- Discover how businesses hold a sale online
- Learn how member discounts sell products
- Explore online sales tools
- Learn how educating a consumer can help make a sale

NOTES

Special Offers Keep Customers Buying at HarryandDavid.com.

- You might design the prettiest Web site in the world and give your customers great navigation tools to get around it. But although those elements make a site pleasant to visit, they don't necessarily close a sale. Just as traditional retailers have created a science of laying out the floorplan of a store to encourage customers to buy, so E-Commerce is evolving methods to sell on a Web site.

- Harry and David's Web site offers fruits and gourmet gifts to customers, with a focus on special events, such as holidays, and ease of shopping. One look at their home page reveals several sales promises:

  - Their **slogan** is "We make it easy to give the Best," which is a sales promise of ease of use and quality.

  - They guarantee on-time delivery of holiday gifts.

  - They push certain products at customers on their home page by featuring seasonal gifts on their home page and including a list of Great Gift Ideas by price levels.

HarryandDavid.com Home Page

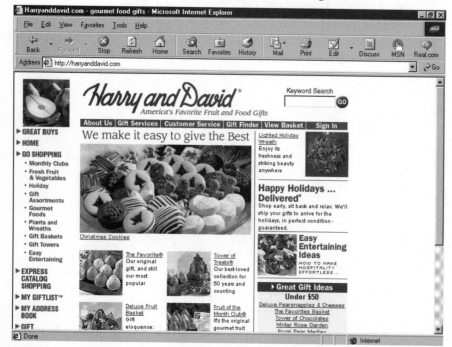

Buzzword

A *slogan* for a business is a phrase that encapsulates the unique qualities or benefits of doing business with that business. For example, Visa's slogan is "We're everywhere you want to be;" Gateway Computer's slogan is "Technology is great...but people rule;" and FedEx's slogan is "When it absolutely, positively has to get there."

Technical Note

HarryandDavid.com customer support indicates that you must order from their site while using certain browsers. That's because in order to place a secure order online, you must have a browser that supports secure sockets layers (SSL). Internet Explorer and Netscape Navigator both have this feature, which directs you to a secure environment for transactions, and HarryandDavid.com provides links for downloading either browser for customer convenience.

See How Promotions Sell at SharperImage.com

- Sharper Image is a store catering to unusual or luxury items such as executive CD players, air purifiers, and personal care items. Their Web store is a good example of how a site can sell by offering several types of promotions to customers. Promotions are special deals that can motivate customers to buy; they are typically offered for a limited time. A promotion might be in the form of a sale price, free shipping, or special two-for-the-price-of-one-type offers. Other ways to promote products are by simply highlighting them for the customer; for example, on Sharper Image's Web page, there are special categories for New Products and Best Sellers, which make the customer feel there is something special about these products even though no savings are attached.

SharperImage.com Home Page

- E-Commerce promotions typically take advantage of time and variety. That is, promotions last only a short time, and promotions are rotated so that virtually every time a customer visits a Web site, they see a different set of promotions. The limited timeframe is a motivator for a customer to purchase now; the variety ensures that if a customer wasn't attracted to one promotion, another might hit the mark. Traditional retail stores also use these approaches, however with the speed of change online, and the fact that a customer can easily visit your Web store every day rather than a few times a month, the pace of rotating promotions is even faster online.

- SharperImage.com offers what they call a dynamic browser. This is simply a page with thumbnail pictures of several items. The customer can scroll his or her mouse cursor over a picture and the name and price of that item appears at the bottom of the page. This is done using the onmouseover and onmouseout functions of HTML.

Note

Typical sales motivators work on customer need: the need to purchase now due to limited availability, the need to be among the first to own this product to impress friends, or the need to own a product everybody else has so as not to be left out, to name a few.

BMG Music Service Promotes Sales with Member Discounts

■ Companies that sell music have come up with an interesting approach to locking in repeat customers. Because people who buy CDs typically buy music on a regular basis and within certain categories, a club or membership model was created. This club model allows customers to buy music throughout the year from one company and enjoy significant savings because of the volume of their purchases. It also allows a music Web site to target promotions to member tastes, highlighting specials in jazz, classical, or rock, for example. This model has also been extended to books, videos, gourmet fruit baskets, and other products that people buy on a regular basis.

BMGmusicservice.com Home Page

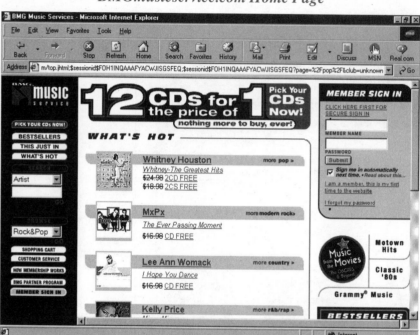

■ On BMG's Web site, the main selling message is that new members get twelve CD's for the price of one. This is the hook used to get new members to sign up for the service. In the early days of this sales approach members were then obligated to buy a certain number of additional products over the course of a year. To some extent, member sales models have moved away from that kind of commitment, because people became leery of getting locked in to future purchases. However, even though BMG and other clubs now promise that there is "nothing to buy, ever!", the membership model still allows them to send promotions and offers to members on a monthly basis. Over time, members are likely to make several purchases simply because they are being bombarded with offers.

■ Sometimes, impulse buying mentality comes into play; an **impulse buy** is the purchase of something the customer didn't necessarily want or need, but when the product was put in front of him or her, he or she had an impulse to own it. In retail stores this is done by placing racks of items at the checkout counter. On a Web store, it is done by offering items of interest targeted to consumers either on the Web site, or by e-mail. Buying clubs gain the right to e-mail their members with special offers, thereby motivating impulse sales.

Buzzword

An *impulse buy* is when a customer purchases something that he or she didn't want or need, but decided to buy on the spur of the moment simply because it was made available.

TheNewWayToShop.com Provides Advice About Online Selling

■ Several sites offer advice about effective online selling. The New Way To Shop Web site is focused on 'netpreneurs'. The site includes not only articles about selling online, but also a Sales & Marketing Toolbox with links to affiliate selling programs, sales newsletters, contact management software, and sales courses.

TheNewWayToShop.com Selling Online Page

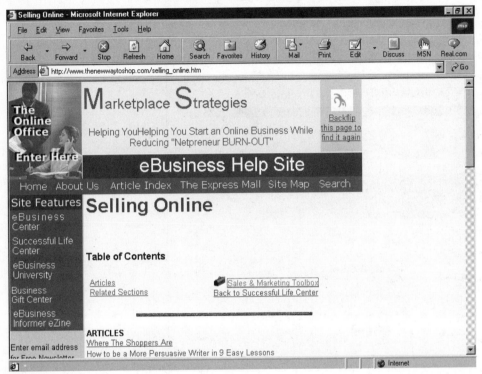

■ One of the articles on this site is titled "How to Be A More Persuasive Writer in 9 Easy Lessons." That's because writing good site content is one of the most important tools for selling online. Luckily, sales writing has been around for years to produce print advertisements and direct mail offers; some of the same guidelines for these sales pieces work well for Web content. For example:

- be concise and get to the point so you don't waste the customer's time

- know your customer and anticipate his or her concerns or questions

- sell benefits, not features (i.e., talk about how a car feels when you drive it, not about what kind of shock absorbers it has)

- ask for the sale

■ On the Web, asking for the sale might simply mean placing a button on the Web site that says "Buy Now", or even "Add to Cart." These terms use an imperative structure; that is they are essentially a command to the customer to do something that can motivate the customer to buy.

Technical Note

In designing a Web store, you also have the ability to use design elements such as color or even sound files to drive sales. In HTML you use the tag <FONTCOLOR="X"> in front of text, with X being the name of the color you'd like to use. HTML accepts both standard color names such as red, or a color code expressing a color value. There are currently 16 colors that can be specified by name (aqua, black, glue, gray, green, lime, fuchsia, maroon, teal, white, yellow, olive, purple, red, silver, navy).

Charles Schwab Encourages Customers by Educating Them

- In some cases, a Web business can get customers to buy by making them comfortable with the process. At Schwab.com, for example, which is an online investment broker, there is a Smart Investor feature, as well as free stock quotes and charts. The idea here is that if a customer doesn't feel comfortable buying shares of stock because he or she doesn't really understand how to choose the right stock or make a purchase, the customer will leave the site without buying. In addition, an investor who makes poor investments will have a bad experience and stop investing. Businesses such as Charles Schwab must provide free advice and information to customers to make the sale and keep customers buying from them in the future.

Schwab.com Home Page

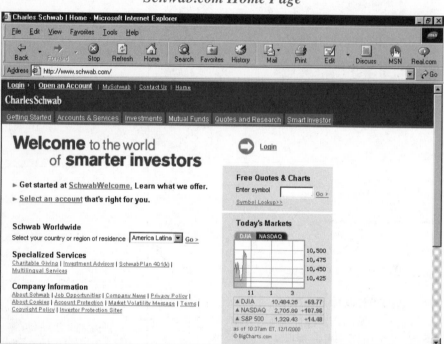

- In general, E-Commerce sites face an education challenge with most of their customers, simply because buying products online is such a relatively new activity. Customers are concerned with placing an order they didn't mean to by clicking the wrong button, as well as having their credit card or personal information made public when completing online transactions. It's a good idea to include general advice about how to buy products on your site as well as a privacy statement explaining the measures you have put in place to protect customers.

E-BUSINESS ANALYSIS

> *Take a look at each of these sites (full URLs are located at the end of the exercise), then read the site analysis below and answer the questions.*

CASE STUDY 1: HARRYANDDAVID.COM

■ Harry and David is a gift food company that has traditionally sold by catalog mail order. Their Web store offers a complementary online catalog of products, and the added advantage of allowing customers to look for products by various categories, or to search by keyword. Harry and David has always put strong sales emphasis on the Christmas season, sending out its largest quantities of catalogs by mail at this time and offering a large number of Christmas gift food baskets. It's no surprise, then, that their online store offers seasonal specials and items grouped by holiday as well. This sales strategy is no fluke; customers are aware that food items are perishable. By promoting items by season, Harry and David suggests to its customers that its products are fresh and appeals to their holiday gift-giving spirit.

HarryandDavidcom Christmas Sale Page

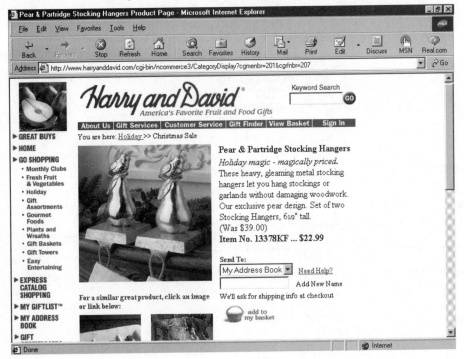

- Harry and David offers savings on items which customers can reach by clicking the Great Buys link on their home page. Notice that they have included the original product price, the sale price, and even an indication of the percent savings customers will get by ordering each product. Reminding customers of how much they will save plays into their desire to get a bargain and save money. Sometimes Web sites feature discounts on overstocked items, that is, items a store has too much of and wants to get rid of. Other times a new item will be sale priced in an introductory promotion.

HarryandDavid.com Sale Page

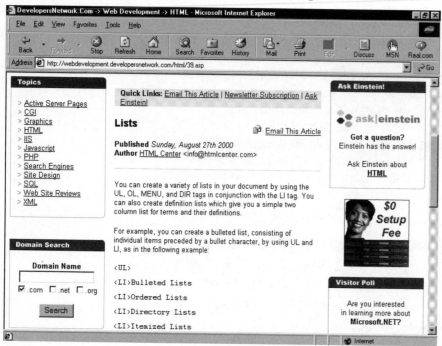

1. What are Harry and David monthly clubs?

_____

2. What variables does the Gift Finder feature allow customers to search by?

_____

3. How does the My Address Book feature on HarryandDavid.com make the shopping experience easier for customers and help close a sale?

_____

CASE STUDY 2: SHARPERIMAGE.COM

■ The Sharper Image is another company that has sold through catalog in the past and also maintains retail stores around the country. Their Web site sports a low-key, elegant, and uncluttered look to match their executive customer base. Although promotions and special offers appear throughout the site, there is a special page devoted to Promotions that spotlights a handful of products. Typical promotions might be a discount price for an item when another item is purchased, or free shipping. Offering a discount for purchasing more than one item is a great sales strategy; it is a way to sell overstocked or out of season products with minimal impact on the company profit.

SharperImage.com Promotions Page

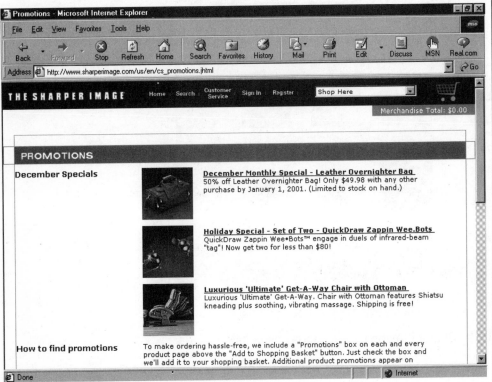

■ The Sharper Image Web site also offers Gift Guides. These are basically visual catalogs organized by typical buying needs, such as gifts for men, women, or kids; or gifts within a certain price range. This is another opportunity for a company to spotlight products it most wants customers to buy. Providing suggestions of gifts for certain occasions or recipients also makes the customer feel the Web store is helping him or her out, much as salesperson would help a customer shop in a traditional store.

SharperImage.com Gift Guides Page

1. What is a "Promotions" box on Sharper Image product pages used for?

   _____

2. How does the contents of the On Sale/Monthly Special page differ from the Promotions page?

   _____

3. One of the Gift Guides lists the top 10 holiday gifts; why would a customer be drawn to purchasing a gift many other people are purchasing?

   _____

CASE STUDY 3: BMGMUSICSERVICE.COM

- BMG Music Service has traditionally sold by direct mail (that is solicitations sent to people's homes). Its Web site offers current members the ability to manage their membership and place orders for additional CDs quickly and easily. It also promotes membership to visitors who are not currently members. BMG mentions its Web site in its mailings, offering a way for someone considering membership to search for products to see if BMG has the kind of music they want to buy. It also allows new members to sign up and pick their 12 free CDs online. Where a direct mail piece might be limited in the amount of space it provides to explain how membership works, the Web site can provide more details without overwhelming the potential customer, because the customer picks and chooses what information he or she wants to read.

BMG Music Service Information Page

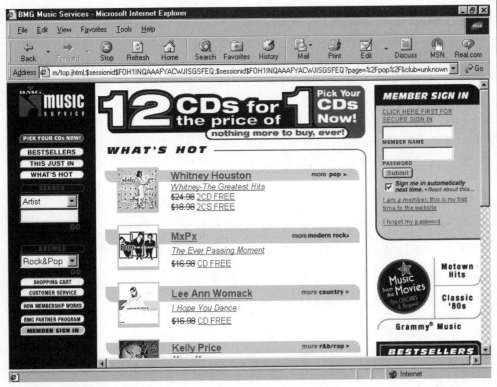

- When a visitor looks at information about a product on BMG's site, there is an added benefit that only the Internet can offer; a customer can play audio selections from a CD before buying. This is done by placing a link to a sound file on the product page. By clicking on the link the customer opens a Real Audio list of tracks that are available. When a customer clicks on a particular track, the Real Player opens and plays a sound clip. This one feature makes the Web a tremendous sales tool for any company selling music to the public, because it lets customers hear what they're buying to be sure the product is right for them.

1. What incentives does BMG offer people to become a BMG member rather than buying their CDs from any other music store?

   _____

2. How many CDs are members committed to buying in their first year of membership?

   _____

3. What criteria can you use to search for music on this site?

   _____

http://harryanddavid.com
Harry and David

http://www.sharperimage.com/
Sharper Image

http://www.bmgmusicserivce.com/
BMG Music Service

http://www.thenewwaytoshop.com/
TheNewWayToShop.com

http://www.schwab.com/
Charles Schwab

334

Web Design Building Blocks: HTML, XML, Java, and CSS
- **Get an overview of Web page design**
- **Learn about the basic structure of HTML**
- **See how scripts and style sheets make life easier**
- **Discover how Java makes Web pages accessible to all**
- **Explore how browsers behave**

NOTES

Take a Look at the World of Web Developers at DevelopersNetwork.com

- The essential language of the Web is **HTML**, or hypertext markup language. Web pages are built by creating HTML documents. HTML can be used to specify the text on a page, hyperlinks, and various characteristics of text such as bold, italic, font, font color, and so on. HTML doesn't offer sophisticated control of page layout, and browsers interpret HTML slightly differently, so browsers display HTML documents in slightly different ways.

- **XML** (extensible markup language) is a more recently developed language for creating Web pages, and it provides more flexibility than HTML. Where HTML mainly defines the appearance of a page, XML is better at defining information in a precise way that can be displayed more accurately by browsers. XML doesn't replace HTML; in fact, a Web developer would typically build a document template in HTML, then place XML content in that template.

- **Style sheets** are sets of code that make programming a Web page easier. Where HTML defines elements of a page tag by tag (for example defining a table), a style sheet can define sets of attributes (a table with bold heading, italicized text in cells, and dark blue lines, for example). Because style sheets, once saved, can be applied to any Web page, they save programmers a great deal of time. Cascading style sheets (CSS) has been the standard style sheet language for a several years, and XSL (extensible style language), developed for use with XML, is coming into general usage.

- **Java** is a programming language that allows software created on different platforms (Windows, Macintosh, UNIX, and so on) to run on different computers and devices such as personal digital assistants or even TV control boxes. Java programs can be used in Web design, either referenced within HTML documents or on their own. Because Java is built into all browsers, the programming is read by browsers on a variety of computer platforms with more accuracy. Sites such as the Developer's Network provide information on all of these Web programming options and more.

Buzzwords

HTML is the basic language for building Web documents.

XML is a language used with HTML to provide more accuracy and flexibility.

Style sheets (including CSS and XSL) save time in creating Web pages because they are sets of characteristics (such as bold, blue, and capitalized, for example) that can be applied with a single command.

Java is a programming language for the Web that overcomes certain browser and platform compatibility issues.

WinEdit.com Offers One Text Editor Choice

- At its core, the World Wide Web is made up of HTML documents and browsers such as Netscape Navigator and Internet Explorer, that interpret and display those documents. HTML is a computer language that uses **tags** to instruct browsers about how to display a Web page.

- HTML tags are surrounded by brackets <> to designate the start and end of each tag. The end tag uses a slash before the end bracket /> (although a few tags don't use an end bracket at all). Certain tags also have **attributes**. An attribute is a specific variable for that tag; for example, the <FONT> tag has a COLOR attribute.

- HTML is created within a text editor; a text editor is simply a program you can use to enter the tags and attributes of HTML with text and characters. Many programmers have relied on the simple word processing program built into Windows, called Wordpad, over the years. However, today there are more sophisticated editors available. For example, there are Wysiwyg (what you see is what you get) editors that let you enter page content much as you would in a word processor, but they translate that text into HTML commands. There are also text-based editors that contain more sophisticated code entry and editing tools than WordPad. WinEdit is one such editing program.

Buzzwords

A *tag* is an instruction to a browser in an HTML document.

An *attribute* is a characteristic applied to a tag, such as color applied to a font.

WinEdit.com Home Page

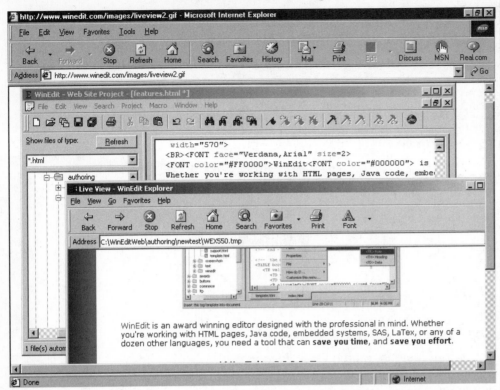

- Beyond text editors there are more robust programs for Web design, such as FrontPage. These programs not only help you build your HTML documents, but also create the overall structure of your Web site and manage and make changes to the site with simple to use controls.

ScreamDesign.com Offers Shortcuts for Web Page Creation

- Cascading style sheets offer not only time savings in building Web pages, but also more control over formatting and page layout. To add CSS to a document created with HTML, you have to declare the style and apply the style to the HTML element. Using this method you could specify a style of bold, red, uppercase text, then apply it to all headings on the page.

- Two types of cascading style sheets, inline and embedded, work a bit differently. Inline styles are applied to individual HTML elements, affecting only that occurrence on the page. Embedded style sheets are placed in the heading of a document, defining a style block. This block establishes a set of style rules for a group of elements. Using embedded style sheets you can apply a style to all elements of a certain type throughout the document.

- Scripts are small pieces of code that build a certain feature into a Web page. They are basically a list of commands to be executed, such as rotating a banner or placing a calculator function on a page. Scripts are written in scripting languages such as JavaScript or CGI. Scripts make dynamic HTML (DHTML) possible: DHTML creates Web content that can change each time it's viewed based on who's viewing it, the time of day, or other variables. Programmers are always sharing scripts; ScreamDesign.com makes a whole library of them available to you.

ScreamDesign.com Form Script Page

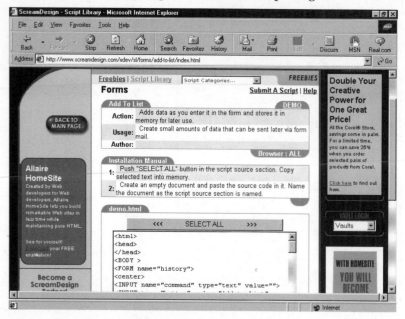

Java.Sun.com Explains the Power of Java

- Java is based on the older programming language C++. Java was originally created as a language for intelligent devices such as TV set-top boxes. To service the wide variety of programming options in these different kinds of hardware, one of Java's key characteristics is that it is compatible with many different kinds of computers and other devices.

- Java attains this universal usability because of something called the Java Virtual Machine. This is essentially a machine code that is built into platforms and browsers that can execute Java programming code. So, instead of Java code being played by Windows or UNIX, it is played by this virtual machine build into all of these systems. The Java Tutorial on Sun's Web site can help you explore the basics of using Java to build Web pages.

Java.Sun.com Page

Note

For detailed instruction in building Web pages check out these books from DDC Publishing:

Learning HTML
(Cat. No. Z59)

Learning Java
(Cat. No. Z66)

Learning to Create a Web Page with Microsoft Office 2000 (Cat. No. Z43)

Learning Microsoft Publisher (Cat. No. Z47)

See How all This Programming Looks on a Web Site at Microsoft.com

- Browsers are the window through which you view all this Web page coding. If you have a clean window, you see one thing, if there's a curtain in front of the window, you see it differently. Understanding how the major browsers are set up to view pages is essential to Web design that works well for most or all of the visitors to a site. Microsoft.com contains a gallery of pages that use various cascading style sheets. These pages will be viewed accurately with Internet Explorer 3+ or any other browser that supports CSS. Although these samples were created several years ago, this feature of the Microsoft site is of use to those trying to understand the basics of Web page layout. You can display a page in the gallery then display the style sheets that were used to build it by selecting View, Source from Internet Explorer's menu bar.

Microsoft CSS Gallery page

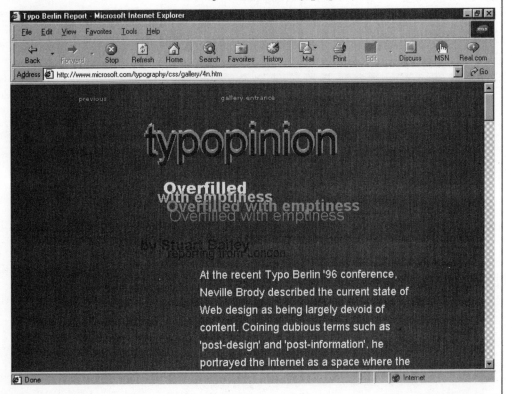

- Another issue related to browsers is how they read various fonts. HTML specifies a font to appear on a page, but those fonts have to be available to a browser. There are two options for enabling a browser to read more than standard fonts: a user can install Web fonts on his or her own computer, or Web sites can link font objects to their site, offering these fonts to any browser. Because a Web developer can't count on all visitors having all fonts installed, the second option is the better of the two.

E-BUSINESS ANALYSIS

> *Take a look at each of these sites (full URLs are located at the end of the exercise), then read the site analysis below and answer the questions.*

CASE STUDY 1: DEVELOPERSNETWORK.COM

- DevelopersNetwork.com is a site that provides information and resources for Web developers. An interesting feature of this site is Ask Einstein. Visitors can submit questions by category and experts from the site will answer them. What's useful about this feature is the table of question listings it provides. You can browse for a question by topic such as hyperlink or space tag, see who posted the question, if it was answered, and when. If the question seems useful and the response was recent enough to still be valid you can follow a link to read it.

DevelopersNetwork.com Ask Einstein Question Listings Page

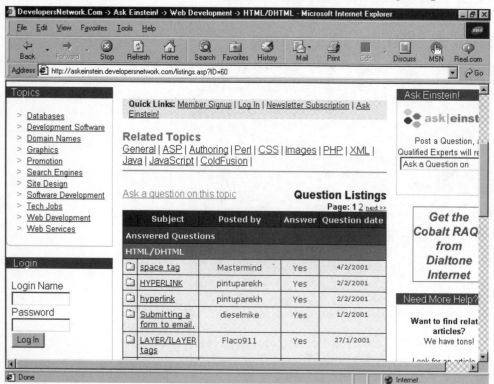

- Articles on this site provide information about specific HTML tags and attributes in an area called HTML Center. Sample HTML helps you see exactly how HTML tags are used to create certain effects, such as bulleted or other styles of lists. If a piece of HTML code looks useful to you, perhaps requiring only minor changes, you can always copy and paste it from these articles into your own HTML editor.

DevelopersNetwork.com HTML Center Page

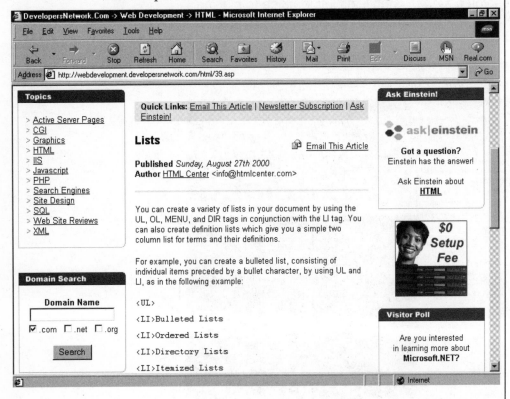

1. What is DHTML?

   _____

2. What are some of the tags you can use to create lists?

   _____

3. What is a characteristic of a definition list?

   _____

CASE STUDY 2: SCREAMDESIGN.COM

■ ScreamDesign.com also offers some useful resources for Web designers. One set of resources is a script library. This area includes scripts by categories such as animations, backgrounds, and banners. What's especially nice about this feature is the information it provides: it describes the action the script will cause and how it might be used on a Web page. Then, it gives you a step-by-step installation guide to placing the script on your page. You can also demo the script, which opens a separate window with the script function executing, as with this spaceship animation script.

ScreamDesign.com Animation Script Page

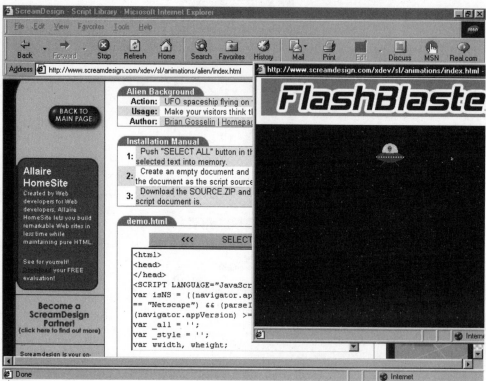

■ Using the Internet Explorer View, Source command, you can see the same page from ScreamDesign.com in its HTML format. Note various HTML tags such as <title> and <head>. Also notice where scripts are included, between the <script> tag and </script> ending. There are also JavaScript elements to this page and even a script to deal with a Netscape browser bug.

ScreamDesign Script Libraries Page Viewed in HTML

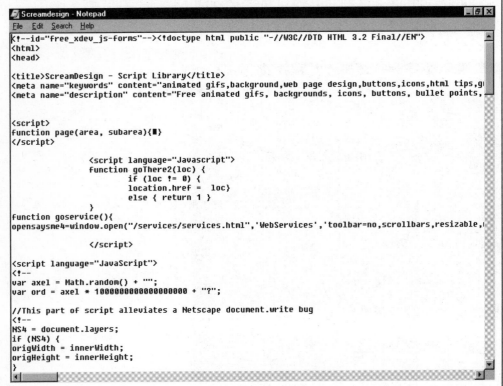

```
Screamdesign - Notepad
File  Edit  Search  Help
<!--id="free_xdev_js-forms"--><!doctype html public "-//W3C//DTD HTML 3.2 Final//EN">
<html>
<head>

<title>ScreamDesign - Script Library</title>
<meta name="keywords" content="animated gifs,background,web page design,buttons,icons,html tips,g
<meta name="description" content="Free animated gifs, backgrounds, icons, buttons, bullet points,


<script>
function page(area, subarea){■}
</script>

                <script language="Javascript">
                function goThere2(loc) {
                        if (loc != 0) {
                        location.href =  loc}
                        else { return 1 }
                }
function goservice(){
opensaysme4=window.open("/services/services.html",'WebServices','toolbar=no,scrollbars,resizable,

                </script>

<script language="JavaScript">
<!--
var axel = Math.random() + "";
var ord = axel * 10000000000000000 + "?";

//This part of script alleviates a Netscape document.write bug
<!--
NS4 = document.layers;
if (NS4) {
origWidth = innerWidth;
origHeight = innerHeight;
}
```

1. What is a script?

   _____

2. What is a tag?

   _____

3. How can you put a script from the ScreamDesign.com script library into an HTML document? (The site includes directions to do this.)

   _____

CASE STUDY 3: MICROSOFT.COM

■ Microsoft's CSS Gallery shows you how you can use cascading style sheets to quickly change the look of a Web page. The gallery shows several versions of the same page as in the following two figures; the only change is the replacement of the style sheets used in each. Notice the things that change instantly with the application of a new style sheet: the background color, font, paragraph format, and alignment of the text on the page.

Microsoft.com CSS Gallery Sample Page

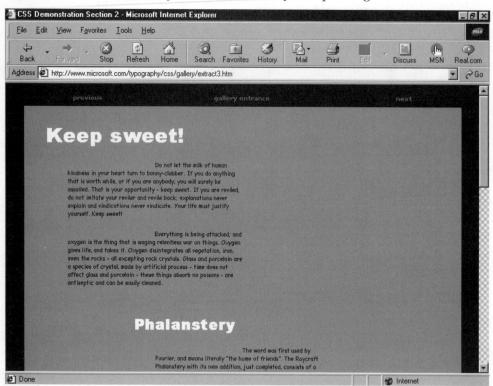

Microsoft.com CSS Gallery Sample Page

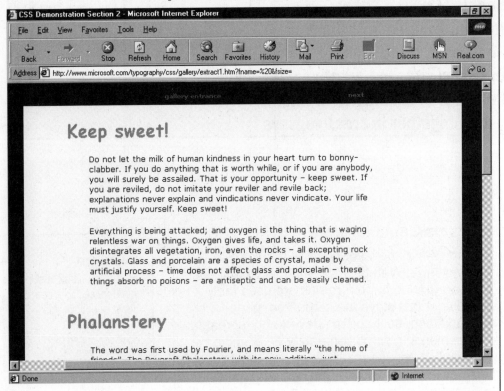

■ Making changes with style sheets is easier than with simple HTML code. For example, to change the text color of the background for all headings in a document you only have to change the value of the background-color property.

1. What is CSS?

_____

2. What is an attribute in HTML?

_____

3. Can you place links on a page by using HTML?

_____

http://www.developersnetwork.com
DevelopersNetwork.com
http://www.winedit.com/
WinEdit.com
http://www.screamdesign.com
ScreamDesign.com
http://java.sun.com/
Sun Java
http://www.microsoft.com/
Microsoft.com

Theme

29

The Elements of a Web Page
- Learn about working with frames
- See how tables bring order to a page
- Discover how sites get creative with menus
- Use headings to emphasize or inform
- Bring it all together in creative ways

NOTES

CNET Builder.com Describes How Frames Work

- One of the tools you can use to control the layout of a Web page is a **frame**. A frame is a way to divide up a Web browser window so that each section of it can contain a separate Web page. Frames are used for a variety of reasons: to place content that stays the same from page to page, such as the site name and logo, so it doesn't have to be recreated on each page; to allow for documents to scroll separately on a single page; or to help with navigational design, keeping navigation tools available in the same window all the time. CNET's Builder.com page gives Web developers information about how to use frames.

CNET Builder.com Fund with Frames Page

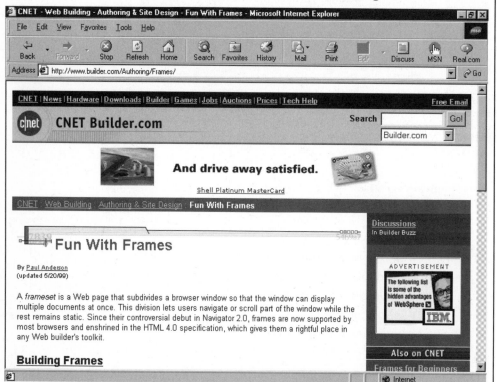

- To create frames you must first create a Web page for each piece of the frame, then build a Web page that specifies how your frames will appear on the page. Generally it's not wise to use too many frames on a page, partly because they can offer your visitor information overload and partly because it can make updating your page cumbersome, because you actually have to make changes to several pages. Also, some browsers have difficulty dealing with frames; for that reason many Web designers offer the visitor the option of displaying a page with or without frames.

- Peerless-faucet.com Uses Tables to Create Order

- Another way to control the layout of a page is with **tables**. Tables are very similar to tables in a word processing program: they are sets of rows and columns that form cells. Information can be placed in the cells to control their placement on a page. The sets of icons and text links on the home page of Peerless Faucet that provide access to the various areas of the site are laid out on a simple four column, four row table.

Peerless-faucet.com Home Page

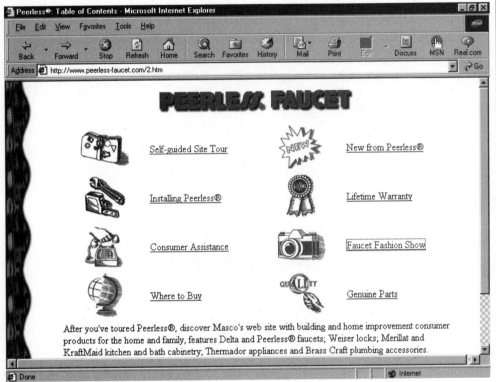

Buzzword

A *table* is an HTML – created element that functions like a word processing table, allowing you to place text or images in cells to help organize your page contents.

- Tables help you achieve various effects, from simple lists of information to the creation of columns or to arrange graphics and text on a page in more creative ways. Although you can add a border to your table and lines delineating each cell, you don't have to. Tables that don't display their borders sometimes don't look like tables at all on the page. Tables can use different formatting and alignment of items in each cell and even different colored backgrounds in each cell.

Technical Note

To create a table you use the <TABLE> tag, as well as tags such as <TR> to create a new table row and <TH> to specify the text of a table heading. To format elements of a table, you'd use attributes, such as this one used to center a heading in a table:
<TH> align="center"

Cocacola.com Offers Creative Menu Design

- Tables and frames are devices that can be used to place a menu or navigation bar on a page. How creative those navigation tools are depends on the Web designer. Cocacola.com uses a scrolling, graphic navigation bar. The images in the middle of the home page scroll past like a filmstrip (while the company name and logo stay onscreen without moving). Some of the images provide links to other pages. By placing your mouse cursor over an image (when it comes around again) you see the name of the item; you can click on the image to go that page. One unique feature of this scrolling navigation bar is that you can reverse the direction of the scrolling by simply moving your cursor in one direction or the other.

Cocacola.com Page

- Menus are sometimes built as a menu list containing links using the <MENU> tag. These lists of links take a viewer to different pages in the site or even to other sites. Menus and navigation bars are essential elements of Web site design; they are the methods by which users move around from page to page. Build them well and visitors will feel comfortable getting around; build them badly or inconsistently and visitors will get frustrated.

- E-Commerce sites should be especially careful about how their navigation tools work because there's usually a lot going on on their pages. The trick to good navigation is to keep in mind what you want the reader to be able to do. If your main goal is to have them buy something, you should have a shopping cart link placed prominently on every page. If you want them to be able to jump to other products in a category from a catalog page, you should include a menu of links to do that.

Soundblaster.com Offers a Variety of Headings to Visitors

- In addition to menus, tables of information, and frames to help display those elements, all Web pages also use headings. Headings function just as they do in your newspaper: they serve as a break in the action for readers and a flag that something new is starting. This break might be used to mark the beginning of a new element, call out important information, or create an outline-like organization of information on a page.

- SoundBlaster.com's home page shows several uses of headings and several different levels of heading styles. Headings are created using the <HEAD> tag. You can use a series of tags, <H1> to <H6> that specify attribute sets for headings; all of these use the Times font, flush left, in various sizes:

<H1>	24 pt.
<H2>	18 pt.
<H3>	14 pt.
<H4>	12 pt.
<H5>	10 pt.
<H6>	8 pt.

SoundBlaster.com Page

The X Files Brings it all Together

- The best way to understand how to orchestrate all of these elements on a page is to look at examples out there on the Web. The X Files Web site is an interesting combination of frames, tables, and heading styles. The navigation bar along the right side of the screen offers three links for each item: a text link, a photo link, and a link to the graphic of the double arrows. These elements are organized on a table.

TheXFiles.com Home Page

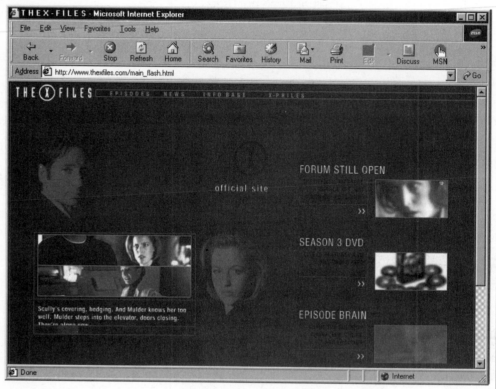

- The box on the left of the home page is actually a separate frame, in which a transcript of an episode of the TV show scrolls constantly, while all other elements of the page stay still. The preview frame also contains its own horizontal scrollbar that controls only the document within it. When the people who run this site want to put next week's episode on the page, they simply change the document that's called into this frame.

- When you visit Web pages try to notice how all the elements, color, text, graphics, and animations, are orchestrated on the page. How is information organized? What information stays on every page and what changes? How are headings used? Are menus and links simple to understand? It is often not the individual pieces of a Web site but the overall organization and display of that information that makes for an interesting and appealing Web experience.

E-BUSINESS ANALYSIS

> *Take a look at each of these sites (full URLs are located at the end of the exercise), then read the site analysis below and answer the questions.*

CASE STUDY 1: CNET BUILDER.COM

- Builder.com includes not only information about tools to build Web sites, but also about the people and disciplines required to do so. Builder.com includes a ten-part series on Information Architecture, the discipline that has evolved to provide structure and flow to Web site creation. Where the Web designer uses tools to divide and order a Web page, an information architect lays down the roadmap for the structure of that page.

Builder.com Information Architecture Page

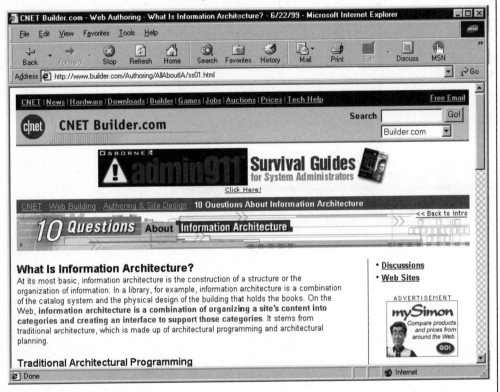

- CNET Builder.com sponsors a Web developer conference called CNET Builder.com Live!. The Web brochure for that event includes a practical use of a frame with scrolling information surrounded by static content. Only the conference details scroll; the conference links stay on the screen at all times. When you click on a link, the document contained in the scrolling frame changes but everything else stays on screen. This is an interesting way to fit a lot of information on a site without making the visitor feel like he or she is constantly having to move from page to page.

CNET Builder.com Live! Web Brochure Page

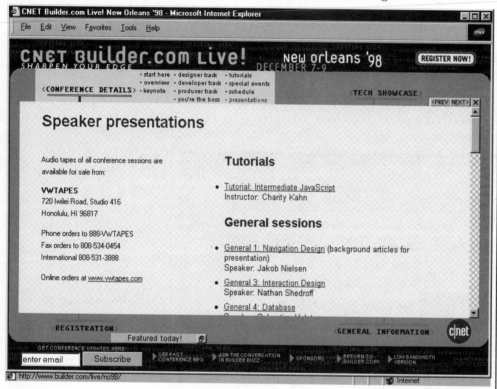

1. What is information architecture?

   _____

2. What does each frame on a page contain?

   _____

3. Can a frame contain its own scrollbar?

   _____

CASE STUDY 2: PEERLESS-FAUCET.COM

- Peerless Faucet uses a simple table with links on its home page. It also uses a table structure for its product catalog. If you look at the kitchen showroom page, you'll see that the table has four columns, with the first and third containing images and the second and fourth containing text. The images are all set up with links; if you click on any of them you go to a page with a larger version of the image on it.

Peerless Faucet Kitchen Faucet Showroom Page

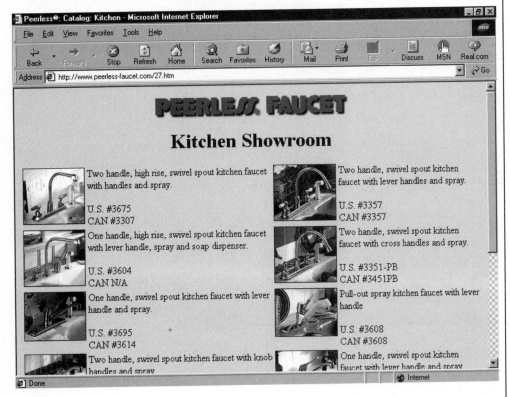

■ Take a look at the HTML code behind this table. You can see the use of the <HEAD> tag right near the top. Then comes the code that sets the background color of the page <BODY BACKGROUND>. The table begins with the ninth line of the code and the <TABLE> tag. Notice that the programmer has used the <HREF> tag to place a photo in the first cell using an imagemap (in this case the first image is called "pics/9.gif"). An imagemap is a reference to an image file.

Peerless Faucet Kitchen Faucet Showroom HTML Code

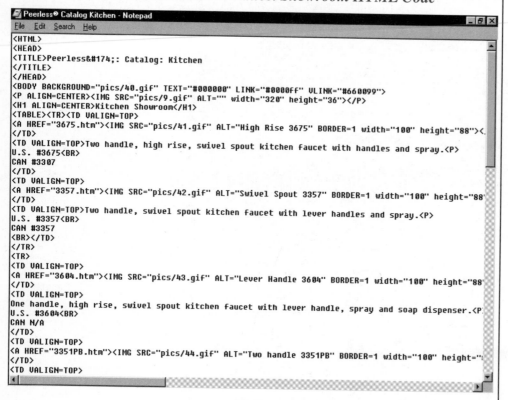

1. What does the <TR> attribute control in a table?

   _____

2. Can tables contain images and text?

   _____

3. How do you enlarge a picture on the showroom page?

   _____

CASE STUDY 3: COCACOLA.COM

- Coca-Cola's Web site is fun no matter where you go. The Coca-Cola Store sports the look of a soda fountain, with one of its menus taking on the look of a booth-sized jukebox. Yet with a lot of graphic elements and a shopping cart, link to specials, contest for winning a year of Coca-Cola, a link to a gift section, search feature, and three navigation menus, it doesn't feel the least bit busy. That's partly due to the way the designer has organized content in neat lists and hidden detailed information on its own pages, which you get to by following these links.

Coca-Cola Soda Shop Page

- The Coca-Cola Investor's page has a different feel; in fact, except for use of a red background and the Coca-Cola logo on each page, consistency isn't the approach of this site. The Investor's area loses the soda fountain metaphor for a more business-like look, and several distinct frames, each with its own scrollbar. One consistent piece of fun on this site is the bubble animation that occasionally pops up, seemingly from your mouse cursor, as you move it around the page.

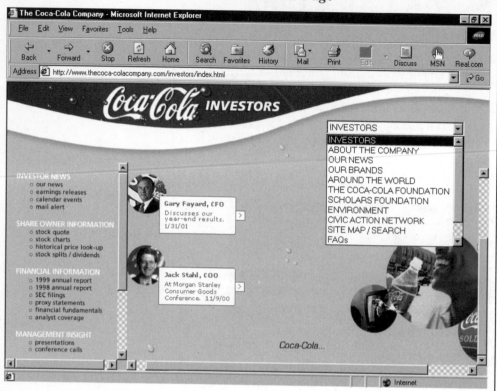

1. What are two ways you can get to the Gift Ideas page from the Soda Fountain?

   _____

2. Who is the CFO of Coca-Cola?

   _____

3. Can you resize the frames on the Investor's page?

   _____

http://www.builder.com
Builder.com

http://www.peerless-faucet.com
Peerless-faucet.com

http://cocacola.com
CocaCola.com

http://www.soundblaster.com
SoundBlaster.com

http://www.thexfiles.com
TheXFiles.com

Theme 30	**Creating Effective Web Page Content** ■ Learn about writing style for the Web ■ Find out where content writers and publishers connect ■ Explore how sites use newsfeeds ■ Learn how conciseness and scannability improve Web writing ■ See how basic rules of writing pertain to Web writing

NOTES

WiredStyle Offers Advice About Working with the Language of the Web

■ **Content** on a Web site is considered by many to be the most important key to bringing customers back—more important than flashing animations and beautiful graphics. What is content? Content can include articles, news items, charts and graphs of information, FAQs, catalog copy, or explanations of customer service policies. Content is essentially the information a site provides, outside of the design elements used on a page, though on a graphic design site content could certainly include photo samples or clip art available for download.

■ Although in its infancy, writing for the Web has developed some special rules for what works and what doesn't. For example, Web sites need to make proper use of Web lingo, that is, terms and phrases related to the Web itself. Do you hyphenate E-Commerce, and should the E or C be capitalized? Should you capitalize Web in the phrases Web browser, Web page, or World Wide Web? Is hotspot one word or two? Wired Magazine, a hip publication about technology, has produced a style guide specifically covering terms and phrases related to the Internet. Their Web site contains some style guidance and is also an interesting example of dramatic Web design.

Buzzword
Content is the information provided on a Web page, outside of the design elements on the page.

Note
Many new terms in Cyberspace have yet to reach an agreed-upon form. What if you can't figure out whether to hyphenate e-mail and style guides disagree? One important guideline is, whichever form you feel is correct, be consistent with it across your site.

Wiredstyle.com Home Page

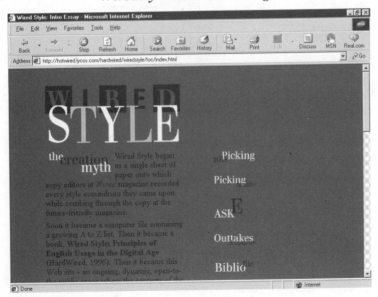

- Although it may seem like a small detail, correct spelling and punctuation on a Web site speaks volumes to visitors. A company that is sloppy on its Web site and makes blatant errors may do the same when it comes to handling a customer order or manufacturing its products. Accuracy and consistency across a Web site are very important to how customers feel about an E-Business.

Find Out Where Companies Get Content at Content-Exchange.com

- Content doesn't come from a single source. Typically some is produced within a company, some is added to a page through sources such as news organizations, still other content might be reprinted from an article, book, or other Web site with permission. Some companies keep Web writers on staff, while others hire freelance writers to contribute content. Some sites use technical or product experts to write, some use marketing people, and it is often easy to spot which is which by the informational or promotional tone of a site. It is also easy to spot a Web site for which content is written by non-writers: such a site is often wordy, uses run-on or incomplete sentences, and is riddled with grammatical errors and disorganized information.

- If companies can't afford the expense of on-staff writers to create with their Web content, they sometimes look to resources such as Content-Exchange.com. Here a business can search for freelance writing talent, place an ad for a writer, or hire content consultants. Another option is to contact a syndicate such as AP Digital from Associated Press and pay a fee to use an article in their archives.

Content-Exchange.com Home Page

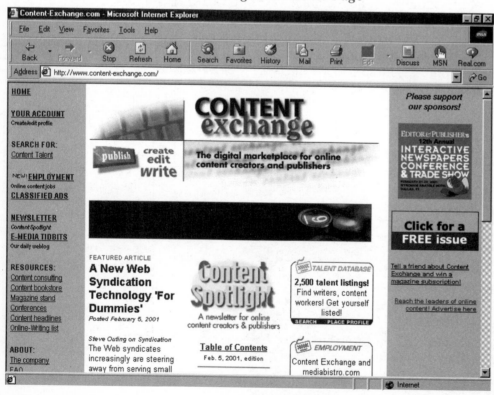

358

- Don't forget sound and motion in your content strategy. AP Digital, for example, offers audio and video files of breaking or historical news events that you can use for a fee. If you choose to place such files on your Web site, be sure that you also provide the player on your site so it can be downloaded for free. RealPlayer and RealAudio are two of the most popular multimedia players.

Moreover.com Provides Newsfeeds Directly to Web Sites

- In addition to hiring somebody to write content for your E-Business, you can place a newsfeed on your site. A newsfeed is a **dynamic** listing of current headlines with links to full articles on the source's Web site. You can find newsfeeds that pick up news items from various publications by different topics, such as business news or technology news. Moreover.com is one provider of a newsfeed product and editorial service.

Moreover.com Page

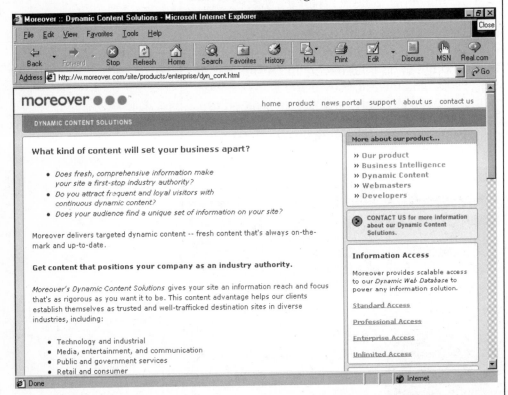

Buzzword

Dynamic content is content that is continually updated at frequent and regular intervals. Dynamic content is typically not text placed on a site but text drawn from another source in real time.

- One of the greatest benefits of a newsfeed is that it is constantly updated, providing fresh content. A software consulting company might put a technology newsfeed on its site, for example; a site that sells movie videos might include entertainment news. Stock data is another form of content feed a site can use, with continually updating numbers on stock market performance, which might be ideal for a bank or investment company Web site. For those with sites that they hope visitors will return to frequently, this kind of fresh content is very important. The goal is that people see new information or offers every time they go to the site.

- Moreover.com and companies like it provide newsfeed options that require only that you place a simple piece of code on your Web site. Content can be provided in various formats, such as Java, HTML, or

XML. Some newsfeeds are free, but services such as Moreover.com edit content somewhat, making sure there are no dead links, or that stories in a certain category really fit that category. Moreover also makes custom feeds available, to place a combination of different kinds of stories on a site.

SharperImage.com Provides an Example of Good Web Writing

- So what exactly makes good Web writing? It's not the same as writing good product manuals or advertising copy. There are actually some unique rules to writing for the Web because of the way people read online. Generally, people don't read every word; they scan a Web page, similar to the way they scan newspaper headlines. They are likely to have come online for a specific piece of information or to make a purchase, though they will take side trips if you grab their attention. People browsing the Web are often in a hurry, ready to take off to the next site if they don't find what they want on your site quickly.

- Because of the way people read online, when writing for the Web it's important to be concise and provide scanning aids like frequent break up of information with headings and bullets lists. Sharper Image's Web site uses a nice balance of graphics and text. Where they do provide text on product pages, they are brief, and break up information into bulleted lists. If there is more information a visitor might want, they place a link on their product page so the visitor can choose to read more, but isn't forced to. Information about related products, like accessories, are also placed on a linked page. In this way a customer can find out the most important details about a product and make a buying decision quickly, or take his or her time and get more details.

Sharper Image Home Page

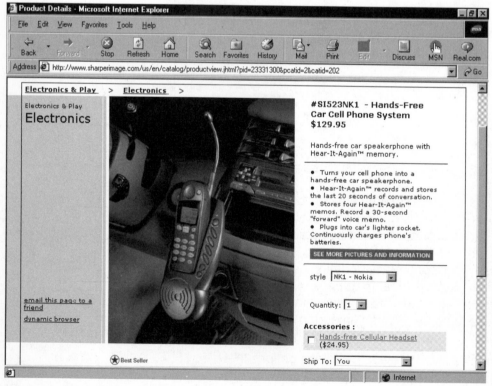

> **Note**
>
> There are several types of organizational patterns you can use in writing; they include chronological, alphabetical, priority (most important to least important or vice-versa), spatial, and cause and effect.

- Because of the need for scannable Web pages, calling attention to certain information on a Web page is something of an art. Use of short, meaningful headings and highlighted keywords within sentences are two ways to do that. Repetition of a key phrase or product name can also be useful for drawing the readers' attention where you want it.

- Certain standard rules of good writing pertain to how writing is organized on a page, for example covering one idea per paragraph of text, and placing information in some logical order such as chronological or cause and effect. If you want to draw the reader to a conclusion, put the conclusion right up front in a paragraph and then build the argument for it. That way the reader sees the key ideas right away if they are merely scanning the first line of each item on the page.

Loudeye.com Proves that Grammar and Mechanics Count

- One site that doesn't produce quite as good content is Loudeye.com, a digital media company. This site uses hardly any graphics to break up information. Their headings are lengthy, and their sentences tend to be run-on, even for an offline publication. For example, look at this sentence on their digital media services page:

  > Whether you are looking to generate additional content for online distribution or you are looking to enhance communication and knowledge sharing by extending your analog content for online use, Loudeye can help you get there.

  Compare this to a sample benefit statement from SharperImage.com:

  > Turns your cell phone into a hands-free car speakerphone.

Loudeye.com Home Page

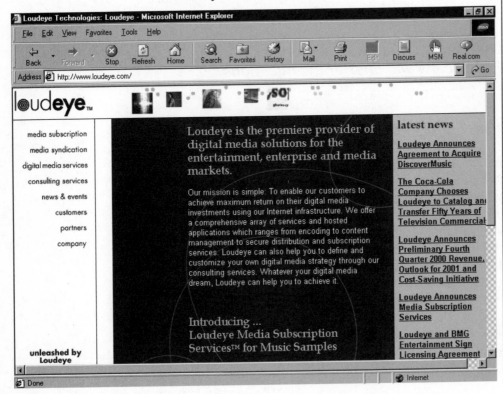

- When you put content on a Web site, always keep in mind what you want every visitor to your site to do. On a product site, you want a customer to buy something. On a site providing information about a service, such as Loudeye, you probably want visitors to contact you and speak with a salesperson. Loudeye's site includes a contact link, but way at the bottom of the page. If you want people to buy, tell them how to do it or put a shopping cart prominently at the top of the page. If you want them to call you, put your 800 number near the top of every page, not behind a link at the bottom. All the content in the world won't help if your customers aren't sure what they should do once you've peaked their interest.

- One good rule of Web writing to keep in mind is you shouldn't pack all of your best content on your home page, but make sure every page on your site has interesting material. This is one way to divide up your information in chunks that are easily read and digested by the reader. Short headings, short paragraphs, and links to related or additional information all help to modularize information on your site.

E-BUSINESS ANALYSIS

Take a look at each of these sites (full URLs are located at the end of the exercise), then read the site analysis below and answer the questions.

CASE STUDY 1: LOUDEYE.COM

- Loudeye.com, a site that is attractive and has obviously had some professional design input, has a few content problems. First, they are guilty of marketing-ese, which is typified by grandiose promises or claims, such as "Whatever your digital media dream, Loudeye can help you to achieve it." Studies have shown that visitors to Web sites are turned off by wild claims and respond more favorably to clear, simple facts. In addition, the writing style on Loudeye.com violates certain rules of good writing, such as using incomplete sentences with unclear subject ("Though it might also mean encryption and digital rights wrapping of your content to ensure protection of your ownership rights and secure file transfer.") and redundancies ("Through our partner network, Loudeye has partnered with leaders in technology....").

Loudeye.com Digital Media Services Page

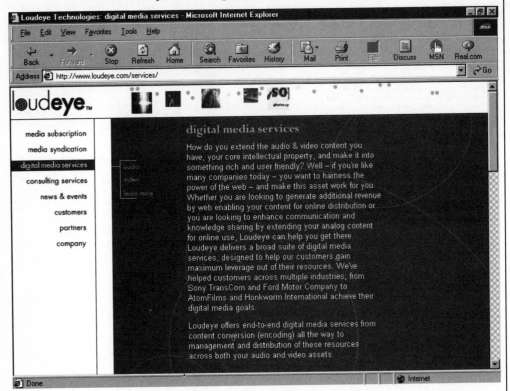

- Loudeye.com also includes copies of online press releases about the company. At the end of one of these a lengthy legal disclaimer assaults the reader. Although it may be required to include this kind of information on your site, you may have a few options: you can create a page for legal disclaimers and company policy information, or you can place such language behind a link at the bottom of a document. Those who want to read it can, those who don't, won't. Although there are some occasions when you will be legally or ethically required to feature this data front and center, do what you can to put the fine print in a convenient, but out-of-the-spotlight location.

Loudeye.com Press Release Page

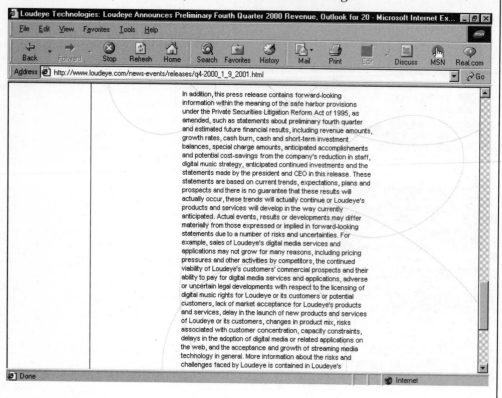

In addition, this press release contains forward-looking information within the meaning of the safe harbor provisions under the Private Securities Litigation Reform Act of 1995, as amended, such as statements about preliminary fourth quarter and estimated future financial results, including revenue amounts, growth rates, cash burn, cash and short-term investment balances, special charge amounts, anticipated accomplishments and potential cost-savings from the company's reduction in staff, digital music strategy, anticipated continued investments and the statements made by the president and CEO in this release. These statements are based on current trends, expectations, plans and prospects and there is no guarantee that these results will actually occur, these trends will actually continue or Loudeye's products and services will develop in the way currently anticipated. Actual events, results or developments may differ materially from those expressed or implied in forward-looking statements due to a number of risks and uncertainties. For example, sales of Loudeye's digital media services and applications may not grow for many reasons, including pricing pressures and other activities by competitors, the continued viability of Loudeye's customers' commercial prospects and their ability to pay for digital media services and applications, adverse or uncertain legal developments with respect to the licensing of digital music rights for Loudeye or its customers or potential customers, lack of market acceptance for Loudeye's products and services, delay in the launch of new products and services of Loudeye or its customers, changes in product mix, risks associated with customer concentration, capacity constraints, delays in the adoption of digital media or related applications on the web, and the acceptance and growth of streaming media technology in general. More information about the risks and challenges faced by Loudeye is contained in Loudeye's

1. What link on the top of the Digital Media Services page allows you to send an e-mail to the company? Is this obvious?

   _____

2. Cite an instance of misuse of punctuation in the Digital Media Services page.

   _____

3. Read the fine print disclaimer from Loudeye.com; does this make you feel comfortable doing business with the company? Why or why not?

   _____

CASE STUDY 2: MOREOVER.COM

■ Moreover.com provides edited newsfeeds to Web sites. They provide a Webfeed Wizard on their site to help customers create the newsfeed that's right for their sites. The Wizard, which is very simple to use, offers 15 channels of news within 18 categories. For example, you could choose Finance news in the technology category to get news on stock market or other financial activities in the technology sector. Once you make these choices you can preview your newsfeed and see if it meets your needs, edit it, or get the code that will place it on your Web page.

Moreover.com Webfeed Wizard Page

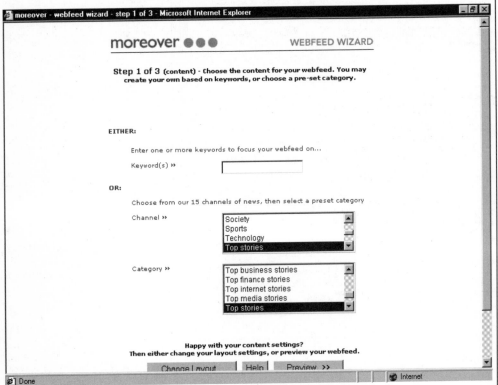

- Moreover.com also offers a tool called Newsblogger. This program allows companies to integrate their own commentary with news stories in Moreover.com's database. This gains exposure for the company as an expert on a topic in the news and draws visitors to their Web site. Another tool that Moreover.com can provide to customers is Email Alerts. Using this feature, a site can e-mail stories of interest to customers.

Moroever.com NewsBlogger Page

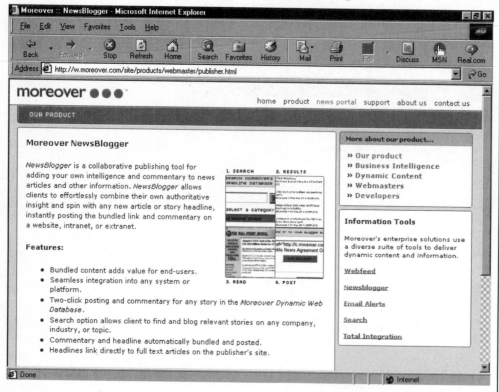

1. What is a newsfeed?

   _____

2. Can NewsBlogger be used on an intranet?

   _____

3. What is dynamic content?

   _____

CASE STUDY 3: SHARPERIMAGE.COM

■ One of the strengths of the Sharper Image Web site is its balance of images and text to create a quick and easy shopping experience. Their Gift Guides provide a good example of this. Rather than wordy advice about gift giving, or even much in the way of product descriptions, these highly visual guides simply show the products they recommend in each category with the name of the product and a picture. The names of their products are very descriptive: not Elegance Hair Dryer but Ionic Conditioning Quiet Hair Dryer, placing clear information about the features of the product right in the name.

SharperImage.com Gift Guide Page

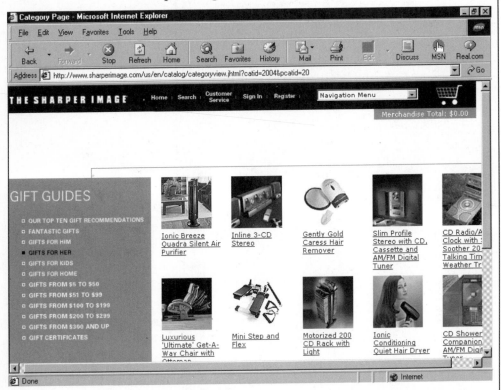

■ SharperImage.com is as concise in presenting information about its company as it is in describing its products. When you click on the Investor Relations link you get a simple table with a wealth of stock performance information at a glance and only one simple disclaimer sentence below. They have placed additional investment information on linked pages so the visitor can find exactly what he or she needs without weeding through several paragraphs of self-serving text about the company.

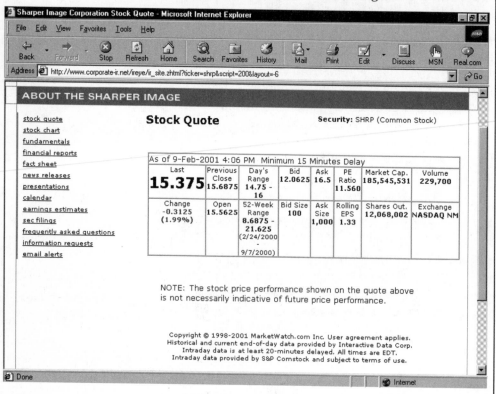

1. Why is it important to be concise when writing for the Web?

   _____

2. How can using pictures on a site support written content?

   _____

3. How often is the stock information for Sharper Image updated?

   _____

http://hotwired.lycos.com/hardwired/wiredstyle/
WiredStyle

http://www.content-exchange.com/
Content-Exchange.com

http://www.moreover.com/
Moreover.com

http://www.sharperimage.com
SharperImage.com

http://www.loudeye.com
LoudEye.com

Theme 31	Designing Effective Web Page Layout ■ Discover the importance of a consistent look and feel ■ See good and bad examples of Web page navigation ■ Learn how tables bring order to a page ■ Break a page into sections to make the most of horizontal space ■ Determine how long a Web page should be

NOTES

Take a Look at a Consistent Overall Design at Sentosa

- When someone coined the term 'surfing the Web' they were a good observer of human nature. People don't move logically from place to place online, they slide around on a wave of impulse. That's why it's a good idea to give a visitor a sense of place when he or she lands on one of your Web pages. Visitors should know when they've entered a unique space and when they've left it. They should have consistency not only to identify the space, but to give the Web site a personality through design that sends a clear message on every page. In addition, consistency of the pages within a site makes that site easier to use, because navigation tools are identified in the same way and located in the same place, and a visitor doesn't have to reorient him- or herself every time he or she moves to a new area.

- Sentosa is the Web site for an Asian restaurant that provides a remarkably consistent look and feel. The design and its consistency have an Asian flair, in keeping with the style of the restaurant, and a sense of calm and comfort for the prospective diner. The site creates its consistency through the use of a single color palette, placement of the restaurant logo, use of fonts, and a consistency to graphic images. When you enter this space you could never stumble out of it unknowingly.

Note

It's important to test your page design with several browsers from a few different computers. That's because browsers deal somewhat differently with colors, and some browsers, like Netscape, will view the same page slightly differently on different platforms, such as Mac, PC, and UNIX.

Sentosa Home Page

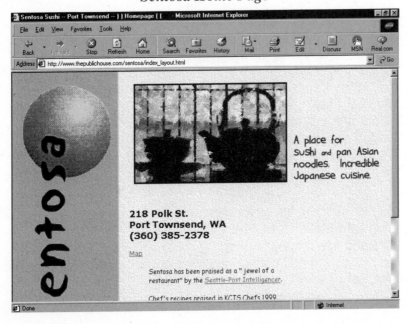

- Consistency of graphics is important for more than just a unity of look and feel. If you use a single graphic several times on a site, even if you place it differently or resize it, you can reduce the download time for each page on your site. That's because a graphic only has to be downloaded once; then it can be used again and again. Once a visitor has viewed a page with that graphic, any other page utilizing it will load more quickly.

See the Good and Bad of Web Design at WebPagesThatSuck.com

- There are many factors that contribute to good Web page design: use of color and graphics, length of each Web page, navigation tools, logical organization of content, good use of fonts, and so on. One site that takes a look at all of these with a critical eye is Web Pages That Suck. Because one of the best ways to get ideas for good page design is by seeing what works and what doesn't, it's helpful to view the examples shown on this site and read the analyses of sites that are doing it wrong, and a few that are doing it right.

Web Pages That Suck Home Page

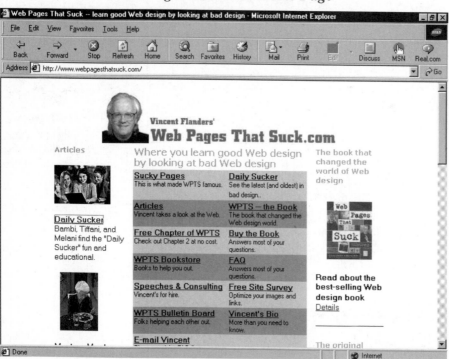

- Because Web pages are interactive, in the sense that those viewing them can control their display to some degree, they have to be both attractive and useable. Some of the best E-Commerce Web sites may not be the prettiest from a graphic design standpoint, but they make effective use of the space allotted to them to get information across to a customer and sell a product. They also make navigating around the page and the site easy and intuitive.

- Planning the layout of your Web pages has benefits beyond creating logical navigation tools and providing a consistency of look: by building a logical layout you can create one file and use a copy of it for every page on your site. Then you simply have to add and edit content appropriate to each page. This makes for much less work, especially if your basic layout is at all complex.

SaabUSA.com Makes Good use of Horizontal Space

■ On any Web page you have two dimensions to the real estate you can build on: the horizontal and the vertical. Horizontal space runs across the page, vertical runs from top to bottom. Some sites, such as SaabUSA.com, find creative ways to maximize the horizontal area of a page. In this way users get all they need on one short page and never have to scroll anywhere to see more. This site is organized so that information is broken up into several shorter pages, with links to move easily among them. Depending on the amount of information you have to get across on your site, you may find ways to make the most of the horizontal space available to you.

SaabUSA.com Home Page

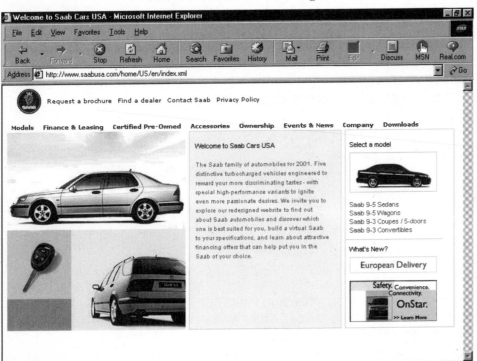

■ One tool that helps Web designers make good use of the whole page is tables. Tables are created using HTML tags and are pretty much like the tables you create in a word processing program. Each cell of a table can contain its own graphics or text. On Saab's home page you can clearly make out the separate portions of the table that divide the content up for the reader. You can essentially use tables to create separate columns across a page.

Harry and David Fits a lot of Information into its Pages

■ Visit some E-Commerce sites and you'll think you're in Times Square: flashing animations, floating banner ads, a dozen photos, and linked headlines screaming for attention. It can be a challenge to get a great deal of information, perhaps a full catalog of products and the sales tools to promote them, onto a Web page. But by using organizational tools such as tables, attractive and easy-to-read fonts, and appropriate layout, it is possible to pack a lot of information into one place and not give all your visitors a headache.

Note
Studies have shown that people read 25% more slowly online, and most people aren't that comfortable with reading from a computer screen. Keeping the content short and to the point should be a goal of any Web site designer.

Technical Note
Tables, though useful, do present some problems for Web designers. Some browsers might have trouble reading complex tables, or might cut off a portion of a table. Although flexible in the sense that you can modify the size of each cell of the table, they don't accommodate overlapping columns or less logically arranged grids of content. However, tables are a relatively simple way to bring a sense of order to a Web page and control the placement of elements on the page.

- HarryandDavid.com is one such site. Looking at their home page, you see a balance of ordered design and scannability. **Scannability** makes the most out of the way people look at Web pages, reading only short pieces of text, such as brief headings, and glancing at pictures or graphics for a clue as to the content behind a link.

HarryandDavid.com Home Page

- E-Commerce Web sites are constantly changing, providing variety of content to returning customers, offering new promotions on a regular basis, or providing fresh news or other information. It's a good idea to plan your page for this constant updating. Pick a spot for a larger photograph of the latest product you're promoting, and designate a column for constantly updating news story links. This not only makes updating the page easier, it helps returning visitors to find this week's promotion or the latest headline at a glance.

Maison Europeenne De La Photographie Uses a Visual Approach to Web Page Layout

- Determining page length on a Web site is a challenge. Shorter pages keep the important information in front of the reader and avoid constant scrolling. However, breaking up a lengthier document into segments that appear on separate Web pages can be jarring to somebody who is reading and causes a delay while a new page loads. Plus, breaking information up too much can make for a very big site and cause navigation difficulties.

Buzzwords

Scannability relates to how easily a reader can quickly review a Web page and get the information he or she needs. Graphics, short headings, and concise text all add to the scannability of a Web page.

Note

If you break up a lengthy document to fit on several separate pages, be sure to include links to go to the next page and previous page at the bottom of the text. In this way readers move quickly from the bottom of one page to the top of the next, causing minimal interruption of their reading experience.

■ Web designers have come up with a few solutions. One, used on the collections page of Maison Europeenne De La Photographie, is to create a hyperlinked list of portions of a long document at the top of the page. On this site the links are all photographs, in keeping with the focus of the site. If you actually scrolled down this collections page, you would go through multiple screens of information. But you can easily jump to any piece of the collection page by clicking on its link at the top.

Maison Europeenne De La Photographie Home Page

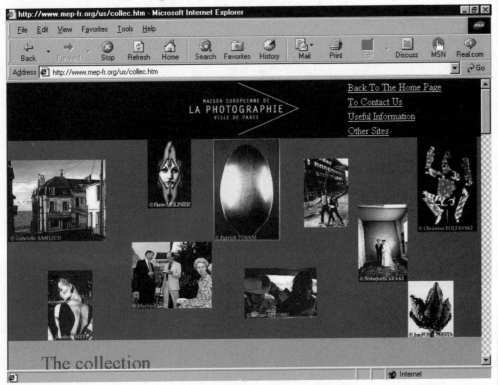

■ Many sites use this link index approach for glossaries, alphabetical listings of store locations, or other information. By clicking on a letter link, a reader moves to that section of a store locator, for example. Pages designed this way should also include a top of page link on every page, so that once you've jumped to, say, the Walla-Walla store in a store locator listing, you can move back up to the linked index with a single click.

E-business Analysis

Take a look at each of these sites (full URLs are located at the end of the exercise), then read the site analysis below and answer the questions.

CASE STUDY 1: THEPUBLICHOUSE.COM.SENTOSA

- Sentosa's Web site has the luxury of being able to focus on beauty of design on its Web pages, because the information is minimal and can be contained on about six Web pages. Not all E-Commerce sites have this space for design, but the methods this site uses to create a consistent look and feel can be used by even the most information-intensive site. First, the Sentosa logo appears on every page; with one exception it's in the upper-left hand corner. Also, the handmade paper-look background with a darker brown border along the left hand side of the page is used consistently throughout the site. There are only two fonts used on this entire site, which makes for a very clean look on each page.

Sentosa Menu Page

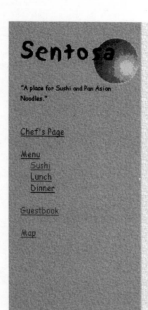

Sentosa

"A place for Sushi and Pan Asian Noodles."

Chef's Page

Menu
   Sushi
   Lunch
   Dinner

Guestbook

Map

Menu

Many centuries ago, the people of Japan began preserving fish in fermented rice because of a lack of refrigeration. As refrigeration became available this food faded from popularity. Tastes changed and the people of Japan were looking for a fresh, healthy food source. Thus, the interest in what is now talked about as "sushi" resurfaced. Sushi began being presented at joyous occasions such as weddings and births. Contrary to popular American thought, sushi does not mean raw fish, but reflects its celebratory connotation.

The two most popular styles of sushi are handheld rice presentations called "maki" and "nigiri". Maki denotes the roll of rice and nori (a pressed, dried sheet of seaweed high in protein and trace minerals) filled with assorted fish and vegetables. Nigiri implies a ball of rice which has been topped with egg or fish. "Chirashi" is a third method of preparation offered traditionally in Japan where an assortment of fish is place on a bed of sushi rice. The fare served at sushi bars usually reflects that of local procurement including seafood such as crab, octopus, prawns, surf clams, mussels, geoduck, salmon and tuna. These items may just as likely be offered cooked as uncooked.

■ Sentosa uses a simple menu system to navigate its small number of Web pages, located on the left side of most pages. Graphics are used well: although size and placement of a graphic on each page might vary for visual interest, the colors and style of each graphic are identical. The graphic elements are photos with effects applied, such as dithering. Dithering is a photo imaging technique that essentially repeats pixels of color in a photo to create a soft, smudged effect.

Sentosa Luncheon Menu Page

1. What is dithering?

   _____

2. What tools does this site provide for navigation?

   _____

3. What purpose does consistency of look and feel serve for visitors to a site?

   _____

CASE STUDY 2: HARRYANDDAVID.COM

- Harry and David is an E-Commerce site that has a lot of information to get across to visitors. It is typical of a site built around a catalog of products and shopping cart function. Where the home page sports several different sizes of photos and promotions, pages of the catalog itself provide a certain order to the page by using neat rows of identically-sized product photos. The text below them is kept to the essentials: discount, item name, and price.

HarryandDavid.Catalog Page

■ As visitors drill down through this site to more specific product information, they are rewarded with a less busy page design. The two navigation devices across the top and along the left side of the page stay consistent, but the central portion of the page now contains only one product photo and a reasonably brief product description. A handy **You are here** line above the photo helps the customer know where he or she is in this information-rich site.

HarryandDavid.com Product Page

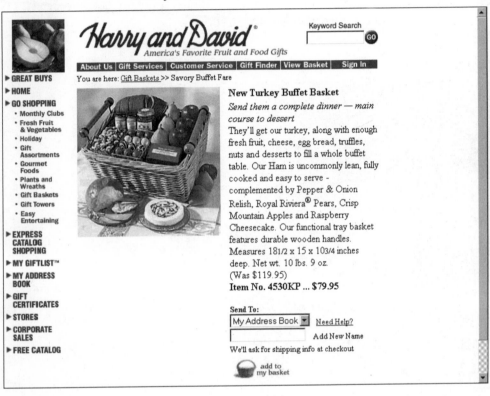

1. How many fonts can you identify on the Harry and David site?

   _____

2. What design device is used to create columns of content on this site?

   _____

3. How can you send information about a product to a friend from the product pages?

   _____

CASE STUDY 3: MAISON EUROPEENNE DE LA PHOTOGRAPHIE

- This site has the dual challenge of maintaining an attractive design to appeal to its visually-oriented visitors and fitting a lot of information into one place. The photo catalogue on this site places the entire catalog on one Web page. If you paged down you'd go through about 40 screens of information. To help the reader use the catalogue, the site offers a set of alphabetical links. Each catalogue entry also provides a link to a separate image page.

Image Catalogue Page

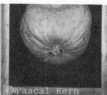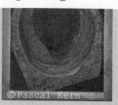

The Image Catalogue

Reproduction is strictly prohibited.

According to the law of 11 March 1957 and 3 july 1985, the author rights for all creative works are protected. In particular photographic works and those created by similar technical means as the photography. Any representation, reproduction or exploitation of a photography as a whole or in parts, carried out without consent and written permission by the author or his eligible party is strictly prohibited and can be charged with imprisonment from 3 months to 2 years and a fine from 6000 to 120 000 FF

A B C D E F G H I J K L M N O P Q R S T U V W X Y Z

ANONYME
"Aley, 1936"
"Le Liban intime, photographies 1850-1860", Institut du Monde Arabe, Mois de la Photo 1998
© Collection El Khoury-Pharaon/FAI

- Consistency isn't the strong suit of this site. Where the image catalog and some other pages cram several screens of information on a single page, other pages, such as the Library page, use devices to fit everything on a single screen. One device used on this page is a frame; a frame is a way to split a Web page into sections, allowing for independent scrolling of each section and separate documents in each frame. On this page the text is in a separate frame; the two arrows to the left of the text allow the reader to scroll the text up and down, independently from the rest of the page. The visitor doesn't even have to click on the arrows; by passing a mouse over an arrow the scrolling is activated.

The Library Page

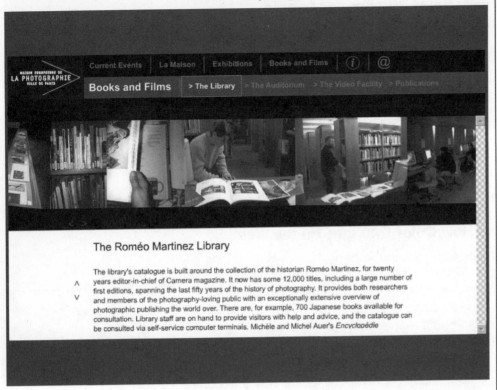

1. What is a frame?
   _____

2. Where is the Musee Europeenne de La Photographie located?
   _____

3. Where on the Library page is a table used?
   _____

http://www.thepublichouse.com/sentosa
Sentosa

http://www.webpagesthatsuck.com/
Web Pages That Suck

http://www.saabusa.com/
Saab USA

http://HarryandDavid.com/
Harry and David

http://www.mep-fr.org/
Maison Europeenne de La Photographie

Working with Color, Images, and Fonts
- ■ Learn about how the Web affects color
- ■ Explore how fonts get a message across
- ■ See how to use graphics and type to appeal to your audience
- ■ Learn about the importance of a consistent look and feel
- ■ Use images to add elegance to a site

NOTES

ColorMatters.com Shows How Color Changes on the Web

- ■ In the early days of the Web, way back in the early 1990s, Web pages all sported white backgrounds. In 1995 Netscape Navigator came out in a new version that supported some HTML tags that allowed designers to modify the background of a Web page in various ways. The bgcolor= attribute could be used to designate a specific color, instead of a graphic. Web sites today use every color of the rainbow—or at least of available color **palettes**—to catch a visitor's attention.

- ■ One of the challenges designers still face, however, is the way that colors appear to users of the Web. There are several variables that make color on the Web problematic. When an image is scanned into a computer originally, it might or might not have been color corrected for a computer screen. Different operating systems and monitors handle colors differently. To make things worse, Web browsers deal with colors in different ways, so viewing the same page with Netscape Navigator and Internet Explorer might display slightly different colors. Web sites such as ColorMatters.com try to help you sort through the confusion.

Buzzword

A *palette* is an array of color choices. In traditional painting, a palette is an actual board on which an artist places various paint colors. On the Web, palettes are sets of colors that are available to Web designers based on various combinations of numerical values for red, green, and blue.

ColorMatters.com Home Page

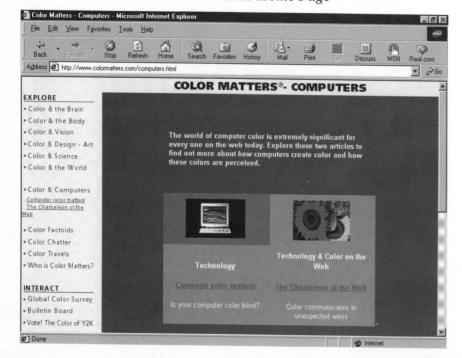

- Windows offers a 256-color palette. Netscape Navigator reduces colors to 216 colors. UNIX varies its color palette based on how many colors are available to it, but typically uses 125 colors. A more recently developed Reallysafe palette promises that its 216 colors will all be displayed accurately with any computer and any browser, but it hasn't been the complete solution to the problem. The bottom line is that a Web designer must understand these palettes and stick to the colors that most computers and browsers can read accurately.

- Beyond the technical requirements for color, Web designers must also consider the psychological impact of color. Studies have been done that suggest that orange makes people irritable; blue is soothing; brown suggests dependability; and green suggests prosperity. Choosing a color selection for a Web site that matches the style of your business or product and needs of your visitors is an important consideration for E-Commerce Web sites.

Choosing Fonts Wisely at Wallpaper.com

- **Fonts** are families of style applied to text, such as Times New Roman or Arial. Fonts can be playful or plain, artistic or conservative, and they can create a definite feel to a Web page. There are literally thousands of fonts that have been designed, and many of those are available to even the most basic computer today. Graphic designers spend a lifetime mastering the art of using fonts well. Web designers are just beginning to explore the power of fonts on the Web. A site such as Wallpaper.com is an interesting example; it makes a statement with its use of fonts and the artistic positioning of text on a page.

Buzzword

A *font* is a family of style applied to text. Font's can be *serif* or *sans serif*; a serif font has small lines that extend off of certain portions of letters, and a sans serif font is missing those lines.

Wallpaper.com Home Page

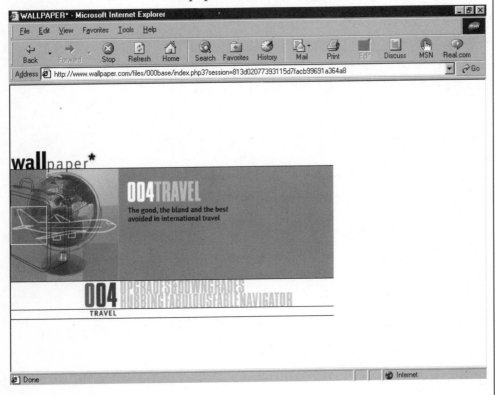

- Fonts are typically broken into two categories: serif and sans serif. A serif font, such as Times New Roman, uses small extensions off of letters, such as the little lines extending off of the legs of a capital n (N). A sans serif font, such as Arial, is missing these extensions (N). Serif fonts tend to have a more conservative, traditional look, and work well in lengthier documents, such as books, where the small extensions help the eye keep moving from one word to another. Sans serif fonts are often used on headlines, to help the reader stop and focus on the clean-looking letters.

- Fonts are more than fashion for text: they become an important design element on any page, print or Web. The type and variety of fonts, together with font effects, such as bold or italic formatting, can make a pleasing page, or a busy, difficult to read page. A site such as Wallpaper, a design magazine, makes creative use of fonts, modifying one font for size, boldness, and even space between letters and lines of text. However, it makes the reader work to find his or her way around the page. For this design site, that might be okay; for an online bank, it might be disastrous.

Note

Traditional wisdom is that you should never use more than three font styles on a page and might be better off sticking to two. You should also avoid too many font effects, such as use of italic and bold, variation in size or upper- and lowercase letters, and shadows, unless, of course, your goal is to create a sense of chaos or excitement.

Scholastic Books Breaks all the Rules

- So how are people using color and fonts on the Web? If a Web site is well designed, that depends on the product and audience to which they want to appeal. Scholastic Books' Web site is meant to appeal to kids and have a fun feel. For that reason, they have broken all the rules about use of font and color, because they want to create a sense of excitement and fun. They combine orange, blue, green, purple, and pink on one page. They have fonts with shadows, serif and sans serif fonts, various font sizes in a single sentence, and use at least four fonts on the same page. Does it work? Yes, for this product and this audience, it does.

Scholastic Books Home Page

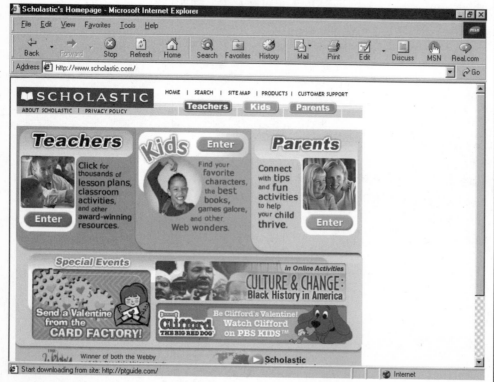

- Online businesses should first analyze the mood they want to create as well as practical concerns such as whether visitors can easily read content and figure out how to navigate around the site. A company that sells rare books to typically wealthy, older customers, would probably use a conservative color palette with dependable colors, such as brown, and fonts that are simple and easy to read. They would want an elegant, uncluttered feeling, with a reasonable amount of white space on each page. White space on a printed page is the blank space around the text or images. On the Web, white space isn't always white: it is simply empty background with no text or graphics, whether that background is white or purple. Leaving blank white space on a page creates a sense of calm in the reader. Fonts used on a site with this kind of visitor would tend to be conservative and elegant, such as:

Antique Olive

Book Antiqua

Century Gothic

COPPERPLACE GOTHIC LIGHT

- A Web site that sells CDs of the latest music to teens would avoid the cute feel of Scholastic and the elegant feel of a rare bookstore. The music site might use darker colors, such as black with flashes of bright red, and graphics that appeal to a teen audience. There would be a lot going on on each page to entertain this hip, young visitor. Font choices for such a page might include:

CHILLER

Bauhaus 93

KRISTEN ITC

RAVIE

Creating a Consistent Look and Feel at Guggenheim.org

- Once you know what feeling you want to create and make some choices about color and font for your site, another important element is a consistency across the site. Think of a Web site as being like a house. It would be jarring to move from room to room suddenly being assaulted by different styles of furnishings and uncomplimentary colors. A Web site, like a home, is an environment your visitors move around. Consistency drives home your basic goals for the site and makes visitors comfortable moving around from page to page.

- A good example of a site that provides a consistent look and feel is Guggenheim.org, online home of the Guggenheim Museums. The visitor to this site is interested in the visual arts, so a modern, graphically pleasing look with simple fonts is appropriate. One device this site has used for consistency is in the way the visitor uses the graphic image menu at the top. When you click on one of these choices, only the text in the bottom half of the screen changes; the photo menu stays in place. The visitor is in the same environment, but the information has changed. Different areas of the site, such as Education or Exhibitions, use a similar graphic menu device with different choices, making the site easy to use.

Guggenheim.org Programs Page

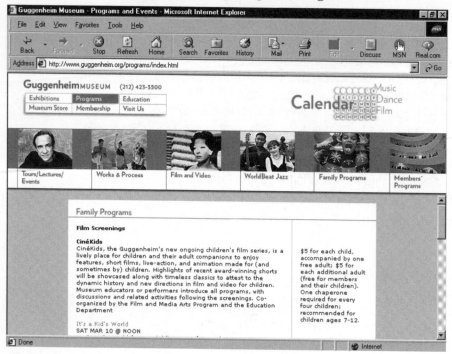

Watershedwines.com.au Makes Good Use of Images and Graphics

- Designing a Web page involves more than just text and color. It also involves use of graphics in the form of illustrations, photos, or design elements. It's the combination of all of those that produce the final impression of a site such as Scholastic.com or Watershedwines.com.au, an Australian Web site for investors in a new winery venture.

Watershedwines.com Home Page

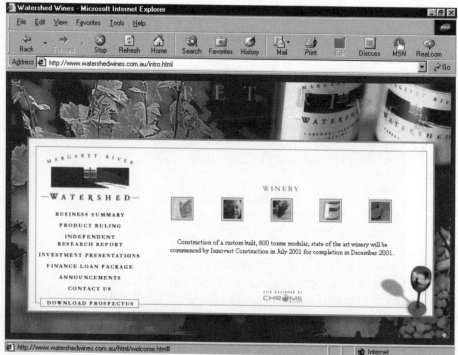

Technical Note

You can use the same HTML tags to create consistent backgrounds on all of your pages. Backgrounds are set using the bgcolor= attribute. Colors are designated by a value for red, green, and blue (RGB). Most word processors include color palettes that use the RGB value system for backgrounds in drawing objects; this is a good place for you to experience the way that color values are specified. Designers can build style sheets for Web pages that include values for a page background, font color, and font colors for links, then used on every page of a Web site for consistency.

- This site uses an image rather than solid colors for its background; in this case a photograph is used as a backdrop for the contents of the page. The font used is traditional and elegant. Each of the small photos in the middle of the home page is used to display different information about an aspect of the winery, its people, marketing, and so on. When a visitor passes his or her mouse over an image, text appears beneath the image relevant to that topic. There is also a text-based menu on the left of the page that offers access to other pages with more detailed information.

- Web designers use graphic elements for a variety of reasons: to create a feeling on a page, as with the background image on Watershed Wines' site; to help the visitor find a topic with a visual clue; to inform visitors as with a news article photo; and to provide visual interest. The decision to use a graphic should involve the appropriateness of the graphic to the mood of the site and the usefulness of the graphic in navigating the site.

E-BUSINESS ANALYSIS

Take a look at each of these sites (full URLs are located at the end of the exercise), then read the site analysis below and answer the questions.

CASE STUDY 1: SCHOLASTIC.COM

- Scholastic Books publishes books for younger readers, and its site reflects that audience's interests. One area of the site is the Harry Potter Discussion Chamber. Notice that this page differs from the rest of the site: it uses the look and feel of the Harry Potter book series, with fonts and images from those books. This provides a virtual book experience for the visitor who instantly recognizes these elements. Although consistency of look and feel is usually important, Web sites that provide information about distinctly branded products, such as a book series or lines of clothing, might consider allowing a unique look to certain pages on the site to support that brand recognition.

Harry Potter Discussion Chamber Page

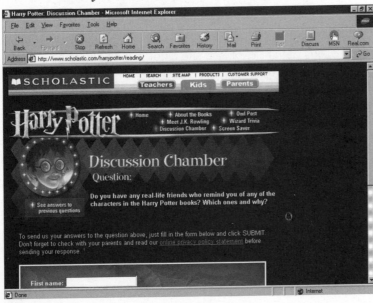

- The Scholastic site also includes a feature called Get Quizzy, a quiz on various books where a visitor can show off his or her knowledge of a book and possibly get his or her name listed on the site. When you select a book on the Get Quizzy page, you are taken to a page that looks like the one on the following page, with the book cover image and a brief description of the plot. All of the pages in the quiz sport this same look. Although the background uses orange and purple swirls, there are few graphics on these pages. Instead, the sense of fun is created by the use of casual fonts and cartoon-like numbers.

Scholastic.com Get Quizzy Page

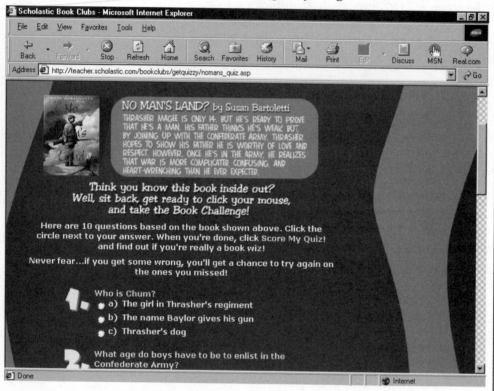

1. What is branding?

   _____

2. How do the Teachers, Kids, and Parents pages of the Scholastic site differ in look and feel?

   _____

3. How do you make a selection of an answer in the Get Quizzy quiz?

   _____

CASE STUDY 2: GUGGENHEIM.ORG

- The Guggenheim site is really five sites for the various Guggenheim museums around the world and a virtual museum. The New York museum site includes a museum store. Product pages in the museum store appeal to the visually-oriented visitor, with a picture of the product front and center and minimal text to describe it. A simple Order button leads to the purchasing process. Simple white or light gray backgrounds on the site's pages let the all-important pictures stand out.

Guggenheim Museum Store Product Page

- The Exhibitions page of the Guggenheim New York site offers similar simplicity. Photo images serve to display different exhibition information, and the area containing information and photos from the exhibitions has the same clean white background. Because color on the site comes to a great extent from the photographs and artwork, colors in the backgrounds and fonts are kept to a minimum, with simple borders of solid colors such as red, blue, green, and orange providing elegance to the page layouts.

Guggenheim Museum Exhibitions Page

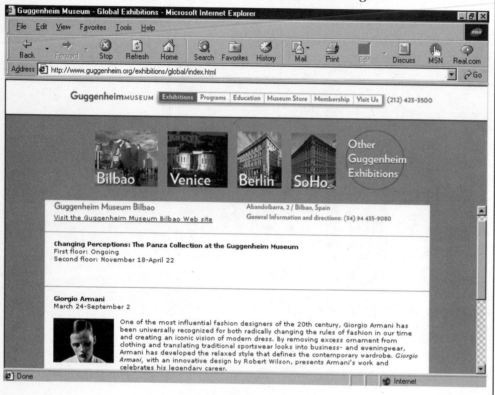

1. In what cities around the world are Guggenheim museums located?

   _____

2. What is white space?

   _____

3. What can affect how a visitor to a Web site sees color?

   _____

CASE STUDY 3: WATERSHEDWINES.COM.AU

- Watershed Wines' site is focused around elegance and luxury to match the wine connoisseur audience. Colors used are greens and purples, to suggest vines and grapes and complement the photo background. The graphic images of the Watershed logo and the wine glass in the right hand corner are consistent on every page of the site, as is the background image. On the home page, depending on which photo image you place your cursor over, the name of that topic and information about it will be displayed. This doesn't require moving to a new Web page for each topic, but a simple HTML command to display different text depending on your mouse location.

Watershedwines.com.au Home Page

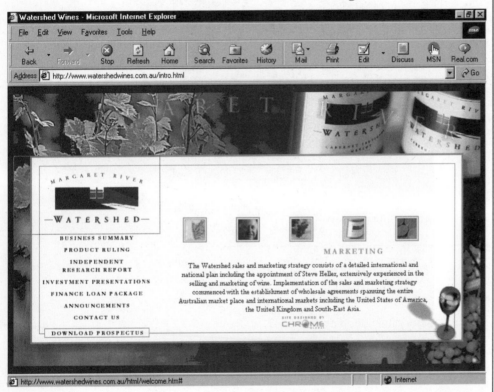

- When you first go to the Watershedwines.com.au site, an introductory animation appears. This animation shows a beautiful picture of grapes hanging on a vine and text floating in and out of the picture with key marketing messages. This movement of text adds to its impact. Notice that the current text is slightly smaller and bolder than the text that is moving off the screen and fading away. This creates a collage affect that is both attractive and helps the visitor focus on several layers of information presented over 30 seconds or so of animation.

Watershedwines.com.au Introductory Animation

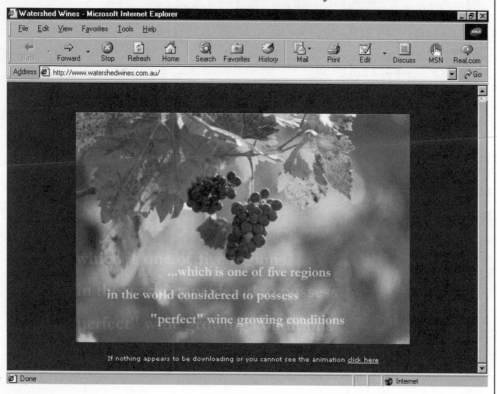

1. Is the font used on this site serif or sans serif?

   _____

2. How do the fonts on this site match the character of the typical visitor?

   _____

3. How can a visitor bypass the introductory animation on this site?

   _____

http://www.colormatters.com/
ColorMatters.com
http://www.wallpaper.com
Wallpaper.com
http://www.scholastic.com
Scholastic Books
http://www.Guggenheim.org/
Guggenheim Museum
http://www.watershedwines.com.au/
Watershedwines.com.au

Working with Animation, Photography, and Video on the Web
- **See how 3-D animations bring life to the Web**
- **Learn how animations are used to get across a business message**
- **Look at streaming interactive media created with Shockwave**
- **Explore how sites are using media to promote products**
- **Discover how video is used online**

NOTES

Learn All About Flash Animations at FlashResource.com

- **Animations** began in the world of movies, where series of images were shown in quick succession, forming the animated cartoons we all grew up with. Animation on the Web can be created in a similar way, but the technologies that are used to create animations vary and browsers work with them differently. These include animated GIFs, Dynamic HTML, Java applets, and **plug-ins** such as Flash and Shockwave from Macromedia.

- Animated GIFs (an image file format) are the closest to cartoon animation: they are essentially a series of bitmap files that a browser plays back in sequence. GIF animation is easy to create, and most browsers can work with GIF images easily. However, because a GIF animation contains settings for each **pixel** in an image, and every image in the sequence is a full bitmap image, it's easy for one of these files to become very large. It's also not possible to add sound to a GIF animation. GIF animation is best used in simple, short animations.

- Dynamic HTML, referred to as dHTML, uses scripting languages such as JavaScript that work with your browser to display images. Browsers contain an element called the document object model (DOM), which controls the way the browser displays a Web page. dHTML essentially works with the DOM to tell a browser to change the location of an image on a page, creating the sense of movement. dHTML is rather complicated to script, but one benefit of this form of animation is that it's recognized by most browsers. dHTML is not that robust: all you can do with it is move images around a screen. To create more complex animations, users have to move beyond their browsers' built-in capabilities and use a plug-in program.

- Two other methods of building animations are with Java applets (a small add-on program for your browser) or two very popular plug-ins from Macromedia called Flash and Shockwave. Java applets have the benefit of working on any platform and are a great way to cause animations to interact with other elements on a Web page. Flash and Shockwave are vector-based animation viewers. Vector-based graphics can be smaller because rather than describing every pixel in an image, they describe sections of an image mathematically. In addition, not every frame of an animation needs to be created because vector-based animation players can calculate in-between frames (called tween frames) that occur from one point to another in an animation. In this way they can build those

Buzzwords

Animation is the playing back of a series of images in sequence.

Plug-ins are programs that help your Web browser software do something it can't do on its own. For example, the browser may need a plug-in program to play a certain type of video file. Some plug-ins download and install automatically when you need them. In other instances, you will need to download and install the plug-in manually.

Pixels are very small elements that in combination make up an image.

calculated tween frames on the fly. Flash is built into most browsers these days, so it has become a very popular animation format. Many sites such as FlashResource.com have been started to support the enthusiastic Flash designer community.

FlashResource.com Home Page

Explore How E-Commerce Sites are Using Animation at Spheranetworks.com

- Any use of animation, sound, or video on a Web site has an upside and a downside. The downside is that these files can take a long time to play back and may cause visitors with a standard telephone connection to become frustrated. Some of the formats and players cause a jerky quality in the playback that seems amateurish. Streaming and compression help to some extent. Compression is a way of making a file smaller by simplifying the information contained in it; streaming is an approach to playing back video, sound, or animation that allows a portion of the sequence to play while the rest of the file is loading in the background. This is one reason why many Web sites, such as Spheranetworks.com, include an animated introduction to their page; the introduction plays while all the other images and text for the Web site load in the background. This entertains the visitor and diffuses his or her impatience from waiting for a Web site to appear.

Spheranetworks.com Introduction Page

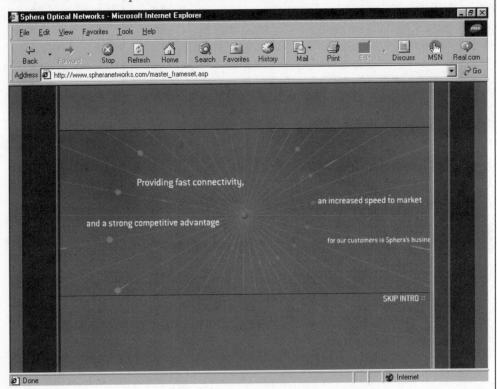

- Animations are used for a variety of reasons by E-Businesses. Sphera Networks' animated introduction delivers key marketing messages for the company and manipulates the company logo to help build brand recognition. Some businesses use animation to show a process in action. Others animate product catalogs to create filmstrip effects, moving products across the screen to add motion to the flow of the page.

- 3-D Web graphics are the next step after Flash animations. 3-D graphics allow a user to interact with the animation, moving objects around and actually resizing them or causing certain actions to take place. 3-D content brings up interesting possibilities for E-Commerce because customers can do more than look at a static picture of a product. They can move it around and view it from all sides. This may help overcome objections of customers that they can't actually pick up and look at items when shopping online.

Shockwave Takes the Animation Model Further at Shockwave.com

- Flash and Shockwave are both vector-based animation programs, and they're both from Macromedia. But they have some important differences. Flash was built from the ground up for the Web and intended for transmission of animations over telephone lines. Shockwave has been around longer and was originally used for building animations for CD-ROMs. Shockwave allows you to create more complex multimedia, with more detailed animations and interactivity. Shockwave has some built-in abilities to work with 3-D graphics that make it more flexible for more advanced animations. Flash wins out over Shockwave when it comes to its availability, because it's built into most browsers, but the Shockwave plug-in is easily downloaded from the Web. In reality, these two products will probably merge somewhere down the road, but for now, each is popular with Web designers for its own strengths.

- Macromedia's Web site includes a showcase of sites using Macromedia technology. You can follow links here to see Shockwave in action, as with the featured animation for Sony Music. These case studies explain the business goal for the animation, the technology used, and the results of using the animation on the site. As with any element of a Web page, it's important to have a good reason for including animation or video. Because they involve large files and can slow down your site's performance, they should make a strong impression on your visitor and provoke some action, such as a purchase, return visit, or request for information from your company.

Macromedia Showcase Page

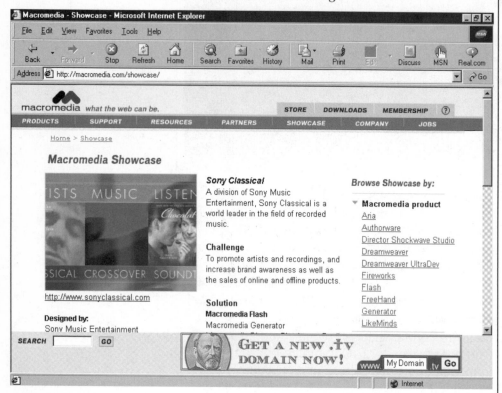

Barneys.com Puts its Site into Motion

- The technology to create sophisticated animations and video movies online exists. What keeps Web sites from implementing those complex technologies is the ability of Internet users to receive the information in a seamless way. The move towards higher **bandwidth** connections in the form of cable modems or high-speed telephone access will pave the way to a much more multimedia-rich Web.

- Some animations, such as the animated filmstrip on Barneys.com, manipulate photographic images. With improvements in computer monitors over the years, photographs can now be rendered online with excellent quality, and photo manipulation software such as Photoshop allows graphic designers to create amazing effects. Photos can also be made part of interactive animations, or used to create visual navigation elements on a page.

Buzzwords
Bandwidth is the transmission capacity of a connection such as telephone line. Bandwidth is counted in cycles per second (Hertz) or in bits per second.

Barneys.com Home Page

- Don't neglect the power of still photos online. Many businesses put photographs of their executives on their Web site in the About Us area to give a face to their corporate persona. Online catalogs make good use of product photographs. Some uses of photography in traditional advertising translate nicely to the Web. Sites such as investment brokers or cell phone companies might place photos of happy customers using a product or benefiting from a service, creating the sense in visitors that their lives will be better if they do business with this company.

Watch TV Online at Streamsearch.com

- Video must be digitized before it can be put on a Web site using one of several formats such as MPEG or QuickTime, a video standard developed by Apple can be played back on both the PC and Mac. Video still has a way to go on the Web, because video files are so large that they must be compressed, losing some information from the files in the process and causing a jerkiness in their playback.

- Video is used on business Web sites to make media coverage such as television interviews of a company executive or speeches to investors available to visitors. Some companies use videos of a manufacturing process or product at work (for example a car driving down a winding road on a car company site) on their sites. On StreamSearch.com, a provider of multimedia content to Web sites, video clips from movies and television shows are offered for viewing.

Note

The better the source of video the better it will look online. Video cameras run the gamut from the kind you use to keep a record of your high-school graduation, to high-end professional equipment. If a business is going to place video on a Web site, it should consider investing in good quality video.

- The size of the video image on your Web page has an impact on how good it will look. Because compression used with most video files online removes certain information, a smaller image on your Web page will not show the gaps and glitches as a larger one will, which is why many video players offer such a small image area for viewing. When video is captured for use online, a small image size, such as 160 x 120 pixels, will provide the best reproduction.

E-BUSINESS ANALYSIS

Take a look at each of these sites (full URLs are located at the end of the exercise), then read the site analysis below and answer the questions.

CASE STUDY 1: SPHERANETWORKS.COM

- Sphera Networks is an optical networks consulting company. When the introductory animation on their page finishes playing, their home page appears. This page also sports an animation of a lighted rectangle that moves around an illustrated network of computers, suggesting a network connection. The page allows the user to scroll through recent news story links by clicking on the up and down arrows on the upper right. This scrolling menu keeps the page clearer of text, so that the combination of too much text and a continual animation doesn't make the page feel cluttered.

Spheranetworks.com Home Page

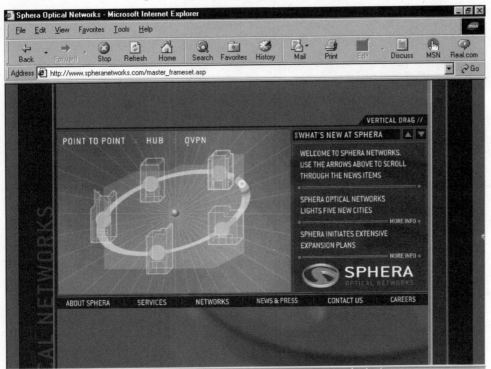

- The Spheranetworks.com Web site first appears with a screen that lets the visitor know the technical requirements for viewing the site with optimal results. This site requires Flash Player version 4 or higher, a 24-bit display, and 800 x 600 screen resolution. Many sites display messages like this when a visitor arrives. In some cases sites incorporate software that can detect what plug-ins a visitor has on his or her hard drive and can offer to download required updates or players. In this way people who move around the Web gain the tools they need to playback sophisticated multimedia. However, configurations such as 24-bit display and 800 x 600 screen resolution are a factor of the visitor's operating system and can't be changed by the Web sites.

Spheranetworks.com Site Requirements Page

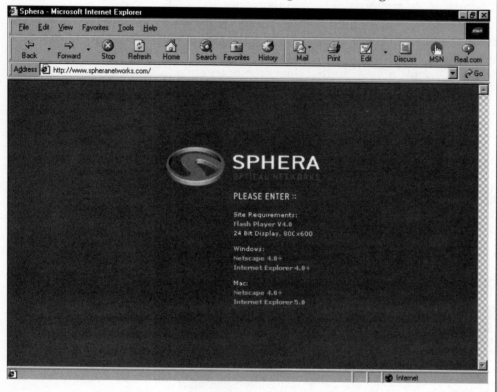

1. What is an optical network?

   _____

2. What is an animated GIF?

   _____

3. What adverse affect can it have to let visitors to a site know that their computer setup won't let them view the site optimally?

   _____

CASE STUDY 2: BARNEYS.COM

- At the writing of this book Barneys.com was not yet set up for shopping online, so the goal of the site is simply to showcase products, provide the visitor with a feeling for the business and its merchandise, and provide information, such as store locations and the history of the company. Barneys.com uses scrolling photographs of various images to achieve this overview. Visitors can't control the animations, which just continue to scroll as the visitor moves around the site. Although this is attractive and interesting, after a while it's frustrating: you want to know how to stop the pictures from moving and do something on the site. Continuous animations should be used judiciously, if at all.

Barney's Co-Op Page

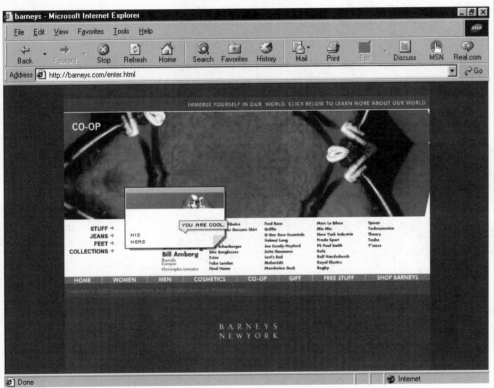

■ One feature of Barney's site is the floating menu. This menu appears on top of the scrolling animation. When you move your mouse over an item on the menu a little message appears explaining what you can do if you go to this page. What's somewhat unique is that this menu box isn't anchored: you can click and drag to move it around the Web page.

Barney's Store Location Page

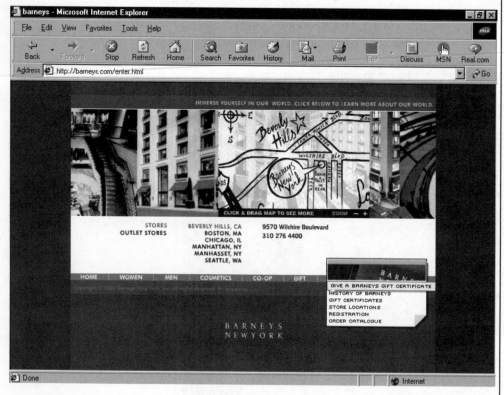

1. Identify various navigation devices offered on Barney's site.

   _____

2. What happens if you click and drag the store locator map?

   _____

3. What are the benefits to a visitor of having a floating menu they can move around the page?

   _____

CASE STUDY 3: STREAMSEARCH.COM

- StreamSearch.com is a content provider for ISPs and other Web sites. The site showcases products ranging from animations and video to audio files. When you select an item to playback, StreamSearch opens your media player and plays the clip. Someone viewing the video can use the simple controls on the player to stop, rewind, or playback the clip.

StreamSearch.com Playback Page

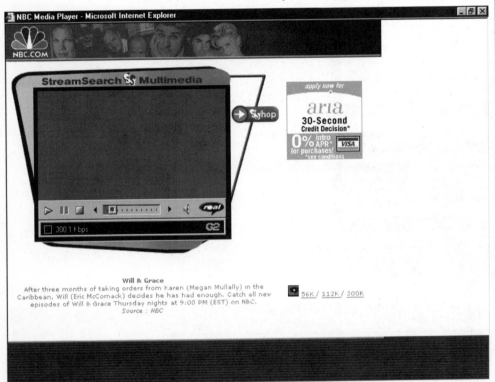

- One feature of StreamSearch.com is player detection. The site can look at your computer system and analyze which players you have on your hard drive. The site then offers to download players you don't have to your computer. Once downloaded, players are usually set to install themselves without the user having to close his or her browser, or be involved in any way. Occasionally you will see a message that indicates that new settings for an updated player won't take effect until you restart your computer.

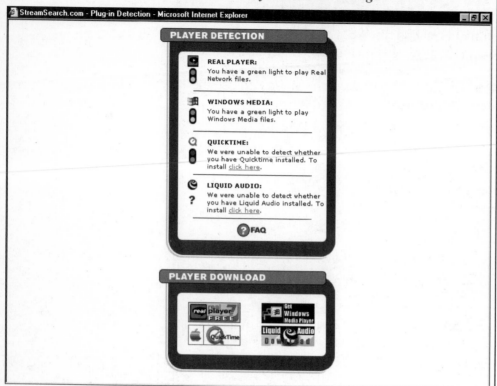

StreamSearch.com - Plug-in Detection - Microsoft Internet Explorer

PLAYER DETECTION

REAL PLAYER:
You have a green light to play Real Network files.

WINDOWS MEDIA:
You have a green light to play Windows Media files.

QUICKTIME:
We were unable to detect whether you have Quicktime installed. To install click here.

LIQUID AUDIO:
We were unable to detect whether you have Liquid Audio installed. To install click here.

FAQ

PLAYER DOWNLOAD

1. What do the 56K/112K/300K noted at the bottom of the player page represent?

   _____

2. What shape is the button you use on RealPlayer to pause playback?

   _____

3. What reasons would a visitor to a site have for not wanting to download media players?

   _____

LIVE ON THE WORLD WIDE WEB!

http://www.flashresource.com
FlashResource.com

http://www.spheranetworks.com/
Spheranetworks.com

http://macromedia.com/
Macromedia

http://barneys.com/
Barneys.com

http://www.streamsearch.com
StreamSearch.com

Adding Sound to Web Pages
- **Learn about sound file formats**
- **Explore how audio players work**
- **Discover how Web sites are using sound**
- **Hear speeches online**
- **Learn how sound is being used in online training**

NOTES

Liquidaudio.com Helps People Play Music Online

- The use of sound on a Web page can add fun, provide information, narrate training, or demonstrate an audio product. Although a lot of advances are being made in sound formats, many sound files on the Web are still in two formats that have been around for a while, WAV and MIDI. MIDI files are usually smaller than WAV files, but this format is really meant for music because it records commands that create sounds in MIDI-compatible instruments. WAV files can get large even with short sound clips. As with graphics files, you should be careful not to make sound files so large that they cause site performance issues when visitors try to play them.

- MP3 files are the hottest thing in the music business. Digital formats store immense amounts of data, as much as 1.4 million bits per second of music. The MP3 format is essentially a way to compress digital audio while maintaining the CD-like quality of the music. This is possible because certain pieces of information in a recording aren't missed by listeners, such as harmonics of music that the human ear can't actually hear. LiquidAudio.com is the site of a system to distribute CD-quality audio files.

LiquidAudio.com Home Page

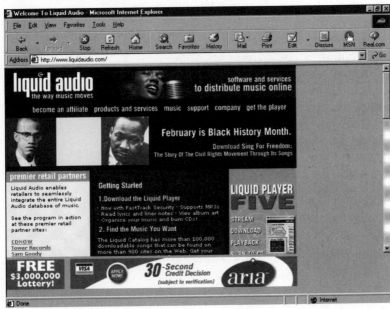

Note
MP3 has caused quite a stir, not because the technology is all that sophisticated, but because it has made distribution of music cheap and easy. This has caused stirrings in the music industry and several copyright-focused law suits.

Technical Note
You can use HTML to add a link that a visitor clicks to play a sound file. The HTML tag for this is the A HREF tag, which points to the audio file. A typical link to an audio file might look like this:
`<A HREF="Beethoven.wav"> Click here to hear Fur Elise.</A>`

Amazon.com Previews Musical Selections for Customers

- Amazon.com sells more than books; it also sells electronics, video, and CDs. When you go to a CD product page, there are quite often samples from the CD that you can play to preview the product before you buy. You play these clips by clicking on a song title link. An audio player called Real Audio then opens on the visitor's screen, allowing him or her to start, stop, and pause the music. Audio players are usually free downloads from the site containing audio files, or from the site of the manufacturer of the player.

Amazon.com CD Page

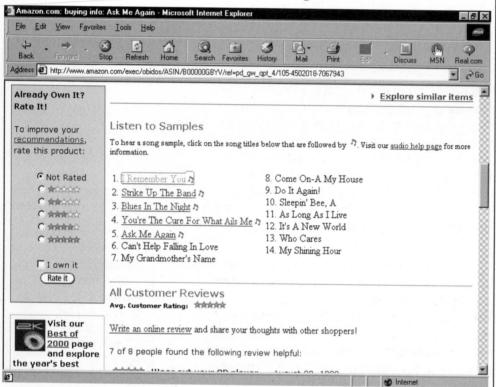

- Not all audio files are played by clicking on a link. Some audio plays automatically, perhaps when an animated introduction to a Web site loads or when some specific action is initiated on a site. It's possible to make audio files **loop**; that is, they play from beginning to end, then go back and start playing from the beginning again until you either cancel the action or leave the page. One problem with automatic audio on a site is that it doesn't let the visitor choose whether to take the time to listen to the audio or not, as they do with a clickable link. For that reason, and because large audio files can cause delays while waiting for the file to load, it's not advisable for Web designers to build in a great deal of automatic audio.

GetMusic.com Offers Music Clips, Interviews, and More

- How can an E-Business make good use of sound on a site? Some play music behind certain segments of the site to create a mood; others place comments or short speeches from executives on a page. Companies in the business of selling music such as Amazon and GetMusic.com use

Buzzword

To *loop* music is to set it to play continuously, starting again at the beginning every time the end of music is reached.

audio files to allow customers to sample the music and to hear interviews with musicians.

GetMusic.com Home Page

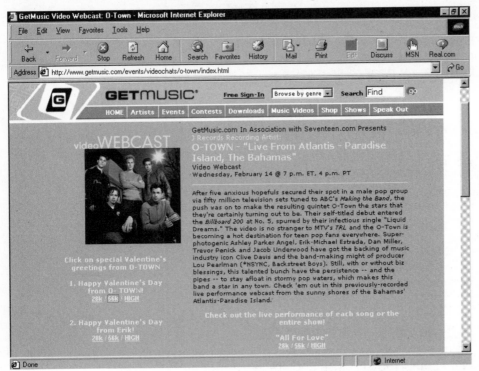

- Some businesses use sound effects on their sites. In fact, business presentation software such as PowerPoint allows you to associate sounds such as a camera click with the switching of slides or the crashing of glass with a chart showing sales breaking through the roof. These presentations can then be placed on a Web page for viewing. You can associate a sound effect on any Web page with the clicking of a button or link. These types of effects usually fit in pretty small files, so they aren't too cumbersome to use on a site.

- GetMusic.com offers visitors the opportunity to select a playback option that matches their modem speed for optimal performance. When somebody with a 56K modem wants to play a song, for example, he or she would click on the 56K link under the song title. HIGH would include those computer systems with cable modems or a form of high-speed telephone access.

Hear How PBS.org Uses Audio for the Spoken Word

- Not all sound on Web sites is music. Quite a few sites include audio for speeches or discussions. PBS.org is one site that uses lots of audio, from presidential speeches to news talk shows. Because they use a variety of multimedia, the site offers little icons to help visitors know whether a clip is an audio clip (a small megaphone) or a video clip (a video camera graphic).

Note

For Web visitors with vision disabilities, voice recognition software can turn the text on any Web page into audio.

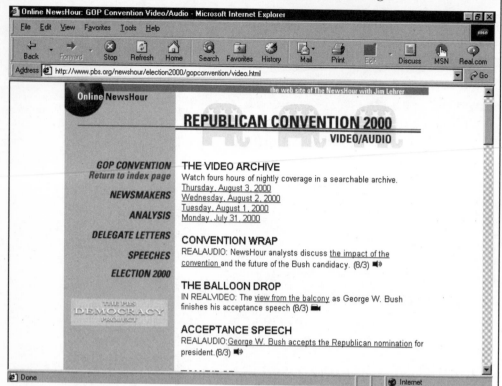

- If you want to put audio clips on your Web site, you should be aware that some visitors will have trouble playing the audio if they are working on a computer that is on a network protected by a firewall. That's because the audio server is on your Web site and, even though the audio player is on their computer, their security won't let the two communicate. You can set an audio server to send files in HTTP format, which is accepted through most firewalls, just as they allow Web sites and e-mail to enter.

Consider the Uses of Sound in Online Training at Click2Learn.com

- The area of **distance learning**, which involves teaching students who are located remotely from an instructor, is making interesting use of audio. Online courses often include an audio narration of processes or concepts being shown in text or through illustrations on screen. Online training companies such as Click2Learn.com use this approach on some courses. If an E-Commerce business wants to offer how-to information to help customers use its products successfully, or even train remote employees, it might consider building in an audio narration in training materials.

Buzzword

Distance learning involves education where the students and teacher are located remotely from each other. Distance learning can be done using regular mail, videotapes, audio tapes, or over the Internet.

Click2Learn.com Home Page

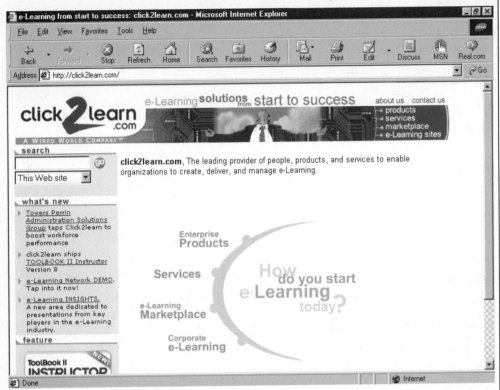

- Audio is also being used in live meetings held online using products such as NetMeeting. An E-Commerce company might hold a live product launch allowing customers or investors to attend and hear announcements as they happen. In distance learning, some software products set learners and instructors up to interact with audio and video in real time. Video files can contain sound so no separate audio file or player is involved.

Technical Note

Digital audio formats (MIDI, WAV, AU, AIFF) save values of sound digitally. Digital formats record sounds by sampling it at regular intervals. Sampling frequency is important for quality of digital formats: the higher this frequency, the more information per sample of sound in the digital code. Frequency is measured in megahertz; common frequencies are 11KHz, 22KHz, and 44Hz.

E-BUSINESS ANALYSIS

> *Take a look at each of these sites (full URLs are located at the end of the exercise), then read the site analysis below and answer the questions.*

CASE STUDY 1: GETMUSIC.COM

- GetMusic.com is a distributor of music and music videos. Their site includes a regular feature, The A List. This is a show where the host explores various aspects of today's music scene through interviews. The page on the GetMusic.com site for The A List includes links to listen to archived shows using RealPlayer.

GetMusic.com The A List Page

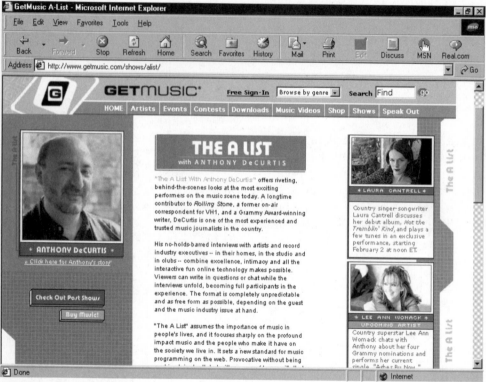

■ GetMusic.com also includes a list of events including live audio chats. Audio chats are another interesting use of sound on a Web site. Listeners must use an audio player and have speakers and a sound card on their computers. Using live audio chat you could set up an event to have your CEO speak live to customers or vendors through your Web site. For those who don't have audio-ready computers, it's a good idea to provide a text version of any live audio chat.

GetMusic.com Events Page

1. What is live audio chat?

_____

2. Of AU, MIDI, and WAV, which format is better suited for music than speech?

_____

3. How could use of audio on a site benefit visitors with vision disabilities?

_____

CASE STUDY 2: PBS.ORG

■ PBS.org uses sound on its site in a variety of ways, from offering recorded interviews, to political speeches, and audio transcripts of radio programs. The PBS Kids area includes a Karaoke section, where kids can play popular tunes or TV theme songs and sing along. This area uses graphic links in the form of small icons to play the files, and visitors have to have Real Player or Shockwave, which can be downloaded from this site.

PBS.org Kids Karaoke Page

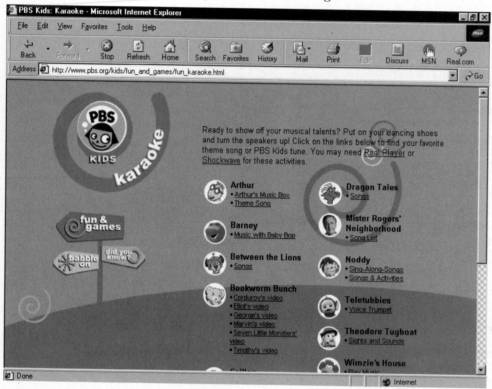

- Another creative use of audio on this site is in the feature called Fooling with Words with Bill Moyers. In this series there is a page called The Poets Read where you can play files of poets reading their own works, and interviews with poets. Depending on a visitor's computer system, there could be a short delay in starting to play larger audio files, but because a visitor must click to initiate the playing of an audio file, they don't cause any delay in loading Web pages on the site.

The Poets Read Page

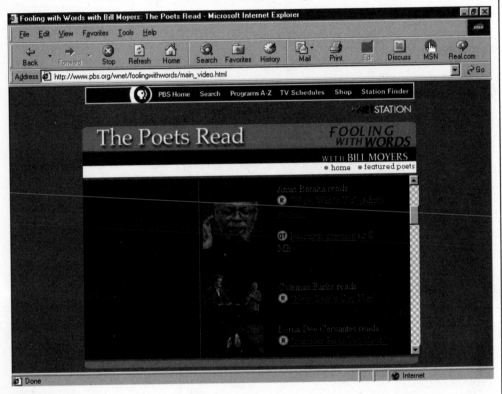

1. What is RealPlayer?

_____

2. What is PBS?

_____

3. Of audio, video, and photos, which uses more bandwidth to play online?

_____

CASE STUDY 3: CLICK2LEARN.COM

- Click2Learn offers a wide variety of courses on technical topics such as computer software, as well as management and job skills training. Some of the courses they offer use audio, as with the DiscoverWare course on Outlook 98 shown here. As the cursor moves around the Outlook screen opening menus and making choices, the narration describes what's happening. The user can control the narration using the controls built right into the course page.

Click2Learn.com Discover Outlook 98 Course Page

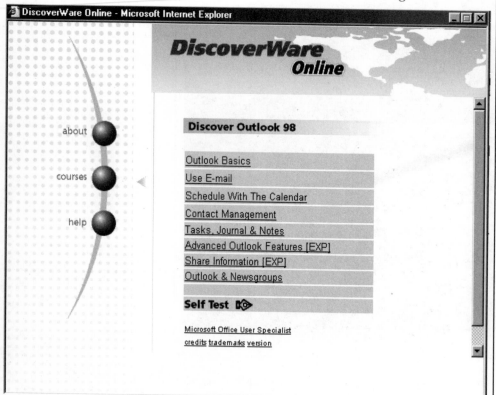

- When a course uses multimedia, it's a good idea to let those taking it know right up front about any technical requirements. For example, Click2Learn.com outlines technology requirements including a sound card, minimum screen resolution, and minimum speed of modem they recommend for taking the course. It may also be necessary to build technical help files into a Web site that uses multimedia in case visitors have difficulty with multimedia players or files.

Click2Learn DiscoverWare Help Page

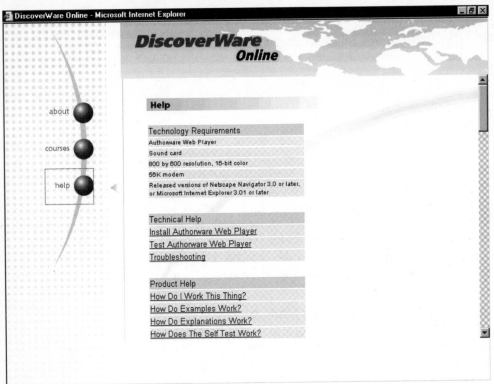

1. What is distance learning?

   _____

2. What kind of technical support does Click2Learn provide?

   _____

3. What benefit is there to a student in being able to control the playback of narration for an online course?

   _____

http://www.oanda.com
Oanda.com
http://www.harrodsonline.com/
Harrods Online Shopping
http://chase.com/
Chase
http://www.sothebys.com/
Sothebys.com
http://www.wto.org/
The World Trade Organization

Learning E-Commerce
Part VI, Web Site Design
Capstone Project

Summary of Concepts

- The design of an E-Commerce Web site involves many elements, but the foundation of a good site is to understand what you want your visitors to be able to do and provide them with the tools to do that easily. Navigation is one important element of that: how easily can visitors find their way around your site and get what they came for? Placing useful tools and information in logical places is also important. For example, include a shopping cart link or contact information for customer support on every page.

- The basic language of Web design is HTML (Hypertext Markup Language), which allows you to place text on a page, format it, add links, and build elements such as tables and frames. XML adds some functionality and control to HTML. Style sheets allow you to build in sets of attributes into an HTML document, and scripts execute a command, for example, to place a calculator on a Web page. Java is a language that allows you to build Web pages that are viewed uniformly by various browsers and platforms.

- The structure of a good Web page is an evolving art, but certain concepts are fundamental to good Web design. It's important to build consistency on a site to make visitors feel more comfortable and enable them to find their way from page to page. Pages can be split into sections to provide order to information contained there and break up the content for visitors into manageable chunks. Color, graphics, and font characteristics should all be used with an eye towards avoiding clutter and supporting the mood of the site, whether fun or all business.

- Multimedia offers rich possibilities for Web sites, including animations, photography, video, and sound. As with page design, multimedia shouldn't be overdone, both because it can become monotonous and because multimedia files are large and can slow down the performance of a Web site.

Case Study

The Business:

- In early discussions about designing All Creatures Publishing's online bookstore it seemed that everybody had an idea for a design motif. The editorial department thought the bookstore should look and feel like an old style bookstore with little images of book spines lined up on a shelf and a book bag for a shopping cart. The marketing department wanted a more sophisticated, contemporary look with an abstract background, clean fonts, and subdued colors. The owner liked the idea of reinforcing the virtual bookstore idea by making it look like the bookstore of the future with gleaming stainless steel and computer terminals. Finally, the Web design consultant they hired recommended the use of photographs and animations of pets with lots of barking and meowing sounds to support the pet emphasis in the publisher's books. The owner decided to create **storyboards** for each idea.

Buzzword

A *storyboard* is a term used in both film and advertising that is also used in many other types of design projects. It refers to a visual map of the structure of a work. For a movie, a storyboard shows each of the major shots of the movie in sequence, providing a director with a roadmap for the production. In Web design, a storyboard provides a site map, showing all the pages in the site and links between them. A storyboard can be created as rough sketches in a Web design program such as FrontPage or with a desktop publishing program such as Microsoft Publisher.

The Project:

- Have students break into four teams, with each team taking one of the design approaches suggested above. The teams should come up with a sketch or collage to show what the All Creatures' bookstore page might look like based on their theme. The teams should also create a storyboard diagramming the various pages of the site and links between them. Finally, the team should design the main menu and a navigation bar that would appear on every page, trying to incorporate the design theme assigned to them.

The Business Model:

- To complete this project, you must look for examples of good E-Commerce Web design and advice on Web design online. Here are three important things to consider:

    1. ***Consider sites that have a similar audience or feel***: Look for sites that relate to books or pets. If the design theme you are using is a fun one, look for kids sites or crafts sites; if it's a futuristic site, look at science fiction related sites or hi-tech sites.

    2. ***Be alert to how sites have built in functionality within a design theme:*** Notice how sites include navigation tools to make getting around sites easy. Look at Web pages that get too cluttered with graphics or busy fonts and learn from their mistakes. Look at sites that make buying a product simple and understandable. Visit customer service areas of Web sites to see what kind of information you must provide there, including ways for visitors to contact you.

    3. ***See how sites are using multimedia.*** Look for sites that use multimedia in ways that enhance a visitor's experience, without detracting from the goal of the site. Notice how sites with multimedia perform: does it take a long time to load some pages with a lot of graphics or animations? Do some sites include music that plays over and over—is that effective? How do sites use sound effects?

Note

In the early stages of a design project it's sometimes useful to *brainstorm*, that is, to sit down and solicit ideas in a free-for-all discussion. The open nature of brainstorming, where everybody should feel comfortable contributing ideas, no matter how unusual, is designed to spur creativity. However, when the brainstorming ends, a company must find solid criteria to base its final choices on. Focus groups (groups of customers you try ideas out on), customer surveys, and professional consulting advice all come into play in taking early brainstorming and turning it into a professional Web presence.

Technology

- The technologies involved in Web design include the basic languages of HTML and Java, as well as the software used to build Web pages, such as FrontPage. Other software products are used to manipulate photographs (Photoshop), work with fonts (Adobe Type Manager), or create illustrations (Adobe Illustrator). In the area of multimedia, most animations are built today using two products from Macromedia, Flash or Shockwave. Use of video, animation or sound on a site requires a multimedia player, which you should provide to your visitors to download from your site, if they don't already have it.

Books to help:

Learning to Create a Web page With Office 2000 (catalog number Z43)

HTML 4.0 Fundamentals (catalog number DC67)

Creating Web Graphics (catalog number DC87)

Converting Files for the Web (catalog number DC54)

Learning Macromedia Flash 5 (catalog number Z101)

Learning Adobe Photoshop 6 (catalog number Z94)

416

Web sites to explore:

http://www.screamdesign.com /

This site offers libraries of free Web design elements, including graphics, Flash media, and interface designs.

http://www.wpdfd.com

Web Page Design for Designers is a site that focuses on giving advice on topics such as navigation, use of graphics, and page layout with the emphasis on design rather than technology.

http://macromedia.com

This is the site of the publisher of Flash and Shockwave animation software. You can download demos free here, and read about how they work.

http://design-agency.com

A wonderful site to inspire creative ideas, Design-agency.com gathers together some very cool and very out of the ordinary Web design, with links to featured designers' own sites.

http://www.access.nac.net/falken/annoying/main.html

How to Make an Annoying Web Page is an example of learning by looking at what not to do. Pages here overdo on graphics, overdo on bad fonts, and generally provide great examples of common Web design mistakes.

Index

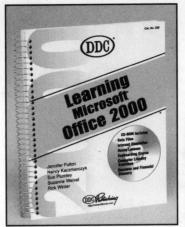

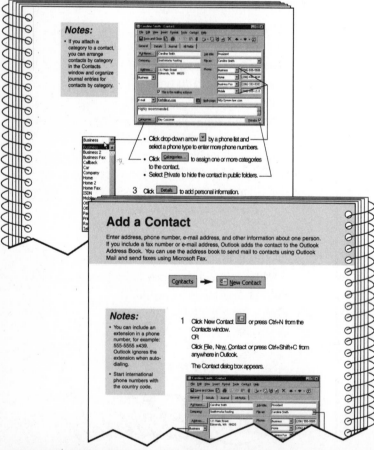

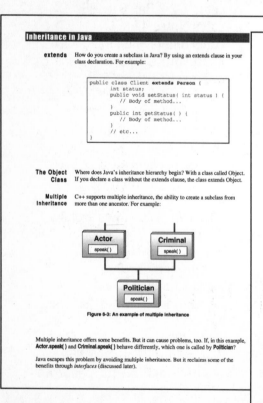
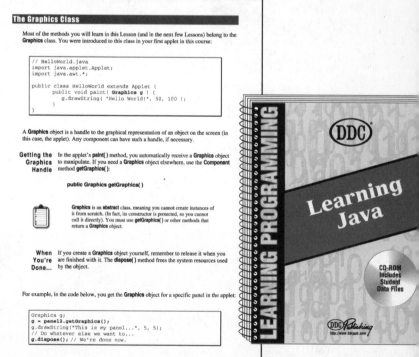